Dyslexia
Theory and Good Practice

Dyslexia

Theory and Good Practice

Edited by

ANGELA J. FAWCETT

Department of Psychology, The University of Sheffield

W

WHURR PUBLISHERS

LONDON AND PHILADELPHIA

© 2001 Whurr Publishers
First published 2001 by
Whurr Publishers Ltd
19b Compton Terrace, London N1 2UN, England and
325 Chestnut Street, Philadelphia PA 19106, USA

British Library Cataloguing in Publication Data
A catalogue record for this book is available from the
British Library.

ISBN: 186156 210 1

Printed and bound in the UK by Athenaeum Press Ltd,
Gateshead, Tyne & Wear

Contents

List of contributors

Steve Chinn, Mark College, Somerset
Angela Fawcett, Department of Psychology, University of Sheffield
Simon E. Fisher, Wellcome Trust Centre for Human Genetics, University of Oxford
Torleiv Hoien, Foundation of Dyslexia Research, Stavanger
Mike Johnson, SEN Centre, Manchester Metropolitan University
Jane Kirk, Moray House Institute, University of Edinburgh
Ray Lee, Bramblewood Educational, County Durham
Geoff Lindsay, Centre for Educational Development, Appraisal and Research, University of Warwick
Ingvar Lundberg, Department of Psychology, Göteborg University
Heikki Lyytinen, Department of Psychology, University of Jyväskylä
David McLoughlin, Adult Dyslexia and Skills Development Centre, London
Rod Nicolson, Department of Psychology, University of Sheffield
Beth O'Brien, Centre for Reading and Language Research, Tufts University
Lindsay Peer, British Dyslexia Association
Steve Reder, Department of Applied Linguistics, Portland State University
Gavin Reid, Moray House Institute, University of Edinburgh
John Stein, Department of Physiology, Oxford University
Shelley D. Smith, Center for Human Molecular Genetics, University of Nebraska Medical Center
Joel Talcott, Department of Physiology, Oxford University
Michael Thomson, East Court School, Ramsgate
Joe Torgeson, Department of Psychology, Florida State University
Priscilla L Vail, Educational Consultant, San Francisco
Aryan van der Leij, Department of Education, University of Amsterdam
Susan A. Vogel, Literacy Education Department, Northern Illinois University
Caroline Witton, Department of Physiology, Oxford University
Maryanne Wolf, Centre for Reading and Language Research, Tufts University
Frans Zwarts, Department of Dutch and Frisan Language and Literature, University of Groningen

Introduction
Developmental dyslexia: into the future

RODERICK I NICOLSON

Introduction

I have found this a difficult chapter to write. I am attempting to present an overview of the dyslexia landscape – the 'helicopter view' in management jargon. But this is rather a challenge. Telling the wood from the trees is difficult in any discipline, but particularly so in dyslexia, where there is much controversy, many theories, and many different roles for the dyslexia community.

I am much aided in this task by the fact that Angela Fawcett and I have been able to persuade a range of outstanding theorists and practitioners to make contributions to this book, and so I am at liberty to refer in passing to their data and insights while focusing more on the twin aims of analysing and persuading. In terms of persuasion I shall use the device of presenting vignettes of occasions that were (in retrospect) persuasive to me, and helped shape my collaborative research with Angela.

The plan of the chapter is as follows. I start by attempting to unmask some potent causes of confusion in dyslexia research and practice. I then outline the progress that has been made under the headings of theory, diagnosis, support and policy over the past decade; and then move on to develop some targets for the next decade, working on the principle that clarity and unity of purpose is one of the key determinants of progress. I will start, though, by a personal view of how to make progress in science.

As we move further into the new century, it is appropriate to take stock of what has been achieved, and to set some targets for the future. It is a time to look back as well as forward. I can claim only a quarter of Professor TR Miles's 50-year perspective on dyslexia research, though I am able to offer over 25 years in learning. When I changed to psychology after a mathematics degree, I seem to have imprinted on two figures, both giants of cognitive psychology: Donald Broadbent and Allen Newell. Broadbent, the most influential British psychologist of his era, explained it was only possible to follow the progress of science by evaluating progress over say a 10 year period (Broadbent, 1971). He also singled out the importance of applied research (Broadbent, 1973), stressing the decisive role that evidence-based research should have in informing policy. Furthermore, he claimed that theoretical insights frequently followed from applied research, because applied work 'kept research honest' in that although many results could be obtained in the laboratory, the real world was a decisive testing ground.

Newell, with his longstanding collaborator and Nobel Prize winner Herb Simon,[1] was a founder of cognitive science research. His particular contribution to my development (at the critical period when I was developing my belief system in psychology) was a playful but devastating critique (Newell, 1973) of almost all the accepted methodologies in cognitive psychology at that time. In particular, he argued that the traditional 'head-to-head' method of testing between theories in psychology was fundamentally mistaken, and led to confusion rather than progress, because it was never the case that theory A was unequivocally better than theory B, but rather that each had its strengths and weaknesses. Second, he argued that the traditional scientific approach of specialists, each carving out their narrow domain, was potentially disastrous unless integrative researchers with broader vision inspired multi-disciplinary teams of researchers to tackle 'big' problems. Third, he argued that the traditional empirical methodology of testing between groups of subjects was potentially flawed if the different subjects were doing the task in different ways. Theoretical psychology was never the same again. Newell followed his own advice and made it his life's work to try to motivate the cognitive science community to collaborate internationally and attempt to build 'unified theories of cognition' that captured the generalities of learning and behaviour (Newell, 1990).

My aim in writing this chapter is to try to apply the advice of these giants to the field of learning disability in general, and dyslexia in particular. I take three propositions as evident. First that progress will follow if all those in the dyslexia community – researchers, practitioners, educationalists, policy makers and dyslexic people – attempt to pull together, respecting each others' insights and roles. Second, that in order to make progress it is necessary to have a vision of what one wishes to achieve, and a method of working towards that vision. Third, there is no 'magic bullet', no single theory, no single 'cure' for dyslexia. With a prevalence of at least 4% in English-speaking countries, there will be multiple causes and manifestations of dyslexia. But, as we shall see in this book, multiple causation does not mean random causation. On the contrary, the only way to progress is to identify the different causes and manifestations of the dyslexias.

Important distinctions in learning disabilities

Different roles

It is apparent that the dyslexia community, broadly defined, includes a number of unlikely bedfellows. Researchers and practitioners; parents and teachers; teachers and educational psychologists; schools and local education authorities; local education authorities and governments – all have different priorities, and much of the time they are thrown into opposed roles. Furthermore, different groups of researchers often need to stress the distinctive nature of their own research, and this can disguise the important commonalities between them. It is important to perceive that this apparent oppositional rivalry reflects an attitude of mind rather than an immutable law. It derives from the normally correct assumption that funding is 'zero sum'. If one group gets more (whether it be one group of researchers, one set of children, or one lobbying group) then the zero sum assumption is that the rest get less.

However, imagine the situation in 2005, with the introduction of a system in which theoretical work led to the introduction of early screening tests that detected dyslexia at pre-school, and these in turn led to proactive and ongoing individualized support. This support would be based on applied research identifying dyslexia-friendly teaching methods, and would, where appropriate, involve specialists. This support would ensure that dyslexic children did not suffer reading failure and subsequent educational disadvantage. Similar scenarios can be foreseen for adult dyslexia, with fuller screening, expert subsequent assessment, especially for job-related goals, and much greater awareness of the requirements for 'dyslexia-friendly' working practices. These innovations would actually be 'win win', rather than 'zero sum', in that they would appeal to all participants – dyslexic individuals, dyslexia support specialists, schools, educational psychologists, funding bodies and governments.

A successful, effective and cost-effective policy will be a major step forward for all the participants in the wider dyslexia community. It is possible to justify the outlay of initial costs if the outcome is thoroughly beneficial, in terms of human resources, educational expenditure, national competitiveness, and scientific progress.

Different theories

One of the most important distinctions in scientific research is that between cause and description. Typically scientific research progresses by first getting a reasonably complete description of the facts, and then by inventing hypotheses considered to account for the facts, and then by evaluating the hypotheses against new data. It is hoped that by this means progress is made towards the true explanation. Hypotheses built on inadequate databases of facts suffer the danger of premature specificity.

The 'medical model' provides a reasonable starting point for investigations of abnormal states. Here the distinction is between cause, symptom and treatment. I normally use the analogy of malaria here, where all three accounts are clearly different.[2] Several diseases have similar-looking symptoms, but the treatments are quite different. It is therefore necessary to use further, more sensitive tests, administered by a trained specialist, to determine the true underlying cause, and thus the appropriate treatment. It is important to realize that, for practitioners, the primary task is treatment, for educational psychologists the primary task is identification of symptoms, and for theorists the primary task remains the discovery of the underlying cause(s). Despite these differences in primary motivations, a full understanding requires the investigation and integration of all three aspects.[3]

Turning to an alternative, complementary perspective from cognitive neuroscience theory, following Uta Frith (1997), it is important to distinguish between three 'levels' of theory: the biological, the cognitive and the behavioural level. The behavioural level is in terms of symptoms – poor reading and difficulty with rhymes for example. The cognitive level gives an explanation in terms of theoretical constructs from cognitive psychology – say reduced working memory, poor phonological processing, incomplete automatization, slow central processing, and so forth. The biological level attempts to identify the underlying brain mechanism – disorganization in cerebral cortex in the language areas, abnormal magnocellular pathways, abnormal cerebellum, and so forth. It is not that any one level of explanation is intrinsically 'better' than another. A complete explanation would involve all three. The cognitive level might at first sight appear to be an unnecessary one, both hypothetical and unobservable, but in much the same way as the cognitive construct of 'thirst' can be used to explain differing behaviours in differing circumstances it provides a valuable and economical explanation of a variety of behaviours and forms a crucial link between brain and behaviour.

Finally, taking yet another perspective, it is important to consider the 'development' in developmental disorders. That is, following Thelen's 'ontogenetic landscape' approach (Thelen and Smith, 1994), a key theoretical requirement is to explain how developmental disorders develop, that is, how initial hypothetical brain/cognitive differences interact with experiences over time to shape brain and behaviour to provide the known symptoms. For this approach, it is important to take repeated observations of the same individual, rather than the 'snapshot' approach that is common in all branches of psychology – see also Lyon and Moats (1993).

All these different perspectives have their merits, and all are indispensable in a complete understanding of a developmental disorder. A mature approach identifies the strengths of the individual research programmes, and attempts to integrate them into a fuller and richer picture. Good research requires teams of specialists, able to co-operate in working towards the 'grand theory', that covers all these aspects.

What's in a name? Dyslexia versus specific learning difficulties versus learning disability versus reading disability

The advantage of the label 'dyslexia' is that it has no intrinsic meaning – it says nothing about the underlying cause, and is neutral as to whether the cause is visual, phonological, motor or some combination. The drawback (for educationalists) is that it has strong political and emotional connotations, that it suggests there is a single relatively uniform syndrome, and that dyslexia is somehow 'special'. From here it is but a short step to saying that dyslexic children need special treatment. While few would dispute this, many educationalists rightly stress the need for equally special treatment for non-dyslexic children with equally special educational needs (Siegel, 1989).

Furthermore, there was (and remains) considerable controversy over how distinct dyslexia may be as a syndrome. In the telling analogy of Andrew Ellis (Ellis, 1993), is dyslexia like obesity, with varying degrees and with arbitrary cutoff? If dyslexia is special somehow, is it then a collection of subtypes (Boder, 1973; Castles and Holmes, 1996) or do the majority actually show a common 'core' deficit (such as phonology)? Miles has termed this debate that between the 'splitters' and the 'lumpers'. Possibly in response to these problems in definition, UK educational psychologists preferred to use the term 'specific learning disabilities'.

Some time in the 1980s, influential US dyslexia researchers redesignated dyslexia as 'reading disability' rather than 'specific learning disability'. At first sight this seems entirely reasonable. After all, the specific problem is with reading. However, there is a deep consequence of the name change. The result is a change of emphasis from process to skill, from a 'specific learning' disability – that is a deficit in some (specific but not yet determined) form of the learning processes – to the skill of reading. Clearly if the problem is one of reading, then the solution must surely reside in a painstaking analysis of the reading process.

This is certainly a legitimate approach, but it is not the only approach. It has led to a schism between those who want to find the cause of dyslexia and those who want to find the cause of the reading problems. Given hindsight, it is clear that both approaches are needed for the 'grand vision' of dyslexia, as we discuss below.

Science, research and politics

When I first entered dyslexia research, I naively assumed that dyslexia research was science, science was search for the truth, and that nothing else really mattered. This is not so. Even in academia, scientific research is at least as much about academic politics as about science – as Medawar put it, science is the art of the soluble. If no one will fund the research, the scientific progress will not be made. Consequently, astute academics spend much time cultivating influential acquaintances and building their power base. Dyslexia research spans a particularly broad spectrum, including a range of 'pure science' theories, to a range of treatments and support that if successfully marketed might make their inventors millionaires, to overt lobbying of governments. Politics is the art of persuasion, and persuasion is most effective if a simple, coherent message is given. This is normally achieved by 'special pleading' – cherry picking the arguments in favour of one's position, and ignoring or denigrating inconvenient facts and alternative approaches. It is all too easy to apply the logic of politics (or, worse, marketing) to matters of science. Again, I emphasize that each has its place, and its specialists, but many dyslexia researchers have to wear several of these hats. Perhaps the way forward to maintain the credibility of the field is to introduce some system of 'kite marking', or declaration of interests, allied to clear dissociations of function, so that lobbying, marketing and science are kept well apart.

The situation in 1990

In 1990 the most powerful theoretical framework for dyslexia research, both in the UK and internationally, was in terms of phonological deficit. In the UK the approach was inspired by seminal research by Bradley and Bryant, by Frith and by Snowling. In the US it reflected the results of a concerted effort by dyslexia researchers and educationalists to 'sing from the same hymn book', providing a coherent and unified vision that was instrumental in persuading US policymakers to provide substantial long-term funding via the NICHD Learning Disabilities program – funding that is still continuing at around $20 million per year. The phonological message was a simple but powerful one: the core deficit for dyslexic children is with phonological processing, probably attributable to brain abnormalities in the language areas. This deficit means that, at school age, they have greater difficulty hearing the individual sounds in spoken words, and this makes it more difficult for them to learn to read, because of poor awareness of phonological features such as rime, which are very important when building up the rules of grapheme (written letters) to phoneme (corresponding sounds) translation rules. Clearly the key teaching requirement is to present more systematic and more thorough training in phonological awareness for children (especially those at risk of reading failure). The key research priorities were to investigate more fully the causes of the phonological difficulties. The key teaching priorities were to introduce better methods of assisting children to acquire phonological awareness. The key policy requirements were to support the phonological agenda by providing the necessary backing in terms of funds and statutes. See the chapter by Lundberg for an elegant review of the more recent literature.

By contrast, my theoretical background was in theories of learning, and I had just started dyslexia research, working with Angela Fawcett who has extensive experience of dyslexia in her family. We considered that the phonological account, although accurate and important, did not fully capture what Miles (1983) had caused the 'profile' of difficulties associated with dyslexia. We were struck by the fact that many dyslexic children and adults seemed to find many tasks difficult – even tasks that they had mastered seemed to be less fluent, more effortful. Crucially, many of these skills were not related to literacy, with motor skills featuring strongly in the reviews by (Augur, 1985; Haslum, 1989). We therefore formulated and tested the automatization deficit hypothesis – that dyslexic children have problems becoming automatic at any skill, irrespective of whether it is related to reading. The sharp way to test the theory was in some domain unrelated to language, and so we chose balance. Rather to our surprise, and precisely as predicted by the hypothesis, we did establish that the dyslexic children whom we tested showed problems in balance, especially if they were prevented from concentrating on balancing by having to do another task at the same time. We considered it particularly interesting that phonological skills are built up (without explicit instruction) over several years. We then published the results, arguing that automatization deficit could provide a broader framework for dyslexia research, integrating the phonological deficits within mainstream theories of learning.

The reaction of many dyslexia theorists was of considerable hostility to this view, which at the time we found puzzling and dismaying. We realized eventually (this may be no more than a process of rationalization) that many teachers and dyslexia researchers interested in the teaching of reading were concerned that a simplistic reading of our research might indicate that we advocated that it was more important to teach children to balance than to learn to read. We had not even considered such a possible interpretation! By contrast, many dyslexia practitioners and parents of dyslexic children resonated strongly with our automatization difficulty analysis – often giving the reaction that Miles has called the 'that's our Johnny' affirmation.

In 1991–2 we had the opportunity to talk to many influential dyslexia researchers and practitioners via an international survey (Nicolson, Fawcett and Miles, 1993) designed to assess the feasibility of large-scale screening for dyslexia in adults. The scenario that the respondents were asked to consider was initial testing by trained professionals in a job centre (with computer support), and probably involving subsequent referral to an appropriately qualified psychologist or adult literacy specialist for further testing and support. The project involved a complete literature survey of the field of adult literacy and diagnosis of dyslexia; a series of interviews with British experts on theoretical and applied aspects of dyslexia; and finally an international questionnaire study conducted with a wide range of dyslexia practitioners and researchers.

The survey established a clear consensus in the dyslexia community that was particularly impressive given that the respondents were specialists whose opinions spanned the spectrum of approaches to dyslexia and adult literacy. There was consensus that new developments in computer technology made it feasible to introduce computer-supported testing procedures that do not require the direction of a trained clinician/diagnostician, and could therefore be carried out cost-effectively in centres such as adult literacy centres, units for young offenders or job centres, subject to the provisos that a follow-up second stage testing procedure was available, and that the screening was integrated within a support framework. The survey was a landmark learning event for us, and led us to make the following recommendations (adapted from a talk given at the Third BDA International Conference – Nicolson and Fawcett, 1994). We present the complete figure, because it formed the basis for our subsequent applied research strategy, as we discuss later.

There are two further vignettes I would like to note from the interviews in the survey. First, Harry Chasty, then director of the Dyslexia Institute, stressed the importance of understanding dyslexia from a range of viewpoints. If you are trying to support dyslexic people, you must always find out what it is they want support in. Many adults do not want yet more literacy support – they want help with their lives and jobs. If you want to persuade the local education authority to provide better support for dyslexia, you have to persuade them that it will save them money in the long run, compared with the alternative. If you want to persuade the

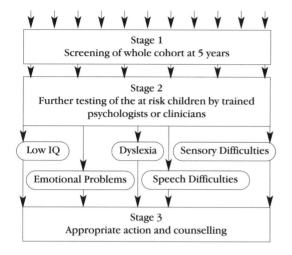

Figure 0.1: Objective: introduction of systematic screening, diagnosis and support. This diagram is taken from our early screening project, but our objective is to provide similar facilities at all ages – pre-school, junior school, secondary school and adult dyslexia.

government to support you, you have to persuade them it will be popular and generally beneficial.

Second, Jean Augur, an outstanding dyslexia practitioner who has been sorely missed, lamented the overreliance on reading problems in diagnosis of dyslexia. She recounted a story that ended: 'and then the Headmaster turned to me and said "Well, you taught him to read, Jean, so he can't be dyslexic."' In short, the success of her attempts to help with the reading meant that the head no longer considered that continuing support was needed.

We consider this the central paradox of dyslexia research. A farsighted, proactive approach will ideally lead to detection of dyslexia in time to prevent reading failure. The child would never be diagnosable as dyslexic, and so dyslexia would have been 'prevented' (Bryant, 1985). I believe that the answer to this paradox involves recognition that dyslexia will exist at the biological and cognitive levels whether or not the reading-related symptoms are alleviated. Consequently, the real diagnostic requirement is to move away from behaviour-based symptoms to cognitive- and brain-based symptoms. This will require development of new measurement tools and techniques.

Progress since 1990

In the light of the above analyses, I shall consider progress from four perspectives: policy, theory, diagnosis, and support.

Policy

Policy is the area where dyslexia has made incontrovertible progress during the 1990s, a tribute to the dedication and adroitness of the Dylexia Institute and the British Dyslexia Association. At the start of the decade, dyslexia was not recognized by the political and educational authorities, and many educational psychologists were openly and explicitly sceptical of the concept. In 1994, the Education Act was passed, and the following Code of Practice for Children with Special Educational Needs made it the responsibility of the schools to identify and support children with special educational needs. Furthermore, a series of stages, interventions, and procedures was introduced that was designed to ensure that children received appropriate and effective support.

The Code provides a valuable summary of these early stages:

2.119 In summary, schools should adopt a staged response to children's special educational needs and:

- employ clear procedures to identify and register children whose academic, social or emotional development is giving cause for concern
- identify children's areas of weakness which require extra attention from their teachers or other members of staff
- develop, monitor, review and record, in consultation with parents and involving the child as far as possible, individual education plans designed to meet each child's identified needs.

    Such plans should include written information about:

    - individual programmes of work
    - performance targets
    - review dates, findings and decisions
    - parental involvement in and support for the plans
    - arrangements for the involvement of the child
    - information on any external advice or support

- assess children's performance, identifying strengths as well as weaknesses, using appropriate measures so that the rate of progress resulting from special educational provision can be assessed
- call upon specialist advice from outside the school to inform the school's strategies to meet the child's special educational needs in particular, but not necessarily only, at stage 3.

Furthermore, the Code does consider dyslexia specifically under the heading of 'Specific learning difficulty (for example, dyslexia)' when considering criteria for making a Statutory Assessment (§3.60–3.63). A key requirement is that '... there is clear, recorded evidence of clumsiness, significant difficulties of sequencing or visual perception;

deficiencies in working memory; or significant delays in language functioning' (§3:61iii).

In short, although the situation regarding dyslexia in UK schools remains far from ideal, exceptional progress has been made. It is fair to say that the situation for a dyslexic child in the UK is one of the most favourable in the world. The UK situation is considerably in advance of that in the US, where the devolution of power to the individual states appears to have hindered the introduction of a coherent policy, despite the best efforts of the US dyslexia community.

While the situation in the UK regarding adults is less advanced, there is reason to believe that the situation may soon be improved. The 1998 Adult Disability Act made it a requirement that most large firms introduce a systematic disability support system. Recently, the Moser Report (Moser, 2000) has highlighted the importance of adult literacy and numeracy skills and has led to the introduction of an ambitious programme of government support.

Theory

There have been major developments in several theoretical areas related to dyslexia. In particular, neuroscience, brain imaging, and genetics have made outstanding progress. This progress is reflected in several ways in dyslexia theory, as is clear from the other chapters of this book. Following Frith (1997) it is valuable to classify theories at the biological level, the cognitive level and the behavioural level. I shall additionally introduce the genetic level.

Genetic level

A range of new and intriguing findings have emerged, indicating that dyslexia is likely not to be caused by a single gene but through the interaction of multiple genes, with possibly different gene sets being involved with different phenotypes (behavioural symptoms). It is not clear what bearing these genes have directly on behaviour or even on the development of the brain. It is, for instance, possible that one gene might lead say to birth complications, and so it would have only an indirect effect upon the child's brain. Another gene might lead to sinus problems or 'glue ear' in infancy. The poor quality auditory input during the critical period for development of speech-related auditory cortex might lead to poorer quality auditory representations of speech, and thus phonological deficit – again an indirect effect. The chapter by Fisher and Smith provides a valuable though difficult overview of these issues. See also Elman et al. (1997) for an incisive analysis of the links between genes and behaviour.

Biological level

New theories have been suggested, both in terms of magnocellular deficit (Stein) and cerebellar deficit (Fawcett and Nicolson), as discussed in this volume. Both theories have a good deal in common, and both suggest that problems will be more widespread than just phonological deficit. A good deal more research is needed to establish the extent to which these theories account for dyslexia and, in particular, we need to establish the 'prevalence' of the different subtypes that might be expected under the different accounts.

Cognitive level

In addition to the automatization deficit and phonological deficit account, the major newcomer to the cognitive level accounts is the 'double deficit' hypothesis (Wolf and Bowers, 1999) that suggests that dyslexic children suffer not only from a deficit in phonological processing but also in central processing speed (see the chapter by Wolf in this volume). An intriguing and underevaluated new analysis is also provided in my chapter (with Fawcett) on learning. Rather than automatization per se, it now appears that there may be abnormalities in fundamental learning processes such as classical conditioning, habituation, response 'tuning' and error elimination. A particularly striking finding is our 'square root rule', that dyslexic people may take longer to acquire a skill in proportion to the square root of the time normally taken to acquire it. If a skill takes four practice sessions to master, it would take a dyslexic child eight sessions to reach the same standard. If it normally took 400 sessions, it would take the dyslexic child 8000 sessions! If replicable, this finding would have striking implications for dyslexia support in that it mandates progression in terms of small, easily assimilated steps. This would not only provide theoretical support for existing good practice in dyslexia support but might also distinguish dyslexia support requirements from those for other poor readers. Clearly considerable further research is needed to investigate these hypotheses.

Behavioural level

We now have a wide range of skills on which groups of dyslexic children show significant impairment. These include sensory deficit (flicker, motion sensitivity, rapid auditory discrimination), motor (bead threading, balance), and cognitive (phonological, working memory, speed). The challenge is no longer to find skills where the dyslexic children perform poorly, but rather those where they perform at normal or above normal levels. These typically include non-verbal reasoning, vocabulary and problem solving. What is still not clear is whether there are different 'subtypes' of dyslexia, each corresponding to a different 'profile' of skills, and to what extent dyslexia is distinct from other learning disabilities.

Screening and diagnosis

Screening

The situation regarding diagnosis is mixed. There have been several valuable screening tests introduced. These include Singleton's COPS computer-based screening tests for school-age children and adults, together with a range of phonological tests (see the chapter by Lindsay for a brief review of these tests).

Naturally, however, I choose to focus on our own screening tests – the Dyslexia Early Screening (4.5 to 6.5 years), the Dyslexia Screening Test (6.5 to 16.5) and the Dyslexia Adult Screening Test (16.5 to 65). Again, I digress somewhat to give anecdotes aimed at explaining why they take the form that they do. Each of these tests was explicitly designed to form the first stage in a systematic screening–assessment–support procedure, as described in Figure 0.1. As we explained to amused conference audiences, we wished to introduce tests that appealed to educational psychologists, in that they were normed, reliable, and provided important and objective information; we wanted tests that appealed to school teachers in that they 'empowered' them to undertake the tests themselves, and gave informa-tion that was understandable and related to teaching objectives; tests that appealed to schools in that they were quick, cheap, effective, and fitted into the Code of Practice; tests that appealed to the dyslexia community in that they represented an amalgam of all the 'positive indicators' for dyslexia; and tests that appealed to the children, in that they were fun, varied, and non-threatening. We also wished to start by developing an early screening test for dyslexia that could be administered in a child's first year at school (from 4.5 years upwards), before dyslexia can formally be diagnosed, but was a valid predictor of subsequent reading difficulty. Such a test would address the central dilemma of dyslexia research by addressing the reading problems before dyslexia could be diagnosed.

We believe that we succeeded in this apparently impossible balancing act. The key insight is that, rather than being adversaries, all these very different constituencies have the same core interest – a rapid, informative and cost-effective indicator of whether a child needs more help. Following extensive pilot work and discussion, we designed the tests to be administered by the child's teacher, to be fun, to include 10 to 11 short sub-tests of ability for skills 'across the board', and to take no more than

30 minutes to administer. We had originally intended them to be computer administered, but following pilot work, we decided the greater accessibility and 'hands-on' immediacy and transparency of traditional testing methods outweighed the advantages of computer presentation. This decision led to some limitations – we were unable to design a simple but effective kit for testing speed of reaction (trivial for a computer program); and some key advantages – it's hard to design a computer-based method of testing bead threading or balance!

Figure 0.2 illustrates data from a six-year-old child whom we tested. It illustrates the operation of the test and also a rather deeper point. The child took 87 seconds to say the names of the 24 common objects on a card. This is very slow for a child of that age. In fact it's within the bottom 10% for the norms for the age, which is why it has a '– –' label. The 'sound order' test was 15 out of 15, which merits a O 25th–75th percentile, which suggests that the auditory magnocellular system is fine. The only other test with reasonable performance is recognition of digits (seven out of seven) again in the normal band (O). The '–' band represents performance in the eleventh to 25th percentile, an 'at risk' score, but not as serious as the double minus. The combination of 'at risk' scores on the individual sub-tests (six at double minus, two at minus) leads to a total 'at risk' score of 14 $((6 \times 2) + (2 \times 1))$, and an 'at risk quotient' of 1.4 (dividing by 10). An ARQ of 0.9 or more is scored as 'clear risk of dyslexia' and so the 1.4 ARQ indicates that the child needs extra support, and should enter stage 1 or 2

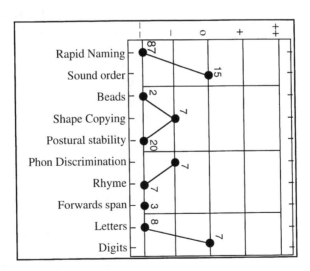

Figure 0.2: Illustrative DEST profile and at-risk Quotient age: 6:2 Outcome: 6 @ – –, 2 @ –, total 14. Hence at-risk quotient 1.4.

of the support procedure of the Code of Practice. This leads naturally to inclusion within the special educational needs procedures, with probable referral for a full diagnosis by an educational psychologist at stage 4.

The deeper point may be perceived by inspection of the right hand portion of Figure 0.2. In addition to the poor recognition of letters there are marked difficulties in phonological discrimination, rhyme and memory span. These are all precisely as expected on the phonological deficit hypothesis. If we had not tested bead threading, balance (postural stability) and rapid naming, we would have said 'typical phonological deficit profile'. As it is, we would say 'typical dyslexic profile, with problems in speed, phonology and motor skills'. The deep point, however, is that some (too many!) teachers have said to us 'we like the test very much, but we can't see the point of the postural stability. What's more, it's fiddly to do, so we don't bother.' Naturally, we're upset by this. We rationalize the explanation as follows: the teaching implications of problems in the right hand five tests are clear – one teaches the appropriate skills. But the teaching implications of the left hand five tests are unclear. If a child is slow at bead threading, one surely doesn't give systematic training therein, in the forlorn hope that this will help with reading! Indeed not! Most of the left-hand tests are purely diagnostic, rather than diagnostic/remedial. They suggest that the child is dyslexic, and therefore that standard teaching approaches may have to be modified, as we discuss in the support section.

Diagnosis

In comparison with screening, where there is now a varied set of possible tests, the situation with regard to diagnosis is now very confused. It is important to distinguish between two forms of diagnosis: a diagnosis for formal/legal purposes (formal diagnosis), and a diagnosis for personal development/treatment purposes (support diagnosis). In our adult screening survey, we established that most diagnosticians attempted to combine both functions, by starting with a structured interview, then moving to various formal diagnostic tests, then ending with further discussions aimed at specific problems. It is fair to say that there is no set approach to support diagnosis (unfortunately), and in this section, therefore, I will focus on formal diagnosis.

The traditional definition of dyslexia emphasizes both discrepancy (a difficulty in learning to read not explicable on the basis of lack of opportunity, low general ability, or emotional trauma). Practitioners normally tested both reading and IQ, and then used one of two methods: the cutoff method, commonly used in the UK, takes a criterion such as 'IQ of at least 90, and reading age at least 18 months behind chronological age'. The regression method appears more sophisticated, and commonly involves 'reading age that is at least 1.5 SD below that expected on the basis of the child's IQ'. It is clear that semi-arbitrary cutoffs are used in both definitions (cf. Ellis' analogy with obesity). The key difference between the two is that the regression method explicitly takes account of the child's IQ – so a child with an IQ of 140 and reading standard score of 100 (exactly normal) may turn out to be dyslexic. By contrast, the cutoff method might classify a child of IQ 92 and reading standard score 90 as dyslexic, whereas the regression method would not.

However, in the US, the field is in turmoil owing to the fact that poor readers without discrepancy (those with low IQ) show pretty much the same sort of phonological problems as poor readers with discrepancy (dyslexic poor readers). Indeed, both sets just don't seem to be very good at reading! This has led a number of influential US researchers to suggest that there is no point distinguishing the two groups. A poor reader is a poor reader is a poor reader. Geoff Lindsay (this volume), following the recommendations of the Working Group of the BPS Educational Section, also notes this suggestion. Now I personally consider this a retrograde and unjustified move (Nicolson, 1996). I think its adoption confuses the three issues: cause, symptom and treatment. The empirical finding is that the reading-related symptoms are similar.[4] Clearly, if there are different underlying causal factors for the two groups, lumping the two groups together can only obscure this. Equally, if the optimal treatment approach is different for the two groups, failing to distinguish them will prevent this critical fact being discovered.

Irrespective of my personal view, it would appear that the situation with regard to screening for dyslexia and other special needs has improved over the past decade, but the situation with respect to formal diagnosis has become less clear, with continuing concerns over the value of reading-related symptoms, grave concerns over the legitimacy of using IQ-related measures, and serious apparent problems in use of the discrepancy criterion.

Support

From the viewpoint of a dyslexic person (especially an adult) one of the most frustrating aspects of support is that there is an implicit assumption that literacy problems are the only area where support is needed. In fact, if one listens to the dyslexic individuals, quite the opposite is the case. Dyslexic adults will have spent years of their life struggling with literacy tasks. The last thing they want is more of the same. The key aspect to providing support is to generate and maintain motivation. Consequently, I distinguish here between literacy support and life support, starting with the former.

Life support

Dyslexia does not go away when one is adult – even though one's reading may become good enough to get by. Many routine skills will be less automatic than normal and so require more effort than normal. As we have argued in another chapter, being dyslexic may be a bit like living in a foreign country, where one can cope with the problems, but everything requires more effort, more thought than at home. When driving in France, I can drive pretty fluently, but it takes effort – remember to drive on the right, give way to all comers, work out the route beforehand, get a passenger to read the traffic signs, and so on. It's more effortful, stressful and tiring. Dyslexic adults will have developed methods of working that are essentially strategies for coping with these problems. One common symptom (McLoughlin, Fitzgibbon and Young, 1994) is the apparent reduction in working memory – it's hard to keep several things in mind at the same time. Another is a tendency to focus on the task in hand, to the extent that an impression of surliness may unwittingly be created. Constant task focusing and preferences for explicit knowledge can also lead to a failure to pick up semi-automatically the 'corporate culture', leading to workmates thinking that 'he [or she] is not one of us'. A further characteristic is a tendency to take an independent, 'first principles' approach, which in the right circumstances can be a major creative strength (West, 1991), but in others can be a further irritant. As McLoughlin et al. (1994) observe, diagnosis of dyslexia can be a significant liberator in adults, giving a rationale for a cluster of otherwise baffling characteristics, and providing a large implicit support group. The latter is particularly valuable, because dyslexia may be seen as the 'hidden disability'. Very often neither the workmates nor the individual is aware that he/she is dyslexic, and almost certainly no one will realize that dyslexia has ramifications outside of the literacy domain. It is unlikely that a dyslexic adult will wish to devote further time and effort to literacy – throwing good time after bad. A key requirement for the support of dyslexic adults is to find out (via structured interview) what their major goals are, and then to determine an individual support plan tuned to the specific goals. Needless to say, the plan must be achievable and motivating. The chapter by Kirk, McLoughlin and Reid provides a valuable overview of issues relating to identification and support in adults.

Much the same picture applies to dyslexic children. There is a serious danger that all support resources will be thrown into literacy support. This is of course crucial, but should not be seen as the only requirement. Early school failure has devastating consequences – emotional trauma, loss of self esteem, and family difficulties. Different children develop different coping strategies – avoidance of academic work, clowning, disruption, truancy, withdrawal. There are few who emerge unscathed, and many dyslexic adults harbour deep-seated anger and resentment about their treatment at school. It is valuable to distinguish two forms of coping: problem solving coping and emotional coping. Few people are good at providing both forms. Some prefer to analyse the problems, and suggest solutions. Others are better at providing a sympathetic ear, listening but not rushing in. An optimal approach will include elements of both, tailored specifically to the characteristics of the individual child.

One issue that has not yet been properly addressed in the literature is the effect of these general 'life support' factors on academic performance. Human beings are not machines. A small increase in confidence, having one-to-one sessions with a supportive teacher, a feeling that one is getting a new chance, the belief that one's parents are taking the problem seriously, more time spent on the academic tasks – all these factors are known to have disproportionate beneficial effects. Consequently, when evaluating interventions it is not enough to demonstrate that the intervention has a positive effect, one needs to compare the effect size with that of alternative support treatments, as discussed below. See Chapter 9 for eloquent advocacy of the importance of affect in support.

Literacy support

Much of the early work on reading support for dyslexia children was based on the timeless principles that literacy support needs to be individualized, systematic, explicit and structured, progressing a step at a time, and gradually building the skills needed (Gillingham and Stillman, 1960; Hickey, 1992; Miles, 1989). The difficulty with this approach is that it's hard to maintain motivation given such a gradual regime.

The major development in terms of literacy in the UK in the past decade was the introduction of the 'Literacy Strategy' in all infant and junior schools. The core feature of the strategy was the 'Literacy Hour', a dedicated hour every day devoted to literacy teaching, and with a systematic associated teaching methodology intended to make sure that all children progressed through the stages in reading in a predetermined sequence based on established good practice.

There is no doubt that introduction of the Literacy Strategy has had beneficial effects on overall literacy in UK schools. However, the sceptic might say that this is hardly surprising given that very much more time and resources are now being allocated to literacy. A dyslexia specialist might also enquire, with reason, whether there is evidence that the teaching methods used are in fact tuned to the teaching of dyslexic children.

In order to address these questions, it is necessary to consider evidence – controlled studies of the comparative effectiveness of different methods for teaching reading, especially for dyslexic children. Before evidence may be considered, however, it is necessary to devise a methodology for evaluating the evidence. In an ambitious series of controlled studies, US researchers have established high quality data on the effectiveness of a range of different interventions, recently published as (NICHD, 2000). See Joe Torgesen's chapter for an excellent review of the methods involved. For my purposes here, however, I provide a vignette from the third phase of our research programme, aimed at systematic screening–assessment–support.

Our main aim was to inform policy decisions on providing cost-effective support for dyslexic children, and we investigated two issues: first we needed to establish baseline data on how much improvement one might reasonably expect via a low cost standard intervention; and second we wished to establish whether such an approach was suitable for dyslexic children. From the viewpoint of policy, one needs to establish the cost-effectiveness of any intervention. It is clear that if more resources are devoted to teaching reading, then that should lead to significant improvements in reading. The sharp policy question is: how can we best invest the resources so as to maximize the benefits per unit cost?

Rather to our surprise, despite decades of educational research, there appeared to be no accepted methodology for assessing cost-effectiveness. In particular, no extant research appeared to have noted the obvious point that the longer the intervention, the more effect it is likely to have.

In an initial study, we took children in infant and junior schools in Sheffield and Harrogate, identified those at risk of reading problems, and gave them reading-related support in groups of three for two 30 minute sessions per week for 10 weeks, and monitored how much they improved on standard tests of reading and spelling over that period. Naturally we also used matched control groups in matched schools who did not have an intervention, so that we could establish the relative improvement. The intervention used was the balanced 'step by step' approach to tailoring the reading support to the individual capabilities of each reader developed by Reason and Boote (1994).

Figure 0.3 provides an overview of the effects of the various interventions. The outcome measure displayed is the 'composite literacy score', which is the average of the standard scores for reading and spelling. A standard score is age-normed, with a mean of 100. The children under investigation were all struggling with reading, as indicated by their low scores of below 90 initially (worse for the junior school study than the infant school study). Two interventions were compared, Reason's 'traditional' (in the sense that it was not computer-assisted) intervention described above, and a computer-based intervention named RITA

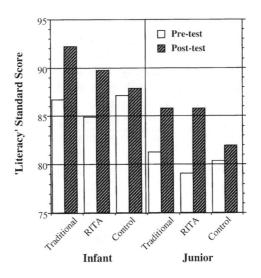

Figure 0.3: Effects of the Interventions on the Composite Literacy Standard Scores.

(Readers' Interactive Teaching Assistant) that I had developed myself and was designed to allow the teacher complete latitude in whether to use the computer, use traditional methods, or some combination thereof.

In all studies the intervention group made significantly more progress than the control group as measured by mean literacy standard scores. The overall effect sizes were 0.95 for the infant school and 0.67 for the junior school for the traditional interventions. Corresponding figures for RITA were 0.92 (infant) and 1.01 (junior). Effect sizes for the control groups were 0.23, both for infant and junior, demonstrating that the literacy strategy was having some beneficial effects.

The effect size alone indicates effectiveness (and if one subtracts the effect size for the control group, one gets the 'added value' of the intervention). An effect size in the region of 1.0 is considered 'large' statistically. The programmatic 'Reading Recovery' methods pioneered by Clay in New Zealand had added value effect size of between 0.70 and 1.30 (Nicolson, Fawcett, Moss, Nicolson and Reason, 1999). However, from the viewpoint of educational policy the key indicator is cost-effectiveness not just effectiveness. For cost-effectiveness one must divide the benefits (effect sizes) by the costs (teacher hours per child). The fact that our interventions took place in small groups for relatively short times (10 hours per group) means that both of our interventions were very much more cost-effective than reading recovery.

Finally, we considered the results relating to dyslexia. Are there some children who do not benefit much from the traditional intervention? In

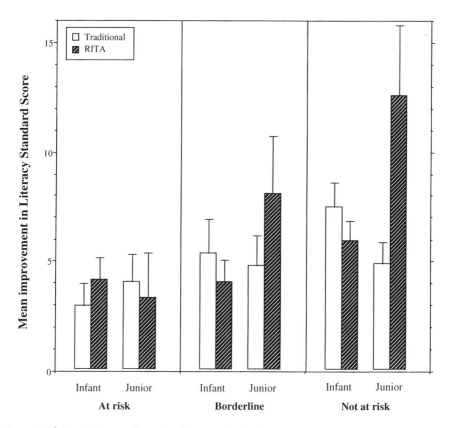

Figure 0.4: Breakdown of standard scores for the different 'at risk' categories.

fact in all studies there were children who did not improve much. Of these, almost all had 'at risk' scores on the DEST (infant) or DST (junior) tests. In the infant school traditional study, children at risk or borderline risk made very much less progress than the remainder (effect sizes 0.40, 0.35 and 0.96 respectively). For the junior school traditional study, at-risk children made very much less progress than the borderline or not at risk groups (0.35, 0.63 and 0.65 respectively). We had hoped that use of RITA would prove particularly helpful to the at-risk children, but this was not the case. It may be seen (Figure 0.4) that RITA was actually particularly beneficial in junior school for those poor readers who were not at risk, leading to an enormous mean improvement in standard score of around 12.5 points!

We concluded that the results confirm the importance and cost-effectiveness of early intervention in a child's initial school years – the 'stitch in time' approach. While cost-effective improvements in reading can be achieved at junior school, a significant proportion of junior children will fail to achieve lasting benefits from a relatively short intervention of this type.

I have spent too long on these illustrations since reading is not the primary focus of this chapter. As noted earlier, Torgesen's chapter, the comprehensive report of the US National Reading Panel and classics such as (Adams, 1990; Goswami and Bryant, 1990; Rayner and Pollatsek, 1989) provide excellent overviews. A broader account is given in (Nicolson, 1999).

The situation in 2000

In summary, outstanding progress has been made in the 1990s. Phonological deficit remains a central concept from the viewpoint of theory, diagnosis and early support. There is, however, an emerging consensus that a broader framework is needed for causal explanations and for diagnostic aids. In reviewing the 'state of the art', I will first note briefly the state of knowledge, and then consider in more detail the areas where knowledge is lacking, or there are unresolved difficulties.

Theory

Theoretically, at the cognitive level, hypotheses including slower speed of processing and abnormal fundamental learning processes have been added to phonological deficits. At the biological level, hypotheses including magnocellular deficit and cerebellar deficit have been proposed as alternatives to deficits in the cerebral language areas. Descriptions are now being introduced in terms of underlying genes, though the links to theories at biological, cognitive and behavioural levels are not yet established.

The new theoretical developments raise more questions than they answer. This is a strength rather than a weakness, reflecting the opening up of fruitful new research avenues. Limitations on knowledge are described below.

Lack of quantitative data on tasks 'across the board'

It is not enough to show that a group of dyslexic children differs significantly from controls on a particular skill. There will be significant impairments for most skills. What is needed is the profile of deficits (effect sizes), so that we can identify for which skills there are the most extreme deficits. A few small-scale studies have been completed, but it is not clear how representative these data are for the general dyslexia population.

Lack of quantitative data on prevalence and comorbidity

It is puzzling that despite a decade and more of intensive research, there are still few clear-cut data on whether individual dyslexic children and adults show one, two or more of the key indicators of phonological deficit, sensory deficit, speed deficit, and cerebellar deficit. What is needed is a large-scale study where all the children in a particular cohort are given standardized tests that cover the range of above skills, together with the different forms of learning, so as to assess the relative incidence and overlap ('comorbidity') of the possible different subtypes.

Lack of quantitative data on dyslexia and other learning disabilities

There are intriguing data that suggest there is unexpectedly high comorbidity between dyslexia and ADHD, dyslexia and specific language impairment, and dyslexia and dyspraxia. It is also likely that there would be comorbidity between dyslexia and generalized learning difficulty, if some measure other than IQ discrepancy could be established. Unfortunately, the underlying causes of these other developmental disorders are less well understood than those for dyslexia, but there is intriguing evidence of cerebellar abnormality in all of the specific disorders including ADHD (Berquin et al., 1998; Mostofsky, Reiss, Lockhart and Denckla, 1998). Clearly there is considerable scope for studies comparing and contrasting different disorders, using the techniques outlined above.

Lack of complete, integrated accounts

Perhaps a key requirement is to develop the accounts at the biological, cognitive and behavioural levels, with the intention of providing not only explanations at the different levels, but also providing an account of how the various symptoms develop as a function of genes, brain and experience.

Lack of links with mainstream developmental cognitive neuroscience

There is a real danger that dyslexia research in the UK remains seen as something of an isolated backwater. It takes too long for concepts from mainstream science – development, cognition and neuroscience to become accepted in dyslexia research. An outstanding example of the benefits that can accrue from infusion of new scientific approaches derived from the Rodin Remediation Dyslexia Society, which organized a series of exceptional scientific conferences on themes related to dyslexia over the 1990s.

Screening and diagnosis

In terms of diagnosis, there are now good screening tests available that can be used by a teacher or adult specialist to identify quickly the profile of strengths and weaknesses of an individual. This information, when augmented with interview data, may be able to form the basis of an initial individual development plan. Furthermore, a good case can be made for screening for 'dyslexia' before a child reaches school, especially if appropriate support regimes can then be introduced so as to maximize the chances of the child learning reasonably normally at school.

Difficulties over discrepancy

Unfortunately, the situation regarding diagnosis (both formal diagnosis and support diagnosis) is unsatisfactory. Formal diagnosis depends on assessment both of reading and of IQ. There are longstanding and valid objections to the use of IQ as an indicator, but in the absence of positive indicators for dyslexia it is hard to see how a discrepancy definition can otherwise be maintained. There is a movement in the US and the UK to abandon the discrepancy criterion, but this appears to me to reflect confusion between theory, diagnosis and support. Failure to maintain discrepancy would prevent analysis of the key issues of whether dyslexia does have underlying cause(s) distinct from other developmental disorders, and whether a dyslexia-friendly support regime is in fact significantly different from a generalized special-needs-friendly support regime. The movement to abandon discrepancy should be resisted strenuously until these key issues have been resolved.

Lack of positive indices of dyslexia

In my view, the reliance on 'reading' as a primary determinant is misplaced. Reading is a learned skill. Despite their difficulties, dyslexic children do learn to read (fortunately). Nonetheless, they remain dyslexic. What is urgently needed is an index of dyslexia that is based on a more fundamental attribute than is reading. It seems likely that a range of indicators – speed of processing, fundamental learning processes, magnocellular system operation – will be needed. Current diagnoses are based on a 'snapshot' of performance at one time. As with the current Code of Practice, it is important to augment these tests with tests of response to learning opportunities.

Lack of clarity regarding diagnosis relative to other learning disabilities

A further key requirement is comparison of dyslexia with other learning disabilities. At present the diagnosis a child receives is too dependent upon the specialist to whom s/he is first referred. Early speech difficulties will lead to a diagnosis of specific language impairment. Early clumsiness may lead to a diagnosis of dyspraxia. A child with mild problems in speech and motor skill may be diagnosed as dyslexic or maybe attention deficit. Development of more fundamental diagnostic criteria should illuminate this vexed issue.

Difficulties regarding diagnosis in multilingual children

It is currently very difficult to know how to diagnose dyslexia in children whose first language is not English. Clearly some degree of reading impairment is likely. We would hope that identification of fundamental criteria should significantly alleviate this vexed issue.

Difficulties regarding diagnosis in non-English-speaking countries

It is important to stress that dyslexia is somewhat differently defined in countries where the language spoken has a more transparent (regular) orthography. In Spanish and German, for instance, the rules for pronouncing the written word are straightforward, with few exceptions. Consequently, most children are able to read, albeit slowly in some cases. One approach to the problem of diagnosis is to identify those children who read slowly as dyslexic (Wimmer, 1993). It is not clear whether this approach leads to the same classifications as would obtain if the children were English-speaking. Again, it seems likely that cross-linguistic research, finding commonalities between dyslexia in different languages, is likely to advance the search for fundamental positive indicators of dyslexia.

Support

There has been considerable progress in literacy and numeracy teaching. Nonetheless, there seems to be a lack of clear knowledge on a number of crucial issues.

Clarifying principles of dyslexia-friendly teaching

The central question is whether the techniques introduced are in fact dyslexia friendly. In my view, the 'one pace suits all' approach implicit in the UK literacy strategy is unlikely to be appropriate for dyslexic children. At the very least they will require considerable extra support. There is a clear need for carefully controlled evaluation studies aimed at identifying the cost effectiveness of different support methods for different groups of children with reading problems. Standard instructional theory established many years ago that if one wants to teach a complex skill, it is necessary to perform a balancing act – to try to automatize the component subskills while also teaching the skill as a whole (Nicolson, 1998). This is pretty obvious in the case of a skill such as tennis – one needs to be able to practise the forehand as well as the backhand, and one needs to play a game in order to maintain interest. The consensus of studies in the past decade is that this is also true of reading. One needs to develop fluency and knowledge as well as phonological skills. It remains to be established whether the optimal dyslexia-friendly methods are the same as the optimal normal-reader-friendly methods or the optimal non-dyslexic-poor-reader-friendly methods. I doubt it.

Harnessing new technology

Computer-based opportunities (including voice recognition, multimedia and the Internet) have improved out of all recognition over the decade. One of the key support requirements is the issue of how to harness these opportunities to supporting dyslexic people. I believe that the computer provides the method to maintain enjoyment and fun while delivering the adaptive, carefully crafted and systematic schedules needed to develop automaticity. The challenge is to identify how best to use computer, human teacher and learner as a team.

How to exploit strengths as well as remedy weaknesses

It may be that dyslexic and non-dyslexic poor readers have a similar profile of weaknesses on reading. They certainly do not have the same strengths, and instructional science (and common sense) make it clear that good learning normally builds on strengths rather than weaknesses.

Policy

Finally, then, policy. In this area it would appear that successive UK governments have performed outstandingly, in terms of education Acts and adult disability discrimination Acts. It is unfortunate that UK research councils have failed to capitalize on this by dedicated funding for 'pure' dyslexia research.

What is the best dyslexia-friendly policy?

The thrust of the above review is that the UK government would be more than willing to introduce a popular, justifiable and cost-effective policy towards the identification and support of dyslexic individuals, and those with other special needs. The question, however, is, what should such a policy be? What would be the main objectives for theory, diagnosis and support? How would it be evaluated? It is surely time for the UK dyslexia research community to attempt to provide the answers – to design, propose and undertake a comprehensive and united research programme aimed at a complete and inclusive analysis of dyslexia theory, diagnosis and support. I outline below some considerations that may be relevant. My main aim, however, is to stimulate discussion of these issues, in the expectation that those with greater expertise in the specific areas will be able to improve significantly on the proposed framework.

Into the future

I start with 10 sober questions for dyslexia research, in the hope that researchers will attack these with relish, thereby significantly advancing the field. I move on to six 'injunctions' for dyslexia research, following the lead of Allen Newell. I then present a somewhat fanciful portrayal of the future, using the style of a third giant of my formative years, Isaac Asimov, in the hope that the artistic licence granted will illuminate the possible objectives for the next few years. I conclude with a plea for a concerted effort at a coherent, inclusive and integrated research programme into dyslexia theory, practice and policy.

Ten questions for dyslexia research

Q1. Is there a better way to teach reading, one that combines the important aspects of the systematic approaches known to help dyslexic children, but designed also to be intrinsically motivating, and natural?

Q2. How we can diagnose dyslexia as early as appropriate? In particular, how much can studies of development in infancy and in the preschool period inform our understanding and identification? See the chapters by Van der Leij, Lyytinen and Zwarts and by Johnson, Peer and Lee for theory and identification in infancy.

Q3. Are there different forms of dyslexia? Do some children have only phonological problems, others magnocellular plus phonological, others cerebellar etc? How do differences relate to different genes?

Q4. If there are different forms, what are the implications for teaching and support?

Q5. How about 'alternative' methods of support? What credence should one attach to tinted lenses, travel sickness pills, dietary supplements, reflexology and other methods? For whom are they successful, and if so, why?

Q6. Does intelligence matter for diagnosis and/or support?

Q7. How about other learning disabilities/developmental disorders? What is the overlap with dyslexia, and how important is it?

Q8. How can we develop and introduce a systematic, cost-effective and valuable system for screening, assessment and support that is respected by all?

Q9. How can we integrate dyslexia research within mainstream developmental, cognitive and neuroscience research?

Q10.Can we really 'prevent' dyslexia? That is, can we develop a series of 'learning experiences' that 'scaffold' brain development on to an optimal track? For instance, is it possible to present speech sounds in such a sequence during infancy that the 'optimal' brain representation for speech sounds is ensured.

Injunctions for dyslexia research

Following Allen Newell, whose 1973 analysis of the way forward for cognitive psychology was formative for me, I offer five 'injunctions for dyslexia research'.

Injunction 1: be open minded and inclusive

Too little is known about the mechanisms of brain development (normal or abnormal) to allow us the luxury of rejecting alternative support methods out of hand. Many will have a kernel of good sense that can be integrated into a fuller support system, or may provide a valuable perspective suggesting new research avenues.

Injunction 2: Gather quantitative evidence, using objective methods

As in other spheres, evidence-based research is the key requirement for progress. We need to evaluate the effectiveness of support methods using standardized criteria such as effect sizes and cost-effectiveness. Of course, if evidence suggests that a particular approach is not good, that approach should be discouraged, injunction 1 notwithstanding.

Injunction 3: Be inquisitorial, not adversarial

The adversarial (head to head) approach is largely discredited in psychological theory. Its overuse in psychological research derives more from politics than science. The inquisitorial (pursuit of truth) approach is the only way to hope to make cumulative progress.

Injunction 4: Groups are made of individuals

From Piaget's studies of his children to the sophisticated methods of cognitive neuropsychology, detailed case studies of individuals have presented fascinating insights into development, abnormal and normal cognitive processes. By contrast, traditional empirical psychology has studied differences between groups. When studying a heterogeneous syndrome such as dyslexia it is necessary to combine the techniques, studying both groups and individuals within groups.

Injunction 5: Respect differing roles and work together

Newell argued that, in order to make cumulative progress on a complex problem, it was necessary to integrate teamwork from diverse specialists. For dyslexia the teams should involve theoreticians (neuroscience, developmental, and cognitive), educationalists, and policy makers. Furthermore, people with first-hand experience of dyslexia may often have unique and distinctive insights that short laboratory tests may miss.

Injunction 6: Aim for a unified, complete approach

Newell made a convincing case that one needed to know where one was aiming for in order to get there (a theme going back to his classic work on means–ends analysis). He also took the view that it was better to think big, to aim for a complete explanation of a complex problem, than to mess around with a series of partial solutions. As with learning to read, one needs to perceive and play the whole game, rather than merely parts thereof.

2011: a Dyslexia Odyssey

Susan Seldon was worried. Her husband Matthew had been diagnosed as dyslexic following the introduction of the mandatory 'dyslexia in the workplace' screening and support procedures. There was a 50% chance that their toddler son Hari would also be dyslexic. She checked the World Dyslexia Association Website. She downloaded the testing software on to the Cube, worked through the interactive DVD-manuals. Hari climbed into the control pod and expertly adjusted the joystick. Susan calibrated the Webcam was working and booted up the TV wall. The programs took 30 minutes. They monitored eye movements and tracking, rapid auditory screening, balance, dexterity, verbal and visual working memory, mental rotation, letter recognition, and phonological discrimination. Within a couple of minutes the software analysed the data, and came up with an outline profile and diagnosis. At risk. She clicked the 'see specialist' option and watched the data transfer to the clinic. An appointment was made for the next day.

Hari enjoyed the visit to the clinic. There was a funny moving platform, a strange net they kept on his head while he listened to some noises and then played a strange game where he had to save the good rabbits – it was hard because you couldn't tell which ones were the good ones at first. There were a couple of things he didn't really like – a boring game where there was a beep and then something blew in his eye, and a toy that pricked his thumb.

The clinician explained the diagnosis to Susan. 'We've checked all the signs and the DNA. It looks as though the cerebellum is fine. The conditioning, memory, eye control and speech are fine. Everything points to a problem in the auditory magnocellular system. We've picked up difficulties with the sound sequence task, and there's no mismatch negativity when we play two slightly different tones. This is also consistent with the presence of the magnocell gene on chromosome 1, same as his father.

'Our main aim is to make sure that he's up to speed on his phonological skills by his next birthday. Take this DVD game, and let him play on it for 20 minutes per day – you'll have trouble keeping him off! What it does is it trains up his auditory system to be exceptionally good on making the phonological discriminations. It was specially developed by the Speech Science Foundation to ensure optimal phonemic categorization for English. He'll be much better than all his friends by next birthday, but bring him in again in three months and we'll check again.'

Fanciful!? Maybe – the next-day appointment is a bit optimistic! In terms of the screening and diagnosis, though, we have the technology to do this now (though not as smoothly as suggested!). What we do not have is the integration of the different approaches, or the evidence needed to guide the development of the differential testing procedures, and the links from the diagnosis to a specific age-appropriate adaptive and enjoyable support regime.

Targets for dyslexia research

On re-reading the chapter, I feel I have not done justice to reading – a wonderful and elusive skill that is the 'queen and servant' of human cognitive achievement. Unlike language, the human cognitive architecture was not designed for learning to read. Of course the study of reading and the teaching of reading is central to the understanding and support of dyslexia. I have been arguing the need for a wider perspective largely because this view has been under-represented. Before it is too late, then, and the dedicated and skilled body of teachers, educationalists, and reading theorists is further alienated, I need to highlight the crucial role that the reading community must play in any coherent strategy for assessing and supporting learning disabilities and dyslexia.

In order to do this I shall bring in one further diversion. In 1980 a wonderful book was published (Papert, 1980). Papert attempted to revolutionize the learning of mathematics by harnessing the power of computers to allow children to discover concepts for themselves. His analyses were convincing and uplifting. He argued that a major aim of education should be to allow children to learn 'naturally', as in the real world – the best way to learn French is to live in France, to be immersed in it. He attempted to create a 'Mathland' where children were immersed in mathematical concepts.[5] Unfortunately, the educational world was not ready for such innovation then (or now!), the technology was too rudimentary, and arguably the children themselves were not ready. In one telling analogy, Papert described the 'ski revolution':

> Twenty years ago parallel skiing was thought to be a skill attainable only after many years of training and practice. Today it is routinely achieved in the course of a single skiing season. [This revolution was partly achieved via technological improvements – shorter skis, lighter materials, but primarily by reconceptualisation of the process of skiing) . . . when the parents learned to ski, both vacation skiers and Olympic champions used turning techniques based on a preparatory counter-rotation, thought to be necessary for parallel turns. The realisation that more direct movements could produce a more effective turn was a fundamental discovery, and it rapidly transformed skiing, both for the vacation skier and the champion.

The above passage highlights one of the fundamental difficulties in learning a complex skill – often one has to scaffold the skill by learning an intermediate skill which, in due course, must be unlearned so that the complete skill may be performed more fluently. It is well established that unlearning a bad habit is much more difficult than learning a new one. Our research on long-term learning suggests that dyslexic children are even more severely affected than normal by any need to unlearn. Learning to read (traditionally) involves a large number of transitional stages. Adding some common-sense thoughts to Uta Frith's brilliant analysis of learning to read (Frith, 1986) one can adduce a whole range of stages: first, the logographic stage (recognizing a whole word as an integral shape); next the 'alphabetic' stage, where one picks out the individual letters in an unfamiliar word, and, using the principles of grapheme–phoneme translation, blends them together into the corresponding spoken form, and finally recognizes the word corresponding to the spoken sound. Frith calls the third stage the 'orthographic' stage, where strings of letters are recognized as a unit, and so, rather than analysing say 'catapult' into eight letters, then blending the corresponding 8 sounds into one word, one analyses it into 'cat', 'a' and 'pult', each of which can be read as a chunk, and then combined. On top of these major changes there are several other changes needed for fluent reading: first one has to wean oneself off the need to articulate the letters (by using an internal speech representation – inner speech). Next, one has to learn to move one's eyes in an efficient manner across the page. A skilled reader, reading aloud, will have an 'eye-voice span' of up to seven words – the eyes have read the rest of the sentence while the voice is still on the beginning, thereby allowing the meaning to have been determined in time to sort out the appropriate intonation patterns. Frith speculated that dyslexic children have difficulty moving from the logographic to the orthographic stage. I speculate that dyslexic children have difficulty moving from any stage to the next, whenever any unlearning is required.

Reading is a complex, learned skill. It can perhaps be compared to a range of mountains, with rolling foothills leading to a range of snow-covered peaks. As with any other skill, there are many routes up the reading mountain. Some faster, some slower. Some may not reach the top, leaving the learner stuck on a plateau with no means of reaching the next peak. Surely a mature science of reading instruction should be able to streamline these processes, to reduce the amount of unnecessary unlearning and relearning, to identify the places where readers 'get stuck' in their ascent of the mountain, and to devise 'bridges' to assist children to get across these crevasses. We need to devise the analysis tools that help identify where a child is on the reading mountain, and to help them reach a safe route. Above all, we need to be able to select a route of ascent that suits the child in question. In order to achieve this, it is necessary for teachers, theorists and educationalists to work together to map the terrain.

Conclusions

It has been a difficult chapter to write. It's probably a difficult chapter to read. In attempting to provide an overview from a range of perspectives, I lay myself open to the justified charge that I have gone beyond my sphere of expertise. That is so. I hope nonetheless that these outline analyses will prove a solid enough foundation for specialists to construct a more fully informed, more coherent, and better framework to guide research for the next ten years.

In conclusion, dyslexia research has made considerable progress. I think, though, we're at the start of a revolution in the learning disabilities field, where the different sciences and techniques of development, of neuroscience, of cognition and of education come together with the needs and opportunities of policy and government. The way forward is to be clear about what we need to achieve, and have a coherent strategy to move towards it. There is a need for consensus, for foresight, for an attitude of partnership, for inclusion. Balancing those characteristics, there is a need for objectivity, for comparative evaluation, for 'kitemarking', for better analysis and evaluation tools. Above all, we need to be able to respect and motivate the individual, as well as analysing the group.

The stage is set for undertaking ambitious, multi-disciplinary, multi-perspective projects aimed at redefining the field of dyslexia and learning difficulties as the field of learning abilities.

Notes

1. Simon gained the Nobel prize for his work in economics, in which he developed the concept of a human as a 'rational' decision maker, essentially applying a cost benefit analysis to the alternatives in any given situation. As we shall see, dyslexia research can also benefit from rational analysis.
2. Perhaps, though, a more appropriate analogy is with allergy. The same allergy can lead to different symptoms in different people and the mechanisms by which allergies arise are poorly understood. Traditional medical science has had difficulties with allergies, and progress has been made primarily via the development of systematic procedures for narrowing down the potential causes.
3. A good example of the application of theory in diagnosis is the need for early diagnosis, before a child fails to learn to read. In order to diagnose dyslexia before reading failure, one needs to have a theoretical approach that indicates positive indicators in addition to reading.
4. Some might argue that, theory aside, the fact that the two groups have similar reading symptoms is hardly surprising given that they were defined in terms of the symptom of poor reading.
5. As it happens, I think Mathland would be a poor environment for dyslexic children as they appear to be relatively weak at learning from the real world and relatively strong at learning by being told.

References

Adams MJ (1990) Beginning to Read: Thinking and Learning about Print. Cambridge MA: MIT Press.

Augur J (1985) Guidelines for teachers, parents and learners. In M. Snowling (ed.) Children's Written Language Difficulties. Windsor: NFER Nelson.

Berquin PC, Giedd JN, Jacobsen LK, Hamburger SD, Krain AL, Rapoport JL, Castellanos FX (1998) Cerebellum in attention-deficit hyperactivity disorder – a morphometric MRI study. Neurology 50: 1087–93.

Boder E (1973) Developmental dyslexia: a diagnostic approach based on three atypical spelling-reading patterns. Developmental Medicine and Child Neurology 15: 663–87.

Broadbent DE (1971) Decision and Stress. London: Academic Press.

Broadbent DE (1973) In Defence of Empirical Psychology. London: Methuen.

Bryant P (1985) The Question of Prevention. In MJ Snowling (ed.) Childrens' Written Language Difficulties. Windsor: NFER Nelson, p. 42.

Castles A, Holmes VM (1996) Subtypes of developmental dyslexia and lexical acquisition. Australian Journal of Psychology 48: 130–5.

Ellis AW (1993) Reading, Writing and Dyslexia: A cognitive analysis. 2 edn. Hove: Erlbaum.

Elman JE, Bates EA, Johnson MH, Karmiloff-Smith A, Parisi D, Plunkett K (1997) Rethinking Innateness: A connectionist perspective on development. Cambridge MA: MIT Press.

Frith U (1986) A developmental framework for developmental dyslexia. Annals of Dyslexia 36.

Frith U (1997) Brain, mind and behaviour in dyslexia. In C Hulme, M Snowling (eds) Dyslexia: Biology, Cognition and Intervention. London: Whurr.

Gillingham A, Stillman B (1960) Remedial training for children with specific difficulties in reading, writing and penmanship. Cambridge MA: Educators Publishing.

Goswami U, Bryant P (1990) Phonological Skills and Learning to Read. Hillsdale NJ: Lawrence Erlbaum Associates.

Haslum M (1989) Predictors of dyslexia? Irish Journal of Psychology 10(4): 622–30.

Hickey K (1992) The Hickey Multisensory Language Course. 2 edn. Ed. J Augur, S Briggs. London: Whurr.

Lyon GR, Moats LC (1993) An examination of research in learning disabilities. In GR Lyon, DB Gray, JF Kavanagh, NA Krasnegor (eds) Better Understanding Learning Disabilities: New views from research and their implications for education and public policies. Baltimore MA: Paul H Brookes, pp. 1–13.

McLoughlin D, Fitzgibbon G, Young V (1994) Adult Dyslexia: Assessment, counselling and training. London: Whurr.

Miles E (1989) The Bangor Dyslexia Teaching System. London: Whurr.

Miles TR (1983) Dyslexia: the pattern of difficulties. London: Granada.

Moser C (2000) Better basic skills – Improving adult literacy and numeracy. London: Department for Education and Employment.

Mostofsky SH, Reiss AL, Lockhart P, Denckla MB (1998) Evaluation of cerebellar size in attention-deficit hyperactivity disorder. Journal of Child Neurology 13: 434–9.

Newell A (1973) You can't play 20 questions with nature and win: comments on the symposium. In W Chase (ed.) Visual Information Processing. London: Academic Press.

Newell A (1990) Unified Theories of Cognition. Cambridge MA: Harvard University Press.

NICHD (2000) Report of the National Reading Panel: Teaching children to read. Washington DC: National Institute for Child Health and Human Development.

Nicolson RI (1996) Developmental dyslexia; past, present and future. Dyslexia: An International Journal of Research and Practice 2: 190–207.

Nicolson RI (1998) Learning and Skill. In P Scott, C Spencer (eds) Psychology: A contemporary introduction. Oxford: Blackwell, pp. 294–343.

Nicolson RI (1999) Reading, Skill and Dyslexia. In D Messer, S Millar (eds) Exploring Developmental Psychology. London: Arnold.

Nicolson RI, Fawcett AJ, Miles TR (1993) Feasibility study for the development of a computerised screening test for dyslexia in adults (Report OL176). Sheffield: Employment Department.

Nicolson RI, Fawcett AJ, Moss H, Nicolson MK, Reason R (1999) An Early Reading Intervention Study: Evaluation and Implications. British Journal of Educational Psychology 69: 47–62.

Papert S (1980) Mindstorms: Children, computers and powerful ideas. New York: Basic Books.

Rayner K, Pollatsek A (1989) The Psychology of Reading. London: Prentice-Hall.

Reason R, Boote R (1994) Helping Children with Reading and Spelling: A special needs manual. Oxford: Routledge.

Siegel LS (1989) IQ is irrelevant to the definition of learning disabilities. Journal of Learning Disabilities 22: 469.

Thelen E, Smith LB (1994) A dynamic systems approach to the development of cognition and action. Cambridge MA: MIT Press.

West TG (1991) In the Mind's Eye: Visual thinkers, gifted people with learning difficulties, computer images, and the ironies of creativity. Buffalo NY: Prometheus Books.

Wimmer H (1993) Characteristics of developmental dyslexia in a regular writing system. Applied Psycholinguistics 14(1): 1–33.

Wolf M, Bowers PG (1999) The double deficit hypothesis for the developmental dyslexias. Journal of Educational Psychology 91: 415–38.

PART ONE
BIOLOGICAL BASES

Progress towards the identification of genes influencing developmental dyslexia*

SIMON E FISHER, SHELLEY D SMITH

Introduction

The observation that reading disability tends to run in families was first reported at the turn of the last century (Thomas, 1905) only a few years after publication of the first case study of what was then referred to as 'congenital word blindness' (Morgan, 1896). As we enter the twenty-first century, the isolation of gene variants that may be involved in developmental dyslexia remains a major challenge for research into this important trait. The potential benefits of achieving this goal include early diagnosis of individuals who are at increased risk for reading disorders and the identification of novel biological targets for therapeutic intervention. Such research promises to provide a firm foundation for exploring how environmental factors may interact with genetic predisposition. The ultimate aim of these investigations is to gain insight into the neurological pathways that underpin our ability to learn to read.

The past 15–20 years have seen dramatic advances in the field of human molecular genetics, allowing scientists to identify the mutations[1] responsible for the majority of the single-gene disorders known to man (such as cystic fibrosis, several forms of muscular dystrophy, Huntington's chorea and fragile-X mental retardation). Many of these discoveries are due to the success of an approach known as 'positional cloning' (Collins, 1992). In the initial part of the process scientists track the inheritance

---

*Editor's note – This chapter contains complex material, which readers from a variety of backgrounds may find difficult. In order to make it more accessible I have added a series of endnotes to explain some of the more technical terms. Those readers who have the determination to persist will access some fascinating material.

patterns of chromosomal[2] regions in families affected by the trait of interest, in order to map the location of the gene[3] responsible. This first stage exploits naturally occurring variation (polymorphisms) in DNA sequence at anonymous genetic markers and is referred to as 'linkage[4] mapping', because it evaluates whether the markers are linked to the trait of interest. With enough linkage data from families it is possible to zero in on a specific chromosomal region containing a small subset of genes, each of which can then be tested for mutations until the gene responsible for the trait is pinpointed. The power of positional cloning is that it allows identification of a gene involved in a particular trait without any prior knowledge of the biochemical basis of the trait, or the function of the gene. This is in contrast to pure candidate-gene approaches, where hypotheses regarding the relevant biological pathways are used to choose a known gene as a candidate for involvement in the trait, without any information about chromosomal location. It is also possible to combine strategies, initially using linkage mapping to isolate a chromosomal region of interest, and then targeting particular candidate genes from the region on the basis of their likely function (Ballabio, 1993; Collins, 1995).

Now that many of the human single-gene disorders have been successfully tackled by the above approaches, molecular geneticists are turning their attention to more common diseases including heart disease, diabetes, asthma and psychiatric disorders, which constitute major health and sociological problems for the modern world. The study of these common traits is complicated by the fact that they are multi-factorial, that is resulting from interactions between a number of different influences, which may be genetic, environmental or stochastic[5] in nature, thus requiring development of novel techniques and statistical methodologies (Lander and Schork, 1994; Weeks and Lathrop, 1995). This chapter will describe how the recent advances of molecular genetics have been applied to studies of developmental dyslexia, and will give an overview of progress to date towards identification of gene variants involved in the trait. No specific gene has yet been implicated in reading disability, but there have been remarkable successes in mapping the approximate positions of a number of loci[6] that may be important. As the sequencing of the human genome nears completion we are now in a unique position to begin dissecting out the relevant genetic variants from these chromosomal regions.

We will begin by highlighting the genotypic and phenotypic[7] complexity of dyslexia, then outline the gene localization strategies that have been critical for recent successes, before reviewing the latest findings in this burgeoning field.

Developmental dyslexia is a complex trait at the genetic level

There is substantial evidence from many studies demonstrating that relatives of probands with dyslexia have an increased risk of developing reading and spelling disorders (for example Hallgren, 1950; Lewitter et al., 1980; Pennington et al., 1991; Lubs et al., 1993). It is important to realize that the well-documented familial clustering of reading disability does not, by itself, implicate genetic factors in the etiology of the trait, because clustering may also be due to shared family environment. However, strong support for genetic influences has also come from studies that compare the concordance[8] of developmental dyslexia in monozygotic[9] (MZ) twins (who have an almost identical genetic make-up) with that observed in dizygotic[10] (DZ) twins (who share approximately half of their genes). For example investigation of a large sample of twins identified by the Colorado Learning Disabilities Research Center has shown a concordance rate of 68% in MZ twins, as compared to 38% in DZ twins (DeFries and Alarcón, 1996). This same twin sample has been used to pioneer quantitative approaches to define dyslexia for genetic analyses (DeFries et al., 1987; DeFries and Gillis, 1993). A composite discriminant score for overall reading performance was constructed from a number of psychometric tests administered to the twins and normalized with respect to an unselected control population. Reading-disabled probands[11] were selected from the twin pairs if their discriminant score lay at the extreme end of the distribution, below a predetermined cutoff. The extent to which co-twins of the probands regressed towards the mean of the normal population was examined as a function of relatedness (MZ versus DZ). This method, known as DeFries-Fulker (DF) regression, assesses whether DZ co-twins are more similar to the control population than MZ co-twins, and gives estimates of the heritability[12] of extreme deficits in the measure – the proportion of variation which can be attributed to genetic factors (DeFries and Fulker, 1985). The Colorado study has thereby estimated a heritability of ~50% (±11%) for reading disability (DeFries and Gillis, 1993). DeFries-Fulker regression has since been applied to specific subtests of reading performance, as well as a number of other quantitative traits, and has also been extended for use in linkage analyses, as described later in this chapter (Olson et al., 1994; Cardon et al., 1994, 1995; Gayán et al., 1999).

Given that there is strong evidence for the involvement of genetic factors in dyslexia, how do we go about identifying them? A pure candidate-gene approach is unlikely to be fruitful, because there are a very large number of potential candidates that would have to be tested (although there are several hypotheses regarding the neurological or physiological etiology of the trait, which might suggest subsets of genes to focus on). A more promising strategy to adopt is that of linkage mapping and positional cloning. Linkage analysis that has been successful in mapping single-gene disorders is model based (or parametric), because it requires one to make a number of assumptions about how the trait is inherited in order to map it with any confidence. For example, the analyses may depend on correctly specifying the mode of transmission (dominant, recessive, sex-linked,[13] and so forth), the frequency of the mutation causing the trait, the likelihood of an individual showing the trait when they inherit the mutation (known as the *penetrance*) amongst other parameters. In addition the analysis explicitly assumes that predisposition to the trait is caused by a single major gene. Unfortunately it is clear from many studies that dyslexia is a 'complex trait', a phrase used to refer to any phenotype that does not always display a classical Mendelian inheritance pattern – one that can be attributed to a single gene (Lander and Schork, 1994). Genetic complexity can arise as a consequence of a number of different factors. It is very likely that dyslexia is genetically heterogeneous, meaning that there are different genes (possibly with different transmission patterns) predisposing to reading disability in different families. Linkage studies often increase their power by combining data from numerous families, so mapping by traditional model-based methods might be confounded if there is significant *genetic heterogeneity,* because different families will give conflicting mapping data. Another source of complexity is *oligogenic inheritance,* where predisposing alleles of several different genes interact with each other within the same family to increase risk for the disorder. Further problems arise from *reduced penetrance,*[14] where an individual with a predisposing genotype does not manifest the disorder, either due to other modifier loci in their genetic background, or environmental/random factors. Conversely, there may also be cases of *phenocopy,*[15] where an individual who does not have a predisposing genotype nevertheless does develop reading disability. Therefore traditional model-based linkage mapping, requiring knowledge of the mode of transmission, level of penetrance and rates of phenocopy, and relying on the assumption of single-gene inheritance, often runs into difficulties when handling a trait like dyslexia. As outlined later in this chapter, recent developments in study design, genetic technology and statistical methodologies have offered alternatives to traditional linkage analyses and are providing new opportunities for mapping genes of complex traits.

Complexity of phenotype – defining dyslexia

An essential prerequisite for successful genetic analysis is the reliable classification of the trait under investigation (see Pennington, 1997). At the most basic level this involves making a diagnosis of 'affection status' –

designating within a pedigree which individuals manifest the trait and which individuals do not. Accurate model-based mapping of a locus involved in a trait will depend on genetic data from some key affected or unaffected members of a family, so it is obviously important that these individuals have been given the correct diagnosis. A trait like dyslexia may show considerable variability in nature and severity between different affected individuals, particularly with respect to age, because dyslexic adults often compensate for their overall reading difficulties. Furthermore, there is not yet a strong consensus about exactly what constitutes the core deficit in reading disability, although it is clear that visual problems, phonological difficulties and/or impaired temporal processing are likely to be important factors (reviewed in Habib, 2000). Opinion is also divided about whether dyslexia is a single disorder or a cluster of related traits, a critical question for genetic studies that pool data from several or many different families. A further cause for concern is that different genetic studies often use different diagnostic tools and varying definitions of affection status. For example, different investigations have classified on the basis of varying phenotypes such as phonological deficit (Field and Kaplan, 1998), spelling difficulty (Schulte-Körne et al., 1998), or dyslexia associated with speech delay (Froster et al., 1993). Sometimes the lack of conformity between the diagnostic tools of different studies is an unavoidable consequence of language differences. The psychometric tests used to study reading and spelling in English-speaking families (for example, Smith et al., 1983) are inevitably not the same as those adopted for German (Froster et al., 1993; Schulte-Körne et al., 1998), Danish (Bisgaard et al., 1987) or Norwegian pedigrees (Fagerheim et al., 1999). Given all of the above issues, comparison of linkage data from multiple studies can be difficult, and it is not surprising that independent groups are often unable to replicate linkage findings.

The application of non-parametric linkage techniques to qualitative definitions of dyslexia (described below) can only partially ameliorate the above problems of uncertain affection status and phenotypic heterogeneity. In recent years there have been two key developments in the field of definition of reading and spelling disability for genetic studies. The first involves the use of quantitative psychometric test data directly for linkage mapping, thereby exploiting the full variation of the trait (for example, Cardon et al., 1994, 1995). This is known as quantitative trait locus (QTL) analysis, and is discussed in more detail in the next section. The second retains a qualitative definition of affection status, but fractionates the overall dyslexia deficit into a number of partly overlapping, but partly distinct phenotypic components, such as phoneme awareness, phonological coding, rapid automized naming and single-word reading (Grigorenko et al., 1997). Perhaps the most powerful approach to phenotype definition is a combination of these strategies, employing direct QTL analyses of several continuous measures which should correlate with different components of the dyslexia phenotype (Fisher et al., 1999a, 1999b; Gayán et al. 1999; Fisher et al., 2000; Francks et al., 2000).

Strategies for localizing genes influencing dyslexia

Since the first report of a dyslexia linkage to chromosome 15 in 1983 (Smith et al., 1983), a variety of methods have been used to map genes involved in this disorder. One way of dealing with the complexity of the trait is to identify very large families containing multiple severely affected members, where the transmission pattern looks very similar to classical monogenic Mendelian inheritance. This allows one to apply traditional qualitative model-based linkage analysis in the hope that there will be a major gene predisposing to dyslexia that segregates in the pedigree under study. Once a chromosomal region is implicated in a large pedigree, it can be tested in a wider range of families in order to demonstrate whether or not the proposed locus plays a significant role in common forms of dyslexia. There has been some success using this approach for reading disability (for example, the locus on chromosome 2 identified by Fagerheim et al., 1999), but the most convincing example actually comes from studies of a three-generation family affected with a severe monogenic form of speech and language disorder, in which the gene responsible was localized to a small interval on chromosome 7q31 (Fisher et al., 1998; Lai et al., 2000). Unfortunately, for traits such as dyslexia and language impairment, large families of this kind with sufficient power for model-based linkage analysis are very rare, and heterogeneity presents problems for pooling of data from smaller families.

However, if it is not possible to assume single-gene transmission and to reliably estimate parameters for model-based linkage analyses of families, an alternative is to use recently developed non-parametric or 'model-free' techniques. Qualitative non-parametric linkage methods are essentially based on assessing whether or not affected relatives inherit identical copies of a polymorphic[16, 17] genetic marker from a common ancestor more often than that which would be expected by chance. For example if the marker under investigation is unlinked to the trait of interest then two affected siblings will, on average, share ~50% of their alleles identical-by-descent (IBD) as a consequence of random Mendelian segregation.[18] By contrast, if the marker under investigation is in the vicinity of a gene involved in the trait, affected siblings will tend to show increased IBD sharing. Simple statistical tests can be used to assess the significance of any observed excess IBD sharing. In order to have sufficient power to detect a susceptibility gene using this technique large collections of hundreds of affected sib-pair[19] (ASP) families are needed. Allele-sharing methods can also be applied to arbitrary affected members of extended pedigrees, although the assessment of statistical significance of increased sharing is more complicated (Weeks and Lathrop, 1995). Such qualitative non-parametric methods have been employed in a number of recent dyslexia gene mapping efforts (for example, Grigorenko et al., 1997; Schulte-Körne et al., 1998; Fagerheim et al., 1999).

A powerful extension of the sib-pair design is the QTL approach alluded to above, where continuous phenotypic measures are used, instead of a qualitative definition of affection status. As with qualitative ASP methods, QTL analysis relies on estimating IBD allele sharing. With two copies of each gene, a given pair of sibs may share either 0, 1 or 2 alleles IBD at any particular locus. If the marker under investigation is close to a gene influencing the measure, then siblings who share more alleles IBD should be more similar in phenotype than those who share fewer alleles. A simple way of assessing this relationship is to regress D^2 against x, giving a straightforward method for estimating statistical significance (Haseman and Elston, 1972). For sib-pair samples that have been selected on the basis of a proband with an extreme phenotypic score, a modification of the DeFries-Fulker method (described earlier) can increase power for detecting linkage. In this case the extent to which scores of co-sibs regress towards the unselected population mean is examined as a function of x at the locus of interest (Fulker et al., 1991). One of the disadvantages of these sib-pair trait difference approaches is that they are unable to properly accommodate multiple sib-ships or use the full information from extended families. This can be overcome by use of a method based on variance components (VC), which is more computationally intense, but can simultaneously examine all relationships in a pedigree (Amos, 1994). The VC approach uses maximum-likelihood techniques to partition the full variability of the trait observed in the data-set into separate components due to major gene unlinked polygenic and residual environmental factors. At any particular genetic locus, the likelihood of the data when allowing for a major gene effect is compared to the null hypothesis of no major gene effect. Significance of QTL linkage can be estimated from the ratio between these two likelihoods. Although VC approaches have been shown to be more powerful than those based on sib-pair trait differences, their theoretical estimates of statistical significance assume multivariate normality, which may be violated under certain sampling strategies. The application of all these types of QTL analyses has been particularly important in demonstrations of linkage of dyslexia to 6p21.3 (Cardon et al., 1994, 1995; Fisher et al., 1999a; Gayán et al, 1999).

An important consideration when reviewing the findings of linkage analyses of dyslexia is the fact that the majority of studies have analysed only a small part of the human genome, or targeted specific chromosomal regions, for example on the basis of hypothetical associations between reading disability and autoimmune disorders (Hugdahl et al., 1990). Although they have sometimes been successful, these focussed investigations do not exploit the full power of the positional cloning approach, which has the potential to identify loci influencing dyslexia at any region on any chromosome, in the complete absence of an etiological hypothesis. Whilst early studies were limited by a lack of available polymorphic markers, a systematic search for dyslexia genes can now be done by performing a complete genome-wide scan of all the chromosomes in a set of families, using a panel of several hundred polymorphic markers. As well as evaluating linkage at each specific genotyped marker (single-point analysis) it is possible to infer genetic information from the intervals between the markers, allowing full multi-point analysis of entire chromosomes (Kruglyak and Lander, 1995). Genome-wide scanning of the large sample sizes required for complex traits was until recently highly labour intensive and time consuming, but in the past few years there have been major advances in fluorescent semi-automated genotyping technology (Reed et al., 1994). Therefore it is now feasible to run large-scale genome searches in substantial data sets.

Another strategy that complements the above approaches is the identification of individuals who have chromosomal abnormalities associated with the disorder. These include deletions[20] and inversions[21] of specific chromosomal regions, and translocations, where part of one chromosome breaks and becomes attached to part of another chromosome. Molecular cyto-genetic[22] techniques can now be used to map the breakpoints of many of these chromosomal rearrangements to remarkable accuracy (see Lai et al., 2000). Any genes identified in the vicinity of such chromosomal breakpoints might be considered as candidates for the trait in question. Note, however, that the observation of a chromosomal abnormality in an individual affected with a particular trait does not necessarily implicate the rearrangement in the etiology of the disorder; sometimes deletions, inversions or translocations can arise with no phenotypic consequences. Most children who are diagnosed with a severe developmental disorder will have their chromosome make-up (called a 'karyotype') checked as a matter of routine, whereas many unaffected individuals who have never had their karyotype investigated may harbour silent chromosome rearrangements that remain undetected. In order to increase confidence that the site of a breakpoint is really relevant to the disorder, converging evidence is needed from multiple cases or from other types of studies (such as linkage investigations) that implicate a common region (for example the 15q translocation cases reported by Nopola-Hemmi et al., 2000).

A final approach that has not yet been used very extensively in dyslexia research, is that of association analysis. In its most basic form this involves testing whether a specific allele of a gene or marker occurs at a higher frequency among affected cases versus unaffected controls (case-control studies). In contrast to linkage studies, which look for co-segregation within a family, association studies assess correlation at the population level. Positive associations may indicate that a specific allele itself is a high-risk factor for the disorder, but can also be observed for alleles at loci that map very close to the true susceptibility gene (a phenomenon known as 'linkage disequilibrium' or LD). In a mixed population trait and allele frequencies may differ between ethnic groups, and this can lead to false positive associations, so reliable case-control studies are highly dependent on very careful matching of ethnicity between cases and controls. To prevent such spurious associations arising, there are a number of family-based association study designs that can be used instead, in which the parental alleles that are not transmitted to an affected child act as artificial 'internal controls'. A commonly used example is the transmission disequi-librium test (TDT), which is based on the premise that if a specific allele (for example, 'A1') is associated with a disorder, then a heterozygous parent (for example, A1/A2) should transmit the A1 allele more often than the A2 allele to an affected child (see Lander and Schork, 1994). One advantage of family-based association tests over linkage analyses is that the former only requires samples of trios (a single affected child plus both parents). However, because linkage disequilibrium extends over relatively small distances in outbred populations, it is not yet technically feasible to run a comprehensive scan for association across the entire genome, since this would involve screening of prohibitively large numbers of markers (>100 000) along with considerable multiple testing issues (see Abecasis et al., 2001). Although this is likely to change in the coming years as technology improves, at this stage association studies are more appro-priate for targeted analyses of specific candidate intervals that have already been identified by linkage analyses.

Key gene localizations to date

To date there are three key chromosomal regions that have each been implicated by a number of studies and are likely to contain genes predis-posing to dyslexia. Note that although corroborating evidence for linkage at these loci has come from multiple investigations, in each case there have also been several well-designed studies that have been unable to replicate

Table 1.1: Summary of the main approaches that have been adopted for localizing genes involved in developmental dyslexia

Phenotype definition	Method	Sampling	Advantages	Disadvantages
Qualitative	Model-based parametric lod-score linkage	Extended families	High power if correct model is known and assumptions are met; can detect trait locus up to ~20 cM from marker	Success depends on correct specification of mode of inheritance; requires estimates of parameters such as penetrance and phenocopy rates; power reduced by heterogeneity and oligogenicity; large extended families with multiple affected members may be rare
	Allele-sharing non-parametric linkage	Affected sib-pairs	Doesn't require assumptions about mode of inheritance, penetrance, phenocopy; easy to ascertain families; can detect trait locus up to ~20 cM from marker	Large sample sizes required to give sufficient power; multiple sib-ships may not be properly accomodated
		Extended families	Doesn't require assumptions about mode of inheritance etc.; can detect trait locus up to ~20 cM from marker	Some approaches are sensitive to specification of allele frequencies; large extended families with multiple affected members may be rare; not as powerful as parametric when correct model is known
	Family-based association	Parent/proband trios, affected sib-pairs	Doesn't require assumptions about mode of inheritance etc.; easy to ascertain families; can detect genes with only minor effect	Marker locus must be very close to trait locus (<1 cM) in order to detect it; genome-wide scans currently unfeasible
	Mapping chromosomal rearrangements	Single cases or extended families	Chromosomal breakpoints can be very accurately mapped	Rearrangement can be unrelated to the trait; converging evidence may be required from multiple cases; breakpoints can influence genes that are up to ~1 Mb away (position effects)

Table 1.1: (contd)

Phenotype definition	Method	Sampling	Advantages	Disadvantages
Quantitative	Haseman-Elston regression	Phenotyped sib-pairs	Doesn't require assumptions about mode of inheritance etc.; easy to ascertain families; increased power due to continuous nature of trait	Large sample sizes required to give sufficient power; multiple sib-ships may not be properly accomodated
	DeFries-Fulker regression	Phenotyped sib-pairs; extreme proband	Doesn't require assumptions about mode of inheritance etc.; easy to ascertain families; increased power due to continuous nature of trait; exploits selection of sample	Multiple sib-ships may not be properly accomodated; no obvious basis for choosing best cut-off for selection
	Partitioning of variance components	Phenotyped sib-pairs or extended families	Doesn't require assumptions about mode of inheritance etc.; easy to ascertain families; increased power due to continuous nature of trait; handles any pedigree structure	Tests of significance assume multivariate normality; analysis is much more computer-intensive than other QTL approaches

linkage, and even where linkage has been supported it has often been very sensitive to the mode of analysis employed. Thus, the effects of each putative locus on the phenotype of reading disability might actually be quite subtle and difficult to reliably observe in any single data set. Nevertheless, the level of concordance between the linkage studies is encouraging for a complex trait such as this. Before describing the results we should briefly outline a few guidelines for interpreting them. Geneticists assess strength of linkage by determining the probability of observing a given genotype-phenotype relationship by chance. Thus many of the following results are accompanied by *p values*. An alternative way of reporting linkage is using *lod* (log of the odds) scores, originally developed for maximum-likelihood-based parametric linkage analysis. (An attraction of lod scores is that, under certain specific circumstances, the results for a particular marker from separate families can be combined by simply adding them together.) For reasons that are too complex to go into detail in this review, a lod score of 3 or above has usually been taken to indicate 'significant' linkage for traditional parametric linkage analysis, whilst a significance cut-off of 3.6 has been recently proposed for allele-sharing methods. As a general guide, a lod score of 1 corresponds to a theoretical nominal p value of ~0.02, a lod of 2 has a p value of ~0.001, and a lod of 3 has a p value of ~0.0001. For more information about why such low p values are required for declaring linkage and detailed discussion of assessing significance for complex traits see Lander and Kruglyak (1995). Genetic distances are usually reported as centi-morgans (cM), which are estimated from linkage studies, or megabases (Mb), which are actual physical distances of DNA. Although the relationship between these types of units varies at different chromosomal regions, on average an interval of 1 cM corresponds to ~1 Mb, and would be expected to contain around twenty or so different genes. A standard nomenclature is adopted for referring to specific genomic regions (such as 6p21.3), which is related to chromosomal banding patterns, where 'p' and 'q' denote the short and long arm of the chromosome respectively.

Chromosome 15q21 (DYX1)

The first report of linkage analysis in reading disability was by Smith et al. (1983) who studied nine US families with three-generation histories of dyslexia. This was prior to the development of DNA-based genotyping, so only a sparse map of markers was investigated, comprising enzyme polymorphisms, red blood cell antigens and chromosomal heteromorphisms. Traditional parametric model-based analysis using a qualitative definition of affection status yielded a lod score of 3.24 with heteromorphisms at the centromere of chromosome 15. These families, plus an additional 10 multi-generational pedigrees,

Table 1.2: Summary of the main studies that have investigated the DYX1-3 loci

Locus		Sample	Method	Findings
15q21	Bisgaard et al. (1987)	5 extended families (Denmark)	Model-based parametric linkage analysis	Negative
	Smith et al. (1991)	19 extended families (US)	Qualitative and quantitative non-parametric sib-pair analysis	Positive
	Fulker et al. (1991)	19 extended families (US)	DF regression of discriminant score in selected sibs	Positive
	Grigorenko et al. (1997)	6 extended families (US)	Model-based parametric linkage of component qualitative phenotypes	Positive
	Schulte-Körne (1998)	7 extended families (Germany)	Model-based parametric linkage and non-parametric allele-sharing methods	Positive
	Morris et al. (2000)	178 parent/proband trios (UK)	Family-based association analysis	Positive
	Nopola-Hemmi et al. (2000)	2 families (Finland)	Mapping of chromosomal translocations	Positive
6p21.3	Smith et al. (1991)	19 extended families (US)	Model-based parametric linkage analysis; qualitative and quantitative non-parametric sib-pair analysis	Positive
	Cardon et al. (1994,1995)	19 extended families, 46 DZ twin pairs (US)	DF regression of discriminant score in selected sibs	Positive
	Grigorenko et al. (1997)	6 extended families (US)	Non-parametric allele-sharing methods with component qualitative phenotypes	Positive
	Schulte-Körne (1998)	7 extended families (Germany)	Model-based parametric linkage and non-parametric allele-sharing methods	Negative
	Field and Kaplan (1998)	79 families (Canada)	Model-based parametric linkage and non-parametric allele-sharing methods	Negative
	Fisher et al. (1999a, 2000)	82 nuclear families (UK)	HE and VC quantitative analysis of multiple reading-related measures	Positive
	Gayán et al. (1999)	79 DZ twin-based families (US)	DF regression of multiple reading-related measures	Positive

(contd)

Table 1.2: (contd)

Locus		Sample	Method	Findings
	Petryshen et al. (2000a)	79 families (Canada)	HE and VC quantitative analysis of multiple reading-related measures	Negative
	Grigorenko et al. (2000a)	8 extended families (expansion of previous sample) (US)	Non-parametric allele-sharing methods with component qualitative phenotypes	Positive
2p15-16	Fagerheim et al. (1999)	1 large extended family (Norway)	Model-based parametric linkage analysis and non-parametric allele-sharing methods	Positive
	Petryshen et al. (2000b)	96 families (Canada)	Qualitative non-parametric allele-sharing methods; quantitative analysis of multiple reading-related measures	Positive
	Francks et al. (2001)	119 DZ twin-based families (US)	HE and VC quantitative analysis of multiple reading-related measures	Positive

were further investigated by Smith et al. (1991) using several DNA-based markers from chromosome 15. Non-parametric sib-pair analysis of a qualitative diagnosis and a quantitative discriminant score implicated two markers from 15q (pYNZ90.1 and pJU201) both of which map quite a large distance (>50 cM) from the centromeric region where evidence for linkage had first been found. Selection of sib-pairs in which at least one sib was severely affected and application of DeFries-Fulker regression methods to the discriminant score increased the evidence for linkage to these markers (p<0.005) in this sample (Fulker et al., 1991). The analysis also gave some weaker evidence (p<0.05) for another marker mapping nearer to the centromere. Unfortunately, the DNA-based markers employed by Smith et al. (1991) and Fulker et al. (1991) were RFLPs (restriction fragment length polymorphisms), which have not been precisely localized with respect to the STS (sequence tagged site) markers that are now commonly used for linkage mapping. This presents some difficulties when comparing the results of these early studies to those from more recent investigations.

Following up these findings, two studies reported an absence of linkage to chromosome 15 in their data sets (Bisgaard et al, 1987; Rabin et al., 1993). The Rabin et al. (1993) sample included one of the linked families from the original Smith et al. (1983) study, but excluded linkage to the centromeric part of 15q using DNA-based markers.

Grigorenko et al. (1997) investigated chromosome 15 in six large extended families from the US, using qualitative analyses of five different theoretically derived dichotomous phenotypes. They ran both traditional parametric analysis and non-parametric allele-sharing methods. With parametric methods, assuming an autosomal dominant model with sex-dependent penetrance they obtained a single-point lod score of 3.15 at marker D15S143 for the phenotype of single-word reading, but did not observe any significant results for their other four phenotypes. D15S143 maps to 15q in a region similar to that implicated by the Smith et al. (1991) and Fulker et al. (1991) studies. However, it should be noted that Grigorenko et al. (1997) observed very highly negative parametric lod scores with markers that should map very close to D15S143. They did not find evidence for linkage to this region when using non-parametric methods. (Apparently non-parametric analysis *was* significant for a marker D15S128, close to the centromere, but they did not report the strength of this result, nor the phenotype with which it was associated.) Grigorenko et al. (1997) proposed on the basis of this data that the putative chromosome 15 locus may be specific to the single-word reading phenotype (see below for further discussion of this). Schulte-Körne et al. (1998) analysed chromosome 15 in seven extended German families segregating spelling disability, employing a qualitative definition of affection status. Their data supported linkage to the D15S132–D15S143 region on 15q21 with both parametric (multipoint p = 0.0042) and non-parametric (multipoint p = 0.03) methods.

Further support for DYX1 has come from two complementary approaches for gene localization. Morris et al. (2000) performed a family-based association study of eight markers from an ~8cM region containing 15q21, using a dichotomous phenotypic definition of reading disability. In a first sample of 101 parent-proband trios they observed association for a marker D15S994 (p = 0.004 with TDT), which is nearly 5 cM away from the D15S132–D15S143 peak of Schulte-Körne et al. (1998). However this could not be confirmed in a second sample of 77 trios. Morris et al. (2000) also examined the transmission of combinations of alleles at different markers (haplotypes), detecting association with three marker haplotypes of D15S146/D15S214/D15S994 (p < 0.001; corrected to p = 0.03 to account for multiple testing). This result was successfully replicated in their second sample of trios (p = 0.0059). They were unable to define a specific set of D15S146/D15S214/D15S994 alleles associated with reading disability, possibly indicating the presence of more than one susceptibility mutation and/or multiple founders for the putative 15q risk locus in their samples. It is worth noting that the extent of linkage disequilibrium (the maximum distance from a susceptibility locus at which you can expect to detect a true association) can vary in different regions of the genome and for different populations. In outbred populations, although LD occasionally exceeds 0.5 Mb (~0.5 cM) it is usually nearer 0.05 Mb and is often as low as 0.005 Mb (Abecasis at al., 2001). So additional studies employing a denser set of markers in 15q21 may yield further interesting results.

Nopola-Hemmi et al. (2000) identified two Finnish families with a clinically defined history of dyslexia who were found to have translocations involving chromosome 15. In one family a translocation between 15q21 and 2q11 was found in a father and three of his children, all of whom had histories of reading problems. A fourth sib who did not inherit the translocation had no reading difficulties. In the other family, the father and all three children had a translocation involving 15q22 and 2p13, but only one of the children was diagnosed with dyslexia. This could reflect reduced penetrance, or it may indicate that the reading problems are unrelated to the translocation in this second family. In both families, the breakpoints were located between D15S143 and D15S1029, a 6–8 Mb region that overlaps with that implicated by Schulte-Körne et al. (1998), but is distinct from the interval associated with dyslexia in the Morris et al. (2000) study. Taken together, these studies provide evidence for the presence of a gene (or genes) influencing reading and spelling disability on chromosome 15, but as yet there is no overall consensus on exactly where this locus maps.

Chromosome 6p21.3 (DYX2)

Perhaps the most compelling evidence thus far for a gene involved in dyslexia comes from studies of the HLA region on chromosome six. The first suggestion of linkage to 6p resulted from analyses of the 19 extended kindreds of Smith et al. (1991) using both traditional parametric qualitative methods, and also standard sib-pair analysis of a quantitative discriminant score. However, the markers that were typed for this study were not very polymorphic. Cardon et al. (1994, 1995) followed up analyses of the discriminant score in these same 19 families, plus a sample of 46 DZ Colorado twin pairs, using a selection of more informative markers from the region, coupled with the DeFries-Fulker regression method of evaluating linkage. In addition, they employed an interval mapping procedure that allowed assessment of linkage at the regions between the typed markers. These results suggested the presence of a QTL in 6p21.3 between the markers D6S105 and TNFB ($p = 0.0417$ for the kindred sample; $p = 0.0094$ for the twins).

Grigorenko et al. (1997) investigated this region in the same six large extended families that they used for their chromosome 15 analyses (described above), again employing both parametric and non-parametric approaches for their five dichotomous phenotypic definitions. In this case, the results of parametric analyses were not significant, but their non-parametric results strongly supported the existence of a 6p locus influencing dyslexia; the highest significance ($P < 10^{-6}$) was found for the phoneme awareness phenotype, whereas the weakest results came from investigation of single-word reading. On the basis of this and their chromosome 15 findings (described above) Grigorenko et al. (1997) hypothesized a dissociation of genetic effects in their families, such that phoneme awareness is specifically linked to 6p whereas single-word reading is linked to 15q. Although an attractive idea, this interpretation of their data has since been questioned on a number of grounds (see Pennington, 1997; Fisher et al., 1999a). Note that the effects observed by Grigorenko et al. (1997) for the 6p locus could not be specific to phoneme awareness, since significant results were also obtained for all other phenotypes tested, including phonological decoding, rapid automized naming, single-word reading and IQ-reading discrepancy. Certainly they observed varying levels of significance for the different phenotypes (highest for phoneme awareness, weakest for single-word reading) but the actual difference in linkage between these phenotypes was not in itself significant (Pennington, 1997).

It can be difficult to make accurate inferences about the relative effects of a
locus on different phenotypes, because significance levels may differ as a
consequence of variation in methodological factors such as sample size and
reliability of phenotypic testing (Fisher et al., 1999a). Finally, alternative
statistical approaches may respond differentially to the use of different
phenotype information from the same family sample; Grigorenko et al.
(1997) found linkage to 6p only with non-parametric techniques, and to
15q only with traditional parametric analysis. Interestingly, a follow up of
this study by the same authors, in which two extra families and more
individuals from the original families were added to the sample, confirmed
evidence for linkage to 6p, but in this larger data set it was found that
single-word reading was now the most significant phenotype (Grigorenko
et al., 2000a). Therefore the new findings from this set of families do not
support the dissociation of phenotypic effects between 6p and 15q that was
originally proposed. Nevertheless, the work of Grigorenko et al. illustrates
the value for genetic analyses of dissecting out a complex behavioural
phenotype into components.

Two further studies in independent samples have provided support for
the 6p locus, both of these adopting QTL methods. Fisher et al. (1999a)
investigated 82 nuclear families selected on the basis of a dyslexic
proband, in which at least one sib also showed some evidence of reading
impairment. All sibs were assessed with tests of word recognition, irregular word reading and non-word reading and linkage to markers on 6p was
evaluated using Haseman-Elston (HE) and variance components (VC)
analyses of these quantitative measures. Evidence was observed for a
6p21.3 QTL influencing both phonological and orthographic processing,
with peak significance at markers D6S276–D6S105 for reading of irregular
words (multipoint HE, $p = 0.00035$; multipoint VC, $p = 0.007$) and non-
words (multipoint HE, $p = 0.0035$; multipoint VC, $p = 0.0038$). (A follow
up of this study has shown that the 6p QTL also influences a test of
phoneme awareness and an additional test of orthographic coding in this
set of families, but at weaker levels (Fisher et al., 2000).) Gayán et al.
(1999) analysed 6p markers in 79 new families identified from the
Colorado twin project, with several different reading-related measures.
For each measure they selected probands scoring 2 SDs below normal
controls and used DeFries-Fulker regression methods to assess linkage,
reporting lods of 3.1 for orthographic choice, 2.42 for phonological
decoding and 1.46 for phoneme awareness, with peak significance again
around D6S276–D6S105. Thus, both these QTL studies indicate that the
6p21.3 locus influences multiple measures of reading ability.

A striking aspect of the 6p results is the remarkable concordance in
localization of the trait locus between the various positive studies – an

extremely unusual finding in complex trait genetics (Cardon et al., 1994, 1995; Fisher et al., 1999a; Gayán et al., 1999; Grigorenko et al. 2000a). However, a number of investigations have been unable to replicate linkage to 6p. Schulte-Körne et al. (1998) observed a p value of only 0.21 around D6S105 for non-parametric analysis of their seven spelling-disability families. Field and Kaplan (1998) ascertained 79 Canadian families containing at least two siblings affected with phonological coding dyslexia and found no evidence for a 6p21.3 QTL with qualitative parametric and non-parametric techniques. Petryshen et al. (2000a) further studied the same 6p markers in these 79 families, but investigated measures of spelling, phoneme awareness, phonological coding and rapid automized naming using the same QTL-based techniques as Fisher et al. (1999a), in order to increase power to detect linkage. Although they did not obtain any significant results there was a weak suggestion of linkage to 6p21.3 for the spelling trait, with a single-point HE p-value of 0.07 at marker TNFB and a multipoint VC lod of 0.82 in the region implicated by previous studies. Lack of significance in the latter study may be partly due to the low density of marker coverage but is more likely a consequence of genetic heterogeneity between the different study samples.

Chromosome2 p15-16 (DYX3)

Fagerheim et al. (1999) identified a large four-generation Norwegian pedigree in which dyslexia was inherited in a manner that was consistent with autosomal dominant transmission. A computer-administered test battery was used for diagnosis, and cut-off points for determination of qualitative affection status were developed empirically by comparing results between subsets of clearly affected and clearly normal adults from the family. A genome scan in 36 members of this pedigree revealed strong evidence for a locus on chromosome 2p15-16 using traditional parametric methods, assuming sex dependent penetrance and phenocopy values. A maximum single-point lod score of 3.525 was observed when analysing all generations of the pedigree. Although there was perfect co-segregation between 2p15-16 markers and dyslexia in the adults of the pedigree, the younger generation included two distinct cases of phenocopy; children with positive histories of reading problems and positive current test-based diagnoses who had not inherited the putative 2p risk locus. In addition, one child with a predisposing genotype had a negative history of reading difficulty and had a normal current diagnosis, presumably a case of non-penetrance. The authors postulated that their diagnosis in the youngest generation of the family was less accurate than in the older generations, because the empirical cut-offs had been established in adults. Indeed, investigation of an older subset of the family, including only adults over the age of 20, increased the maximum parametric lod score to 4.32. Non-parametric multipoint analyses suggested a 4 cM region between D2S2352 and D2S1337 as the most likely location of the 2p gene (p = 0.023 for the complete pedigree; p = 0.0009 for adults only).

A complete QTL-based genome scan of a set of 119 families from the Colorado twin study has just been finished (Francks et al., 2001, see below). Intriguingly, the strongest linkage identified by this search was on 2p, in a region that was extremely close to that implicated by the Fagerheim et al. (1999) study. Thus two completely separate genome searches, one using a dichotomous qualitative diagnosis to investigate a single large Norwegian pedigree, the other employing quantitative analyses of multiple measures in a large epidemiological sample of small nuclear families from the US, have independently identified DYX3 as their most significant locus. In addition, preliminary attempts to replicate the 2p15-16 findings in a large Canadian data set have yielded some encouraging results (Petryshen et al., 2000b) It is therefore highly likely that DYX3 is a general risk locus for developmental dyslexia in the wider population.

Large-scale QTL-based genome screens

There have been a few additional regions that have been suggested to contain genes influencing dyslexia, such as 1p34–36 (Rabin et al., 1993), 1p22 or 2q31 (Froster et al., 1993) and 6q13–16.2 (Petryshen et al., 1999). However, as this chapter has highlighted, there can be considerable difficulties in integrating the findings from the many separate genetic mapping studies that have been undertaken to date, even when they do appear to implicate the same chromosomal regions. This is because there is a lack of consistency of phenotypic definition and diagnostic tools between studies, sampling strategies and pedigree structures differ, some studies use qualitative definitions whilst others use quantitative, and many alternative methods of genetic analyses have been employed (often several within a single study). Most importantly, the vast majority of investigators have only analysed limited parts of the human genome in their family samples and they therefore have to make conclusions about genetic etiology in their data set on the basis of incomplete information. There are considerable advantages to be gained by performing a systematic scan of all chromosomes using the same sets of families, measures and statistical methodologies. Firstly, it is highly likely that previous large-scale studies, having focused on specific chromosomal regions, will have missed important loci mapping elsewhere in the genome. Secondly, it is widely acknowledged that complex trait linkage analysis is very prone to false positive results (Lander and Kruglyak, 1995); the genome-wide approach allows judgement of the relative strength of positive results against the general background levels produced by the linkage statistics in the sample. Thirdly, complete genome data for each measure may help to evaluate whether there are indeed different loci influencing different components of the dyslexia phenotype.

The first large-scale QTL-based full genome searches have been very recently completed, one in the set of UK families described by Fisher et al. (1999a,b), the other in a subset of families from the Colorado twin study (combined from Cardon et al., 1994 and Gayán et al., 1999). Both scans have used direct linkage analysis of quantitative measures, and simulation methods to determine empirical significance of results (Fisher et al., 2000; Francks et al., 2001). These studies implicate loci on chromosomes 2, 4, 6, 9, 13 and 18 in components of developmental dyslexia, and will be described in full elsewhere (manuscripts in preparation).

The future

Even before the specific mutations that increase risk for reading disability are identified, we can go some way towards dissecting out the genetic etiology. For example, it is possible to explore the effects of a single locus on several different measures by simultaneous multivariate linkage or association analyses. Furthermore, combined investigation of multiple chromosomal regions in a single set of families may allow modelling of interactions between risk loci (for example, Grigorenko et al., 2000b). Another interesting area of study involves the evaluation of whether loci for developmental dyslexia may also influence co-morbid conditions such as attention deficit hyperactivity disorder (Smith et al., 2000). A large amount of data from many families will be required in order to pinpoint the specific gene variants that predispose to developmental dyslexia in the general population. For complex traits, whilst linkage analysis remains a powerful tool for initial detection and mapping of loci, the regions implicated by the method typically contain hundreds of genes. Association-based analyses of candidate intervals using new types of genetic markers known as single nucleotide polymorphisms (SNPs) will be crucial for zeroing in on mutations. Studies will be able to exploit the wealth of candidate gene data that are already available for many chromosomal regions as a result of human genome sequencing. Although a large proportion of monogenic disorders are caused by mutations that severely disrupt a gene (for example by cutting it short or changing the amino acid encoded at a critical point), it is probable that many of the mutations involved in complex traits have only subtle effects on the relevant gene, such as an elevation or reduction of gene expression. Therefore, functional studies will be needed to provide definitive proof that a specific change is responsible for increased risk of reading disability. Finally, it is important to note that these linkage mapping and association studies can not exist in isolation and that an understanding of the etiology of developmental dyslexia can only result from the integration of behavioural, neurological and genetic approaches.

Acknowledgements

We thank Professor Anthony Monaco for his helpful comments on this manuscript.

Notes

1. Mutation: a change in the genetic material, either a single gene or the number or structure of the chromosomes.
2. Chromosome: thread-like deep-stained bodies composed of DNA and protein and carrying genetic information.
3. Gene: a part of the DNA that directs the synthesis of the specific chain.
4. Linkage: two genes at different loci on the same pair of homologous chromosomes are said to be linked. Homologous chromosomes pair during cell division and contain identical loci.
5. Stochastic: Skillful in guessing, probabilistic.
6. Loci: Plural of locus. The site of a gene on a chromosome.
7. Genotypic and phenotypic. Genotype is the genetic constitution of an individual. Phenotype is the appearance (physical, biochemical and physiological) of an individual that results from the interaction of environment and his genotype. In dyslexia, the genetic vulnerability (genotype) for dyslexia may not be expressed if the environment is sufficiently favourable, producing a phenotype of dyslexia that shares the dyslexic genetic endowment but with near normal literacy skills.
8. Concordance: when both members of a twin pair exhibit the same trait.
9. Monozygotic twins: identical, from same egg.
10. Dizygotic twins: from two eggs, and therefore not identical.
11. Probands: index case. The affected individual through whom the family came to the attention of the investigators.
12. Heritability: the proportion of the total variation of a character attributable to genetic as opposed to environmental factors.
13. Dominant: a trait that is expressed in individuals who are heterozygous for a particular gene. This means that they have two different

alleles, alternative forms of genes found at the same locus making them carriers.

Recessive: a trait that is expressed in individuals who are homozygous for a particular gene and not in those who are heterozygous. This means that they have two identical alleles. Sex linked. These are genes carried on the sex chromosomes, usually X linked.

14. Penetrance: expressing a genetic trait, even mildly.

15. Phenocopy: a condition due to environmental factors that resembles a genetic condition. An example in dyslexia might be phonological deficits, which can be caused by a variety of factors such as glue ear or sensory impairment.

16. Polymorphic: the occurrence in a population of two or more genetically determined forms in such frequency that the rarest of them could not be maintained by mutation alone.

17. Allele: alternative form of gene found on same locus.

18. Segregation: the separation of alleles (genes) during meiosis (cell division) so that each gamete (sex cell) contains only one member of each pair of alleles.

19. Sib pair: a pair of siblings, brother or sister.

20. Deletions: a type of chromosomal aberration in which there is a loss of part of a chromosome.

21. Inversions: a type of chromosomal aberration in which a chromosome is inverted.

22. Cytogenetic: A branch of genetics involving the study of chromosomes.

References

Abecasis GR, Noguchi E, Heinzmann A, Traherne JA, Bhattacharyya S, Leaves NI, Anderson GG, Zhang Y, Lench NJ, Carey A, Cardon LR, Moffatt MF, Cookson WOC (2001) Extent and distribution of linkage disequilibrium in three genomic regions. American Journal of Human Genetics, in press.

Amos CI (1994) Robust variance-components approach for assessing genetic linkage in pedigrees. American Journal of Human Genetics 54: 535–43.

Ballabio A (1993) The rise and fall of positional cloning? Nat Genet 3: 277–9.

Bisgaard ML, Eiberg H, Moller N, Niebuhr E, Mohr J (1987) Dyslexia and chromosome 15 heteromorphism: negative lod score in a Danish sample. Clin Genet 32: 118–19.

Cardon LR, Smith SD, Fulker DW, Kimberling WJ, Pennington BF, DeFries JC (1994) Quantitative trait locus for reading disability on chromosome 6. Science 266: 276–9.

Cardon LR, Smith SD, Fulker DW, Kimberling WJ, Pennington BF, DeFries JC (1995) Quantitative trait locus for reading disability: correction. Science 268: 1553.

Collins FS (1992) Positional cloning: Let's not call it reverse anymore. Nat Genet 1: 3-5.

Collins FS (1995) Positional cloning moves from perditional to traditional. Nat Genet 9: 347–50.

DeFries JC, Fulker DW (1985) Multiple regression analysis of twin data. Behav Genet 15: 467–73.

DeFries JC, Fulker DW, LaBuda MC (1987) Evidence for a genetic aetiology in reading disability of twins. Nature 329: 537–9.

DeFries JC, Gillis JJ (1993) Genetics of reading disability. In Plomin R, McClearn G (eds) Nature, nurture, and psychology. Washington DC: APA Press, pp. 121–45.

DeFries JC, Alarcón M (1996) Genetics of specific reading disability. Mental Retard Dev Disabilities Res Rev 2: 39–47.

Fagerheim T, Raeymaekers P, Tonnessen FE, Pedersen M, Tranebjaerg L, Lubs HA (1999) A new gene (DYX3) for dyslexia is located on chromosome 2. J Med Genet 36: 664–9.

Field LL, Kaplan BJ (1998) Absence of linkage of phonological coding dyslexia to chromosome 6p23-p21.3 in a large family data set. Am J Hum Genet 63: 1448–56.

Fisher SE, Vargha-Khadem F, Watkins KE, Monaco AP, Pembrey ME (1998) Localisation of a gene implicated in a severe speech and language disorder. Nat Genet 18: 168–70.

Fisher SE, Marlow AJ, Lamb J, Maestrini E, Williams DF, Richardson AJ, Weeks DE, Stein JF, Monaco AP (1999a) A quantitative trait locus on chromosome 6p influences different aspects of developmental dyslexia. Am J Hum Genet 64: 146–56.

Fisher SE, Stein JF, Monaco AP (1999b) A genome-wide search strategy for identifying quantitative trait loci involved in reading and spelling disability (developmental dyslexia). Eur Child and Adolesc Psych 8(S3): 47–51.

Fisher SE, Francks C, Marlow AJ, Williams DF, Ishikawa-Brush Y, MacPhie IL, Talcott JB, Weeks DE, Cardon LR, Richardson AJ, Stein JF, Monaco AP (2000) A genome-wide screen for quantitative trait loci involved in developmental dyslexia in a large sample of sib-pairs from the UK. Eur J Hum Genet 8(S1): 160 (abstract).

Francks C, Fisher SE, Marlow AJ, Richardson AJ, Stein JF, Monaco AP (2000) A sibling-pair based approach for mapping genetic loci that influence quantitative measures of reading disability. Prostaglandins, Leukotrienes and Essential Fatty Acids 63: 27–31.

Francks C, Fisher SE, Marlow AJ, Cardon LR, Ishikawa-Brush Y, MacPhie IL, Williams DF, Gayán J, Olson RK, Pennington BF, Smith SD, DeFries JC, Monaco AP (2001) A genome-wide screen in families from the Colorado twin study of reading disability, with evidence that a quantitative trait locus on chromosome 2p influences multiple measures of developmental dyslexia. Tenth International Congress of Human Genetics (abstract)

Froster U, Schulte-Körne G, Hebebrand J, Remschmidt H (1993) Cosegregation of balanced translocation (1;2) with retarded speech development and dyslexia. Lancet 342: 178–9.

Fulker DW, Cardon LR, DeFries JC, Kimberling WJ, Pennington BF, Smith SD (1991) Multiple regression of sib-pair data on reading to detect quantitative trait loci. Reading and Writing: An Interdisciplinary Journal 3: 299–313.

Gayán J, Smith SD, Cherny SS, Cardon LR, Fulker DW, Brower AM, Olson RK, Pennington BF, DeFries JC (1999) Quantitative trait locus for specific language and reading deficits on chromosome 6p. Am J Hum Genet 64: 157–64.

Grigorenko EL, Wood FB, Meyer MS, Hart LA, Speed WC, Shuster A, Pauls DL (1997) Susceptibility loci for distinct components of developmental dyslexia on chromosomes 6 and 15. Am J Hum Genet 60: 27–39.

Grigorenko EL, Wood FB, Meyer MS, Pauls DL (2000a) Chromosome 6p influences on different dyslexia-related cognitive processes: further confirmation. Am J Hum Genet 66: 715–23.

Grigorenko EL, Wood FB, Meyer MS, Pauls JED, Hart LA, Pauls DL (2000b) Linkage studies suggest a possible locus for developmental dyslexia on chromosome 1p. Am J Hum Genet 67 (suppl): A1882 (abstract)

Habib M (2000) The neurological basis of developmental dyslexia. An overview and working hypothesis. Brain 123: 2373–99.

Hallgren B (1950) Specific dyslexia ('congenital word blindness'): a clinical and genetic study. Acta Psychiatr Neurol 65: 2–289.

Haseman JK, Elston RC (1972) The investigation of linkage between a quantitative trait and a marker locus. Behav Genet 2: 3–19.

Hugdahl K, Synnevag B, Satz P (1990) Immune and autoimmune disorders in dyslexic children. Neuropsychologia 28: 673–79.

Kruglyak L, Lander ES (1995) Complete multipoint sib-pair analysis of qualitative and quantitative traits. Am J Hum Genet 57: 439–54.

Lai CSL, Fisher SE, Hurst JA, Levy ER, Hodgson S, Fox M, Jeremiah S, Povey S, Jamison DC, Green ED, Vargha-Khadem F, Monaco AP (2000) The SPCH1 region on human 7q31: genomic characterisation of the critical interval and localisation of transloca-tions associated with speech and language disorder. Am J Hum Genet 67: 357–68.

Lander ES, Schork NJ (1994) Genetic dissection of complex traits. Science 265: 2037–48.

Lander E, Kruglyak L (1995) Genetic dissection of complex traits: guidelines for inter-preting and reporting linkage results. Nat Genet 11: 241–7.

Lewitter FI, DeFries JC, Elston RC (1980) Genetic models of reading disabilities. Behav Genet 10: 9–30.

Lubs HA, Rabin M, Feldman E, Jallad BJ, Kushch A, Gross-Glenn K, Duara R, Elston RC (1993) Familial dyslexia: genetic and medical findings in eleven three-generation families. Annals of Dyslexia 43: 44–60.

Morgan WP (1896) A case of congenital word-blindness (inability to learn to read). Br Med J 2: 1543–4.

Morris DW, Robinson L, Turic D, Duke M, Webb V, Milham C, Hopkin E, Pound K, Fernando S, Easton M, Hamshere M, Williams N, McGuffin P, Stevenson J, Krawczak M, Owen MJ, O'Donovan MC, Williams J (2000) Family-based association mapping provides evidence for a gene for reading disability on chromosome 15q. Hum Mol Genet 9: 843–8.

Nopola-Hemmi J, Taipale M, Haltia T, Lehesjoki AE, Voutilainen A, Kere J (2000) Two translocations of chromosome 15q associated with dyslexia. J Med Genet 37: 771–5.

Olson RK, Forsberg H, Wise B (1994) Genes, environment, and the development of orthographic skills. In Berninger VW (ed.) The varieties of orthographic knowledge I: Theoretical and developmental issues. Dordrecht: Kluwer Academic Publishers, pp 27–71.

Pennington BF, Gilger JW, Pauls D, Smith SA, Smith SD, DeFries JC (1991) Evidence for major gene transmission of developmental dyslexia. JAMA 266: 1527–34.

Pennington BF (1997) Using genetics to dissect cognition. Am J Hum Genet 60: 13–16.

Petryshen TL, Kaplan BJ, Field LL (1999) Evidence for a susceptibility locus for phono-logical coding dyslexia on chromosome 6q13-q16.2. Am J Hum Genet 65 (suppl): A32 (abstract).

Petryshen TL, Kaplan BJ, Liu MF, Field LL (2000a) Absence of significant linkage between phonological coding dyslexia and chromosome 6p23-21.3, as determined by use of quantitative-trait methods: confirmation of qualitative analyses. Am J Hum Genet 66: 708–14.

Petryshen TL, Kaplan BJ, Hughes ML, Field LL (2000b) Evidence for the chromosome 2p15-16 dyslexia susceptibility locus (DYX3) in a large Canadian data set. Am J Med Genet 96: 472 (abstract).

Rabin M, Wen XL, Hepburn M, Lubs HA, Feldman E, Duara R (1993) Suggestive linkage of developmental dyslexia to chromosome 1p34-p36. Lancet 342: 178.

Reed PW, Davies JL, Copeman JB, Bennett ST, Palmer SM, Pritchard LE, Gough SC, Kawaguchi Y, Cordell HJ, Balfour KM, Jenkins SC, Powell EE, Vignal A, Todd JA (1994) Chromosome-specific microsatellite sets for fluorescence-based, semi-automated genome mapping. Nat Genet 7: 390–5.

Schulte-Körne G, Grimm T, Nothen MM, Muller-Myhsok B, Cichon S, Vogt IR, Propping P, Remschmidt H (1998) Evidence for linkage of spelling disability to chromosome 15. Am J Hum Genet 63: 279–82.

Smith SD, Kimberling WJ, Pennington BF, Lubs HA (1983) Specific reading disability: identification of an inherited form through linkage analysis. Science 219: 1345.

Smith SD, Kimberling WJ, Pennington BF (1991) Screening for multiple genes influencing dyslexia. Reading and Writing: An Interdisciplinary Journal 3: 285–98.

Smith SD, Pennington BF, Willcutt E, Deffenbacher K, Hoover D, Smolen A, Moyzis R, Olson RK, DeFries JC (2000) Linkage of an ADHD phenotype to 6p21.3 in a population with reading disability. Am J Hum Genet 67 (suppl): A1951 (abstract).

Thomas CJ (1905) Congenital 'word-blindness' and its treatment. Opthalmoscope 3: 380–5.

Weeks DE, Lathrop GM (1995) Polygenic disease: methods for mapping complex disease traits. Trends Genet 11: 513–19.

CHAPTER 2

The sensorimotor basis of developmental dyslexia

JOHN STEIN, JOEL TALCOTT, CAROLINE WITTON

Overview

In this chapter we advance the hypothesis that reading problems are a consequence of impaired development of a system of large neurones in the brain (magnocells) that is responsible for timing sensory and motor events, and we will argue that their proper development is essential for reading. We will first describe how the visual demands of reading draw on the capabilities of the visual magnocellular system, and how any weakness can lead to visual confusion of letter order and poor visual memory for orthography. We will then discuss how there may be an auditory equivalent of the visual magnocellular system that is essential for meeting the phonological demands of reading, and how weakness in this can lead to auditory confusion of letter sounds, hence weak phonology. After this we will briefly consider the prolific projection of magnocellular/transient systems to the cerebellum, and how these may explain why many dyslexics are clumsy and unco-ordinated. This will help to explain why it is becoming increasingly apparent that the cerebellum plays an important role in the reading process. Finally, we will briefly discuss how the development of magnocellular neurones is likely to be under genetic control and how this may involve the immunological system, how brisk magnocellular function depends on their content of membrane polyunsaturated fatty acids, and how diets poor in these may further impair the development of magnocellular neurones.

Scope of developmental dyslexia

Numerous studies have shown that about 30% of the variance in children's reading ability can be explained by their IQ (for example Yule et al., 1973).

Therefore we define children as having developmental dyslexia if their reading and spelling is significantly below that expected from their age and IQ, unless there is an obvious alternative medical or social explanation, such as lack of schooling. Following Thompson (1982) we compare children's single word reading skill on the British Ability Scales (BAS) with their scores on the BAS similarities or matrices subtests. If their reading is significantly behind that expected from the latter we classify them as dyslexic. In addition we test their orthographic and phonological abilities, as we shall see. However, many of the adults that we see have overcome their reading problems to some extent; they have 'compensated'. Therefore, in adults, in addition to looking for a history suggestive of dyslexic problems in childhood we lay more emphasis on the speed with which they can carry out phonological and orthographic tests.

As first pointed out by Tim Miles (1970, 1993) developmental dyslexia is not just a language or literacy problem. Most dyslexic children have other difficulties in addition to unstable vision leading to orthographic weakness and difficulties with sequencing sounds leading to phonological problems. They tend to have problems with focusing visual and auditory attention. They tend to have poor sequencing in general so that they find it difficult to recite the days of the week or the months of the year in the correct order, particularly backwards. Moreover they tend to be unco-ordinated and clumsy. Many show mixed handedness and left/right confusions, indicating incomplete establishment of cerebral dominance. Furthermore it is well known that dyslexia runs in families; and twin studies have shown a hereditability of 60% (Pennington and Smith, 1988). Linkage to chromosomes 1, 2, 6 and 15 has been described, of which the best evidence is for alleles on the short arm of chromosome 6 (Cardon et al., 1994; Grigorenko et al., 1997; Fisher et al., 1999). Furthermore, reading problems are often found in children with other diagnoses. So developmental dyslexia overlaps with developmental dysphasia (specific language impairment), developmental dyspraxia, attention deficit disorder (ADD), Asperger syndrome and autism (Pennington, 1991a), and often the diagnosis children end up with is really just a consequence of the kind of specialist they first happen to be referred to.

The wide-ranging manifestations of this syndrome together with the strong evidence for its genetic basis suggest that, biologically speaking, impaired literacy is probably a by-product of a much more fundamental neurodevelopmental syndrome. We believe that it may result from impaired development of magnocellular neurones throughout the brain, perhaps as a consequence of immunological attack (Galaburda and Livingstone, 1993; Stein and Walsh, 1997; Stein and Talcott, 1999). The brisk transient responses required of magnocellular neurones demand rapid membrane dynamics; these in turn depend on their possessing flexible membranes that can accommodate rapid conformational changes in their channel proteins. This flexibility requires a high content of polyunsaturated essential fatty acids. The relative deficiency of these that characterizes modern diets may thus exacerbate any hereditary weakness in the development of these cells (Stein, 2000).

Normal reading

There are two partially independent mechanisms for reading, the lexical and sub-lexical (Morton, 1969; Ellis, 1984; Castles and Coltheart, 1993; Seidenburg, 1993; Manis et al., 1997). For reading familiar words that are in your sight vocabulary you see the whole visual form of the word without having to separate it into separate letters and you derive its meaning directly from this orthographic visual form. However for unfamiliar words, and all words are unfamiliar to beginning readers, each individual letter of the word has to be analysed visually; then converted into the sounds that each letter stands for; and then those sounds have to be melded together in inner speech to give the meaning of the word. This is the so-called phonological or sub-lexical route. Thus for both the whole word, lexical route and for the sub-lexical, phonological, route visual analysis is required first. However the role of vision is probably greater for the faster whole-word, lexical route compared with the sublexical route, because for the latter, phonological translation of letter to sound can help at each stage.

Visual fixation for reading

All the linguistic information conveyed by print is obtained during brief (300 ms) fixations on words. The eyes are then advanced by a rapid saccade to the next word; during these movements no detailed information about the next word is available. Thus successful reading depends greatly upon achieving stable visual perception during each fixation on the word to be read and rapid shifts of visual attention to the next. The saccades between fixations and the drifts that occur during fixations cause letter images to move around on the retina a great deal; yet, for good readers, the print remains stationary on the page.

In 1896, Pringle Morgan described the case of Percy who often spelt his own name as 'Precy' and did not notice the difference. He habitually misordered letters in words and Morgan described him as having 'word blindness'. A great many poor readers have similar problems with correctly sequencing the letters in words, and they often complain that the reason is that the letters seem to move around on the page, so that they cannot work out their correct order (Fowler and Stein, 1979; Simons and Gordon, 1987; Garzia and Sesma, 1993). The following are some comments made by children with visual reading problems:

- 'the "c" moved towards the "l" so that it looked like a "d"';
- 'the "d" and the "g" changed places';
- 'the "g" moved above the line so that it looked like a "p"';
- 'the "o" looked as though it was hovering over the page';
- 'the "m" moved in and out of the page.'

Clearly these children were experiencing unstable perceptions of print. The most likely explanation is that their attention and their eyes were moving around in an uncontrolled way when they were trying to fixate on the words.

For intended eye movements 'corollary discharge' signals are generated that inform visual centres that an eye movement is about to take place. For uncontrolled movements, however, there is no such corollary discharge and so the resultant motion of images across the retina is easily mistaken for the letters actually moving on the page. In good readers such unintended eye movements are quickly reversed because they generate powerful motion signals that are fed back to the fixation system to reverse the unwanted movements and thus stabilize the eyes. These motion signals are generated by the visual magnocellular system. But in dyslexics development of the visual magnocellular system is often impaired. Clearly this could interfere both with the reliable direction of visual attention and of eye movements.

The visual magnocellular system

Although 90% of retinal ganglion cells are small parvo cells that signal the fine detail and colour of objects, 10% are much larger magno cells that signal the timing of visual events, not their form. Hence they are important for detecting visual motion (Enroth-Cugell and Robson, 1966; Shapley and Perry, 1986; Merigan and Maunsell, 1993). Their dendritic area, hence receptive field size, is some 500 times that of parvo cells; they have rapid membrane dynamics so that they can signal sharply the onset and offset of stimuli. They have heavily myelinated axons, which conduct signals to the cerebral cortex some 10 ms faster than parvo cells. They project to the magnocellular layers of the thalamic visual relay nucleus (the lateral geniculate nucleus – LGN) and from there onwards to layer IV C (of the primary visual cortex in the calcarine fissure of the occipital lobe).

Although after this there is much intermingling of parvo and magno pathways in the primary and in the other visual cortical areas, two main output streams of visual processing have been distinguished (Ungerleider and Mishkin, 1982). The ventral stream is devoted to identifying objects on the basis of their fine detail and colouring. This pathway is therefore often called the 'what' pathway. It culminates in the inferior temporal cortex; and it receives almost equal quantities of magno and parvo input.

The dorsal pathway passes via the middle temporal motion area to the posterior parietal cortex. It is dominated by magnocellular input (Maunsell et al., 1990). Since these signals provide information about the timing of visual events and of the motion of visual targets, the dorsal system is important for the guidance of both eye and limb movement (Milner and Goodale, 1995). Accordingly the further projections of this 'where' system are to motor structures including the frontal eye fields, the superior colliculus; and it provides a very large input to the cerebellum (Stein and Glickstein, 1992). All these areas then project to the ocular-motor nuclei, which controls the movements of the eyes. Hence the magnocellular system is crucial for controlling eye movements during reading, and particularly for the rapid motion feedback that prevents the eyes slipping off their fixation on a word.

Peripheral visual magnocellular system in dyslexics

Over the last few years evidence has accumulated that development of the visual magnocellular system may be slightly impaired in dyslexics. Galaburda and his colleagues studied the histology of the lateral geniculate nucleus *post mortem* in the brains of known dyslexics. The magnocellular layers were clearly separate from the parvocellular layers in control brains, but parvo and magno layers were seen to merge together in the dyslexic brains. Moreover the size of the magnocellular neurones was reduced by 30% in the dyslexic brains compared to the controls (Livingstone et al., 1991).

It was Bill Lovegrove and his colleagues who provided the first psychophysical evidence that implicated the peripheral visual magnocellular system in dyslexics' problems. They showed that it is functionally slightly weaker in dyslexics than in good readers (Lovegrove et al., 1980). Testing dyslexics under mesopic conditions they found that they needed greater contrast between stationary black and white bars separated by a 1° visual angle (a low spatial frequency grating – 1 cycle per degree), whereas they were actually slightly more sensitive than controls at high spatial frequencies (10 cycles/degree). These findings are consistent with a mild weakness of the peripheral magnocellular system. If the gratings were flickered the dyslexics needed greater contrast than good readers to see gratings of any size – in other words, they had lower sensitivity at both high and low spatial frequencies, again as expected of a magnocellular deficit. All these findings have been confirmed by others, including us (Mason et al., 1993). Likewise, Martin and Lovegrove (1987) showed that dyslexics' sensitivity to flicker, assessed by measuring their flicker fusion thresholds, tends to be lower than controls, and we were able to confirm this also (Mason et al., 1993, Talcott et al., 1998). Dyslexics also tend to have reduced and delayed visual evoked potentials recorded over the primary visual cortex (Livingstone et al. 1991; Maddock et al, 1992; Lehmkuhle et al. 1993). All these findings are consistent with the conclusion that dyslexics have reduced sensitivity of the peripheral magnocellular system.

This conclusion, however, has been hotly disputed (Skottun, 2000). The dyslexic magnocellular deficit is mild, and it only occurs in about two-thirds of dyslexics, so that the difference from controls tends not to be statistically significant if only small numbers are used. Nevertheless if large enough samples of dyslexics are studied and especially if those who display visual symptoms are selected, then this impairment of the peripheral visual magnocellular system can be demonstrated reliably (Stein et al., 2000a).

Cortical magnocellular system

As noted earlier the dorsal 'where' pathway from the primary visual cortex to the temporal motion area (MT) and to the posterior parietal cortex (PPC) is dominated by magnocellular input. Newsome et al. (1988, 1989) showed by recording single neurones in monkey MT and PPC that a most effective way of measuring the sensitivity of the whole magnocellular system, including both its peripheral pathway and central components as far as the motion temporal area, is to use random dot kinematogram (RDK) stimuli. These consist of dots moving around randomly. If enough of the dots are moved together in the same direction, 'coherently' rather than randomly, we see a cloud of dots moving in that direction, like snowflakes driven by the wind. This coherent motion can only be perceived if the motion signals are integrated over a wide area, which is a function of the visual magnocellular system (Talcott et al., 2000b). Thus the density of the dots that have to be moved together for a subject to see the coherent motion gives the sensitivity of that subject's magnocellular system. So when the number of dots moving together has been reduced to such an extent that the subject can no longer reliably determine which of two side by side panels contains the coherent motion, we define this as the subject's threshold and his sensitivity is the reciprocal of this.

Using these random dot kinematograms we have shown that two-thirds of dyslexics have higher than normal thresholds for perceiving coherent motion – they have reduced magnocellular sensitivity (Cornelissen et al., 1994; Talcott et al., 1998, 2000a,b). This has turned out to be a more reliable measure of overall magnocellular sensitivity than using grating contrast sensitivity or flicker fusion thresholds, and there have been many replications of the finding that dyslexics have reduced RDK motion sensitivity. As we have seen the psychophysical results have been corroborated using visual evoked potentials and also by functional imaging (Eden et al., 1996; Demb et al., 1997, 1998).

Static form coherence

It is often argued, however, that dyslexics are simply bad at all psychophysical tasks because of general inattention, nervousness or some other reason. It is important, therefore, to be able to demonstrate that in some control task not involving the magnocellular system, but in other respects as similar to the RDK task as possible, the dyslexics perform as well as controls. We have therefore developed a static form coherence test that is handled mainly by the parvocellular system. In this task the subjects are shown patches of stationary short line segments. Most of these are randomly orientated but some are organized to form a series of concentric circles, and we reduce the proportion of the line segments that form the circles to find the subjects' thresholds for perceiving them. As expected we found that dyslexics, even those with poor motion sensitivity, were just as sensitive as good readers in this static form coherence task.

However some researchers have remained unconvinced that there can be any causal connection between subjects' motion sensitivity and their reading ability; so they suggest that poor motion sensitivity is merely an epiphenomenon, not connected with reading (Hulme, 1988). Therefore we not only have to show that there is a correlation between individuals' motion sensitivity and their reading, but also that there is a clear causal chain that explains why visual motion sensitivity is important for reading.

Motion sensitivity and reading ability

The first step is to show that there is a correlation between subjects' motion sensitivity and their reading ability. We have therefore compared motion sensitivity with reading and spelling ability in groups of adults and children, both good, average and poor readers. We found strong correlations with reading and even higher ones with their spelling ability (Witton et al., 1998, Talcott et al., 2000a). Thus these high correlations are found not only in dyslexics, but over the whole range of reading ability, so that good spellers tend to have high motion sensitivity, average spellers, average motion sensitivity, and poor spellers tend to have low visual motion sensitivity.

In order to examine the visual requirements of reading and orthographical skill more specifically we have used a pseudohomophone test (Olson et al., 1989). In this subjects are presented with two words that are identical phonologically; but one is a pseudohomophone – incorrectly spelled but sounding the same (for example 'rain' and 'rane'). This task cannot be solved by sounding out the letters phonologically; instead the correct visual form of the word must be recalled. After controlling for age and IQ we found that in both children and adults covering the whole range of reading ability there was a high correlation between subjects' visual motion sensitivity in the random dot kinematograms and their ability to carry out this orthographic task (Talcott et al., 2000a).

Visual motion sensitivity correlates highest of all with this orthographic task and with spelling ability. In fact we have shown that visual motion sensitivity can by itself account for over a fifth of the variance in children's literary skill. Furthermore after statistically controlling for covariance between orthographic and phonological skill, we found that visual motion sensitivity continued to account for unique variance in orthographic skill that phonological ability could not account for. In other words these results provide strong evidence that visual motion sensitivity plays an important role in determining how well children can develop the visual skills required for reading.

Visual instability

Nevertheless correlation does not prove causation, and despite these strong relationships it is still argued by some that dyslexics' visual magnocellular impairments are irrelevant to their reading problems. This is partly because Breitmeyer's original hypothesis (1993) to explain the role of the magnocellular system in reading has turned out probably not to be correct. He suggested that magnocellular activity during each saccade is necessary to erase the parvocellular products of the previous fixation; hence weak magnocellular responses might fail to do so and the forms seen on the previous fixation might superimpose on those derived from the next fixation. However it has been shown that magnocellular activity does not inhibit parvo during saccades (Burr et al., 1994); hence Breitmeyer's explanation is unlikely. Nevertheless there are plenty of other potential causal connections between visual motion sensitivity and reading. The magnocellular system is known to be important for direction of visual attention and therefore of eye movements, hence for visual search also. But it is often argued that, during reading, the page is usually stationary and information about each word is taken in during fixations when the eyes are stationary, suggesting that the direction of visual attention, eye movements and visual search are not important for reading.

However this is an illusion; the eyes are not stationary when reading. Even during fixations they move around by a small amount and in dyslexics this wobble during attempts to fixate is much more marked (Eden et al., 1994). Thus one way that has interested us in which a magnocellular deficit might lead to reading difficulty is that it could lead to unsteady eye fixation. The retinal motion signal generated by any unwanted movement of the eyes is the main signal that is used to compensate and reverse such eye movements. Thus between saccades motion feedback keeps the eyes fixated steadily on the word being read. Hence impaired motion sensitivity due to magnocellular weakness may lead to unstable binocular fixation. Such uncontrolled eye movements could cause letter images to move around on the retina. Because they were not intended, these eye movements would not be accompanied by corollary discharge indicating that the eyes had moved. Hence the image movements could easily be misinterpreted as the letters themselves moving, and their order and so forth could become confused. So the visual scene may appear unsteady and this visual instability might make it very difficult for children to determine the order of letters in a word in order to lay down reliable memorized representations of their orthography. That may be why we find that poor motion sensitivity leads to poor orthographic skill. In contrast good motion sensitivity should enable children to lay down a crisp and reliable orthographic representation of words, which could be accessed quickly and reliably.

Control of fixation

As discussed earlier, one of the main functions of the visual magnocellular system is known to be to guide eye movements and in particular to mediate stable eye fixation. But we need to prove each link in the causal chain linking low visual motion sensitivity with poor orthography: we would like to show that poor motion sensitivity leads to poor fixation; that this causes unsteady visual perceptions; and that this in turn interferes with children's ability to acquire orthographic skills. To confirm that these relations are causal, ideally we also need to find an intervention that will improve binocular stability, so that we can demonstrate that improving the steadiness with which the two eyes fixate on words actually improves children's reading. In fact we have been able to establish most of these links.

In the poor readers that we study we measure their motion sensitivity using the random dot kinematograms. In addition we record how steadily their two eyes can fixate a small target at the reading distance, and we also give them a visual symptom questionnaire asking them whether letters move, shake or blur when they are trying to read. As expected we find that there is a marked tendency for those with poor motion sensitivity to have unstable binocular control and unsteady visual perceptions when attempting to read (Stein and Fowler, 1981; Riddell et al., 1990; Eden et al., 1994; Cornelissen et al., 1991, 1994, 1997). The unstable binocular control of dyslexics has been confirmed by numerous other researchers (such as Benton et al., 1969; Bigelow and McKenzie, 1985; Evans et al., 1994).

Binocular vergence control

Unsteady eye control is particularly problematic for reading because the eyes need to be converged to read words at the normal reading distance of about 30 cm. Unsteady fixation can therefore cause the two eyes' views of the letters to vary from moment to moment and even to cross over each other (Stein et al. 1988; Riddell et al. 1990). Hence letters can appear to move around and to change places, so that their order can become very confused.

This leads to the possibility of a very simple treatment. If an important problem is that the two eyes' images tend to cross over each other and thus confuse the child, then simply blanking one eye when reading should help. Accordingly we have been giving children with unstable binocular control spectacles with the left eye occluded to wear for three months just when reading and writing. We have been able to show in four separate studies (Stein and Fowler, 1980; Stein and Fowler, 1985; Cornelissen et al., 1992; Stein et al., 2000b) that this simple treatment helped them permanently to improve their binocular fixation, so that their eyes wobbled less when they were trying to fixate on print. Thus the somewhat paradoxical result was that occluding one eye improved the fixation control of both eyes. This probably resulted from the seeing eye gaining utrocular control over its own eye muscles (Ogle, 1962) – that eye's retinal signals now began to be able to adjust its own muscles to maintain accurate fixation independently of what the other eye was doing.

More importantly, from the children's point of view, if their binocular fixation improved their reading also improved, sometimes dramatically. In the first, open, study we found that this treatment doubled the rate of reading progress compared with children who received no occlusion (Stein and Fowler, 1980). We achieved similar gains in two subsequent randomized controlled studies in which the children did not know which spectacles might help them, nor did the orthoptist examining them know what treatment they had been receiving (Stein and Fowler, 1985; Stein et al., 2000b). In our most recent randomized controlled study the reading of the children who received the patch actually caught up with that of their normally reading peers. Their reading age advanced 2.3 months per month over the 18 months we followed them, whereas those who received identical treatment apart from the patch improved by only 1.3 months/month. This reading spurt was much greater than for any other remediation programme that we have found.

Auditory/phonological requirements for reading

As mentioned earlier, not all dyslexics have visual problems, however, and many have phonological problems in addition to their visual ones. Indeed, the majority of researchers believe that inadequate phonological skill is the main, if not the only, cause of children's reading problems (Lieberman et al., 1974; Snowling, 1981; Bradley and Bryant, 1983). When reading unfamiliar words we have to match each letter in the word with the sound that it stands for, and then meld them together in inner speech to give the word and its meaning. This phonological route is slower, but it is the only one available for unfamiliar words. The phonological route therefore calls upon inner speech and inner hearing to retrieve the memory of letter sounds and their order.

The acoustic cues that distinguish letter sounds are changes in frequency and changes in amplitude (Tallal, 1980). For instance the only difference between the sounds of 'b' and 'd' is a decrease compared with an increase respectively, during the first 40 to 50 ms in the frequency of the second and third formants of the speech sounds. Just as we can measure a person's sensitivity to visual motion using random dot kinematograms, so we can measure sensitivity to the changes in sound frequency (frequency modulations) that signal phonemic distinctions. We vary the frequency of a tone, and measure by how much the frequency has to change for the person to hear the change compared with a pure tone. If we make these frequency changes twice, 20 times or 40 times per second the actual changes in frequency can be tracked by the auditory system in real time. However at faster frequency modulation rates (for example, 240 Hz) the frequency changes become too fast to be tracked in real time. Instead the pattern of frequencies set up by these rapid changes (the frequency spectrum) is detected by a different mechanism (Moore, 1989).

What we have found is that dyslexics and poor readers in general are significantly worse than good readers at detecting frequency modulations of a 500 Hz tone at 2 and 20 and 40 Hz. But they are no worse at detecting 240 Hz FM since this depends on the spectral processing mechanism (Stein and McAnally, 1996; Witton et al., 1998; Talcott et al., 1999, 2000a). Thus dyslexics seem to be worse at tracking frequency changes in real time, but probably they are no worse than good readers at identifying the frequency composition of sounds. Tracking frequencies in real time seems to be one function of large cells in the auditory system that may be analogous to the magnocellular neurones in the visual system (Trussell, 1998).

Phonological skills

If poor readers are worse at detecting frequency change then they should also be worse at detecting the cues that distinguish letter sounds which depend on such frequency changes – they should be worse at phonological analysis. We have therefore correlated frequency modulation sensitivity in good and poor readers with measures of their phonological ability. Proficient readers can read pseudo-, nonsense, words such as 'tegwop' and 'plint', even though they are totally novel, because they can sound out the letters one by one. But anybody with poor phonological skills who cannot retrieve letter sounds quickly and accurately is going to be slower and make more errors when attempting to read nonwords. Thus this nonsense word reading test is a very good measure of phonological ability (Snowling, 1987).

Accordingly we have compared subjects' FM sensitivity with their nonword reading ability, and as expected found that there is a high correlation between the two (Witton et al., 1998, Talcott et al. 1999, 2000a). As with visual motion sensitivity and orthographic ability, this relationship holds over the whole range of reading ability. Thus good readers tend to have both high frequency modulation sensitivity and high phonological skill; poor readers have low frequency modulation sensitivity and low phonological skill. These associations suggest that proficiency at low level auditory analysis of frequency modulations plays a large part in determining how well the high level phonological skills required for reading develop. Nevertheless there is great controversy over whether deficits in auditory temporal processing can really explain phonological problems (Studdert Kennedy and Mody, 1995).

Letter sounds are also distinguished by changes in the amplitude of the speech signal (amplitude modulations – AM). So we have measured dyslexics' sensitivity to amplitude modulations as well. Again we have been able to show that they have lower sensitivity to AM (Menell et al., 1999; Witton, submitted). And again there is a strong correlation between individuals' sensitivity to amplitude modulations and their phonological ability as measured by non-word reading. This is as true of good as poor readers across the whole range of ability.

Visual and auditory transient sensitivity and orthographic and phonological skills

In fact we found that even after accounting for age and IQ, subjects' sensitivity to visual motion and to auditory frequency and amplitude modulations together account for a highly significant proportion of the variance in their reading skills. Furthermore, when we controlled for the variance in literacy that is common to both auditory and visual processing, then sensitivity to auditory frequency and amplitude modulations accounted for significant amounts of the variance in phonological ability that visual/orthographic ability could not account for. Likewise visual motion sensitivity accounted for a significant amount of the variance in orthographic ability that auditory phonological ability could not. Thus auditory and visual transient sensitivity can account for unique variance in phonological and orthographic processing respectively (Talcott et al., 2000a). These findings again suggest that these low-level sensory processes play important parts in the development of these reading skills.

In other words the quality of the teaching a child receives, or the amount of access to books or other social and cultural influences may play a less significant part in their reading development than used to be thought. Instead individual differences in the brain's ability to carry out these basic physiological processes may be crucial. This does not, of course, mean that teaching and the literacy of a child's household are not important – only that their influence depends greatly on a child's basic perceptual capacities.

Auditory magnocellular system?

As we have seen, sensitivity to visual transients, such as target motion and flicker, is mediated by a system of large neurones in the retina, thalamus and cortex that signal the start, changes and end of visual stimuli. There is no such clearly anatomically distinct set of magnocells in the auditory system. Nevertheless many large neurones in the auditory pathways do seem to be specialized for processing acoustic transients, such as changes in frequency, amplitude and phase. As we have also seen, dyslexics tend to have reduced AM and FM sensitivity. Moreover, they tend to be worse at discriminating pure tones at low frequencies (McAnally and Stein, 1996; Hari et al., 1999). Our remarkable ability to distinguish low frequency tones that are separated by only a few Hz (for example, 500 from 502 Hz) depends partly upon phase locking in the cochlea, the ability of some cochlear neurones to respond only at peaks of the sound pressure wave. Although this is not the only cue to frequency change it plays a major role at frequencies below about 1500 Hz.

Faithful tracking of these peaks, and therefore of frequency changes, seems to be one function of large neurones throughout the auditory system. Accordingly dyslexics seem to be less sensitive to sound phase as measured by the degree of binaural unmasking perceived when the phase of the masker is reversed between the two ears (McAnally and Stein, 1996) or in sensitivity to dichotic pitch (Dougherty et al., 1998); but they are not less sensitive to 80 Hz amplitude modulations of white noise (Hari et al., 1999). Thus the precise nature of their auditory temporal processing problem is unclear.

However it is likely to involve the functions of large cells in the auditory system. Studying dyslexic brains *post mortem,* Galaburda and colleagues (1994) found that the large neurones in the magnocellular division of the left medial geniculate nucleus (the auditory thalamic relay) are smaller than those on the right side or in control brains. In other words it seems quite likely that poor readers, in particular dyslexics, may have in addition to impaired development of the visual magnocellular system, impaired development of magnocells in the auditory system. Thus visual magnocellular sensitivity may help determine how well children develop the orthographic skills needed for reading; but also their auditory magnocellular sensitivity may help to determine the development of their phonological skills.

Implications for early identification and remediation of reading problems

Since these visual and auditory magnocellular functions are fundamental to the operations of these systems and do not depend at all on reading, their development must predate learning to read very considerably. Therefore we are aiming to adapt our tests of visual and auditory sensitivity for use with children before they go to school. This may enable us to identify any weaknesses, and thus predict which children are likely to have problems with phonology or orthography before they begin to fail at reading.

At this age, when the brain is still extremely plastic, we know that perceptual training can greatly improve these functions. Merzenich, Tallal and colleagues (1996) found that in children with specific language impairment slowing and exaggerating the frequency and amplitude modulations that distinguish letter sounds can help them to learn to speak properly. The same is likely to be true of dyslexics. Likewise our success with simply occluding one eye in steadying children's binocular fixation shows that visuomotor control can also be improved, and visual reading problems thereby reduced. These examples demonstrate that if children's sensory weaknesses can be identified simple techniques can be used to remediate them. If these are applied early enough before the downward spiral of failure, loss of self esteem, frustration and misery sets in, then many of the 20% of children who leave school still functionally illiterate might be helped to enhance their lives and society's benefit from their existence.

Motor implications, cerebellum

If reading difficulties are a consequence of disturbed development of this generalized magnocellular system then we should expect to see abnormalities in other systems as well. Thus we and others have produced evidence that touch sensitivity, particularly that relying on rapidly adapting receptors served by large diameter afferents and large neurones in the dorsal column nuclei, is another sense that is slightly impaired in dyslexics (Grant et al., 1999; Stoodley et al., 2000). This is an example of a magnocellular defect that does not directly affect reading: impaired skin sensitivity to touch transients results from impaired magnocellular performance in the dorsal column division of the somaesthetic system. But this does not impact on reading; it correlates with reading only because the somaesthetic deficit is associated with similar visual and auditory deficits that do directly affect the reading process.

Fawcett et al. (1996) have shown that dyslexics perform worse than normal on a wide variety of motor tests including balance and other functions thought to involve the cerebellum. This focus on the cerebellum is particularly significant because this structure is the recipient of heavy projections from all the magnocellular systems throughout the brain. For example, quantitatively the largest output of the dorsal 'where' visual magnocellular route is to the cerebellum via the pontine nuclei (Stein and Glickstein, 1992). Likewise the dorsal spinocerebellar tract is dominated by dynamic signals provided by group Ia muscle spindle fibres. Furthermore antibodies selective for magnocells bind to the cerebellum very heavily. Thus we can view the cerebellum itself as a quintessentially magnocellular structure.

The cerebellum is now known to be important for the acquisition of sensorimotor skills, including reading. Not only is it very important for the calibration of eye movements, and thus for the control of reading fixations, but it may also play a part in the 'inner speech' that is required for phonological analysis – sounding out the letters in a word. Richard Scott observed that children with cerebellar tumours sometimes present with reading difficulties. The left temporo-parietal area projects to the right cerebellum, and both are thought to be particularly involved in language related processes. Catherine Stoodley in our laboratory confirmed that children with right-sided cerebellar lesions had severe language and literacy problems, whereas those with left-sided lesions were more likely to have visuospatial problems (Scott et al., 2001 in press). In fact these cerebellar tumours seem to cause more serious and long lasting problems than lesions of the cerebral cortex. Indeed if cortical lesions occur early enough most children recover from them almost completely.

We therefore compared the metabolism of the cerebellum in dyslexics with controls' using magnetic resonance spectroscopy (MRS). The choline/n-acetyl aspartate ratio measured by MRS gives an estimate of the metabolic activity of different brain regions. We found that this ratio was lower in the cerebellum of the dyslexics compared with the controls, particularly on the right hand side (Rae et al., 1998). Likewise, in dyslexics it was lower in the left temporoparietal region with which the right cerebellum connects, compared with controls. Nicolson et al. (1999) then showed that dyslexics have decreased activation of the cerebellum during motor learning. Using positron emission tomography (PET) scanning they showed that during the acquisition of a five-finger exercise there was very considerably less activation in the cerebellum in dyslexics compared with controls. Thus there is now little doubt that cerebellar function is mildly disturbed in many dyslexics. Since the cerebellum receives a heavy magnocellular input and itself contains magnocells this is further evidence for the hypothesis that impaired magnocellular development underlies dyslexics' problems.

Genetic/immunological regulation

Another exciting implication of our work is that understanding the neural basis of auditory and visual reading problems should enable us to develop animal models of these mechanisms. Transient sensitivity can easily be measured in animals; hence it should be much easier to elucidate the genetic and other mechanisms that regulate the development of magnocellular systems in animals and then transfer the results to human reading.

In all our studies there has been a fairly high correlation between the visual motion sensitivity of individuals and their sensitivity to auditory frequency modulations. This suggests that these two kinds of transient processing may be under some sort of common control. Perhaps some common genetic mechanism underlies the quality of development of all magnocellular neurones. These have evolved to time neural events, to track changes in sound, light and other modalities. They have fast membrane channel kinetics so that they respond rapidly to the onset or offset of signals, rapid adaptation, rapid transmitter release and fast conduction times.

Magnocellular neurones all seem to express the same surface antigen that is recognized by particular antibodies (such as CAT 301 – Hockfield and Sur, 1990) so that they probably all derive from a common lineage that provides them with their large size, their rapid membrane dynamics, rapid adaptation and fast conduction. However as we have seen, there are large differences in magnocellular sensitivity between individuals because there are wide individual variations in the development of magno cells in the different parts of the brain. These differences are probably under genetic and immunological control and, to a large extent, they can account for the wide range of reading abilities found between individuals. This would explain why different individuals have a unique mix of sensitivity to visual motion determining their orthographic ability, to auditory frequency and amplitude modulations which determine their phonological ability, and of motor timing precision determining their cerebellar function and degree of motor co-ordination.

It is clear that variations in magnocellular sensitivity are likely to be under genetic control because reading disability is so highly heritable. Twin studies have shown that 60% of the population variance in reading skill is due to inherited factors (Pennington, 1991b). This is a high value that is similar to the heritability of height and other cognitive abilities such as verbal ability or general intelligence, but much higher than the heritability of diabetes or heart attacks. Although visual orthographic and auditory phonological ability are probably under a high degree of common genetic control a significant proportion of variance in ortho-graphic skill appears to be separately inherited from phonological skill. This implies that at least three genes play a part.

Taking advantage of the large number of dyslexics we have seen over the years we have collected over 200 families with at least two children with reading problems. We are in the process of screening the full human genome for linkage to reading difficulties. But we have already been able to show that there is a strong association with a site on the short arm of chromosome 6 (Fisher et al., 1999). This confirms the results of Cardon et al. (1994) and Grigorenko et al. (1997) from smaller studies carried out in Colorado and Connecticut respectively.

This site is highly significant because it is close to the major histocom-patibility complex (MHC), a region that contains many genes that control presentation of antigen to T lymphocytes; hence they also help to distinguish self from not self antigens, and thus to detect foreign invasions. This region was first targeted in dyslexia because of the evidence that there is a higher incidence in dyslexics and their families of autoimmune conditions that signify imbalance in immunological control, such as asthma, eczema, hay fever and disseminated lupus erythematosus (DLE – Hughdahl et al., 1990) although this high incidence has been disputed.

Since then it has been discovered that MHC molecules are not only involved in immune responses but that they may also play an important part during development in regulating the differentiation of magno cells for their specialized functions. Corriveau and Shatz (1998) found that Class 1 MHC molecules play a role in regulating the development of visual magnocellular neurones in the LGN and also in the hippocampus. Since Hockfield's work suggests that all magnocells throughout the brain derive from a common developmental lineage, it is reasonable to speculate that the development of all of them may be regulated by the MHC system. Hence the finding that reading disability is genetically linked to a site close to or within the MHC complex on chromosome 6 may be hugely significant.

Polyunsaturated fatty acids

Furthermore, recent reports that many of dyslexics' problems may be exacerbated by modern diets that can contain dangerously low quantities of polyunsaturated fatty acids (PUFAs) can be fitted into this schema. Dyslexia in both children and adults is associated with clinical signs of essential fatty acid deficiency (Richardson et al., 2000; Taylor et al., 2000). As we have seen, magnocellular function depends upon the rapid dynamics of their membrane ionic channels. The required conformational changes in channel proteins are facilitated by being surrounded by flexible unsaturated fatty acids. The turnover of these is under the control of phospholipases, in particular PLA2. It has recently been shown that there are increased levels of this enzyme in dyslexics (Macdonell et al., 2000), which may remove PUFAs from the membrane and thus compromise rapid channel responses in magnocells. Furthermore this enzyme may be modulated by the MHC system since immune reactions mobilize PUFAs from cell membranes to provide precursors of the cytokines required for effective cellular responses to foreign material. With the decline of eating fish, modern diets tend to be dangerously low in PUFAs, hence magnocellular function may be particularly compromised. Therefore supplementing dyslexics' diets with PUFAs may relieve their fatty acid deficiency and help them to learn to read (Richardson, submitted).

Summary

We have summarized the evidence that reading problems are fundamentally a consequence of the impaired development of a system of large neurones in the brain (magnocells) that are under common genetic control and responsible for timing sensory and motor events; and we have shown that their proper development is essential for reading. The visual demands of reading draw on the capabilities of the visual magnocellular system that is important for controlling eye movements. Therefore impaired development of these neurones can lead to unsteady fixation when reading, hence visual confusion of letter order. This, in turn, leads to poor memory of the visual form of words – in other words it impedes the acquisition of orthographical skills.

The auditory equivalent of the visual magnocellular system is essential for detecting the frequency and amplitude transients that distinguish different letter sounds – in other words for meeting the phonological demands of reading. Impaired development of such auditory transient (FM and AM) processing can lead to auditory confusion of letter sounds, hence failure to acquire phonological skills.

Visual and auditory transient sensitivity can be measured in young children, and improved by appropriate sensory training. Hence we should be able to identify individual children's weaknesses early and hope to remediate them before they begin to fail at reading.

Magnocellular/transient systems project densely to the cerebellum, and it is now becoming increasingly apparent that the cerebellum plays an important role in the reading process, by contributing both to the control of steady eye fixations during reading and to 'inner speech'.

The development of magnocellular neurones is under genetic control perhaps involving immunological regulation of their differentiation. Brisk magnocellular function depends on their membrane channels' environment of polyunsaturated fatty acids. Hence modern diets poor in these may further impair the development of magnocellular neurones, and taking extra PUFAs may help to counteract this, hence improve reading skills.

References

Benton CD, McCann JW (1969) Dyslexia and dominance. J Pediatric Ophthalmology 6: 220–2.

Bigelow ER, McKenzie BE (1985) Unstable ocular dominance and reading ability. Perception 14: 329–35.

Bradley L, Bryant P (1983) Categorizing sounds and learning to read – a causal connection. Nature 301: 419–21.

Breitmeyer BG (1993) The roles of sustained and transient channels in reading and reading disability. In DM Willows (ed.) Visual Processes in Reading and Reading Disability. Erlbaum: Mawah NJ, pp. 95–110.

Burr DC, Morrone MC, Ross J (1994) Selective suppression of the magnocellular visual pathway during saccadic eye movements. Nature 371: 511–13.

Cardon LR, Smith SD, Fulker DW, Kimberling WJ, Pennington BF, Defries JC (1994) Quantitative trait locus for reading disability on Chromosome 6. Science 266, 276.

Castles A, Coltheart M (1993) Varieties of developmental dyslexia. Cognition 47: 149–80.

Cornelissen PL, Richardson AR, Mason A, Fowler MS, Stein JF (1994) Contrast sensitivity and coherent motion detection measured at photopic luminance levels in dyslexics and controls. Vision Res 35(10): 1483–94.

Cornelissen P, Bradley L, Fowler MS, Stein JF (1991) What children see affects how they read. Develop.Med and Child Neurology 33: 755–62.

Cornelissen P, Bradley L Fowler S, Stein JF (1994) What children see affects how they spell. Developmental Medicine and Child Neurology 36: 716–27.

Cornelissen PL, Hansen PC, Hutton JL, Evangelinou V, Stein JF (1997) Magnocellular visual function and children's single word reading. Vis Res 38: 471–82.

Cornelissen P, Bradley L, Fowler MS, Stein JF (1992) Covering one eye affects how some children read. Develop.Med and Child Neurology 34: 296–304.

Corriveau R, Shatz C (1998) Regulation of Class 1 MHC gene expression in the developing and mature CNS by neural activity. Neuron 21: 505–20.

Demb JB, Boynton GM, Heeger DJ (1997) Brain activation in visual cortex predicts individual differences in reading performance. Proc NY Ac Sc 94: 13363–6.

Demb JB, Boynton GM, Best M, Heeger DJ (1998) Psychophysical evidence for a magnocellular deficit in dyslexics. Vision Research 38: 1555–9.

Dougherty RF, Cynader MS, Bjornson BH, Edgell D, Giaschi DE (1998) Dichotic pitch distinguishes normal and dyslexic auditory function. Neuroreport 9: 3001–3.

Eden GF, Stein JF, Wood HM, Wood FB (1994) Differences in eye movements and reading problems in dyslexic and normal children. Vision Res 34(10): 1345–58.

Eden GF, VanMeter JW, Rumsey JW, Maisog J, Zeffiro TA (1996) Functional MRI reveals differences in visual motion processing in individuals with dyslexia. Nature 382: 66–9.

Ellis AW (1984) Reading, Writing and Dyslexia. London: Erlbaum.

Enroth-Cugell C, Robson JG (1966) The contrast sensitivity of retinal ganglion cells in the cat. J.Physiol 187: 517–52.

Evans BJW, Drasdo N, Richards IL (1994) Investigation of accommodative and binocular function in dyslexia. Ophthalmic and Physiological Optics 145: 5–20.

Fawcett AJ, Nicolson RI, Dean P (1996) Impaired performance of children with dyslexia on a range of cerebellar tasks. Ann Dyslexia 46: 259–83.

Fisher S, Marlowe A, Lamb J, Maestrini E, Williams D, Richardson A, Weeks D, Stein JF, Monaco A (1999) A genome wide search strategy for identifying quantitative trait loci in reading disability with detailed analysis of chromosome 6p. Am J Hum Genetics 64: 146–56.

Fowler S, Stein JF (1979) New evidence for ambilaterality in visual dyslexia. Neurosci Letts (suppl) 3: 214.

Galaburda AM, Menard MT, Rosen GD (1994) Evidence for aberrant auditory anatomy in developmental dyslexia. Proc Natl Acad Sci USA 91: 8010–13.

Galaburda AM, Livingstone M (1993) Evidence for a magnocellular defect in developmental dyslexia. In Tallal P, Galaburda AM, Llinas RR, Von Euler C (eds) Temporal Information Processing in the Nervous System. Ann NY Acad Sci 682: 70–82.

Garzia RP, Sesma M (1993) Vision and Reading. J Opt Vis Dev 24: 4–51.

Grant AC, Zangaladze A, Thiagarajah M, Saathian K (1999) Tactile perception in dyslexics. Neuropsychologia 37: 1201–11.

Grigorenko EL, Wood FB, Meyer MS, Hart LA, Speed WC, Shuster A, Pauls DL (1997) Susceptibility loci for distinct components of developmental dyslexia on chromosomes 6 and 15. Am J Hum Genet 60: 27–39.

Hari R, Saaskilahti A, Helenius P, Uutela K (1999) Non impaired auditory phase locking in dyslexic adults. Neuroreport 10: 2347–8.

Hockfield S, Sur M (1990) Monoclonal CAT 301 identifies Y cells in cat LGN. JC Neurol 300: 320–30.

Hugdahl K, Synnevag B, Satz P (1990) Immune and autoimmune disorders in dyslexic children. Neuropsychologia 28: 673–9.

Hulme C (1988) The implausibility of low level visual deficits as a cause of reading disability. Cognitive Neuropsychology 5: 369–74.

Lehmkuhle K, Williams M (1993) Defective visual pathway in children with reading disability. New England Journal of Medicine 328: 989–95.

Liberman IY, Shankweiler D, Fischer FW, Carter B (1974) Explicit syllable and phoneme segmentation in the young child. J Exp Child Psychol 18: 201–12.

Livingstone MS, Rosen GD, Drislane FW, Galaburda AM (1991) Physiological and anatomical evidence for a magnocellular defect in developmental dyslexia. Proc Natl Acad Sci USA 88: 7943–7.

Lovegrove WJ, Martin F, Blackwood M, Badcock D (1980) Specific reading difficulty: differences in contrast sensitivity as a function of spatial frequency. Science 210: 439–40.

Macdonnell LEF, Skinner FK, Ward PE, Glen AIM, Glen ACA, Macdonald DJ, Boyle RM, Horrobin DE (2000) Increased levels of cytosolic phospholipase A2 in dyslexics. Prostaglandins, Leukotrienes and Essential Fatty Acids 63: 37–40.

Maddock H, Richardson A, Stein JF (1992) Reduced and delayed visual evoked potentials in dyslexics. J Physiol 459: 130P.

Manis F, McBride-Chang C, Seidenberg M, Doi L, Petersen A (1997) On the bases of two subtypes of developmental dyslexia. Cognition 58: 157–95.

Martin F, Lovegrove W (1987) Flicker contrast sensitivity in normal and specifically disabled readers. Perception 16: 215–21.

Mason A, Cornelissen P, Fowler MS, Stein JF (1993) Contrast sensitivity, ocular dominance and reading disability. Clinical Visual Science 8(4): 345–53.

Maunsell JHR, Nealey TA, DePriest DD (1990) Magnocellular and parvocellular contributions to responses in the Middle Temporal Visual Area (MT) of the macaque monkey. J Neurosci 10(10): 3323–34.

McAnally KI, Stein JF (1996) Abnormal auditory transient brainstem function in dyslexia. Proc Roy Soc B 263: 961–65.

Menell P, McAnally KI, Stein JF (1999) Psychophysical and physiological responses to amplitude modulations in dyslexia. J Speech and Hearing Res 42: 797–803.

Merigan WH, Maunsell JR (1993) How parallel are the primate visual pathways? Ann Rev Neuroscience 16: 369–402.

Merzenich MM, Jenkins WM, Johnston P, Schreiner C, Miller S, Tallal P (1996) Temporal processing deficits of language-learning impaired children ameliorated by stretching speech. Science 271: 77–81.

Miles TR (1970) On Helping the Dyslexic Child. London: Methuen.

Miles T (1993) Dyslexia, the Pattern of Difficulties. London: Whurr.

Milner AD, Goodale MA (1995) The Visual Brain in Action. Oxford: Oxford University Press.

Moore BCJ (1989) An Introduction to the Psychology of Hearing. 3 edn. London: Academic Press.

Morgan WP (1896) Word Blindness. Br Med J 2: 1378.

Morton J (1969) Interaction of information in word recognition. Psych Rev 76: 165–78.

Newsome WT, Britten KH, Movshon JA (1989) Neuronal correlates of a perceptual decision. Nature 341: 52–4.

Newsome WT, Pare EB (1988) A selective impairment of motion processing following lesions of the middle temporal visual area (MT). J Neurosci 8: 2201–11.

Nicolson RI, Fawcett AJ, Berry EL, Jenkins IH, Dean P, Brooks D J (1999) Motor learning difficulties and abnormal cerebellar activation in dyslexic adults. Lancet 353: 43–47.

Ogle K (1962) The optical space sense. In Davson H (ed.) The Eye, Vol.IV. New York and London: Academic Press.

Olson RK, Wise B, Connors F, Rack J, Fulker D (1989) Specific deficits in component reading and language skills. J Learn Disabil 22: 339–48.

Pennington BF (1991a) Learning Disorders. Guilford Press, New York.

Pennington BF (ed.) (1991b) Reading Disabilities: Genetic and neurological influences. Dordrecht, The Netherlands: Kluwer.

Pennington BF, Smith SD (1988) Genetic influences on learning disability. J Consulting and Clin. Psychol. 56: 817–23.

Rae C, Lee MA, Dixon RM, Blamire AM, Thompson CH, Styles P, Talcott JB, Richardson AJ, Stein JF (1998) Metabolic abnormalities in developmental dyslexia detected by ^{1}H magnetic resonance spectroscopy. Lancet 351: 1849–52.

Richardson AJ, Calvin CM, Clisby C, Schoenheimer DR, Montgomery P, Hall JA, Hebb G, Westwood E, Talcott JB, Stein JF (2000) Fatty acid deficiency signs predict the severity of reading and related difficulties in dyslexic children. Prostaglandins, Leukotrienes and Essential Fatty Acids 63: 69–75.

Riddell P, Fowler MS, Stein JF (1990) Spatial discrimination in children with poor vergence control. Perceptual and Motor Skills 70: 707–18.

Seidenburg MS (1993) A connectionist modelling approach to word recognition and dyslexia. Psychological Science 4: 299–304.

Scott RB, Stoodley CJ, Anslow P, Paul C, Stein JF, Sugden EM, Mitchell CD (2001 in press) Lateralised cognitive deficits in children following cerebellar lesions. Developmental Medicine and Child Neurology.

Shapley R, Perry VH (1986) Cat and monkey retinal ganglion cells and their functional roles TINS 9: 229–35.

Simons HD, Gordon JD (1987) Binocular anomalies and reading problems J Am Opt Ass 58: 578–87.

Skottun BC (2000) The magnocellular deficit theory of dyslexia; the evidence from contrast sensitivity. Vis Res 40: 111–27.

Snowling M (1987) Dyslexia: A cognitive developmental perspective. Oxford: Blackwell.

Snowling M (1981) Phonemic deficits in developmental dyslexia. Psychological Research 43: 219–34.

Stein JF, Fowler S (1980) Visual dyslexia. British Orthoptic Journal 37: 11.

Stein JF, Fowler S (1981) Visual dyslexia. Trends in Neuroscience 4: 77–80.

Stein JF, Fowler MS (1985) Effect of monocular occlusion on reading in dyslexic children. The Lancet, 13 July, 69–73.

Stein JF, Riddell P, Fowler MS (1988) Disordered vergence eye movement control in dyslexic children. Brit J Ophthalmol 72: 162–6.

Stein JF, Glickstein M (1992) The role of the cerebellum in the visual guidance of movement. Physiological Reviews 72: 967–1018.

Stein JF, McAnally KI (1996) Impaired auditory temporal processing in Dyslexics. Irish J Psych 16: 220–8.

Stein JF, Walsh V (1997) To see but not to read; the magnocellular theory of dyslexia. TINS 20: 147–52.

Stein JF, Talcott JB (1999) The Magnocellular Theory of Dyslexia. Dyslexia 5: 59–78.

Stein JF (2000) The neurobiology of reading difficulties. Prostaglandins, Leukotrienes and Essential Fatty Acids 63: 109–16.

Stein JF, Talcott JB, Walsh V (2000a) Controversy about the visual magnocellular deficit in developmental dyslexics. Trends in Cog Sc 4: 209–11.

Stein JF, Richardson AJ, Fowler MS (2000b) Monocular occlusion can improve binocular control and reading in developmental dyslexics. Brain 123.

Stoodley CJ, Talcott JB, Carter EL, Witton C, Stein JF (2000) Selective deficits of vibrotactile sensitivity in dyslexic readers. Nsc Ltrs 295: 13–16.

Studdert Kennedy M, Mody M (1995) Auditory temporal perception deficits in the reading-impaired: a critical review of the evidence. Psychonomic Bulletin and Review 2: 508–14.

Tallal P (1980) Auditory temporal perception, phonics and reading disabilities in children. Brain and Language 9: 182–98.

Talcott JB, Witton C, McClean M, Hansen PC, Rees A, Green GGR, Stein JF (1999) Can sensitivity to auditory frequency modulation predict children's phonological and reading skills? Neuroreport 10: 2045–50.

Talcott JB, Hansen PC, Willis-Owen C, McKinnell IW, Richardson AJ, Stein JF (1998) Visual magnocellular impairment in adult developmental dyslexics. Neuroophthalmology 20: 187–201.

Talcott JB, Witton C, McClean M, Hansen PC, Rees A, Green GGR, Stein JF (2000a) Visual and auditory transient sensitivity determines word decoding skills. Proc US Nat Ac Sc 97: 2952–8.

Talcott JB, Hansen PC, Elikem LA, Stein JF (2000b) Visual motion sensitivity in dyslexia: evidence for temporal and motion energy integration deficits. Neuropsychologia 38: 935–43.

Taylor KE, Higgins CJ, Calvin CM, Hall JA, Easton T, McDaid AM, Richardson AJ (2000) Dyslexia in adults is associated with clinical signs of fatty acid deficiency. Prostaglandins, Leukotrienes and Essential Fatty Acids 63: 75–9.

Thomson ME (1982) The assessment of children with specific reading difficulties using the British Ability Scales. Brit J Psychology 73: 461–78.

Trussell LO (1998) Cellular mechanisms for preservation of timing in central auditory pathways. Current Opinion in Neurobiology 7: 487–92.

Ungerleider LG, Mishkin M (1982) Two cortical visual systems. In DJ Ingle, MA Goodale and RJW Mansfield (eds) The Analysis of Visual Behavior. MIT Press, Cambridge MA, pp. 549–86.

Witton C, Richardson A, Griffiths TD, Rees A, Green GGR (1997) Temporal pattern analysis in dyslexia. British Journal of Audiology 31: 100–1.

Witton C, Talcott JB, Hansen PC, Richardson AJ, Griffiths TD, Rees A, Stein JF, Green GGR (1998) Sensitivity to dynamic auditory and visual stimuli predicts nonword reading ability in both dyslexic and normal readers. Current Biology 8: 791–7.

Yule W, Rutter M, Berger M, Thompson J (1973) Over and under achievement in reading. BJ Ed. Psych. 44: 1–12.

CHAPTER 3

Dyslexia: the role of the cerebellum

ANGELA J FAWCETT, RODERICK I NICOLSON

Introduction

In this chapter we outline the thinking and evidence behind our hypothesis that the problems suffered by dyslexic people may be attributable to cerebellar deficit. We believe that this approach provides intriguing new answers to some of the important questions in dyslexia research. First, we outline these key questions. We then provide an overview of recent evidence that proposes a central role for the cerebellum in cognitive skills, in particular those scaffolded by spoken language, in addition to its well-recognized role in motor skills. Third, we outline evidence from our laboratory that cerebellar function is abnormal in dyslexia. We consider two specific lines of evidence: behavioural, and neuroanatomical/neuroimaging. Further evidence for abnormalities in learning that appear to derive from the cerebellum is outlined in our chapter on learning below. Finally, we provide an ontogenetic causal chain for the development of dyslexia in terms of cerebellar deficit from birth, considering the implications of this framework for the key questions in dyslexia research and subsequent developments.

Key questions for dyslexia research

The major achievement of dyslexia research over the last decade was the identification and analysis of a phonological deficit (Bradley and Bryant, 1983; Snowling, 1987; Stanovich, 1988; Vellutino, 1979) which became the consensus view of many dyslexia researchers. For a full review of the phonological deficit hypothesis see the chapter by Ingvar Lundberg and Torleiv Hoien in this book, together with Maggie Snowling's latest book (2000). The phonological deficit has led to a recent redefinition of dyslexia by the

Working Party of the Division of Educational and Child Psychology of the British Psychological Society, which states that 'Dyslexia is evident when accurate and fluent word reading and/or spelling is learnt very incompletely or with great difficulty' (Pumfrey and Reason, 1999: p. 18).

Interestingly enough, however, dyslexic children show interesting and unusual deficits in a wide range of domains, be they reading, phonology, writing, spelling, memory, speed, hearing, vision, balance, learning, skill, genetics, brain structure or brain function. The key question is whether these derive from diverse sources, or whether they may be accounted for in a unitary framework.

In our view a major source of confusion in dyslexia research derives from the different motivations of different researchers. Applied theorists are concerned with educational attainment, in particular literacy, and therefore analyse reading and the effectiveness of interventions, and emphasize (correctly) the need for support for all 'at risk' children. By contrast 'pure' theorists are interested in the underlying cause(s) of dyslexia (rather than reading itself) and so they test theories not directly related to literacy. If we use a medical analogy, the causes, symptoms and treatment of, say, malaria are quite different. Although several diseases may have similar symptoms, of course, the underlying causes (and treatments) are quite different. In dyslexia, this distinction is less clear cut, but it therefore becomes even more important to differentiate between cause, symptom and treatment (see Figure 3.1).

Our expectation/hope for the development of research in dyslexia over the next five years is that several subtypes of dyslexia may well be identified, each based on a different brain region, but each leading to core

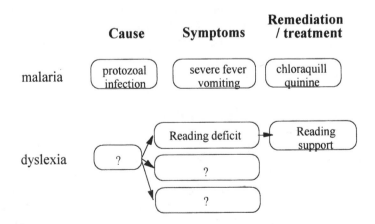

Figure 3.1: Targets for a causal analysis.

phonological difficulties. These may be linked to further and more distinct-ive symptoms (visual, auditory, motor, speed difficulties etc) in line with current theories of dyslexia. Overlaps may be revealed between specific types of dyslexia and other disorders, including ADHD, specific language impairment, dyspraxia, and generalized learning disability. Identification of specific underlying causes might then lead to the specification of the most appropriate intervention strategies for a particular child, in addition to alleviating the reading symptoms. Above all, if a wider range of precur-sors can be identified, we should be able to provide proactive support before children fail, to cut into the cycle of failure for all children with special educational needs. This is the applied challenge for pure theorists – fill in the question marks in Figure 3.1.

We have now made a case for the need for pure theoretical research in order to identify the underlying cause(s) of dyslexia, but what would we need for a causal theory, and specifically a causal theory of dyslexia? Typically scientific explanation moves from descriptive to explanatory theories, which are based on a good description of the symptoms, and specification of the neurological underpin respectively. Similarly, Morton and Frith (1995) distinguish three levels of explanation – biological, cogni-tive and behavioural, with the biological level the deepest level of explana-tion. In our view, an adequate framework for dyslexia must address the following key questions:

- What is the underlying cause of dyslexia?
- Why does it appear to be specific to reading?
- Why do weaknesses appear to be limited to reading?
- Given the wide range of difficulties outlined above, why are there so many high achieving people with dyslexia?

Before addressing these issues, it is important to consider the expanding role of the cerebellum, which until recently has been largely overlooked.

The cerebellum

The cerebellum is a densely packed and deeply folded subcortical brain structure at the back of the brain, also known as the 'hind brain' (Holmes, 1939). In humans, it accounts for 10% to 15% of brain weight, 40% of brain surface area, and 50% of the brain's neurones. The cerebellum is made up of two cerebellar hemispheres, and the lateral zone, known as the neocerebellum has evolved more recently and is much larger in humans than in other primates (Passingham, 1975) in relation to overall brain size. It is involved in the control of independent limb movements and especially in rapid, skilled movements. Damage to different parts of the cerebellum can lead to different symptoms in humans, ranging from disturbances in posture and balance, to limb rigidity, loss of muscle tone, lack of co-ordination and impaired timing of rapid pre-planned, automatic movements. However, one of the key features of cerebellar damage is the plasticity of the system, which means that near normal performance can be regained within a few months of damage (Holmes, 1922).

This concept that the cerebellum is involved in cognitive skills has led to considerable controversy, because the cerebellum has traditionally been seen as a motor area (Eccles, Ito and Szentagothai, 1967; Holmes, 1917; Holmes, 1939; Stein and Glickstein, 1992), involved in learning and the automatization of motor skill (Ito, 1984; Ito, 1990; Jenkins, Brooks, Nixon, Frackowiak and Passingham, 1994; Krupa, Thompson and Thompson, 1993). However, as Leiner, Leiner and Dow (1989) note, the human cerebellum has evolved enormously, becoming linked with areas in the frontal cortex, including Broca's language area. Leiner et al. (1989); Leiner, Leiner and Dow (1991) and Leiner, Leiner and Dow (1993) claimed that the cerebellum is central for the acquisition of 'language dexterity'. They proposed that the cerebellum is critically involved in the automatization of any skill, whether motor or cognitive. The role of the cerebellum in cognitive skills not involving speech or 'inner speech' remains controversial (Ackermann, Wildgruber, Daum and Grodd, 1998; Glickstein, 1993) but there is now overwhelming evidence of the importance of the cerebellum in language (Ackermann and Hertrich, 2000; Fabbro, Moretti and Bava, 2000; Silveri and Misciagna, 2000) including specific cerebellar involvement in reading (Fulbright et al., 1999).

Let us now return to dyslexia.

The Sheffield Dyslexia Research Programme

In our longstanding research programme we were unusual amongst dyslexia researchers in adopting a learning perspective to characterize dyslexia. This led to our 'automatization deficit' hypothesis (Nicolson and Fawcett, 1990) which is outlined in our chapter on learning. Briefly, we argued that it was difficult for dyslexic children to become expert in any skill, whether cognitive or motor. Consequently, they will suffer problems in fluency for any skill that should become automatic via extensive practice.

Primitive skills

A clear description of the range of difficulties 'across the board' for primitive skills is given as Figure 6.2 in our chapter on learning. As noted there, we found that the majority of dyslexic children in our panel had problems not only in phonology, but also in working memory, speed of processing, motor skills and balance. In fact, all the findings are consistent with the automatization deficit hypothesis.

This hypothesis accounts not only for the problems in reading but also for problems with phonological skills (Fawcett and Nicolson, 1995a) and also for deficits outside the literacy domain, which are not easily handled by the phonological deficit, such as motor skill (Fawcett and Nicolson, 1995b) and rapid processing (Fawcett and Nicolson, 1994; Nicolson and Fawcett, 1994). However, the automatization deficit should best be seen as a theory at the descriptive level, because although it provides an excellent account of the symptoms it does not address the neurological underpin of dyslexia. In subsequent research we subsume this 'cognitive level' hypothesis within the 'neurological level' hypothesis of cerebellar deficit, as outlined below.

The cerebellar deficit hypothesis

As noted earlier, deficits in motor skill and automatization point clearly to the cerebellum. However, early findings by Levinson (Frank and Levinson, 1973; Levinson, 1988) arguing for mild cerebellar impairment were largely discounted owing to shortcomings in research methodology (Silver, 1987) allied to the belief that the cerebellum was not involved in language-related skills. Furthermore, if there are indeed problems in the cerebellum, why are the major symptoms specific to the reading domain?

In our attempts to address these issues, we worked with our panel of 'pure' dyslexic children with IQ over 90, and reading age at least 18 months behind their chronological age, with no sign of ADHD, and no significant emotional or behavioural problems, and a control group from a similar social background, matched for age and IQ. These groups feature in all our studies (see our other chapter in this volume). The studies have been reported in detail in the literature so a relatively brief summary must suffice here.

Clinical tests of cerebellar function

If there is indeed a cerebellar impairment, dyslexic children should also show traditional signs of cerebellar dysfunction (see Holmes, 1917, 1939, and Dow and Moruzzi, 1958). Traditional symptoms are dystonia (problems with muscle tone) and ataxia (disturbance in posture, gait, or limb movements). There was no evidence of problems of this type, apart from our own work and Levinson's (1990) controversial findings.

Consequently, in a further stringent test of the cerebellar impairment hypothesis, we replicated the tests described in Dow and Moruzzi (1958), using groups of children with dyslexia and matched controls aged 18, 14 and 10 years (see Fawcett, Nicolson and Dean, 1996). Tasks fell into three types; posture and muscle tone; hypotonia of the upper limbs; and complex voluntary movement, a total of 14 tasks in all.

Analyses showed that the performance of the children with dyslexia was significantly worse than that of the chronological age controls on all 14 tasks, and significantly worse than reading age controls on 11 out of the 14 tests. It was clear, therefore, that there were significant deficits, even compared with reading age controls, on most cerebellar tests. However, we needed to establish how severe the problems were on the various tasks and how many of the children were affected. We therefore normalized the data for each test for each group relative to the corresponding control group.[1] This produces an age-appropriate 'effect size' in standard deviation units (analogous to a z score) for each test for each child (for example, Cohen, 1969). Children were deemed 'at risk' if their performance fell one standard deviation or more below that expected for their age. Note that one would expect around 15% of a normally distributed population to be at least one standard deviation below the mean, and 2% to be at least two standard deviations below. Consequently, if more than 15% of the sample is affected, this suggests an abnormal population.

All but one task (finger to finger pointing) produced an overall effect size for the groups with dyslexia of –1 or worse (at least 1 standard deviation worse than the controls). Reading age, the major criterial deficit in dyslexia on which subjects were selected, was of course severely impaired with an effect size of –2.26, and 100% incidence. Deficits more severe than reading age were for finger and thumb opposition (–7.08, 79%), tremor (–4.44, 80%); arm displacement (–3.59, 100%); toe tap (–3.55, 82%); limb shake (–3.17, 83%); diadochokinesis – speed of alternating tapping the table with palm and back of hand (–3.22, 69%); postural stability – movement when pushed gently in the back (–2.86, 97%) and muscle tone (–2.42, 52%). The performance of the 10-year-old dyslexic children was markedly poorer than that of the older dyslexic children on several tests of muscle tone, with effect sizes of –4 and worse.

Cerebellar function in further groups of dyslexic children

Although the data reported above provided strong evidence of cerebellar impairment, it is important to note that further research with other groups might lead to lower effect size and incidence. We investigated this (Fawcett and Nicolson, 1999), with a further sample of 126 children drawn from private schools specializing in dyslexia. The sample included dyslexic and control children, aged 8–16, divided into four age groups. We administered both a range of cerebellar tasks and other tasks sensitive to dyslexia. In all the cerebellar tests, together with segmentation and nonsense word repetition, the performance of the dyslexic children was significantly worse than controls. Only picture naming speed was not significantly worse. The effect size analyses are also similar to the panel study though (as expected for the larger and more heterogeneous set of control children) lower overall. Spelling had the most extreme effect size (–4.26, 91%), with limb shake (–2.62, 86%) and postural stability (–2.88, 78%) being roughly comparable to reading (–3.56, 92%). Segmentation was somewhat less strong[2] (–1.76, 56%), which in turn was more marked than nonsense word repetition (–1.45, 63%). In line with the earlier study, comparing dyslexic children and controls, some of the most notable results were the exceptionally poor performance of all four groups with dyslexia on postural stability and limb shake.

Direct tests of cerebellar anatomy and function

The above studies provide clear behavioural evidence that dyslexic children do indeed show cerebellar abnormalities. This provides strong evidence that there is indeed some abnormality in the cerebellum or related pathways for many dyslexic children. Nevertheless, these findings provide only indirect evidence of the cerebellar impairment and so an important requirement was to assess cerebellar anatomy and function directly in the hope that this might indicate in which areas of the cerebellum the abnormalities lie. We investigated this in two ways: first by analysing the neuroanatomy of dyslexic brains; second by running a brain imaging study.

Neuroanatomy of the cerebellum

Galaburda's painstaking analysis of the post-mortem tissue derived from the Orton Dyslexia Society 'brain bank' has revealed a fascinating range of differences between dyslexic and control brains. Early work (Galaburda and Kemper, 1979; Galaburda, Sherman, Rosen, Aboitiz and Geschwind, 1985) indicated decreased asymmetry of the planum temporale, together with ectopias or 'brain warts' largely in the language areas of the left hemisphere, but also bilaterally and in non-language areas. More recently, smaller magnocells have been identified in both visual and auditory magnocellular pathways (Galaburda, Menard and Rosen, 1994;

Livingstone, Rosen, Drislane and Galaburda, 1991). Replicating these techniques, Andrew Finch (Finch, Nicolson and Fawcett, 2000) undertook equivalent analyses on the cerebella of the same brain specimens. Interestingly, although significant differences were found, the pattern was opposite to that for the magnocells, with relatively more large neurones and fewer small neurones in the cerebella of the dyslexic brains. Significantly larger mean cell area in the posterior cerebellar cortex was identified (p <0.05), and confirmed in an analysis of cell size distributions (p < 0.0001; effect size 0.730), which also revealed significant differences in the anterior lobe (p < 0.0001; effect size 0.586), again with a pattern of more large and fewer small cells. A similar pattern was found in the inferior olive (p < 0.0001; effect size 0.459) but not in other areas. The pattern of results remained unchanged when analyses accounting for age disparities were undertaken within the groups. Although care must be taken in generalizing from these results, because of the small number of specimens, the areas involved suggest problems in the input to the cerebellum, particularly the error feedback loop, rather than the cerebellar output to the dentate nucleus.

A PET study of automatic performance and learning performance

Our behavioural data suggest clearly that there must be some abnormality within the cerebellum, or perhaps in terms of the input to the cerebellum. In order to investigate this more directly, we ran a functional imaging study of dyslexic and control adults matched for age and IQ while they undertook a behavioural task. However, unlike other researchers in the area, we wanted to examine a task unrelated to reading, so that any differences obtained could not be attributed to idiosyncratic literacy strategies. Naturally we wished to select a task that was known to involve clear cerebellar activation in control subjects. We therefore chose to replicate a study of 'motor sequence learning' (Jenkins et al.,1994), known to induce strong cerebellar activation, which allowed automatic (pre-learned) performance to be investigated as well as new sequence learning.

Brain activation was monitored in matched groups of six dyslexic and six control adults (all male and right handed) while they performed a pre-learned sequence or learned a novel sequence of finger movements (for full details see Nicolson et al., 1999). The task involved learning a sequence of eight consecutive finger presses (with eyes closed), cued by a tone in a trial-and-error process, with computer feedback on whether or not the right key had been selected. Once the sequence of eight presses had been learned, further practice led to increased automaticity. All participants learned the pre-learned sequence two hours before the scan until they could perform it without errors. During the last trial, subjects were given serial digit span tests to assess the automaticity of the sequence performance. Two further trials of the sequence were given immediately prior to scanning, in order to ensure that subjects were able to perform the sequence in the scanner.

Analyses were undertaken using the standard UK image analysis system of that time, SPM96. Comparisons of relative levels of activation between the two groups were particularly striking (see Figure 3.2). For the between-group analysis of areas of significantly greater increase in the pre-learned sequence compared with rest, (p < 0.01, corrected at p < 0.05 for multiple comparisons) only two regions of difference emerged: the right cerebellum, and an area of frontal cortex. No brain areas showed significantly greater increase for the dyslexic group. For the between-group analysis of activation increases during performance of the new sequence learning compared with rest, the right cerebellum was the only area of significantly greater increase for the controls. A number of areas of the cortex (right and medial prefrontal, bilateral temporal and bilateral parietal) showed significantly greater increase for the dyslexic group.

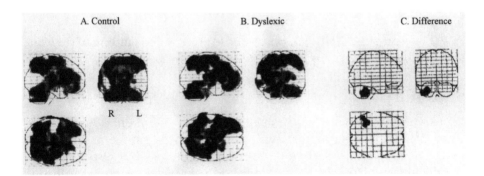

Figure 3.2: Regions of significantly greater activation when learning a new sequence. Location of significant differences in activation (p < 0.01, corrected for multiple comparisons at p < 0.05) between dyslexic and control subjects for the comparisons of new sequence with rest. The images are integrated sagittal, coronal and transverse projections of the statistical parametric maps (SPMs). Images produced by SPM96 (Wellcome Department of Cognitive Neurology, 1996). Figures A and B give the increases in activation all over the brain when the control subjects (A) and the dyslexic subjects (B) are learning a new sequence (compared with the Rest condition). Figure C shows the regions where the dyslexic group showed significantly less relative activation than the controls. The only region of significantly different relative activation in C is the right hemisphere of the cerebellum.

From the blood flow analyses, the control group showed relatively greater activation, compared with rest, in the right cerebellum both during performance of the pre-learned sequence and in learning the novel sequence. By contrast, the dyslexic group showed greater activation in large areas of the frontal lobes when learning the novel sequence. This was in line with the predictions of the CDH, that the dyslexic group activates their cerebella less both in pre-learned and novel sequences. Moreover, it also supported the prediction that the dyslexic group would activate their frontal lobes more in learning a novel sequence. Most strikingly, the dyslexic adults showed only 10% of the level of increased blood flow found in the controls in cerebellar cortex and vermis when performing the tasks. These results are highly significant and would not be predicted by any other theory of dyslexia. They provide direct evidence that the behavioural signs of cerebellar abnormality do indeed reflect underlying abnormalities in cerebellar activation.

A recent study (Rae et al., 1998) has also revealed significant metabolic abnormalities in the cerebellum of dyslexic men – see the chapter by Stein, Talcott and Witton. The authors conclude that 'The cerebellum is biochemically asymmetric in dyslexic men, indicating altered development of this organ. These differences provide direct evidence of the involvement of the cerebellum in dyslexic dysfunction.' These findings provide further support for abnormalities in the cerebellum in dyslexia.

Let us now consider the implications for the understanding of dyslexia, for how dyslexia develops, and for future work in the area.

Summary

Let us start by summarizing the evidence to date. Our behavioural studies showed that a common symptom of performance in dyslexic children is that it is less well automatized, not only for literacy but also for all the other tasks studied. The well-established role of the cerebellum in skill learning and automatization made it a good candidate for investigation, particularly when coupled with evidence from cognitive neuroscience on the central role of the cerebellum in language-related cognitive tasks. We demonstrated not only that our panel of dyslexic children showed clinical symptoms of cerebellar abnormality, but also that these symptoms characterized a much larger group of dyslexic children.

Our neuroanatomical analysis of the Orton Society brain bank showed differences in cell size and cell-size distribution in posterior and anterior cerebellar cortex, and inferior olive with no differences in the output areas (the dentate nucleus). The PET study of motor sequence learning showed that there were indeed abnormalities in cerebellar activation in automatic processing and in new learning, for subjects in our panel who had clinical cerebellar signs. Rather than the expected cerebellar activation in these tasks, the dyslexic subjects showed greater frontal lobe activation in new learning, suggesting they were by-passing the cerebellum to some extent, and relying on conscious strategies. These important findings confirm the behavioural evidence of cerebellar dysfunction, and suggest that dyslexic subjects use different methods in sequential learning and automatic performance. Given that the dyslexic subjects whom we had scanned also showed classic clinical signs of cerebellar deficit, this demonstration that the dyslexic group really did have abnormal use of the cerebellum, in turn lends greater strength to our previous findings that around 80% of dyslexic children show clinical signs of cerebellar abnormality.

Toward a causal explanation

We are now able to start filling in the blanks in Figure 3.1.

In Figure 3.3 (from Nicolson and Fawcett, 1999) the hypothetical ontogenetic causal chain between cerebellar problems, phonological difficulties and eventual reading problems is outlined, accounting for the three criterial difficulties: writing, reading and spelling. Dyslexic children frequently show poor-quality handwriting, which has been hard to explain under other theories, but can be handled naturally by the CDH as a motor skill requiring precise timing and co-ordination of the muscles. Although literacy difficulties arise from several routes, the central route is

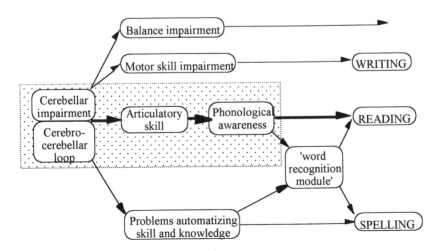

Figure 3.3: Dyslexia: an ontogenetic causal chain.

highlighted as the most important. If an infant has a cerebellar impairment, this will first show up as a mild motor difficulty – the infant may be slower to sit up and to walk, and may have greater problems with fine muscular control. These problems may not seem too serious, unless we appreciate that our most complex motor skill is articulation and, consequently, the infant might be slower to start babbling, and, later, talking. Once speech and walking develop, skills may be less fluent, less 'dextrous', in infants with cerebellar impairment. If articulation is less fluent than normal, it takes up more conscious resources, leaving fewer resources to process sensory feedback. Processing the auditory, phonemic structure of spoken words may be less complete, leading to loss of awareness of onset, rime, and the phonemic structure of language – (see Snowling and Hulme, 1994). Cerebellar impairment would therefore be predicted to cause the 'phonological core deficit' that has proved such a fruitful explanatory framework for dyslexia. Based on this framework, standard explanations of reading deficits apply, coupled with problems in learning and automatization, which lead to impaired fluency and speed of reading, or the double deficit hypothesis (Wolf and Bowers, 1999). One of the keys to fluent reading is the ability to articulate sub-vocally, and the cerebellum is known to be activated in internal speech (Thach, 1996). The third criterial skill, spelling, may be the most resistant to remediation based on a combination of over-effortful reading, poor phonological awareness, and difficulties in automatizing skills and eliminating errors, as well as the simultaneous use of both phonological and motor skills (Thomson, 1984).

This brings us back to the key questions in dyslexia research. We have already addressed the mechanism and direction of causality, and suggest that difficulties appear to be specific to reading and spelling because they involve a combination of phonological skills, fluency, automatization, and multi-tasking – a combination of all the skills that dyslexic children find difficult. Why does performance appear to be normal in other skills? Because literacy is of such critical educational importance it is examined minutely, whereas other skills are largely overlooked. Moreover many skills are unimpaired or even overcompensating, because skills can be acquired without much cerebellar involvement: they simply demand more conscious 'frontal' involvement – precisely the pattern shown in our sequence learning task. Lack of automaticity is only a real problem if rapid processing or multi-tasking is required, because most skills including 'intellectual' skills require frontal involvement – thinking rather than rote learning. This brings us back to an explanation for the discrepancy between the low reading performance and good intellectual functioning of children with dyslexia. There is suggestive evidence that adults with dyslexia may be among the most creative and successful of their generation (West, 1991). How can this be explained in the light of cerebellar impairment, which apparently causes significant difficulties with acquisition of skills, and with linguistic skill? Reasoning ability is not dependent upon fluency. Indeed, fluency may well be the enemy of creativity – trying to solve new sorts of problems that require thinking about the problem and its elements in a different way – in that fluency is in essence the ability to repeat previous actions or thoughts more and more quickly without conscious thought.

Interpretations in terms of alternative hypotheses

We have suggested that the CDH framework naturally subsumes the phonological deficit and that the double deficit hypothesis (Wolf and Bowers, 1999) may also be accounted for in a similar manner, given that the double deficit hypothesis is a cognitive level description. However, the key question remains, why do children become faster as they mature? It seems likely that this reflects improved efficiency of the central processing mechanisms in which the cerebellum will be centrally involved

Stein (for example Stein and Walsh, 1997) has argued that cerebellar impairment might be attributable to faulty input via impaired magnocellular pathways (see Stein's chapter in this book). It seems clear that there is a subtype of dyslexia with magnocellular impairment and Tallal (Tallal, Miller and Fitch, 1993) has suggested that there may be a pan-sensory impairment, including motor output as well as visual and auditory input. Stein notes that there are magnocells in the cerebellum and in the motor output systems, which make it difficult to distinguish these theories from the CDH. However, if one limits the magnocellular deficit hypotheses to the sensory input stage it is not clear why dyslexic children have problems in detecting rhymes, which do not involve rapid processing. From our own work, there is no obvious magnocellular explanation for normal speed of simple reactions, with the same response slowed when a choice needs to be made (Nicolson and Fawcett, 1994); no explanation for difficulties in time estimation, lowered muscle tone or no abnormal cerebellar activation in the motor sequence learning task. Future research may reveal a 'magnocellular' subtype, a 'cerebellar' subtype, and various 'mixed' subtypes.

Conclusions

Both a strength and a limitation of this research is that we have worked with 'pure' dyslexic children, deliberately excluding borderline dyslexic children, or comorbid ADHD/dyslexia children. We included all dyslexic children who met our criteria (and were willing to participate), thus avoiding any selection bias. However, this meant that our groups are small and the results may not generalize completely to further groups. It is clearly a priority to establish the prevalence of cerebellar symptoms in larger populations of dyslexic children (and comorbid groups).

In conclusion, the cerebellar deficit hypothesis is a biological-level hypothesis that is well described at the cognitive level as an automatization deficit hypothesis. The two hypotheses between them have provided a true causal explanation of the varied findings in dyslexia research. No doubt further research will reveal that the story is not yet complete, but meanwhile the CDH generates a number of new and interesting avenues for dyslexia research. These are exciting times!

Notes

1. For example, for the D14 group the data for postural stability for each subject were normalized by obtaining the difference of that subject's postural stability score from the mean postural stability score for group C14, and then dividing this difference by the standard deviation of the C14 group for postural stability.
2. It is important to note that training in phonological awareness and in grapheme–phoneme translation was a central component of the teaching methodology of the school for the children with dyslexia. We interpret the relatively mild deficit on phonological skills as a tribute to the quality of teaching.

References

Ackermann H, Hertrich I (2000) The contribution of the cerebellum to speech processing. Journal of Neurolinguistics, 13(2–3): 95–116.

Ackermann H, Wildgruber D, Daum I, Grodd W (1998) Does the cerebellum contribute to cognitive aspects of speech production? A functional magnetic resonance imaging (fMRI) study in humans. Neuroscience Letters 247: 187–190.

Bradley L, Bryant PE (1983) Categorising sounds and learning to read: A causal connection. Nature 301: 419–21.

Cohen J (1969) Statistical power analysis for the behavioural sciences. New York: Academic Press.

Dow RS, Moruzzi G (1958) The physiology and pathology of the cerebellum. Minneapolis: University of Minnesota Press.

Eccles JC, Ito M, Szentagothai J (1967) The cerebellum as a neuronal machine. New York: Springer-Verlag.

Fabbro F, Moretti R, Bava A (2000) Language impairments in patients with cerebellar lesions. Journal of Neurolinguistics 13(2–3): 173–88.

Fawcett AJ, Nicolson RI (1994) Naming speed in children with dyslexia. Journal of Learning Disabilities 27: 641–6.

Fawcett, AJ., Nicolson RI (1995a) Persistence of phonological awareness deficits in older children with dyslexia. Reading and Writing 7: 361–76.

Fawcett AJ, Nicolson RI (1995b) Persistent deficits in motor skill for children with dyslexia. Journal of Motor Behaviour. 27: 235–40.

Fawcett AJ, Nicolson, R. I. (1999) Performance of dyslexic children on cerebellar and cognitive tests. Journal of Motor Behaviour 31: 68–78.

Fawcett AJ, Nicolson RI, Dean P (1996) Impaired performance of children with dyslexia on a range of cerebellar tasks. Annals of Dyslexia 46: 259–83.

Finch AJ, Nicolson RI, Fawcett AJ (2000) Evidence for a neuroanatomical difference within the olivo-cerebellar pathway of adults with dyslexia. Cortex, submitted.

Frank J, Levinson HN (1973) Dysmetric dyslexia and dyspraxia: hypothesis and study. Journal of American Academy of Child Psychiatry 12: 690–701.

Fulbright RK, Jenner AR, Mencl WE, Pugh KR, Shaywitz BA, Shaywitz SE, Frost SJ, Skudlarski P, Constable RT, Lacadie CM, Marchione KE, Gore JC (1999) The cerebellum's role in reading: a functional MR imaging study. American Journal of Neuroradiology 20: 1925–30.

Galaburda AM, Kemper TL (1979) Cytoarchitectonic abnormalities in developmental dyslexia: a case study. Ann Neurol 6: 94 – 100.

Galaburda AM, Menard MT, Rosen GD (1994) Evidence for aberrant auditory anatomy in developmental dyslexia. Proceedings of the National Academy of Sciences of the USA 91: 8010–13.

Galaburda AM, Sherman GF, Rosen GD, Aboitiz F, Geschwind N (1985) Developmental dyslexia – 4 consecutive patients with cortical anomalies. Annals of Neurology 18: 222–33.

Glickstein M (1993) Motor skills but not cognitive tasks. Trends in Neuroscience 16: 450–51.

Holmes G (1917) The symptoms of acute cerebellar injuries due to gunshot injuries. Brain 40: 461–535.

Holmes G (1922) Clinical symptoms of cerebellar disease and their interpretation. Lancet 1: 1177–237.

Holmes G (1939) The cerebellum of man. Brain 62: 1–30.

Ito M (1984) The cerebellum and neural control. New York: Raven Press.

Ito M (1990) A new physiological concept on cerebellum. Revue Neurologique (Paris) 146: 564–69.

Ivry RB, Keele SW (1989) Timing functions of the cerebellum. Journal of Cognitive Neuroscience 1: 136–52.

Jenkins IH, Brooks DJ, Nixon PD, Frackowiak RSJ, Passingham RE (1994) Motor sequence learning – a study with Positron Emission Tomography. Journal of Neuroscience 14: 3775–90.

Krupa DJ, Thompson JK, Thompson RF (1993) Localization of a memory trace in the mammalian brain. Science 260: 989–91.

Leiner HC, Leiner AL, Dow RS (1989) Reappraising the cerebellum: what does the hindbrain contribute to the forebrain. Behavioural Neuroscience 103: 998–1008.

Leiner HC, Leiner AL, Dow RS (1991) The human cerebro-cerebellar system: its computing, cognitive, and language skills. Behav Brain Res 44: 113–28.

Leiner HC, Leiner AL, Dow RS (1993) Cognitive and language functions of the human cerebellum. Trends in Neuroscience 16: 444–7.

Levinson HN (1988) The cerebellar-vestibular basis of learning disabilities in children, adolescents and adults: hypothesis and study. American Psychiatric Association Annual Meeting New Research Session. Perceptual-and-Motor-Skills 67(3): 983–1006.

Levinson HN (1990) The diagnostic value of cerebellar-vestibular tests in detecting learning disabilities, dyslexia and Perceptual-and-Motor-Skills 71(1): 67–82.

Livingstone MS, Rosen GD, Drislane FW, Galaburda AM (1991) Physiological and anatomical evidence for a magnocellular defect in developmental dyslexia. Proceedings of the National Academy of Sciences of the United States of America 88: 7943–7.

Morrison FJ, Manis FR (1983) Cognitive processes in reading disability: a critique and proposal. In CJ Brainerd, M Pressley (eds) Progress in Cognitive Development Research. New York: Springer-Verlag.

Morton J, Frith U (1995) Causal modelling: a structural approach to developmental psychopathology. In D Cicchetti. CDJ (eds) Manual of Developmental Psychopathology (Vol. 2, pp. 274–98). New York: Wiley.

Nicolson RI, Fawcett AJ (1990) Automaticity: a new framework for dyslexia research? Cognition 35(2): 159–82.

Nicolson RI, Fawcett AJ (1994) Reaction times and dyslexia. Quarterly Journal of Experimental Psychology 47A: 29–48.

Nicolson RI, Fawcett AJ (1995a) Balance, phonological skill and dyslexia: towards the dyslexia early screening test. Dyslexia Review 7: 8–11.

Nicolson RI, Fawcett AJ (1995b). Dyslexia is more than a phonological disability. Dyslexia: An International Journal of Research and Practice 1: 19–37.

Nicolson RI, Fawcett AJ (1999) Developmental dyslexia: the role of the cerebellum. Dyslexia: An International Journal of Research and Practice 5: 155–77.

Nicolson RI, Fawcett AJ, Dean P (1995) Time-estimation deficits in developmental dyslexia – evidence for cerebellar involvement. Proceedings of the Royal Society of London Series B-Biological Sciences 259: 43–7.

Orton Society (1995) Definition of dyslexia; report from committee of members. Perspectives 21: 16–17.

Passingham RE (1975) Changes in the size and organization of the brain in man and his ancestors. Brain Behaviour and Evolution 11: 73–90.

Rae C, Lee MA, Dixon RM, Blamire AM, Thompson CH, Styles P, Talcott J, Richardson AJ, Stein JF (1998) Metabolic abnormalities in developmental dyslexia detected by H-1 magnetic resonance spectroscopy. Lancet 351: 1849–52.

Seidenberg MS (1993) Connectionist models and cognitive theory. Psychological Science 4: 228–35.

Silver LB (1987) The 'magic cure': a review of the current controverisal approaches for treating learning disabilities. Journal of Learning Disabilities 20: 498–505.

Silveri MC, Misciagna S (2000) Language, memory, and the cerebellum. Journal of Neurolinguistics 13(2–3): 129–43.

Snowling M (1987) Dyslexia: A Cognitive Developmental Perspective. Oxford: Blackwell.

Snowling M (2000) Dyslexia: A Cognitive Developmental Perspective. Oxford: Blackwell.

Snowling M, Hulme C (1994) The development of phonological skills. Philosophical Transactions of the Royal Society of London Series B-Biological Sciences 346: 21–7.

Stanovich KE (1988) Explaining the differences between the dyslexic and the garden-variety poor reader: the phonological-core variable-difference model. Journal of Learning Disabilities 21: 590–612.

Stein J, Walsh V (1997) To see but not to read; the magnocellular theory of dyslexia. Trends in Neurosciences 20: 147–52.

Stein JF, Glickstein M (1992) Role of the cerebellum in visual guidance of movement. Physiological Reviews 72: 972–1017.

Tallal P, Miller S, Fitch RH (1993) Neurobiological basis of speech: a case for the pre-eminence of temporal processing. Annals of the New York Academy of Sciences 682: 27–47.

Thach WT (1996) On the specific role of the cerebellum in motor learning and cognition: Clues from PET activation and lesion studies in man. Behavioural and Brain Sciences 19: 411–31.

Thelen E, Smith LB (1994) A dynamic systems approach to the development and cognition and action. Cambridge MA: MIT Press.

Thomson M (1984) Developmental Dyslexia: Its Nature, Assessment and Remediation. London: Edward Arnold.

Vellutino FR (1979) Dyslexia: Theory and Research. Cambridge MA: MIT Press.

Wellcome Department of Cognitive Neurology (1996) Statistical Parametric Mapping SPM96. London: ICN.

West TG (1991) In the Mind's Eye: Visual thinkers, gifted people with learning difficulties, computer images, and the ironies of creativity. Buffalo NY: Prometheus Books.

Wolf M, Bowers PG (1999) The double-deficit hypothesis for the developmental dyslexias. Journal of Educational Psychology 91: 415–38.

PART TWO
COGNITIVE PROCESSES

CHAPTER 4

Dyslexia and phonology

INGVAR LUNDBERG, TORLEIV HOIEN

Reading is primarily a culturally and socially based practice acquired and used in cultural contexts. Some people have difficulty reaching the level of literacy skills demanded by society. The problems they have, however, cannot be completely understood merely as shortcomings of a cultural or social nature; it is also necessary to go beneath the surface of their manifest reading problems and look for explanations at more basic, cognitive and neurobiological levels.

One of the most important underlying explanations, which has become clearer in recent years, is that there is a linguistic problem, in particular a phonological weakness that impairs the process of learning to read and spell. The poor reading observed in dyslexia may be caused by an impairment to a phonological processing system that is not dedicated to reading or spelling tasks per se, but is used in all forms of phonological tasks. Nonetheless, it is debatable whether this phonological deficit is the whole truth of dyslexia. Problems can probably be seen in other areas as well, such as special difficulties with automatization, motor co-ordination, magnocellular deficits, sequencing problems and so forth, some of which are analysed in the present volume. One can even conceive of special abilities or talents as associated with dyslexia (Wolff and Lundberg, 2001). This chapter, however, focuses on the phonological deficit component of dyslexia: how it is developed, how it is expressed and how it constitutes an obstacle for reading acquisition, how it is diagnosed and how it implies guidelines or directives for preventive and remedial measures.

Some of the most characteristic indicators of phonological problems that may play a part in reading difficulties are the following:

- problems in segmenting words into phonemes;
- problems in keeping linguistic material (strings of sounds or letters) in short-term memory;

- problems in repeating back long non-words;
- problems in reading and writing even short non-words;
- slow naming of colours, numbers, letters and objects in pictures;
- a slower rate of speech, sometimes with indistinct pronunciation;
- problems in playing word-games where the point is to manipulate phonemes (games like Pig-Latin: 'Ankay ooya eekspay Igpay Atinlay?' or spoonerisms, whereby 'red book' becomes 'bed rook'.

Strangely enough, this phonological deficit can be very limited in scope; people can have a marked deficiency in dealing with phonemes yet still have perfectly good cognitive abilities in all other areas. Under normal linguistic conditions, when the person is speaking or listening to others the phonological deficit may not be noticeable. But when conditions demand a higher degree of function in the processing of sounds, for example when speaking Pig-Latin, reciting back long non-words, or trying to decipher a spoonerism, then the problem rears its ugly head. The demands made on the phonological module when performing these activities are very much the same as when learning to read and write. So, weakness in the phonological module may be one of the strongest candidate factors in the explanation of reading difficulties.

Why is learning to read a difficult task for some children?

In order to understand what is going on when a child fails to learn to deal with written language, we need to look closely at the specific cognitive and linguistic demands that writing makes, – demands that are different from those that speaking makes.

When children begin to learn to read, they have to be able to deal with phonology more consciously than when they learned to speak. They need to understand the alphabetical principle – that is, to understand that the phonemes of a word can be represented by letters, and that the differences between words are heard in the phonological structures that the letters of written words encode.

Why is it so difficult for some children to understand this principle, and to gain conscious access to the phonology they already master so well in their spoken language? Here we need to take yet another step into the world of phonetics and look at how speakers produce phonemes and how listeners hear them. Phonemes, when we produce them, are movements in the organs of speech. For example, a /b/ is a closing and opening of the lips, accompanied by an explosion of breath and voicing. But before we are finished with one phoneme our speech organs have usually begun preparing for the next phoneme. If you are going to say 'book', you close your lips with a slight rounding because you 'know' your next phoneme is a vowel-sound that needs rounded lips. If you are going to say 'beetle', you don't close your lips rounded, but laterally spread, in anticipation of the bright 'ee' sound. And so it goes all through the utterance, with sounds blurring, overlapping and interfering with each other. This phenomenon is called co-articulation.

Why is spoken language so complex and yet so natural a thing to process and produce? Surely it would have been easier for listeners if all the speakers pronounced their utterances as strings of discrete, tidy, unblurred phonemes. Here we should remember that speech has been around much longer than print, and that speech is obviously the result of a long biological evolution. The good thing about co-articulation is that it lets us speak much faster than if we carefully articulated words one phoneme at a time, and this speed seems to have given us a biological advantage. We usually speak at the rate of 10 to 20 phonemes per second – much, much faster than if we delivered phonemes one at a time, like pearls on a string.

Another advantage of co-articulation is that it provides a higher degree of redundancy. The vowel-sound in book is incorporated in both of the surrounding consonant-sounds, so if the listener doesn't hear the vowel, for example because of some extraneous noise, then nothing is lost. The listener still hears the word 'book'. So the redundancy that is created by co-articulation helps guard against what communication engineers call 'noise' – the inevitable background buzz that accompanies any signal.

Just like other specialized processes that have evolved over great spans of time (another example is depth perception), co-articulation is fully automatic. Neither speakers nor listeners have to know anything at all about it, we just do it. Speakers need only to think of what they are saying, and listeners to what is being said. Phonemes are chosen, blended, and spoken, then heard, unblended, and understood automatically. By way of a preliminary conclusion we can say that our specialized phonological module takes care of these tasks for us. In order to learn to talk, the only thing a child has to do is be around people who talk. But in order to learn to read, the child almost always has to submit to some kind of 'teaching' – in school, or less formally by a parent or an older sibling. We see, then, that writing and speech are not truly analogous functions. Learning to talk is as natural as learning to walk or learning to experience depth perception. Learning to read is more like learning to play chess or program a computer; at least the basic rules have to be taught. But luckily, once the child has grasped the alphabetic principle, he or she has acquired a powerful self-teaching device which allows further explorations of the print environment, where his or her reading skill is developed, refined and automatized (Share and Stanovich, 1995).

We will now turn to some studies that have shown how a lack of phonemic awareness and reading problems are associated. If it is the case that learning to read makes specific demands on the child's phonological system, it should then be possible to predict early on which children will have trouble learning to read and write when they start school.

Can reading and writing problems be predicted in pre-schoolers?

Lack of phonological awareness is related to failure in learning to read and write. This association is in fact one of the most robust findings in developmental cognitive psychology and it has been replicated over and over again across several languages, ages, and tasks used to assess phonological awareness (for a review see Hoien and Lundberg, 2000). One of the earliest demonstrations was presented by Lundberg, Olofsson and Wall (1980). This study was based on an intensive examination of the linguistic abilities of kindergaretners and it addressed the question of whether the children's deficiency in phonological awareness is in fact a specifically linguistic deficiency, or whether it might be attributable to a more widespread deficiency in general cognitive analytical ability. The battery of eleven tests given to 200 children included both linguistic and non-linguistic tasks. The linguistic tasks included word synthesis tasks that varied in two dimensions of two levels each – with or without memory load and using either phoneme or syllable units. Word analysis tasks analogous to those for phoneme synthesis were also used, as were tasks that asked for analysis of phoneme position in words, reversal of phoneme segments in words, and rhyming. The linguistic tasks required the child to shift attention from content or meaning of the words to their abstract form.

This 'mental shift' may possibly reflect a general cognitive function not exclusively limited to language material. For this reason, non-linguistic control tasks that simulated those cognitive demands were also included in the battery. These control tasks made it possible to demonstrate a critical dissociation as support for a modular view of the phonological function.

The most powerful predictors of later reading and writing skills in the entire battery turned out to be those requiring phonological awareness, specifically the ability to manipulate phonemes in words. In contrast, those who later on became poor readers showed no particular deficiency in non-linguistic task.

The causal model hypothesized in the study was thus supported by the data. The longitudinal design implies a causal direction – abilities developed at a later point in time cannot possibly be the cause of the earlier achievement. Thus, phonological awareness seems to be an important prerequisite for learning to read, and non-readers with a low level of phonological awareness at pre-school age have an elevated risk of developing reading disability when they get to school. A strong test of the causality hypothesis, however, would require experimental data to rule out the possible operation of a third, uncontrolled, underlying factor. Before we discuss this possibility further, a few longitudinal studies of the heritability of dyslexia should be mentioned. It is a well-established fact that the heritability of dyslexia is quite strong. Family studies and twin studies have shown that some 50% to 60% of the variation among individuals in reading ability can be attributed to genetic variation. A small child with a dyslexic parent thus runs a considerable risk of developing reading problems in school. Scarborough (1990) studied 32 children of dyslexic parents. She followed the children's development from age two-and-a-half to eight years. As many as 65% were diagnosed as dyslexic at age eight, which indicates that the disorder has a strong genetic component. Already at two-and-a-half years they evinced measurable linguistic disturbances. Their grammar skills and pronunciation were less well developed than a control group of children with normal-reading parents. By age three and a half they had a poorer understanding of words and a poorer ability to come up with the names of items on picture-cards than their cohorts had. And by age five they knew fewer of the letters of the alphabet, had less phonological awareness, and knew the names of fewer items than the controls. Scarborough's study shows that there are early warning signs in the child's linguistic development that signal impending reading and writing problems at school. Other researchers have also studied children of dyslexic parents. Locke's study (Locke et al., 1997) is not yet finally reported, so we don't know how many of his study group will wind up dysexic. But the preliminary results are interesting. Locke started studying the children when they were eight months old. He registered and phonetically analysed their babblings. Strangely, even at this early age there were differences in how 'at-risk' children and a control group (with normal-reading parents) dealt with language-sounds. The 'at-risk' children babbled with fewer different sounds and less complex sequences of sounds. Locke's hypothesis is that children with a strong genetic disposition for dyslexia show a different linguistic development: they base more of their understanding on social signals and contextual information, and derive less information from segmenting and manipulating phonetic segments. Later on the 'at-risk' children had poorer scores on verbal STM-tasks and tasks assessing phonological awareness in pre-school. Snowling has also studied very young at-risk children (Snowling and Nation, 1997). She submitted 71 pre-schoolers (with dyslexic parents) to comprehensive language tests. The children were three-and-a-half years old. Snowling found, as did Scarborough, that at-risk children had more difficulty repeating back non-words than children in the control group. She showed the children pictures of imaginary animals to which she gave fanciful, non-word names. The at-risk children were less adept at using these names, and they had less knowledge of letters and knew fewer rhymes and jingles than the controls.

Elbro, Borström and Petersen (1998) have also employed the strategy of studying children of dyslexic parents. They followed 49 at-risk children from the start of kindergarten (age six) to the start of second grade (age eight), at which time it is possible to diagnose dyslexia. In accordance with the other studies, they found that the children whose parents had reading problems had a much greater chance of developing dyslexia than children with normal-reading parents, and that the level of linguistic competency at kindergarten age is a clear predictor of dyslexia. In particular, they found that children's skills with the sounds of language predict later reading problems. In addition to making various measurements of the children's phonological and morphological awareness, they designed a clever experiment to measure how distinct the children's mental representations of the sounds of words were. They did this by getting the children to interact with a hand-puppet who spoke with a speech impediment, and asking the children to teach the puppet how to pronounce the words correctly.

Among all the tasks they used to chart the linguistic prowess of their kindergarten group, Elbro and his co-workers found that the important skills for learning to read and write were: letter knowledge, phoneme identification, phoneme subtraction, verbal short-term memory, being able to pronounce difficult words precisely, and having a capacious passive vocabulary. All of these were important, but one additional factor stood out as clearly the most important of all: having distinct mental representations of the sounds of words. When all other variables were controlled, this one factor alone could account for much of the child's success or failure at learning to read.

To sum up, we can say that children who are genetically disposed to becoming dyslexics show a delay or a deficit primarily in their phonological development. Their internal representations of what words sound like are fuzzy and lacking in detail (Brady, 1997). Moreover, it is not easy for them to transfer their attention from the meaning of a word (which is what we normally focus on) to its form: to what it sounds like and how it is built up of various well-known sounds. These phonological problems make learning to read and write an exceptionally difficult task (cf. Rack et al., 1994).

The idea of early identification and remediation of reading problems exerts a powerful emotional tug on all of us. Yet there are two conditions that would have to be fulfilled before any sort of screening programme should be implemented. First of all, we have to be fairly certain that we can do something constructive with the probable dyslexics. Secondly, we need to be sure that no great ill will befall our false positives, because our methods for early assessment are far from perfect.

Given the state of our knowledge and capability today, we advise caution. The inadequacy of our individual prognoses can have many causes. Any sort of testing of pre-school children is always rather chancy: some children are inattentive, others lack stamina, and others may not have been listening when the instructions were given. Or the test itself may not be statistically reliable. But above all, we just do not know enough about the causes of dyslexia to be able to devise really good diagnostic tools. In addition, we know that pre-school children develop at different rates. Some of the ones who are lagging behind in phonological skills when we test them in pre-school may develop enough of these skills before they start school to be able to profit from reading instruction.

A longitudinal training study

The interpretation of the causal direction of the relationship between phonological awareness and learning to read proposed above was further strengthened by the results from a study of training (Lundberg, Frost and Petersen, 1988). An experimental group of pre-school children was given the benefit of daily games and exercises designed to promote phonological awareness (see also Adams, Foorman, Lundberg and Beeler, 1998). They had higher reading and spelling skills in school than a control group of children who were not given this type of pre-school training. It was found that the experimental group of pre-schoolers was better prepared when they started formal instruction in reading in the first grade. By becoming aware of the sound structure of spoken language they had already taken an important step toward understanding the alphabetic principle.

The preventive effect of the early pre-school training was demonstrated by Lundberg (1994). Pre-school children with extremely low initial performance on phonological tasks were estimated to be in a high-risk zone for later reading disability. A majority of the high-risk children who participated in the training programme (daily exercises over a period of eight months) benefited considerably and came close to normal performance in reading and spelling several years later in school, whereas non-trained high-risk children showed the predicted severe literacy problems in school.

These positive findings for training in phonological awareness at the pre-school levels do not necessarily imply that this skill should be trained later on in school. Several studies have examined the effect of such training in second, third and fourth grade without finding any particular success (Gustafsson, Samuelsson and Rönnberg, 2000; Niemi et al., 1999; Olson et al., 1997; Torgesen, Wagner and Rashotte, 1997). A substantial proportion of reading-disabled children in the early years of school showed remarkable resistance to the intervention and many merely improved their phonological awareness without being able to transfer much of their new-found insights to reading. One reason for this lack of success might be related to the fact that the length and intensity of training was far from sufficient to be effective. Another reason might be the fact that most dyslexic children have, in fact, understood the alphabetical principle and reached a sufficient level of phonological awareness; further training on phonology might therefore be superfluous. Their main problem is instead related to gaining fluency in word recognition. (This automaticity issue is addressed in other chapters of the present volume, for example Chapter 6 and Chapter 7.)

Phonological problems among older dyslexic children

One might suppose that poor phonological awareness is only typical of very young children with reading problems. Older, teenage dylexics might have overcome their initial deficit, but now be struggling with some other type of problem at a higher level, for example with comprehension. The study we now present shows that this is not the case (Høien and Lundberg, 1989).

On the basis of an exceptionally precise selection procedure, 19 clearly dyslexic pupils were selected from a total population of 1,250 cohorts. They were all 15 years old and in the eighth grade. Two control groups were formed, one of students at the same age but who read normally, and one consisting of younger students who were at the same level of general reading ability as the study group. All three groups were given a comprehensive series of tests. Most of the tests were administered on a computer, which registered both the number of correct/incorrect responses and the reaction time – that is, the number of seconds it took the student to answer the question or complete the task. This study yielded a wealth of data, but here we will only look at the results that have bearing on the question of phonological deficits among teenage dyslexics.

Table 4.1: Comparison of scores and reaction times on tasks of nonword reading, syllable reversals, and phoneme synthesis for dyslexics and two control groups (age matched and a younger reading-level matched group). N = 19 in each group

GROUP	Per cent correct			Reaction time (sec)
	non-word	syllable rev.	phoneme synth	non-word
Dyslexics	76.8	63.1	68.9	3.18
RL-match	88.3	82.0	82.4	1.86
Age-match	94.3	90.7	91.1	1.43

RL = reading level

The proportion of correct responses on the phonological tasks, and the reaction times on the non-word reading are presented in Table 4.1. All the tasks were significantly more difficult for the dyslexics. Most importantly, they had a harder time than the younger readers, who were used as a control group, precisely because they had the same general level of reading ability. Clearly, this tells us that the dyslexics' problem is rooted in phonology. Almost none of the dyslexics attained scores near even the weakest of the control students. In particular, the dyslexics managed to read correctly only a fourth of the non-words, even though they used twice as much time.

The extreme length of the dyslexics' reaction times could be thought to reflect a generally slower tempo in answering all kinds of questions, not only reading-related questions. To find out if this was the case, we measured their reaction times on various other types of tests. The dyslexics turned out to be somewhat slower than the controls, but this difference was not great in non-reading tasks such as visual comparisons, matching letters, naming objects, etc. In lexical decision tasks and in tests of rhyming their reaction times were much longer than the controls.

Compensating for the specific deficit

Other studies have also shown that phonological problems are common among older dyslexics (for example Bruck, 1992; Elbro, Nielsen and Petersen, 1994; Pennington et al., 1990). It is conceivable, at least in principle, that the teenage dyslexics' phonological problems could be due to the simple fact that they haven't had as much practice reading or writing as their cohorts. Perhaps what we thought was the cause really was the effect, for indeed we do know that dyslexics avoid dealing with writing as much as possible because they simply don't like it. Besides, there are some lucky people who had severe dyslexic problems in school but who, thanks to excellent teachers, a supportive home environment, and more than their share of true grit, have achieved an almost normal ability to read and write. We call them compensated dyslexics. The question is whether they still have their phonological handicap and have found techniques to get around their problem, or whether they have truly overcome their initial problem.

Gallagher et al. (1996) has studied well-compensated dyslexics who were attending college, and whose level of general reading ability was within the normal range at the time of their study. These well-compensated dyslexics were compared to a group of normal readers without any dyslexic symptoms who matched the study group quite precisely in all other relevant ways. Gallagher found that the compensated dyslexics were clearly weaker than the control group in a series of phonological tasks. Particularly salient was the difference between the two groups in reading and writing non-words. The compensated dyslexics were also much slower at dealing with spoonerisms and at reading numbers aloud. Their rate of speech was also slower.

This study dealt with talented people who had qualified for university education. Given their high level of general abilities, we may take them as evidence for the notion that the dyslexia deficit is sharply limited in scope and does not affect other intellectual functions. How these college students managed to compensate for their poor reading ability in primary school and ultimately achieve a fairly normal level of general reading ability is a question that needs more study. If we could understand more about the mechanisms whereby some dyslexics manage to compensate, then we would also know more about how to design remedial programmes. In an ongoing study, Lundberg and Wolff (unpublished) are investigating dyslexia among university students. A screening battery included a comprehensive questionnaire, a word recognition test assessing speed and accuracy, and a phonological-choice test (rane – ranp, 'which one sounds like a real word?'). On the basis of the results of the screening battery 30 dyslexic students and 30 non-dyslexic control students were selected from a population of 400 students. A long series of tasks were then used for careful individual assessment. Among the dyslexic and control subjects it was possible to find 10 pairs (one dyslexic and one control) that were perfectly matched on word recognition scores. The dyslexic member of a pair had obviously compensated the reading disability to some degree, whereas the control had a comparatively low but adequate word recognition skill. The matched groups were compared on a number of phonological tasks. The results are presented in Table 4.2.

Although the groups had the same manifest reading skill, they differed dramatically in terms of phonological ability. The non-word tasks were at

Table 4.2: Comparisons of dyslexic and non-dyslexic university students on phonological tasks. The groups have been carefully matched on word recognition. N = 10 in each group

TASK	GROUP		
	Dyslexics	Controls	
Non-word reaction time (seconds)	1.32	0.88	***
Non-word spelling (number of correct answers)	15.3	20.6	***
Making spoonerisms (time/correct answers)	14.5	4.2	***
Reversing spoonerisms (time/correct answers)	8.2	2.6	***
Vocabulary phonologically confusable (number of correct answers)	18.5	22.7	**
Vocabulary general (number of correct answers)	16.1	16.7	n.s.

*** $p < 0.001$; ** $p < 0.01$

least as diagnostic as for the 15-year-olds. Obviously the dyslexics had found a way of reading common natural words that did not require a precise phonological segmentation. However, their spelling was still rather poor, and it was not possible to find a sufficient number of dyslexics and controls matched on this ability. It seems to be the case that the precision requirements in spelling do not permit any circumventing strategies of the kind that is operating in reading. (Spelling is really not symmetrical to word recognition. When you try to spell a word, you are confronted with several potentially correct ways of rendering the word in letters. 'Rane' might be a correct way of spelling 'rain'; it just happens to be wrong. But when you try to sound out a common word with which you are unfamiliar in print, you already have the correct sound-identity in your memory, you just have to find it.)

The time taken to spoonerize word pairs ('long road' becomes 'rong load') seems to be a sensitive indicator of phonological problems not manifested in poor reading among these well-compensated dyslexics. The ability to listen to and 'unspoonerize' a spoonerized word pair might even be more diagnostic, because this task is typically done on the sounds of the words, not on their orthographic renderings. In order to do them quickly, you have to be able to deal with the sounds alone; if you try to imagine the spellings, then mentally switch around the initial letters and pronounce the resulting letter strings, you get a poor score on latency.

Two vocabulary tests were used with the aim of finding a dissociation between phonology and general vocabulary. The first test presented a word and the task was to select one of three alternatives as the most appropriate synonym to the target word. However, the distractors were phonologically highly confusable with the correct alternative (For example: 'What is carried out after someone is sentenced to death: excursion, exclusion, execution?'). A correct selection requires a rather precise phonological representation of the word in question. The other vocabulary test was more conventional and made no particular demand on phonological ability. As can be seen from the table, the predicted dissociation was obtained. The dyslexic group had a significantly lower mean on the phonologically demanding vocabulary task, whereas its performance on the conventional test was comparable to the normal performance. Lundberg (1999) has presented other examples of dissociation tasks.

The basic idea in our testing strategy is to use one type of task that puts the phonological system under severe pressure and another control task that entails almost the same general cognitive operations, but without the phonological load. One would then expect dyslexic individuals to show a low performance on the first task and a fairly normal performance on the control task. Such a demonstration of a dissociation of phonological processing from more general cognitive operations in several types of tasks would give strong support for the modularity hypothesis. Moreover, it would bring us closer to a concept of dyslexia that is more precise and that could be empirically operationalized. However, as an individual with dyslexia grows older all sorts of secondary or additional socio-emotional and intellectual problems will obscure the picture. Perhaps it is even the case that phonological problems to some extent are aggravated by environmental influences. On the basis of the results presented so far, we can conclude with a high degree of confidence that the characteristic trait of dyslexics, even when they are 15 years old or adults, is a slow and inadequate phonological coding and a poorly developed phonological awareness. We can therefore claim to have identified a specific deficit that dyslexics suffer from that is closely related to reading but that does not seem to involve other domains in the cognitive system. The potential of poor phonological awareness to seriously hinder reading ability is strengthened by the fact that this mechanism lies at the very heart of the process of learning to read. Therefore we would strongly suspect that measuring phonological awareness is not merely a way of discriminating dyslexic from non-dyslexic individuals. It tells a powerful story about the individual. The next question that needs to be addressed is this. Why do some individuals have such poor phonological functions in the first place? Is there an identifiable neurobiological basis for the core symptom of dyslexia?

The neurobiological level

In a brain imaging study we made a step in the direction of finding a neurobiological correlate of phonological deficits. We found that reading disabled boys with severe phonological problems had an identifiable cortical anomaly. Their plana temporale were of the same size, while a control group of normal readers had asymmetrical plana (Larsen et al., 1990). Normal readers tend to have asymmetric plana, with the left plana significantly larger than the right plana. The ultimate cause of this deviation from the normal asymmetric brain structure is not yet known, but there are good reasons to assume that the unexpected symmetry must have occurred very early in the development of the nervous system.

It would be tempting to look for a clear-cut dyslexia diagnosis by using brain imaging and categorizing individuals with symmetric plana temporale as dyslexics. Even if we disregard the high cost of this procedure it still would not be feasible. It is certainly very difficult to assess reliably the symmetry in individual cases, and individual variability is indeed considerable. One may also find individuals with strong indications of dyslexia based on other criteria but with perfectly normal asymmetry, as well as normal readers or non-dyslexics with abnormal symmetry.

Differences between dyslexics and non-dyslexics have also been observed in brain function. Paulesu et al. (1996) studied well-compensated adult dyslexics with the PET technique. Although the phonological tasks that they faced were extremely easy to solve (for example, deciding whether letter names rhymed or not), the compensated dyslexics showed a brain activation pattern that was different from what was observed among non-dyslexics. The orchestration of activities in different language-related cortical regions in the left hemisphere was less well developed among the dyslexics, and signs of disconnections between Wernicke's and Broca's areas were observed.

Other signs of disconnection in posterior regions were observed in a PET study by Pugh et al. (2000). In this study the tasks were also extremely simple but involved more visual processing and phonological assembly. In tasks requiring phoneme segmentation (for example, deciding whether two non-words, like LEAT and JETE, rhyme or not) a clear difference between dyslexics and normal subjects was observed. The functional connectivity between angular gyrus and occipital and temporal lobe sites was disrupted in the left hemisphere for dyslexic subjects.

The new imaging techniques have opened up exciting avenues of knowledge development for understanding the neurobiological basis of dyslexia. Chapters in this volume have also indicated how recent advances in molecular genetics will increase the likelihood of identifying different genotypes of dyslexia, which in turn will bring us to finding sharper phenotype characterization of dyslexia. We are facing a new, exciting era in dyslexia research, where neurobiological and behavioural scientists really must co-operate and not just pay lip service to the value of cross-disciplinary work.

References

Adams MJ, Foorman BR, Lundberg I, Beeler T (1998) Phonemic awareness in young children. Baltimore MD: Paul Brookes.

Brady S (1997) Abilities to encode phonological representations: an underlying difficulty of poor readers. In B Blachman (ed.) Foundations of Reading Acquisition and Dyslexia. Implications for early intervention. London: Lawrence Erlbaum.

Bruck M (1992) Persistence of dyslexics' phonological awareness deficits. Developmental Psychology 26: 874–86.

Elbro C, Borstrom I, Petersen DK (1998) Predicting dyslexia from kindergarten. The importance of distinctness of phonological representations of lexical items. Reading Research Quarterly 33: 36–60.

Elbro C, Nielsen I, Petersen DK (1994) Dyslexia in adults: Evidence for deficits in nonword reading and in the phonological representation of lexical items. Annals of Dyslexia 44: 205–26.

Gallagher A, Laxon V, Armstrong E, Frith U (1996) Phonological difficulties in high functioning dyslexics. Reading and Writing. An Interdisciplinary Journal 8: 499–509.

Gustafsson S, Samuelsson S, Rönnberg J (2000) Why do some resist phonological intervention? A Swedish longitudinal study of poor readers in grade 4. Scandinavian Journal of Educational Research 44: 145–62.

Hoien T, Lundberg I (1989) A strategy for assessing problems in word recognition among dyslexics. Scandinavian Journal of Educational Research 33: 185–201.

Hoien T, Lundberg I (2000) Dyslexia: From theory to intervention. Dordrecht NL: Kluwer Academic Publishers.

Larsen JP, Hoien T, Lundberg I, Ödegaard H (1990) MRI evaluation of the size and symmetry of the planum temporale in adolescents with developmental dyslexia. Brain and Language 39: 289–301.

Locke J, Hodgson J, Macaruso P, Roberts J, Lambrecht-Smith S, Guttentag C (1997) The development of developmental dyslexia. In C Hulme, M Snowling (eds) Dyslexia: Biology, cognition and intervention. London: Whurr Publishers.

Lundberg I (1994) Reading difficulties can be predicted and prevented: A Scandinavian perspective on phonological awareness and reading. In C Hulme, M Snowling (eds) Reading Development and Dyslexia. London: Whurr Publishers.

Lundberg I (1999) Towards a sharper definition of dyslexia. In I Lundberg, FE Tonnessen, I Austad (eds), Dyslexia: Advances in Theory and Practice. Dordrecht NL: Kluwer Academic Publishers.

Lundberg I, Frost J, Petersen OP (1988) Effects of an extensive program for stimulating phonological awareness in pre-school children. Reading Research Quarterly 33: 263–84.

Lundberg I, Olofsson A, Wall S (1980) Reading and spelling skills in the first school years predicted from phonemic awareness skills in kindergarten. Scandinavian Journal of Psychology 21: 159–73.

Niemi P, Kinnunen R, Poskiparta E, Vauras M (1999) Do pre-school data predict resistance to treatment in phonological awareness, decoding and spelling? In I Lundberg, FE Tonnessen, I Austad (eds) Dyslexia: Advances in theory and practice. Dordrecht NL: Kluwer Academic Publishers.

Olson RK, Wise BW, Ring J, Johnson M (1997) Computer-based remedial training in phoneme awareness and phonological decoding: effects on the post-training development on word recognition. Scientific Studies of Reading 1: 235–53.

Paulesu E, Frith U, Snowling M, Gallagher A, Morton J, Frackowiak RSJ, Frith, CD (1996) Is developmental dyslexia a disconnection syndrome? Evidence from PET scanning. Brain 119: 143–57.

Pennington B, Van Orden G, Smith S, Green P, Haith M (1990) Phonological processing skills and deficits in adult dyslexics. Child Development 61: 1753–78.

Pugh KR, Mencl WE, Shaywitz BA, Shaywitz SE, Fulbright RK, Constable RT, Skudlarski P, Marchione KE, Jenner AR, Fletcher JM, Liberman AM, Shankweiler DP, Katz L, Lacadie V, Gore JC (2000) The angular gyrus in developmental dyslexia: Task specific differences in functional connectivity within posterior cortex. Psychological Science 11: 51–6.

Rack JP, Snowling MJ, Olson RK (1994) The nonword reading deficit in developmental dyslexia: A review. Reading Research Quarterly 27: 29–53.

Scarborough H (1990) Very early language deficits in dyslexic children. Child Development 61: 1728–43.

Share D, Stanovich KE (1995) Has the phonological recoding model of reading acquisition led us astray? Issues in Education 1: 1–57.

Snowling M, Nation K (1997) Language, phonology, and learning to read. In C Hulme, M Snowling (eds) Dyslexia: Biology, cognition, and intervention. London: Whurr Publishers.

Torgesen J, Wagner R, Rashotte C (1997) Approaches to the prevention and remediation of phonologically based reading disabilities. In B Blachman (ed.) Foundations of Reading and Dyslexia. Implications for early intervention. London: Lawrence Erlbaum.

Van der Leij A, Van Daal V (1999) Automaticity, automatization and dyslexia. In I Lundberg, FE Tonnessen, I Austad (eds) Dyslexia: Advances in theory and practice. Dordrecht NL: Kluwer Academic Publishers.

Wolff U, Lundberg I (2001) Dyslexia and artistic talents– is there a connection? Poster presented at the BDA 5th International Conference, York April 2001.

CHAPTER 5

On issues of time, fluency, and intervention

MARYANNE WOLF, BETH O'BRIEN

One of the most thought-provoking remarks about dyslexia was made some years ago by British psychologist, Andrew Ellis (1985), who said: 'Whatever dyslexia may turn out to be, it is not a reading disorder.' Ellis's prescient remark is supported both by evolutionary logic and the neuroimaging research of recent years. The human brain was never pre-wired to read, and there are no 'reading centres' in the same way that there are cortical centres committed to speech and language comprehension. Rather, as the imaging work instructs us, reading is a three-ring cortical, subcortical, mid-brain, and cerebellar parallel-processing act, which makes biologically novel use of no fewer than seventeen regions in the brain, and integrates them in milliseconds (Shaywitz, Shaywitz, Pugh, Fulbright, Constable, Mencl, Shankweiler, Liberman, Skudlarski, Fletcher, Katz, Marchione, Lacadie, Gatenby and Gore, 1998).

Put another way, sensu Ellis, reading is a vivid example of the brain's Picasso-like capacities to create an evolutionarily new function from other things: like seeing small visual features, hearing discrete sounds, and retrieving names for things. For some years we have argued that the failure to acquire reading in developmental dyslexia and less severe reading disabilities can be based either on an impediment in one of the regions responsible for doing these 'other things', and/or on the ability of these regions to work automatically and in precisely timed synchrony (Wolf, 1991; Wolf and Bowers, 1999). This is because reading requires not only that all its underlying processes operate accurately but also that these processes function at almost unimaginably rapid rates. Without the development of what Sir Edmund Huey in 1908 and LaBerge and Samuels (1974) called 'automaticity' in underlying processes, the entire reading system could never attain fluency and comprehension. And, the end of all our labours – whether, in the research laboratory or in classrooms across

124

the world – is a child who reads not only accurately but also fluently and with comprehension.

Despite this rather obvious fact, for more than two decades many of us have largely focused only on the achievement of accuracy in word recognition processes in reading acquisition (Breznitz, in press). More specifically, we have been investigating phonological processes as the major, core deficit in developmental dyslexia. Indeed, the systematic research in the relationship between phonological awareness processes and reading disability is referred to by Stanovich (1992) as one of the real 'success stories in science'. And rightly so. But a few of us have been following 'a different lead', if you will, about a second core deficit and different source of breakdown in dyslexia: the idea that some children have fundamental difficulties in developing sufficiently rapid processing rates in the components necessary for fluent reading and reading comprehension. Further, there is now a long line of research indicating that these rate-of-processing problems are best indexed by serial naming speed. This essay represents something between a story of 'the second deficit' and the introduction to what we think of as a new chapter in reading disabilities research: the linking of what we know about this second core deficit to problems in reading fluency and comprehension. Toward that end, this chapter will be divided into three sections. First, we will describe some of the naming-speed research that led to the conceptualization of a second core deficit. Second, we will discuss the double-deficit hypothesis, with its integration of phonological and naming-speed research, and the implications of this hypothesis for diagnosis and intervention. Finally, we will link the latter research to issues of reading fluency and its intervention.

The history of the second core deficit

The hypothesis that speed of processing could play a major role in dyslexia was born out of early work in the neurosciences by Norman Geschwind (1974), Martha Denckla (1972) and Rita Rudel (Denckla and Rudel, 1976a and b), and also out of still earlier work in physiology by Donald Hebb (1949). Hebb contributed perhaps the most basic plank underpinning the work to be presented here on fluency. He modelled at the neuronal level how individual cells learn to work together as cell assemblies or working units to increase the automaticity and process-efficiency of various functions.

An example from the visual system will be helpful. Hebb argued that the result of cell assemblies in visual perception areas is a reservoir of mental representations of frequently perceived stimuli. For example, when an unknown visual stimulus is first detected by the retina, there is an activation in the visual cortex of multiple individual cells. These cells correspond to various features of the retinal image and are responsible for coding very specific types of information (such as horizontal, diagonal, or curved lines). After multiple exposures to the same stimulus, the individual cells in the visual areas become a working unit, or cell assembly. These unified groups of neurones learn to work together in precise synchrony, so that recognition of frequently viewed stimuli (like letters) becomes so efficient, it is virtually 'automatic'. One result of these cell assemblies in the visual area is a reservoir of orthographic representations of practised, frequently viewed letters, letter patterns and words.

The second plank underlying the arguments we will be presenting here derives from more structural-level theory in behavioural neurology by Geschwind, and its application to paediatric neurology by his student Denckla. One of Geschwind's many legendary, improbable insights was that the best predictor of later reading would be a child's early capacity at colour naming. Geschwind's logic was based in part on his translation and interpretation of the first case of classic alexia (acquired reading loss resulting from brain lesion) in 1893 by Dejerine. An autopsy of Dejerine's patient revealed two lesion sites: one in the left visual or occipital area, and a second in the splenium or posterior portion of the corpus callosum (those fibre tracts connecting the two hemispheres). This combination of lesions caused alexia and impeded the French businessman-patient from either reading words or naming colours. Geschwind's analysis of the case was a precursor to many later cognitive models: because both colour naming and reading were lost through these discrete lesions, both functions must use similar structures and require many of the same cognitive, linguistic and perceptual processes involved in retrieving a verbal match for a visual stimulus. If this is true, colour-naming ability, Geschwind reasoned, should be a good early predictor of later reading. It was a wonderful, albeit slightly incorrect, hypothesis, which Denckla tested with a small group of dyslexic and average reading children. What she discovered was that dyslexic readers can name colours perfectly well; what they cannot do is name them rapidly in comparison to their peers.

This was the unlikely beginning of what is called 'naming-speed research'. Based on the colour naming-speed finding, Denckla designed the rapid automatized naming (RAN) tasks, in which the child names 50 stimuli as rapidly as possible (for example, five common letters, or five digits, or five colours, or five pictured objects, repeated randomly 10 times on a board). Denckla and Rudel (1974, 1976a,b) found that naming speed for basic symbols differentiated dyslexic children from average readers, as well as other learning-disabled children, a conclusion also reached early on by Spring and Capps (1974). The question for the last 25 years has been why, and the search for an answer has turned out to be a science story all its own. After Denckla and Rudel's findings, the story progresses with a multi-year exploration of the development of naming speed in children with and without developmental dyslexia. Results from a five-year longitudinal study by the first author, Robin Morris, and Heidi Bally indicated that differences in naming speed for children with reading disabilities were visible from the first day of kindergarten (Wolf, Bally and Morris, 1986). Further, differences were most dramatic for letters. In other words, children with dyslexia began the school years with both a general retrieval-speed problem, and a particular difficulty with letter naming retrieval rate. These differences were maintained through Grade 4 for all categories, but especially for the more automatized categories of letters and numbers. We now know from researchers like Meyer, Wood, Hart and Felton (1999) that these differences continue through Gr. 8 into adulthood (see also Scarborough and Domgaard, 1998; Wolff, 1993).

The conclusion that these data indicated another kind of deficit, independent of the well-documented phonological deficit, was challenged by Stanovich (1986). Like many others, Stanovich classified naming speed under the rubric of phonological processes. He suggested several kinds of evidence necessary to show that the processes in serial naming speed represented a truly different cognitive-core deficit from the phonological-core deficit in dyslexic children. First, naming-speed differences would have to distinguish dyslexic from reading-age matched children, in order to eliminate external factors like exposure to print. Stanovich further suggested another 'proof' might be naming-speed differences between dyslexic readers and non-discrepant poor readers. The latter children are sometimes called 'garden-variety poor readers', and are characterized by poor reading that is commensurate with intelligence or achievement measures (Gough and Tunmer, 1986). This second type of evidence is potentially more difficult to obtain because there have been no significant differences found for phonological awareness measures between discrepant and non-discrepant readers. Yet such a dissociative finding would be even more persuasive evidence of a separate core deficit. We pursued both of these lines of evidence. First, we analysed our longitudinal data by comparing older dyslexic readers with children two years younger who were matched on reading level. We were able to demonstrate highly significant group differences: grade 4 dyslexic readers were significantly slower than grade 2 average readers, and grade 3 dyslexic readers were significantly slower than grade 1 average readers. These results clearly demonstrated that greater exposure to print could not explain the naming-speed differences, for older dyslexic children would have had comparable if not considerably more exposure than the younger average-reading children.

Secondly, we compared discrepant dyslexic and non-discrepant poor readers and found significant differences (Wolf and Obregón, 1989; Biddle, 1996). The longitudinal analyses permitted us to observe changes over time in the naming speed of the non-discrepant poor reader group. In kindergarten non-discrepant poor readers were more similar to dyslexic readers in slow naming speed (although dyslexics were still slower). By Grades 3 and 4 non-discrepant poor readers were just like average readers, a finding also shown by Biddle (1996). In other words there appeared to be basic underlying differences in how discrepant dyslexic and non-discrepant poor readers name letters and numbers. In a more recent study, Scarborough and Domgaard (1998) indicated that they also found no significant differences between average and non-discrepant poor readers in letter and number naming speed; however, interestingly there were differences in object-naming speed that were related to IQ.

The next chapter in the story for us concerned the question of the relative universality of naming-speed deficits. Specifically, we wished to know whether naming speed was equally predictive in languages that have orthographies that are more regular than English, and thus have fewer phonological-based demands. Towards that end, we (Wolf, Pfeil, Lotz, and Biddle, 1994) studied German-speaking poor readers in Berlin. We found that not only did naming-speed deficits differentiate reader groups in that language, but that naming-speed performance was actually a better predictor of later reading in German than the most well-known phono-logical measure (a phoneme deletion task), a finding first demonstrated by Wimmer (1993). We now know that across multiple languages – German (Näslund and Schneider, 1991; Wimmer and Hummer, 1990; Wimmer, 1993; Landerl and Wimmer, 2000; Wolf, Pfeil, Lotz and Biddle, 1994), Dutch (Van den Bos, 1998; Yap and Van der Leij, 1993, 1994), Finnish (Korhonen, 1995), and Spanish (Novoa and Wolf, 1984; Novoa, 1988) – serial naming speed is a powerful predictor in transparent languages. The unexpected conclusion of this cross-linguistic work is that when phono-logical skills play a reduced role in the more transparent orthographies, naming-speed performance becomes an even stronger, more important diagnostic indicator and predictor of reading performance.

The issue for the third chapter in the story was and continues to be a perplexing one: that is, at what point in the act of rapid naming are dyslexic children impeded? We have approached this question in varied ways: for example, an analysis of the speech stream during serial naming speed, and cognitive modelling. First, Mateo Obregón (1994) in our lab designed a sophisticated computer program to digitize the speech stream of children performing the RAN task, in order to analyse where in the speech stream dyslexics differed. We investigated a number of potential explanations offered by other researchers about the origins of naming-speed deficits, including: a) articulation; b) end-of-line scanning; and c) fatigue at the end of lines or the task. The results of these investigations indicated that there were no group differences for articulation (see, however, Snyder and Downey, 1995), end-of-line scanning, or fatigue-related effects, but rather group differences were found only for the inter-stimulus intervals (ISIs). The latter represents the 'gap of time' between the response to one stimulus and the response to the next. Within this interstimulus gap occur multiple processes that include inhibiting the response to the previous stimulus (attentional systems within executive functions); shifting the system to anticipate and respond to the current stimulus (for example, anticipatory facilitation (Wood, 2000)); perceiving the current stimulus (perceptual system), and accessing and retrieving a verbal label (semantic, phonological, and lexical retrieval systems).

The results of Obregón's analysis and the cumulative results of earlier work demonstrating an independent core deficit convinced us of the necessity to look beyond previous notions of naming speed as subsumed under phonological processing. We were compelled to consider all other processes that comprise naming speed, including non-linguistic processes that might have little to do with reading, again, like Ellis (1985). We began to reconceptualize naming speed as a small behavioural window on the brain's ability to inhibit, activate, and integrate discrete component operations like visual and auditory perception and representation processes, along with semantic representation and retrieval processes within a very brief period of time (Wolf and Bowers, 1999). With this shift of perspective, naming speed could no longer be categorized as a phonological task, as still held by some today; rather, it appeared best conceptualized as a complex ensemble of multiple processes that clearly included, but certainly was not limited to, phonological processes. The most important conclusion derived from this alternative view of naming speed was that if it could no longer be subsumed under phonology, then there were other critical processes impeding reading in dyslexic children that had to be understood.

During this period we also constructed various cognitive models of letter naming. These models were developed to depict the range of processes involved in naming speed and to illustrate several principles:

- the multiple-componential nature of letter-naming speed;
- the idea that phonological processes represent one set of processes among many that are involved in naming speed; and

- the notion that with multiple component parts, there can be different possible sources of breakdown (for an elaborated discussion of models, see Wolf and Bowers, 1999).

A broader perspective also conveys another conclusion: the components of naming speed represent a mini-version or subset of the components of reading. Within this view, both naming and reading can be considered ensembles of multiple perceptual, lexical, and motoric processes, all of whose subprocesses must function smoothly and rapidly, if the child is to produce a verbal match for an abstract, visually presented symbol. If we conceptualize the processes underlying naming speed as a subset of the processes used by reading, then the naming-speed measure might be thought of as a simple predictor of reading before the child ever begins to acquire reading. It would appear, perhaps unsurprisingly to those of us who knew him, that Geschwind (1974) was not far off in his original, however unlikely, insight.

The double-deficit hypothesis

Along with an extensive number of colleagues, we have now demonstrated in numerous studies across Canada, the United States, Israel, and many countries in Europe, that the processes underlying naming speed represent a second core deficit in dyslexia, largely independent of phonological processes (see Wolf, Bowers, and Biddle, 2000). Further, we have now shown that these problems in rate of processing stretch from kindergarten through adulthood in readers with dyslexia. Perhaps the most unexpected implication of naming-speed's relative independence from phonological deficits was that it allowed a new analysis of potential subtypes in our reading-impaired populations. With our colleague Pat Bowers, we found that within the well-known heterogeneity of dyslexic readers there are three major subtypes who can be characterized by the presence, absence, or combination of the two core deficits in phonology and naming speed. In other words, there are poor readers who have only phonological deficits without differences in naming speed. Conversely, there are readers who have adequate phonological and word attack skills, but who have early naming-speed deficits and later comprehension deficits. First described by Rudel (1985), these are the children who would be missed by the vast majority of our diagnostic batteries, because their decoding is accurate. The most intractable subtype is characterized by both deficits; children with both or 'double deficits' represent the most severely impaired subtype in all aspects of reading, particularly in reading fluency. This part of the story is what we call the double-deficit hypothesis (see special issue on the double-deficit hypothesis in Wolf and Bowers, 2000). Extensive data now replicate the existence of these three subtypes of impaired readers, and in several language systems (for example, German, Dutch, Finnish, and Hebrew). But, there are interesting surprises that are emerging. For example, in English, Lovett, Steinbach, and Frijters (2000) studied a large sample of clinically referred severely impaired readers and found that more than half are double deficit with the remainder fairly equally split across the single deficit subtypes. By contrast, Breznitz (personal correspondence, 13 December 2000) reports that out of 375 dyslexic children studied in Hebrew, the overwhelming majority would be double-deficit readers with only 15 readers classified with solely phonological deficits. Deeney, Gidney, Wolf, and Morris (1999) also report differences in subtype distribution for African-American impaired readers who speak vernacular English. There appear far more double-deficit and phonological subtypes in this population than the distribution of subtypes for Caucasian and African-American children who do not speak vernacular English.

The accumulating data on independent subtypes has led to the most important theoretical and applied implications of the double-deficit hypothesis – that is, the necessity to understand the role of rate of processing and fluency in reading development, and the need to create reading intervention that addresses these issues. Until this time, children with single phonological deficits were adequately treated with current programmes emphasizing phonological awareness and decoding. However, the other two subtypes with their explicit problems in naming speed and reading fluency, were not adequately remediated. These children make up, we believe, at least one significant portion of the children called 'treatment resisters' (Torgesen, Wagner, and Rashotte, 1994). In the final section of this chapter we argue that in addition to a systematic programme of phonological based instruction there should be an equally systematic and comprehensive programme that addresses the development of reading fluency and comprehension. But first there must be an articulated definition of what we mean by fluency, for there are vastly different extant perspectives.

The role of fluency in reading development and reading intervention

Although the history of work on reading fluency is long and complex, research on fluency instruction is in its infancy. Further, definitions of fluency differ substantively, with most definitions approaching it as an outcome of accuracy in other processes like decoding. In an excellent recent review of fluency literature, Meyers and Felton (1999) capsule the most consensual view of fluency as 'the ability to read connected text rapidly, smoothly, effortlessly, and automatically with little conscious attention to the mechanics of reading such as decoding.' This approach to fluency accurately captures the last two decades of researchers' views on the end-goal of fluency – effortless reading with good comprehension (see Carver, 1990; LaBerge and Samuels, 1974; Perfetti, 1985; see however, Torgesen et al., in press). The problems with such a definition are several, including validation issues. In an effort to aid validation, Torgesen and his colleagues (in press) prefer the minimalist definition of 'rate and accuracy in oral reading' (p. 4) used in curriculum-based assessment research (Shinn, Good, Knutson, Tilly and Collins, 1992). Similarly, the National Reading Panel's (2000: 3–5)definition of fluency as 'the immediate result of word recognition proficiency' permits the simple procedure of testing for proficiency in word recognition, just as Torgesen et al.'s view can be assessed by performance on an oral reading measure that incorporates rate and accuracy (such as the Gray Oral Reading Test, Wiederholt and Bryant, 1992). Although we concur in principle with these methodological concerns, we believe that there are still thornier issues to confront. In particular, we believe it is essential to consider the multiple underlying dimensions of fluency, like lower-level subskills that are involved in its development. With the exception of Berninger et al. (in press) and Kame'enui, Simmons, Good, and Harn (in press), few current researchers attempt to define fluency either in terms of its component parts or its various levels of reading subskills – letter, letter pattern, word, sentence, and passage. Together with Kame'enui et al. (in press), we suggest a figure–ground shift for the conceptualization of fluency: that is, as a developmental process, as well as an outcome. In a broad-ranging paper, Kame'enui and his colleagues conceptualize fluency in a more developmental manner as both the development of 'proficiency' in underlying lower-level and component skills of reading (for example, phoneme awareness), and also as the outcome of proficiency in higher-level processes and component skills (for example, accuracy in comprehension). Berninger and her colleagues (in press) take a still broader view, with a systems-approach to fluency. Fluency in this approach is influenced by

- the characteristics of stimulus input (for example, rate and persistence of a visual signal or speech signal);
- the efficiency and automaticity of internal processes (for example, the development of phonological, orthographic, and morphological systems); and
- the co-ordination of responses by the executive functions system.

Berninger is one of the few researchers to place special importance on the role of morphological knowledge about words in facilitating the development of orthographic rate and overall fluency. In an essay on fluency for a special issue on this topic in *Scientific Studies of Reading*, Tami Katzir-Cohen and Wolf (in press) review the modern history of reading fluency research and use the following developmental definition:

> In its beginnings, reading fluency is the product of the initial development of accuracy and the subsequent development of automaticity in underlying sublexical processes, lexical processes, and their integration in single-word reading and connected text. These include perceptual, phonological, orthographic, and morphological processes at the letter-, letter-pattern, and word-level; as well as semantic and syntactic processes at the word-level and connected-text level. After it is fully developed, reading fluency refers to a level of accuracy and rate, where decoding is relatively effortless; where oral reading is smooth and accurate with correct prosody; and where attention can be allocated to comprehension.

Such a developmental, more encompassing view of reading fluency has profound implications for prevention, intervention, and assessment. For, within a developmental perspective, efforts to address fluency must start at the beginning of the reading acquisition process, not after reading is already acquired (as with most current fluency instruction). The importance of working preventatively before difficult fluency problems ever begin is a major theme in the recent studies by Torgesen et al. (in press) and by Kame'enui et al. (in press). As Stahl recently has described (Stahl, Heubach, and Crammond, 1997), most current efforts in fluency do not work within a prevention framework, but rather are based largely on the repeated reading technique (Dahl, 1974; Dowhower, 1994; Samuels, 1985; Young, Bowers, and MacKinnon, 1996). In this approach the already 'reading' child is asked to reread a passage at an appropriate level several times until fluent. Repeated reading methods were designed to increase reading rate for the particular materials being used and also for similar materials. Based on a long history of information processing principles (LaBerge and Samuels, 1974; Perfetti, 1985) the idea is that comprehension skills can be allocated more time when the rate of decoding is increased. From the developmental context we are employing, such a treatment is an important and efficacious tool when used at a particular phase of fluency development.

This type of treatment by itself, however, would be insufficient to address the development of rapid processing in the multiple, sublexical systems, as well as the development of higher level, semantic (vocabulary) systems. Over the last five years we have been developing an experimental, developmental approach to fluency instruction. Described in detail in Wolf, Miller, and Donnelly (2000), the programme has three key aims for each child: first, accuracy and automaticity in sublexical and lexical levels; second, increased rate in word attack, word identification and comprehension; and third, a transformed attitude towards language.

The processes and components described in the research as fluency-related include the following: lower-level attention and visual perception; orthographic (letter-pattern) representation and identification; auditory perception; phonological representation and phoneme awareness; short-term and long-term memory; lexical access and retrieval; semantic representation; decoding and word-identification; morpho-syntactic and prosodic knowledge; and finally, connected-text knowledge and comprehension. In other words, the unavoidable implication of past work on fluency is that reading fluency involves every process and subskill involved in reading. We do not shy away from this conclusion in the RAVE-O programme; rather, like Kame'enui and his colleagues (in press), we emphasize that reading fluency involves the development of accuracy and proficiency in every underlying component. Researchers within connectionist approaches (Adams, 1990; Foorman, 1994; Seidenberg and McCelland, 1989) stress the explicit linkages or connections among the orthographic, semantic, and phonological processes; and Berninger et al. (in press) and Adams (1990) add the connections between morphosyntactic knowledge and these other processes.

The RAVE-O programme (Retrieval, Automaticity, Vocabulary Enrichment, and Orthography) simultaneously addresses both the need for automaticity in phonological, orthographic, morphosyntactic, and semantic systems and the importance of teaching explicit connections among these systems. The programme emerged as the result of a collaboration by Morris, Lovett, and Wolf to investigate the efficacy of theory-based treatments for different dyslexia subtypes.

The programme is taught only in combination with a programme that teaches systematic, phonological analysis and blending (see Lovett et al., 2000). Children are taught a group of core words each week that exemplify critical phonological, orthographic, and semantic principles. Each core word is chosen on the basis of:

- shared phonemes with the phonological-treatment programme;
- sequenced orthographic patterns; and
- semantic richness. For example, each core word has at least three different meanings.

First, the multiple meanings of core words are introduced in varied semantic contexts. Second, children are taught to connect the phonemes in the core words with the trained orthographic patterns in RAVE-O. For example, children are taught individual phonemes in the phonological programme (like 'a', 't', and 'm') and orthographic chunks with the same phonemes in RAVE-O (for example, 'at' and 'am' along with their word families).

There is daily emphasis on practice and rapid recognition of the most frequent orthographic letter patterns in English. Computerized games (see Speed Wizards, Wolf and Goodman, 1996) were designed to allow for maximal practice and to increase the speed of orthographic pattern recognition (onset and rime) in a fun fashion.

There is a simultaneous emphasis on vocabulary and retrieval, based on earlier work in vocabulary development, that suggests that one retrieves fastest what one knows best (see Beck, Perfetti, and McKeown, 1982; German, 1992; Kame'enui, Dixon, and Carnine, 1987; Wolf and Segal, 1992). Vocabulary growth is conceptualized as essential to both rapid retrieval (in oral and written language) and also to improved comprehension, an ultimate goal in the programme. Retrieval skills are taught through a variety of ways including a set of metacognitive strategies called the 'Sam Spade strategies'.

Sam Spade also appears as a character in the series of comprehension stories (for example, Minute Mysteries). These stories accompany each week of RAVE-O and directly address fluency in comprehension in several ways. The controlled vocabulary in the timed and untimed stories both incorporates the week's particular orthographic patterns, and also emphasizes the multiple meanings of the week's core words. The stories provide a superb vehicle for repeated reading practice, which, in turn, helps fluency in connected text. Thus, the Minute Mysteries are multi-purpose vehicles for facilitating fluency in phonological, orthographic, and semantic systems at the same time that they build comprehension skills. In this way all knowledge systems that were taught explicitly earlier in the week in separate domains are being called upon to work together in order to comprehend a story. In conjunction with the other activities, Minute Mysteries encapsulate our goal to facilitate fluency at every level, and in the process contribute to comprehension skills.

There is an additional system too little discussed by many of us – that is, the affective-motivational one. The secret weapon of this programme is the deceptive cover of whimsy over the program's systematicity. There is a daily emphasis for the teacher and the student on having fun with words: we seek in as many ways as we can daily find to empower children who all too often come to us as 'strangers in their own language' (Chukovsky, 1963: 9).

Conclusion

The leitmotiv of this story – that dyslexia is due to something other than a disorder of reading per se – is underscored by the current status of research in reading disabilities. There are decades of evidence that phonological processes are implicated in many cases of dyslexia, and there is growing consensus that the processes underlying naming speed are independently involved in impeding reading in dyslexic children. A growing number of studies document the strong relationship between early naming speed and later reading fluency. We have sought to use our evolving understanding of the component structure of naming speed to help understand its relationship to reading fluency. Rapid naming, which invokes sensory (for example, visual, auditory), representational (for example, orthographic, phonological, morphological), as well as retrieval processes, may fail when any one of these processes or their integration is disrupted. We argue here that reading fluency involves many of these same processes and that a breakdown in any of them can also impede the acquisition of fluent reading. We presented a new definition of fluency that stresses the development of this component structure. Following this line of theorizing, we also described an experimental, developmental fluency intervention aimed at increasing accuracy and automaticity in the components underlying fluent reading (for example, the sensory, representational, and retrieval processes), as well as the overt reading skills (for example, word attack, word recognition, oral reading and comprehension). The RAVE-O programme provides, therefore, a comprehensive approach towards fluency's development and a figure–ground shift from most current intervention methods. The end of this story of naming speed, fluency, and its intervention is not available to anyone; for we are, to be sure, in the very middle of it. It is a story that began improbably but one that has the capacity, we now believe, of illuminating some of the most perplexing reasons why particular children have failed our best past efforts at remediation. An upcoming sequel with data on the RAVE-O programme's efficacy for dysfluent readers will further our progress towards this goal.

Acknowledgements

The authors wish to acknowledge the support of NICHD grant OD30970-01A1 during ongoing intervention research. The authors wish to thank present and past members of the Centre for Reading and Language Research: Heidi Bally, Kathleen Biddle, Zvia Breznitz, Theresa Deeney, Katharine Donnelly, Wendy Galante, Calvin Gidney, Julie Jeffery, Terry Joffe, Tami-Katzir-Cohen, Cynthia Krug, Lynne Miller, Mateo Obregón, Alyssa O'Rourke, and Maya Rom. The work cited in this paper could never have been done without their efforts.

Correspondence to: Maryanne Wolf, Centre for Reading and Language Research, Miller Hall, Tufts University, Medford MA, 02155. Email: mwolf@granite.tufts.edu

References

Adams MJ (1990) Beginning to read: Thinking and learning about print. Cambridge MA: MIT Press.

Beck IL, Perfetti CA, McKeown MG (1982) Effects of long-term vocabulary instruction on lexical access and reading comprehension. Journal of Educational Psychology, 74: 506–21.

Berninger VW, Abbott RD, Billingsley F, Nagy W (in press). Processes underlying timing and fluency of reading: Efficiency, automaticity, coordination, and morphological awareness. In M Wolf (ed.) Time, Fluency, and Dyslexia. New York: York Press.

Biddle KR (1996) The development of visual naming speed and verbal fluency in average and impaired readers: the implications for assessment, intervention, and theory. Unpublished doctoral dissertation. Tufts University, Boston MA.

Breznitz Z (personal correspondence, 13 December 2000).

Breznitz Z (in press) The role of inter-modality temporal features of speed of information processing in asynchrony between visual-orthographic and auditory-phonological processing. In M Wolf (ed.) Time, Fluency, and Dyslexia. New York: York Press.

Carver RP (1990) Reading Rate: A review of research and theory. Boston: Academic Press, Inc.

Chukovsky K (1963) From two to five. Berkeley and Los Angeles CA: University of California Press.

Dahl P (1974) An experimental program for teaching high speed word recognition and comprehension skills (Rep. No. Final report project #3-1154). Washington, DC: National Institute of Education.

Deeney T, Gidney C, Wolf M, Morris R (1999) Phonological skills of African-American Reading-Disabled Children. Paper presented at 6th Annual Meeting of the Society for the Scientific Study of Reading. Montreal, Canada.

Dejerine (1892) Contribution a letude anatomo-pathologique et cliniquedes differents varieties de cecite verbale. Comp Rend Scean Soc Biol 4: 61–90.

Denckla MB (1972) Colour-naming defects in dyslexic boys. Cortex 8: 164–76.

Denckla MB, Rudel RG (1974) Rapid automatized naming of pictured objects, colours, letters, and numbers by normal children. Cortex 10: 186–202.

Denckla MB, Rudel RG (1976a) Naming of objects by dyslexic and other learning-disabled children. Brain and Language 3: 1–15.

Denckla MB, Rudel RG (1976b) Rapid automatized naming (RAN): Dyslexia differentiated from other learning disabilities. Neuropsychologia 14: 471–9.

Dowhower SL (1994) Repeated reading revisited: Research into practice. Reading and Writing Quarterly: Overcoming Learning Difficulties 10: 343–58.

Ellis AW (1985) The production of spoken words: a cognitive neuropsychological perspective. In AW Ellis (ed.), Progress in the Psychology of Language, Vol. 2, Hillsdale NJ: Erlbaum.

Foorman BR (1994) Phonological and orthographic processing: separate but equal? In VW Berninger (ed.) The Varieties of Orthographic Knowledge I: Theoretical and and developmental issues. Boston: Kluwer Academic Publishers, pp. 321–57.

German DJ (1992) Word-finding intervention for children and adolescents. Topics in Learning Disorders 13: 33–50.

Geschwind N (1974) Selected papers on language and the brain. D Reidel: Dordrecht, Holland.

Gough P, Tunmer W (1986) Decoding, reading, and reading ability. Remedial and Special Education 7: 6-10.

Hebb DO (1949) The Organization of Behaviour. New York: John-Wiley.

Huey E (1908) The Psychology and Pedagogy of Reading. Cambridge: MIT Press.

Kame'enui EJ, Dixon RC, Carnine DW (1987) Issues in the design of vocabulary instruction. In MG McKeown and ME Curtis (eds) The Nature of Vocabulary Acquisition. Hillsdale NJ: Erlbaum, pp. 129–45.

Kame'enui EJ, Simmons DC, Good RH, Harn BA (in press) The use of fluency-based measures in early identification and evaluation of intervention efficacy in schools. In M Wolf (ed.) Time, Fluency, and Dyslexia: New York: York Press.

Katzir-Cohen T, Wolf M (in press) Reading fluency and its intervention. Scientific Studies in Reading.

Korhonen T (1995) The persistence of rapid naming problems in children with reading disabilities: a nine-year follow-up. Journal of Learning Disabilities 28: 232–39.

LaBerge D, Samuels SJ (1974) Toward a theory of automatic information processing in reading. Cognitive Psychology 6: 293–323.

Landerl K, Wimmer H (2000) Deficits in phoneme segmentation are not the core problem of dyslexia: Evidence from German and English children. Applied Psycholinguistics 21: 243–62.

Lovett MW, Steinbach KA, Frijters JC (2000) Remediating the core deficits of developmental reading disability: A double-deficit perspective. Journal of Learning Disabilities 33(4): 334–58.

Meyer MS, Felton RH (1999) Evolution of fluency training: old approaches and new directions. Annals of Dyslexia 49: 283–306.

Meyer MS, Wood FB, Hart LA, Felton RH (1998) Longitudinal course of rapid naming in disabled and nondisabled readers. Annals of Dyslexia 48: 91–114.

Näslund JC, Schneider W (1991) Longitudinal effects of verbal ability, memory capacity, and phonological awareness on reading performance. European Journal of Psychology of Education 4: 375–92.

National Reading Panel (2000) Teaching children to read: an evidence-based assessment of the scientific research literature on reading and its implications for reading instruction. Washington DC: National Institute of Child Health and Human Development.

Novoa L (1988) Word-retrieval process and reading acquisition and development in bilingual and monolingual children. Unpublished doctoral dissertation. Harvard University, Cambridge MA.

Novoa L, Wolf M (1984) Word-retrieval and reading in bilingual children. Paper presented at Boston University Language Conference, Boston MA.

Obregón M (1994) Exploring naming timing patterns by dyslexic and normal readers on the serial RAN task. Unpublished Master's thesis. Tufts University, Boston MA.

Perfetti CA (1985) Reading ability. New York: Oxford University Press.

Rudel R (1985) Definition of dyslexia: Language and motor deficits. In F Duffy, N Geschwind (eds) Dyslexia: Current status and future directions. Boston: Little, Brown.

Samuels SJ (1985) Automaticity and repeated reading. In J Osborn, PT Wilson, RC Anderson (eds) Reading Education: Foundations for a literate America. Lexington, MA: Lexington Books, pp. 215–30.

Scarborough HS, Domgaard RM (1998) An exploration of the relationship between reading and rapid serial naming. Poster presented at meeting of Society for Scientific Study of Reading. San Diego CA.

Seidenberg M, McClelland J (1989) A distributed developmental model of word recognition and naming. Psychological Review 96: 35–49.

Shaywitz S, Shaywitz B, Pugh K, Fulbright R, Constable RT, Mencl WE, Shankweiler D, Liberman A, Skudlarski P, Fletcher J, Katz L, Marchione K, Lacadie C, Gatenby C, Gore J (1998) Functional disruption in the organization of the brain for reading in dyslexia. Neurobiology 95: 2636–41.

Shinn MR, Good RH, Knutson N, Tilly WD, Collins VL (1992) Curriculum based measurement of oral reading fluency: a confirmatory analysis of its relation to reading. School Psychology Review 21: 459–79.

Snyder L, Downey D (1995) Serial rapid naming skills in children with reading disabilities. Annals of Dyslexia 45: 31–50.

Spring C, Capps C (1974) Encoding speed, rehearsal, and probed recall of dyslexic boys. Journal of Educational Psychology 66: 780–6.

Stahl S, Heubach K, Crammond B (1997) Fluency-oriented reading instruction. Reading Research Report 79: 1-38.

Stanovich KE (1986) 'Matthew effects' in reading: some consequences of individual differences in acquisition of literacy. Reading Research Quarterly 4: 360–407.

Stanovich KE (1992) Speculations on the causes and consequences of individual differences in early reading acquisition. In PB Gough, LC Ehri, R Treiman (eds) Reading Acquisition. Hillsdale NJ: Erlbaum, pp. 307–42.

Torgesen J, Rashotte C, Alexander A (in press) The prevention and remediation of reading fluency problems. In M Wolf (ed.) Time, Fluency, and Dyslexia. New York: York Press.

Torgesen JK, Wagner RK, Rashotte CA (1994) Longitudinal studies of phonological processing and reading. Journal of Learning Disabilities 27: 276–86.

Van den Bos K (1998) IQ, phonological awareness, and continuous-naming speed related to Dutch children's poor decoding performance on two word identification tests. Dyslexia 4: 73–89.

Wiederholt JL, Bryant B (1992) Gray Oral Reading Test, (GORT-3), Pro-Ed Publishing, Austin, Texas.

Wimmer H (1993) Characteristics of developmental dyslexia in a regular writing system. Applied Psycholinguistics 14: 1–34.

Wimmer H, Hummer P (1990) How German-speaking first graders read and spell: doubts on the importance of the logographic stage. Applied Psycholinguistics 11: 349–68.

Wolf M (1991) Naming speed and reading: the contribution of the cognitive neurosciences. Reading Research Quarterly 26: 123–41.

Wolf M, Bally H, Morris R (1986) Automaticity, retrieval processes, and reading: a longitudinal study in average and impaired readers. Child Development 57: 988–1000.

Wolf M, Goodman G (1996) Speed Wizards. Computerized reading program. Tufts University and Rochester Institute of Technology.

Wolf M, Miller L, Donnelly K (2000) Retrieval, Automaticity, Vocabulary Elaboration, Orthography (RAVE-O): A comprehensive, fluency-based reading intervention program. Journal of Learning Disabilities 33: 322–4.

Wolf M, Obregón M (1989) 88 children in search of a name: a five-year investigation of rate, word-retrieval, and vocabulary in reading development and dyslexia. Paper presented at Society for Research and Child Development conference, Kansas City MO, April 1989.

Wolf M, Segal D (1992) Word finding and reading in the developmental dyslexias. Topics in Language Disorders 13(1): 51–65.

Wolf M, Pfeil C, Lotz R, Biddle K (1994) Towards a more universal understanding of the developmental dyslexias: the contribution of orthographic factors. In VW Berninger (ed.) The Varieties of Orthographic Knowledge I: Theoretical and developmental issues. Dordrecht, The Netherlands: Kluwer, pp. 137–71.

Wolf M, Bowers P (1999) The 'double-deficit hypothesis' for the developmental dyslexias. Journal of Educational Psychology 91: 1–24.

Wolf M, Bowers P (2000) The question of naming-speed deficits in developmental reading disabilities: an introduction to the double-deficit hypothesis. Journal of Learning Disabilities 33: 322–4.

Wolf M, Bowers P, Biddle KR (2000) Naming-speed processes, timing, and reading: A conceptual review. Journal of Learning Disabilities 33: 387–407.

Wolff P (1993) Impaired temporal resolution in developmental dyslexia: temporal information processing in the nervous system. In P Tallal, A Galaburda, R Llinas, C von Euler (eds) Annals of the New York Academy of Sciences 682: 87–103.

Wood F (2000) On the functional neuroanatomy of fluency. In M Wolf (ed.) Time, Fluency, and Dyslexia. New York: York Press.

Yap R, Van der Leij A (1993) Word processing in dyslexics: An automatic decoding deficit? Reading and Writing: An Interdisciplinary Journal 5(3): 261–79.

Yap R, Van der Leij A (1994) Testing the automatization deficit hypothesis of dyslexia via a dual-task paradigm. Journal of Learning Disabilities 27(10): 660–5.

Young A, Bowers P, MacKinnon G (1996) Effects of prosodic modeling and repeated reading on poor readers' fluency and comprehension. Applied Psycholinguistics 17: 59–84.

CHAPTER 6

Dyslexia as a learning disability

RODERICK I NICOLSON, ANGELA J FAWCETT

Introduction

Specific developmental dyslexia is normally identified by unexpected problems in learning to read for children of average or above average intelligence – 'a disorder in children who, despite conventional classroom experience, fail to attain the language skills of reading, writing and spelling commensurate with their intellectual abilities' (from the definition by the World Federation of Neurology 1968: 26).

From a theorist's viewpoint, the challenge in understanding dyslexia is to develop a 'theory'. There are all sorts of theory in science and psychology. In the early days, a theory may be purely descriptive – a clear description and summary of the phenomena involved. This is normally followed by a 'quantification' phase, where methods for measuring the important components are devised, possibly introducing new technical terms and new measurement devices. Many theorists consider that a true theory should go beyond these initial stages to provide some 'model' of the underlying processes, a model from which predictions may be derived and tested, leading in turn to acceptance, modification or rejection of the model. Failure to undertake this initial exploratory work may result in premature theorizing, in which theories are based on incomplete knowledge, and therefore do not cover the full range of phenomena. In terms of psychological theories, one may make a valuable distinction between three 'levels' of theory – the biological, cognitive and behavioural levels (Frith, 1997). In this chapter we present the results of our 'cognitive' investigations of dyslexia. These should be seen as related to, but logically separate from, our work on the biological level framework of the cerebellum. In particular, a range of different biological level explanations might lead to similar cognitive level descriptions. Furthermore, as we shall

141

discuss in this chapter, when considering theoretical implications for intervention, the cognitive level analysis is normally more appropriate than the biological.

The approach that theorists take depends upon their knowledge and interests. Consider the three criterial skills for dyslexia – reading, writing and spelling. What do these skills have in common? Some theorists will stress the language-related components, others the visual components, others the need for rapid cognitive processing, for attention, for motor skill, and so on. Our background was in cognitive theories of learning. We immediately thought: 'These skills are learned skills, they have no special innate status, they are all important school attainments, and they all take hundreds of hours to acquire.' Interestingly, although dyslexia had been investigated from a large range of theoretical perspectives by the late 1980s, no researchers appeared to have adopted a learning framework, systematically assessing the various components of learning ability in dyslexic children. This was something of a puzzle, given that the key difficulty is that of learning to read (and that dyslexia is known as 'learning disability' in the US and 'specific learning difficulties' in the UK). Consequently, in our initial research we adopted a learning, or skill-acquisition, perspective. We preface our dyslexia research with a brief overview of theories of learning. Fuller introductions are given in Nicolson (1998, 1999).

Theories of learning

Humans are learners par excellence. The frog is equipped with innate 'hard-wired' reflexes that equip it perfectly for an amphibious fly-rich existence. If a fly-sized object moves at suitable speed within its range, it shoots out its tongue with marvellous aim and dexterity and swallows it (whether fly or no). Startle it and it will jump towards blue light (a pond typically). Surround the frog with dead flies only and it will starve. Surround it with blue paper . . . Humans have the invaluable gift of adapting to their specific environment, and we appear to exploit all the opportunities offered for adaptation via learning. In particular, we have the ability, through long practice under the right conditions, to 'automatize' arbitrary skills so that they are as fluent as those of the frog. Whereas the frog has a built-in 'fly catching' module specified in its DNA, given appropriate experiences and hundreds of hours of practice we can build our own modules to suit our environment – a process that Karmiloff-Smith (1993) calls 'progressive modularization'. We will outline some of the learning processes available.

Cell-level learning

The brain appears to be specialized for detecting synchronicity. This makes sense. If cells responding to visual stimuli and cells responding to auditory stimuli fire simultaneously, the chances are they are responding to the same event. The Hebb rule states 'cells that fire together wire together', that is, the connection between them is strengthened, and so in due course an assembly of cells may be created. A further law appears to be 'respond or die' in that, if a connection between cells does not provide a changing signal, that connection will wither. These basic processes provide the basis for complex learning possibilities.

Specialization

It is known that a six-month-old infant can discriminate any sound in any human languages. Paradoxically, three months later the infant will have lost the ability to discriminate the majority of sounds, and will have specialized on those categories of sound important in the language(s) it actually experiences. This specialization is an early case of modularization, with the auditory cortex and the language areas of the cortex adapting their cells, synapses and organization to exploit the features of the heard environment. This process may well involve substantial degrees of cell death in the brain. These specialization processes can occur at any time in life, but become progressively more difficult to achieve. A similar process is involved in learning to read, or to play tennis. Once a specialization has occurred, it is difficult to undo. The fact that the human brain is designed to change itself quite fundamentally as a function of experience is an astonishing feature that bestows significant evolutionary advantages. Unfortunately, it is not a feature for which there is a suitable analogy to help us comprehend the implications. The standard modern analogy of 'brain as computer' completely fails to model the self-adaptation aspect. Consequently, there is a real danger that theorists make the apparently reasonable assumption that the processes of adult learning are similar to those of infant learning. This is just not so, and without apology we repeat some purple prose from Nicolson (1999: 341):

> Birth literally draws back the veils from the outside world. The world's finest learning machine, primed and ready, takes centre stage. Inbuilt reflexes let the child root to find the mother's nipple. The combination of touch, sight, taste, smell, sucking sounds, muscular sensation and internal reinforcement combine to create a heady brew of multisensory information rarely equalled subsequently. The newly built cortex receives a volley of information that stimulates

important connections between those areas of cortex and subcortical structures that receive input from the senses. From these input centres, neuronal axons grow, synapses form, then wither or flourish via the Hebb rule, forming an ever increasing network of villages. Pathways between like-minded villages become established, and villages group together into towns of specialists. Eventually, highways between towns become established. Confederations evolve for the efficient processing of important information – eye control, hand control, auditory processing, visual processing, and (later) hand-eye coordination. The mental world is in a constant state of dynamic change, with continual pressure to react faster, to process more efficiently, to deliver a better quality of product. Outdated structures decline and fall, and their workforce is recycled. An awesome blend of capitalism and socialism!

For adults, the situation is very different. The country has been settled, the major cities, institutions and communication networks are established. It is possible still to have significant changes in organisation, as witnessed most starkly, following major damage to the brain, by the really quite exceptional abilities to recover, over time, considerable function, and, more routinely following significant changes in lifestyle. Nonetheless, the inertia of the system, in which modes of thinking and action become more and more strongly established, means that most developments are of an incremental nature, with new knowledge being assimilated into the existing structures, and new skills being developments of those that have already been learned.

Proceduralization

If we are trying to acquire a skill – whether it be walking, talking or driving – a key requirement is to 'proceduralize' it. That is, to develop a series of muscle commands that execute the skill. A child may attempt this by imitation, and typically the first efforts are slow and inaccurate, but with practice the skill becomes more and more fluent. Most parts of the brain are involved in most skills, but for proceduralization the cerebellum is a key structure in increasing fluency and co-ordination. Normally the processes of procedural skill learning and execution are not consciously accessible.

Declarative learning

In addition to learning, humans' major strength is language. Of course language is learned, possibly in much the same way that other skills are learned (see Elman et al., 1997; Pinker, 1995 for opposing views). However, once one has language, this bootstraps a completely new method of learning – by being told. This allows a child to learn about things that are not physically present, and events that have not been physically experienced. Thus arbitrarily complex knowledge structures can be built up over time, leading to the formation of a rich semantic memory.

Declarative (factual/linguistic) learning is thought to be scaffolded by the hippocampus (McClelland, McNaughton and O'Reilly, 1995), and is available to conscious introspection.

Learning complex skills – the three stage model

Based on an earlier model of motor skill learning (Fitts and Posner, 1967), Anderson (1982) provided a major theoretical framework around this analysis of skill with his ACT (adaptive control of thought) architecture for cognition. He argued that the first stage requires the storing of the facts involved (declarative knowledge), and that the key to actually carrying out the task was to convert this declarative knowledge (knowledge that) to procedural knowledge (knowledge how). It is all very well to know that in order to change gear in a car one has to depress the clutch, move the gear stick to the appropriate slot, then release the clutch pedal, synchronizing the release with depression of the throttle. Learners spend weeks trying to acquire the knack of actually doing it. Early efforts require a careful, step at a time procedure, where one has to consciously attend to each step, then remember what the next step is, do that, and so on. Later efforts not only execute each step more efficiently but also combine the sequence of steps into a single, smooth operation. The final stage of learning is known as the autonomous or automatic stage. Once the skill is proceduralized, after much more practice it may become automatic – no longer requiring attention, downloaded to lower centres such as the cerebellum to oversee execution. Using an important distinction introduced by Shiffrin and Schneider (1977), in terms of execution the skill has moved from 'controlled processing' (under conscious, attentional control) to 'automatic processing'.

Acquiring world-class expertise

We all know (either personally or through the television) people whose levels of skill at a particular task are quite extraordinary. Ericsson (for example Ericsson, Krampe and Heizmann, 1993) has made extensive studies of the way in which world-class expertise develops. First he highlights the difference between two different sorts of practice – 'play' (an unstructured, enjoyable method of practice) and 'deliberate practice' (in which individualized training is given on tasks selected by a qualified teacher). Following analyses of people acquiring a range of expertise (including music, sport and chess) Ericsson proposed that there were four phases in acquiring expertise.

In phase 1 practice takes the form of play. Most people never get beyond this stage, but those who are going to progress then typically are taught how to perform the skill better (phase 2). There is rapid improvement to begin with, but then diminishing returns set in, with each hour of practice leading to smaller and smaller amounts of progress. If the person wishes to proceed, it is then necessary to get a coach, an expert, to give further individual training (phase 3). It is rare to get to the final, expert, stage with much less than a thousand hours of practice. This is often referred to as the 10-year rule (Bloom, 1985): it is rare to achieve expert performance without at least 10 years' practice. The point we wish to stress here is that reading is by no means a natural skill. Only a few centuries ago, anyone able to read at all was considered near genius. Our modern educational system requires all our children to acquire routinely a skill that is properly considered 'world class'. It is not surprising that many do not achieve this, whether or not they are dyslexic.

The automatization deficit hypothesis

We are at last in position to return to dyslexia. It is evident that a learning perspective, and in particular the concept of automaticity, should be of use in analyses of reading problems. Consider the conclusions of an influential overview and analysis of the teaching of reading: 'Laboratory research indicates that the most critical factor beneath fluent word reading is the ability to recognise letters, spelling patterns, and whole words effortlessly, automatically and visually. The central goal of all reading instruction – comprehension – depends critically on this ability' (Adams, 1990: 54). There is also evidence that, even when dyslexic children have managed to acquire reasonably good literacy skills, their reading is slower, more effortful, less automatic than normal readers of the same reading age. Consequently we decided to explore the concept of automaticity. As noted earlier, theoretical accounts of skill development made no clear distinction between motor skills and cognitive skills. We therefore boldly proposed the 'dyslexic automatization deficit' hypothesis (Nicolson and Fawcett, 1990) – namely that dyslexic children have abnormal difficulties in making skills automatic, despite extensive practice, regardless of whether the skill is cognitive or motor. The reason that dyslexia theorists had not seriously considered learning as a viable framework is that it fails to explain the apparent specificity of the deficits in dyslexia (Stanovich, 1988). If they have a general problem in learning, why do dyslexic children not show problems in all skills, cognitive and motor? In our approach to this difficulty we were encouraged first by the observation that, whatever skill theorists had examined carefully, a deficit had been observed in dyslexic children. Furthermore, careful observation of dyslexic children suggests that, although they appear to be behaving normally, they show unusual lapses of concentration and get tired more quickly than normal when performing a skill (Augur, 1985). In the words of the parent of one of our subject panel, life for a child with dyslexia might be like living in a foreign country, where it is possible to get by adequately but only at the expense of continual concentration and effort. Therefore, in parallel with the DAD hypothesis, we coined the 'conscious compensation' hypothesis, namely that, despite their more limited automaticity of skill, dyslexic children are able to perform at apparently normal levels most of the time by 'consciously compensating', that is consciously concentrating (controlled processing) on performance that might normally be automatic processing.

Phase 1: balance and automaticity

Our first set of experiments provided a critical test of the DAD/CC hypothesis. We reasoned that there was little point choosing tasks related to reading or language, in that existing empirical data suggested that there should be deficits there. A more rigorous test of the theory was for a skill in which there was thought to be little or no deficit. Consequently, in a rigorous test of the hypothesis, we investigated a range of fine and gross motor skills on the basis that these have absolutely no linguistic involvement and so any deficits found would be hard to explain via the phonological deficit hypothesis. The results with the strongest theoretical interpretation derive from the gross motor skill of balance (Nicolson and Fawcett, 1990), since this is one of the most practised of all skills, and thus the most likely to be completely automatized. The subjects were 23 dyslexic children around 13 years old (defined in terms of a standard discrepancy/exclusionary criterion used in all the studies – namely children of normal or above normal IQ, operationalized as IQ of 90 or more on the Wechsler Intelligence Scale for Children (Wechsler, 1976; 1992), without known primary emotional, behavioural or socioeconomic problems, whose reading age was at least 18 months behind their chronological age – in subsequent work we also screened them to make sure they did not also suffer from ADHD) and eight normally-achieving children, with groups matched overall for age and IQ. Performance was monitored for three tasks: standing on both feet (one foot directly in front of the other); standing on one foot; and walking. The balance tasks were performed under two conditions: single task balance, in which the subjects had merely to balance, and dual task balance, in which they had to balance while undertaking a further secondary task. Two secondary tasks were used: either counting or performing a choice reaction task. Each secondary task was initially 'calibrated' so as to be of equivalent difficulty for each subject, by adjusting the task difficulty (for counting) or by providing extended training (for choice reactions) so that, under 'just counting' or 'just choice reaction' conditions all subjects fell into the same performance band.

The results were exactly as predicted by the automatization deficit/conscious compensation hypothesis. Under single task balance conditions there was no difference in balance between the groups. Under dual task conditions the dyslexic children showed a highly significant impairment in balance (indicating lack of automaticity for balance) whereas the control children showed no deficit (indicating balance automaticity). Even more convincing, in addition to the significant differences at the group level, the pattern of performance also applied to almost all the individuals, with 22 out of the 23 dyslexic children showing a decrement under dual task conditions whereas most of the controls actually improved (owing, no doubt, to the effect of practice).

One problem with the dual task impairments is that it is not clear whether the impairment is attributable to prevention of conscious compensation (as predicted by DAD) or some more general attentional deficit that causes impairments whenever two tasks must be performed simultaneously. In order to discriminate between these accounts we performed a further series of experiments (Fawcett and Nicolson, 1992) in which we blindfolded the subjects, thereby preventing conscious compensation but not introducing the complications of a dual task paradigm. As predicted, the group of dyslexic children showed much greater impairment than the controls when blindfolded, further support for the DAD/CC hypothesis (Figure 6.1).

Phase 2: primitive skills and dyslexia

At this stage in our research programme, on reviewing the literature we found a pattern of results from individual research groups, in which each group came up with an interesting and original hypothesis, tested it, found that their dyslexic group had impaired performance, and concluded that their hypothesis was supported. Different groups had found problems in phonology, speed, motor skill, visual flicker, binocular control, and auditory perception. We considered that an important priority was to see whether a given child was likely to show specific deficits (say phonology only) or a range of deficits.

We developed a research design that included six groups of children – three groups of dyslexic children at ages eight, 13 and 17 years, together with three groups of normally achieving children matched for age and IQ. Furthermore, the two older groups of dyslexic children were also matched

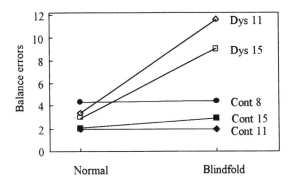

Figure 6.1: Balance and blindfold balance.

for reading age with the two younger groups of controls (D17 with C13, D13 with C8). This design allows a number of different analyses to be performed, and provides a method of investigating the effects of maturation on the skills involved.

The specific issues addressed in the research programme were: first, what proportion of dyslexic children showed each type of deficit; second, whether there is some deficit which is the 'primary' one, which underlies the other deficits, and third, whether it is possible to identify different subtypes of dyslexia, such that each subtype has discriminably different characteristics. Our hope was that the data collected might inform the development of an explanatory framework sufficiently general to accommodate the diversity of the deficits in dyslexia, while sufficiently specific to generate testable predictions, to support better diagnostic procedures, and to inform remediation methods.

Skill tests

One of the problems of investigating a disorder of reading is that the process of reading is so complex, requiring the fluent interplay of a number of subskills together with the smooth integration of lexical, phonological and orthographic knowledge. A deficit in any or all of these components would lead to problems in learning to read. Furthermore, because reading is a crucial school attainment, considerable and varied efforts may be made to train the component skills and this differential training experience leads to further difficulties in interpretation of any differences in reading ability. In an attempt to minimize confounding factors arising from differences in experience together with use of compensatory strategies, we decided to test 'primitive' skills in the major modalities – skills that are not normally trained explicitly, and are not easily subject to compensatory strategies. In addition to psychometric tests, four types of test were used namely tests of phonological skill, working memory, information processing speed, and motor skill (Fawcett and Nicolson, 1994; 1995a; 1995b).

In order to make it easier to compare between tests, the results for each test have been converted to the age-equivalent scores, taking the data from our control groups together with control data from other studies where possible (Figure 6.2).

In almost all tests of naming speed, phonological skill, motor skill, and also non-word repetition and articulation rate, the dyslexic children performed significantly worse than their chronological age controls. In general, the performance of the dyslexic children was somewhat below that of their reading age controls, but significant differences compared with reading age controls were obtained only for simple reaction (better performance than the reading age controls) and phonological skills, picture naming speed, bead threading and balance under dual task conditions or when blindfolded (worse than reading age controls).

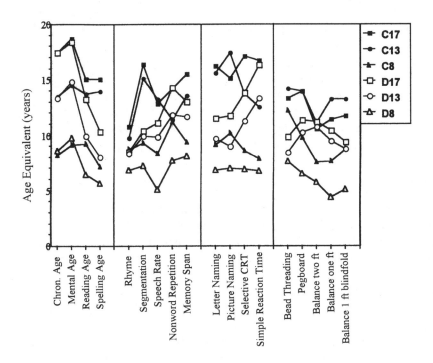

Figure 6.2: Comparative performance of the six groups on selected tests.

Furthermore, it may also be seen that the performance of the oldest dyslexic children is by no means better overall than that of the youngest controls, despite the advantage of around nine years' experience.

A key issue, however, was whether most of the individual dyslexic children showed an impairment in most of the skills, or whether the significant between-group differences derived from just a few dyslexic children. Each child was scored 'at risk' if his or her performance fell more than one standard deviation below the mean score of the same-age control group. Inspection of the individual data revealed that, of the 33 dyslexic children who attempted both one foot blindfold balance and dual task balance, only three (two in the D15 group, and one in the D8 group) were not scored at risk on either task. Even these three showed a deficit in two feet blindfold balance. Balance difficulties, especially when blindfolded, appear therefore to be associated with all our sample of dyslexic children. By contrast, only two out of the 32 controls completing at least two of these tasks showed a marked impairment on two or more tasks. Furthermore, taking three disparate tests (dual task balance, segmentation and picture naming speed), 29 of the 32 dyslexic children (90%) who undertook all three were 'at risk' on at least two. If there are pure phonological dyslexics, they were poorly represented in our sample.

Phase 3: investigating long-term learning

One of the most severe limitations of the above work (and, indeed, of almost all dyslexia research apart from the longitudinal studies discussed in this book) is that the investigations involve a 'snapshot' of the abilities of various groups of children at one point in time. We can infer from differences in performance for children of different ages what the likely development of the skills might be, but for a sensitive analysis it is crucial to follow a child's performance over a period of time, while he or she acquires a skill. This time-consuming (for child and tester) procedure was the basis of the following study.

Blending of primitive subskills into a temporal skill

The above studies led to the intriguing finding that the dyslexic children had normal speed of simple reaction (SRT). However, when a choice needed to be made, the dyslexic children were differentially affected by the increase in task complexity (see also Nicolson and Fawcett, 1994a). In an attempt to identify why this was, we subsequently undertook a further, theoretically motivated, long-term training study investigating the time course of the blending of two separate simple reactions into a choice reaction (CRT) – one of two long-term training studies reported in Nicolson and Fawcett (2000) but completed in 1993.

In order to avoid any problems of left-right confusions or of stimulus discriminability, we used two stimuli of different modalities (tone and flash) and different effectors (hand and foot) for the two stimuli. Twenty-two subjects participated, 11 dyslexic and 11 control matched for age and IQ. In brief, following baseline performance monitoring on simple reaction to each stimulus separately (counterbalanced so that half the subjects had the hand-button paired with the tone, and the foot-button paired with the flash, and the other half vice versa) the two simple reaction tasks were combined into a choice reaction task in which half the stimuli were tones and half flashes, and the subject had to press the corresponding button, using the mapping established in the simple reactions. Each session comprised three runs, each of 100 stimuli, and subjects kept returning every fortnight or so until their performance stopped improving (in terms of speed and accuracy). The results are shown in Figure 6.3.

Analysis of the SRT performance indicated that there were no significant differences between the groups either for foot or hand, tone or flash. By contrast, initial performance on the CRT was significantly slower, and final performance was both significantly slower and less accurate for the dyslexic children. Initially the dyslexic group made slightly (but not significantly) more errors (13.8% versus 10.6%) indicating that the initial deficit

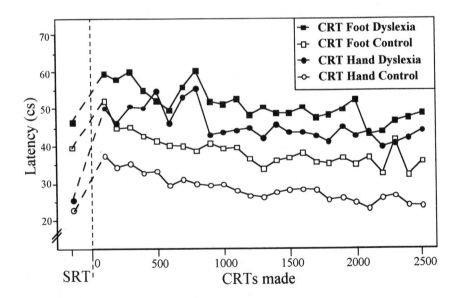

Figure 6.3: Median latencies over the period of CRT training.

cannot be attributable to some speed-accuracy trade-off by one group of children. However, by the final session the dyslexic group made around twice as many errors on average (9.1% versus 4.6%). Average learning rate for latency and accuracy was lower, but not significantly so, for the dyslexic group. Final choice reaction performance was very significantly both slower and less accurate than that of the controls both for hand and foot responses. Comparison of final hand and foot latency with the initial baseline SRT performance led to a dissociation, with both groups having significantly shorter final CRT latency than SRT latency for the foot responses, whereas for the hand responses the control group had equivalent latencies and the dyslexic group had significantly longer final CRT than SRT latencies.

In order to obtain more accurate estimates of the learning rates for completion times and errors, the group data were fitted using a parametric technique which has been established as the most appropriate for fitting human data on practice (Newell and Rosenbloom, 1981). In brief, the curve fitted is the 'power law', $P(n) = A + Bn^{-\alpha}$ – where $P(n)$ refers to performance on trial n, A is the asymptotic performance as n tends to infinity (taken as 0 here), B is a scaling parameter linked directly to initial performance, and α is the learning rate. A parametric learning rate analysis was then performed using the power law equation outlined above. The best fit curves for hand response CRT were $t = 53.9\ n^{-0.073}$ for the dyslexic children and $t = 39.4\ n^{-0.141}$ for the controls. For the foot responses the corresponding best-fit curves were $t = 62.3\ n^{-0.086}$; $t = 50.4\ n^{-0.116}$ respectively. The parameter B was higher for the dyslexic children than the controls (around 30% on average), reflecting the slower initial performance on the CRT. Even more interesting, however, is the difference in learning rate, α which was about 1.5 times faster for the controls than the dyslexic children (0.141 versus 0.073; 0.116 versus. 0.086 for the hand and foot responses respectively). This is a huge difference. Bearing in mind that the learning varies as a function of the time to the power α, if a skill takes a normal child 100 hours to master, it would take a dyslexic child $100^{1.5}$ – or 1,000 hours (10 times as long) to learn the skill to the same criterion!

In summary, the dyslexic children appeared to have greater difficulty in blending existing skills into a new skill, and their performance after extensive practice (such that the skill was no longer improving noticeably) was slower and more error-prone. In other words, they were simply less skilled, their 'quality' of automatized performance was lower. It seems reasonable, therefore, to argue that this group of dyslexic children has difficulties with the initial proceduralization of skill, and with the 'quality' of skill post training. If the CRT training results apply to dyslexic children generally, and apply to tasks other than choice reactions, we are led to a radically new prediction for dyslexic performance, namely that rather than being at the level of children of their own age, or even, as is often considered the appropriate control group, children of the same reading age, the performance of dyslexic children on any task will be comparable with that of much younger children, with the amount of impairment increasing as the square root of the necessary learning time.

Phase 4: fundamental processes of learning

Despite the intriguing findings of the above research, we have barely scratched the surface of learning and its different forms. One fundamental issue is the mechanism by which the learning difficulties arise. One strong possibility, as we discuss in our chapter on the cerebellum and dyslexia, is that the difficulties arise from cerebellar abnormality. Another possibility (Stein and Walsh, 1997) is that cerebellar performance is essentially normal, but that poor quality (in terms of timing or signal to noise ratio) of input to the cerebellum is in fact the true cause. A further fundamental issue is whether there is homogeneity or heterogeneity in dyslexic children regarding the learning difficulties. It is evident that outside the reading domain the symptoms shown by dyslexic people are very variable, a finding that has led many theorists to posit the existence of subtypes of dyslexia (Boder, 1973; Castles and Coltheart, 1993). We consider that these issues can only be addressed by carefully designed studies designed to isolate and investigate the different types of learning, and their relative efficacy in dyslexic children.

Eyeblink conditioning and dyslexia

The eyeblink study (Nicolson, Daum, Schugens, Fawcett and Schulz, 2000) was designed to investigate the above issues directly by examining one of the fundamental processes of learning, namely classical conditioning (Pavlov, 1927). Students of psychology will remember that Pavlov 'conditioned' his dogs to salivate to a tone.

The most frequently used classical conditioning procedure for humans (Steinmetz, 1999) is eyeblink conditioning, which involves presentation of a tone followed after a fixed time interval by a puff of air to the eye. The eye then blinks, following the normal reflex. Interestingly, however, after a number of paired tone–airpuff presentations, the eyeblink occurs to the tone, before the airpuff. The eyeblink to the tone is known as the 'conditioned' response (CR). The essential neuronal circuit underlying eyeblink conditioning is thought to involve the convergence of tone and airpuff information in the cerebellum (for a summary see Thompson and Krupa, 1994).

Thirteen dyslexic subjects (12 male, one female, mean age 19.5 years) and 13 control subjects (11 male, two female) matched for age and IQ participated. The conditioning procedure used was that administered in the studies demonstrating eyeblink conditioning deficits in patients with selective cerebellar damage (Daum et al., 1993). In the experiment, for 60 acquisition trials an 800 ms auditory tone was presented. On 70% of the trials an 80 ms corneal airpuff was presented 720 ms after the tone onset. Following the 60 acquisition trials 10 extinction trials without the airpuff were presented. The cerebellar deficit hypothesis, uniquely of the causal hypotheses for dyslexia, predicts that the dyslexic participants would show abnormal performance in the incidence and/or timing of the conditioned response (CR) of an eyeblink in response to the tone.

Three of the dyslexic group showed no conditioning at all. Furthermore, normally subjects show 'tuning' of the CR, so that, over the course of the conditioning, it occurs closer and closer to the onset of the airpuff. Unlike for the control group, the dyslexic group showed no such tuning from the initial to the final acquisition block ($p < 0.05$). Furthermore, subjects initially make an orienting response (OR) of looking towards the tone source when the tone is presented, but this normally habituates (i.e., they stop making it) rapidly over the first few blocks. The dyslexic group showed significantly slower OR habituation than the controls ($p < 0.05$).

Individual analyses indicated that 3 (23%) of the dyslexic group showed no conditioning at all; a further five (39%) showed no tuning; and a further three (23%) showed poor OR habituation (as did three of the poor tuning subjects). Rather surprisingly, four of the controls showed low conditioning, though all showed relatively normal CR tuning and all bar one showed normal OR habituation. In short, although the procedure revealed inhomogeneity in the dyslexic group, 85% of the dyslexic group showed either: no conditioning; abnormally poor CR tuning and/or abnormally low OR habituation.

Discussion

In summary, generally the findings of our early studies provide strong support for the automatization deficit account at the 'cognitive' theory level. The automatization deficit account holds that the general resource ceiling is normal but that many skills do not become automatized as quickly as normal. Therefore, problems arise primarily for those skills that are not automatic. Furthermore, the relative difficulties of dyslexic children become disproportionately more marked as the length of time needed to master the skill increases (our square root rule, described above). Consequently, if one wishes to minimize the literacy problems of dyslexic children it is necessary to give specialized teaching designed to automatize the subskills involved via carefully designed, carefully monitored and long-term training programmes. This is directly consistent with established good practice guidelines for supporting dyslexic children (Gillingham and Stillman, 1960; Hickey, 1992; Hulme, 1981; Miles, 1989), which stress that an exceptionally structured, explicit, systematic and comprehensive approach is needed, progressing in a series of small steps, with each step mastered before the next one is introduced.

The results therefore do directly support well-established good practice guidelines derived over decades of applied work. The finding is not wholly unexpected therefore, though it should be noted that theoretical and applied educational results do not always match perfectly! More importantly, the automatization deficit account provides an underlying rationale for existing support practice, thereby allowing the full power of the cognitive theories of learning, automatization and their optimization (for example, Anderson, 1982; Eccles, Ito and Szentagothai, 1967; Ericsson et al., 1993; Shiffrin and Schneider, 1977) to be applied to the design of more cost-effective learning procedures for dyslexic children. It is our hope that it will be possible in future to optimize dyslexia support procedures so as not only to foster the development of automaticity but also to avoid the undoubted tedium that is the drawback of many mastery approaches (Nicolson and Fawcett, 1994b).

The more recent findings, and especially the eyeblink conditioning findings, are consistent with the general theme of automatization deficit, but they raise a range of intriguing questions regarding the fundamental processes of learning, and individual differences between dyslexic children. The findings suggest that, while in general the problems can be described as consistent with incomplete automatization, more sensitive learning-based analyses indicate that different dyslexic children may have different fundamental problems. Some show relatively slow habituation, some show little or no conditioning, and others show poor 'tuning' of response to situation. It seems very likely that these factors will have extremely significant implications for support of individual children. We consider that the time is now ripe for very much more systematic analyses, following the approach we adopted for our primitive skills, but this time analysing and investigating the various primitive forms of learning that we outlined in the introduction.

If we were able to devise a 'taxonomy of learning', together with a series of specific tests for each format, we would at last be able to implement the dream of many applied dyslexia theorists. Before a child reached school, and well before he or she failed to learn to read, we would be able to administer a screening test, identify those at risk, carry out a series of further fundamental tests of different processes, and identify the profile of strengths and weaknesses. Then for each child, we could recommend specific interventions – depending on the problems these might involve sensory support (auditory or visual), sensory training, or phonological training. This should then lead to an 'individual support plan' designed to overcome (if possible) the weaknesses, or at least make clear recommendations as to the forms of teaching appropriate to that child. We would then be in position to fulfil the goal of that charismatic figure in early applied dyslexia research, Dr Harry Chasty. Rather than forcing a child to learn the way we teach, we could teach the way the child learns.

References

Adams MJ (1990) Beginning to Read: Thinking and learning about print. Cambridge MA: MIT Press.

Anderson JR (1982) Acquisition of cognitive skill. Psychological Review 89: 369–406.

Augur J (1985) Guidelines for teachers, parents and learners. In MJ Snowling (ed.) Childrens' Written Language Difficulties. Slough: NFER-NELSON, pp. 147.

Bloom BS (1985) Generalizations about talent development. In BS Bloom (ed.) Developing Talent in Young People. New York: Ballantine Books, pp. 507–49.

Boder E (1973) Developmental dyslexia: a diagnostic approach based on three atypical spelling-reading patterns. Developmental Medicine and Child Neurology 15: 663–87.

Castles A, Coltheart M (1993) Varieties of developmental dyslexia. Cognition 47: 149–80.

Daum I, Schugens MM, Ackermann H, Lutzenberger W, Dichgans J, Birbaumer N (1993) Classical conditioning after cerebellar lesions in humans. Behavioral Neuroscience 107: 748–56.

Eccles JC, Ito M, Szentagothai J (1967) The Cerebellum as a Neuronal Machine. New York: Springer-Verlag.

Elman, J. E., Bates, E. A., Johnson, M. H., Karmiloff-Smith, A., Parisi, D, Plunkett K (1997) Rethinking innateness: a connectionist perspective on development. Cambridge MA: MIT Press.

Ericsson KA, Krampe RT, Heizmann S (1993) The role of deliberate practice in the acquisition of expert performance. Psychological Review 100: 363–406.

Fawcett AJ, Nicolson, RI (1992) Automatisation deficits in balance for dyslexic children. Perceptual-and-Motor-Skills 75(2): 507–29.

Fawcett AJ, Nicolson RI (1994) Naming speed in children with dyslexia. Journal of Learning Disabilities 27: 641–6.

Fawcett AJ, Nicolson RI (1995a) Persistence of phonological awareness deficits in older children with dyslexia. Reading and Writing 7: 361–76.

Fawcett AJ, Nicolson RI (1995b) Persistent deficits in motor skill for children with dyslexia. Journal of Motor Behavior 27: 235–41.

Fitts PM, Posner MI (1967) Human Performance. Belmont CA: Brooks Cole.

Frith U (1997) Brain, mind and behaviour in dyslexia. In C Hulme, M Snowling (eds) Dyslexia: Biology, cognition and intervention. London: Whurr.

Gillingham A, Stillman B (1960) Remedial Training for Children with Specific Difficulties in Reading, Writing and Penmanship. Cambridge MA: Educators Publishing.

Hickey K (1992) (eds J. Augur and S. Briggs) The Hickey Multisensory Language Course. 2 edn. London: Whurr.

Hulme C (1981) Reading Retardation and Multisensory Learning. London: Routledge & Kegan Paul.

Karmiloff-Smith A (1993) Beyond Modularity: A developmental perspective on cognitive science. Cambridge MA: MIT Press.

McClelland JL, McNaughton BL, O'Reilly RC (1995) Why there are complementary learning systems in the hippocampus and neocortex: insights from the successes and failures of connectionist models of learning and memory. Psychological Review 192: 419–57.

Miles E (1989) The Bangor Dyslexia Teaching System. London: Whurr.

Newell A, Rosenbloom PS (1981) Mechanisms of skill acquisition and the law of practice. In JR Anderson (ed.) Cognitive Skills and their Acquisition. Hillsdale NJ: Lawrence Erlbaum.

Nicolson RI (1998) Learning and skill. In P Scott, C Spencer (eds) Psychology: A contemporary introduction. Oxford: Blackwell, pp. 294–343.

Nicolson RI (1999) Reading, Skill and Dyslexia. In D Messer, S Millar (eds) Exploring Developmental Psychology. London: Arnold.

Nicolson RI, Daum I, Schugens MM, Fawcett AJ, Schulz A (2000) Abnormal eyeblink conditioning for dyslexic children. Experimental Brain Research, submitted.

Nicolson RI, Fawcett AJ (1990) Automaticity: a new framework for dyslexia research? Cognition 35(2): 159–82.

Nicolson RI, Fawcett AJ (1994a) Reaction times and dyslexia. Quarterly Journal of Experimental Psychology 47A: 29–48.

Nicolson RI, Fawcett AJ (1994b) Spelling remediation for dyslexic children: a skills approach. In GDA Brown, NC Ellis (eds) Handbook of Spelling (Theory), Process and Intervention. Chichester: JohnWiley.

Nicolson RI, Fawcett AJ (2000) Long-term learning in dyslexic children. European Journal of Cognitive Psychology 12: 357–93.

Pavlov IP (1927) Conditioned Reflexes. Oxford: Oxford University Press.

Pinker S (1995) The language instinct :the new science of language and mind. Harmondsworth: Penguin Books.

Shiffrin RM, Schenider W (1977). Controlled and automatic human information processing II: Perceptual learning, automatic attending and general theory. Psychological Review 84: 127–90.

Stanovich KE (1988) The right and wrong places to look for the cognitive locus of reading disability. Annals of Dyslexia 38: 154–77.

Stein J, Walsh V (1997). To see but not to read; the magnocellular theory of dyslexia. Trends in Neurosciences 20: 147–52.

Steinmetz JE (1999) A renewed interest in human classical eyeblink conditioning. Psychological Science 10(1): 24–5.

Thompson RF, Krupa DJ (1994) Organization of memory traces in the mammalian brain. Annual Review of Neuroscience 17: 519–49.

Wechsler D (1976) Wechsler Intelligence Scale for Children Revised (WISC-R). Slough: NFER.

Wechsler D (1992) Wechsler Intelligence Scale for Children. 3 edn. Sidcup, Kent: The Psychological Corporation.

World Federation of Neurology (1968) Report of Research Group on Dyslexia and World Illiteracy. Dallas: WFN.

CHAPTER 7

The study of infant cognitive processes in dyslexia

ARYAN VAN DER LEIJ, HEIKKI LYYTINEN, FRANS ZWARTS

Introduction

In our modern literate society, reading ability is considered to be one of the most important cognitive and communicative skills. For this reason, developmental dyslexia has intrigued educators, linguists, neurologists, and psychologists for over a century. Poor reading skills seriously affect school achievements and interfere with the acquisition of knowledge from written sources, and many thousands of studies have been carried out with the purpose of identifying the core features of this multifaceted disorder. In spite of these efforts and despite considerable progression towards the definition of both the genetic and behavioural phenotype, the etiology of a 'bottleneck' in the acquisition of those complex skills and abilities that underlie the reading process is still not fully understood.

One very important observation is that common forms of dyslexia are hereditary. Large-scale studies have recently confirmed the risk of familial transmission (for example Smith, Kimberling, Pennington, and Lubs, 1983; DeFries, Fulker, and LaBuda, 1987; Gilger, Pennington, and DeFries, 1991; Pennington, 1995). The median risk of a dyslexic son having an affected father is 0.35 and the risk of having an affected mother is 0.15. For daughters, the median risk estimates are 0.41 and 0.33 for an affected father and mother respectively. Unfortunately, family studies are typically retrospective in nature, where the affectation status of parents is determined after the family has been identified through an affected child. Circularly, given that a parent is dyslexic, this means that we cannot directly calculate the probability of offspring being reading-disabled. However, an indirect method using inverse Bayesian analyses, does provide a means of estimating the likelihood that a child will be affected. This shows that given a reading-impaired parent, the posterior probability that a child will be dyslexic is considerable, for example, a median of 0.43 for male offspring of dyslexic men and of 0.19 for female offspring of dyslexic men (Gilger, Pennington, and DeFries, 1991).

Thus, taking children from 'dyslexic' families as subjects, the phenomenon of familial transmission can be used to design prospective studies to uncover the causes of difficulties in the acquisition of reading skills. In her pioneering study, Scarborough (1989, 1990, 1991) followed high-risk children from the age of 30 months and was successful in revealing precursors to dyslexia of a linguistic nature. This was all the more important as it was before an age when more specific markers of dyslexia such as phonemic awareness (see under theoretical and practical considerations) could reliably be observed. Scarborough's findings inspired a prospective longitudinal study in Finland, which started measurements when children were merely a few days old. More than 100 children, born with a familial risk for dyslexia were involved, and were complemented by a matched control group of equal size (Lyytinen H, Ahonen, Leiwo, Lyytinen et al., 1992; Lyytinen H, Ahonen, Leiwo, and Gilger, 1994). The first phase of this project started in 1992, while the second phase (1995–1997) extended until the age of 4 for the oldest subjects. The most recently funded period covers the follow-up of the children up to school age. In turn, the Finnish study, together with Molfese's studies (for example, Molfese and Molfese, 1997), provided the impetus in 1998 for a ten-year Dutch study that commenced measurement of the infants at the age of two months with the aim of following development up to the age of nine years, the time at which a reliable diagnosis of subjects who have developed dyslexia can be made. After some theoretical considerations, the Finnish and Dutch studies will be described in more detail.

Theoretical and practical considerations

Reading is a complex skill and there may be many reasons why children fail. Converging evidence indicates, however, that developmental dyslexia is a language disorder that critically affects the phonological domain of language. Phonological processing entails the segmental analysis of words during ordinary speaking and listening and incorporates and extends to the skills required for a more macro-analysis of the sound structure of speech and its transformation into the phonemic components represented by the alphabet. Many studies have shown dyslexic children to be 'inferior to same-age normal readers on such factors as perceptual discrimination of phonemes, phonological awareness measured by tasks requiring the isolation and manipulation of phonemes within words, speed and accuracy in lexical access for picture names, verbal short-term and working memory, syntactic awareness, and semantic processing in tasks such as listening comprehension' (Olson, 1994). Most, if not all of these weaknesses may arise from a subtle deficit in speech perception. Recent studies have provided ample evidence that heritable differences in spoken language skills – especially awareness of phonemic segments – lead to difficulties in the phonological coding of written language, which is a key prerequisite for word recognition and spelling ability. The processing problems manifested by dyslexics give rise to the most diagnostic symptom of reading impairment: difficulty in the pronunciation of pseudo-words (see Rack, Snowling and Olson, 1992, for a review). Although reading skills also contribute in a reciprocal manner to the development of phonological skills (Wagner and Torgesen, 1987), indications are that a phonological deficit is causal or at least contributes strongly to reading disability (Bradley and Bryant, 1983; Stanovich, 1988; Wagner, 1986).

Of particular importance to the study of early precursors of developmental dyslexia is the work concerning speech-perception deficits in the reading-impaired and which reports deviant patterns of sound identification and discrimination among poor readers. Godfrey, Syrdal-Lasky, Millay and Knox (1981) compared performance on two synthetic sound continua, [ba]-[da] and [da]-[ga], and found that dyslexic children were significantly less consistent in identification, even at the polarized extremes of the continua. Other studies have reported similar results for [ba]-[da] (Reed, 1989; Steffens, Eilers, Gross-Glenn, and Jallad, 1992) and for [sa]-[sta] (Steffens, Eilers, Gross-Glenn, and Jallad, 1992). In several of these studies, inconsistent identification also gave rise to deviant patterns of discrimination along synthetic continua. Impaired readers performed significantly worse than normal controls *between* phoneme categories but not *within*. This indicated that they could not easily exploit the phonological contrast that normally enhances discrimination across a phoneme boundary (De Weirdt, 1988; Godfrey, Syrdal-Lasky, Millay, and Knox, 1981). Such results suggest that perceptual speech categories may be more broad and less sharply separated in reading-disabled than in normal children (Mody, Studdert-Kennedy, and Brady, 1997; Reed, 1989; Studdert-Kennedy and Mody, 1995).

Although poor phonological skills are no doubt a core feature of the disorder, there are reasons for hesitancy in concluding that developmental dyslexia may be *exclusively* explained by deficits associated with phonological processing. A number of studies have shown that non-phonological features also differentiate between dyslexic and normal readers. Byrne (1981), Mann, Liberman, and Shankweiler (1980) and Stein, Cairns, and Zurif (1984) have tested dyslexic children on a variety of linguistic tasks and shown selective impairment along several grammatical dimensions, which Crain and Shankweiler (1987) and Shankweiler and Crain (1986) attribute to limitations in working memory. The hypothesis of limitations in the capacity of working memory has been supported recently by P de Jong (1998) who used a wide range of tasks relating to different aspects of working memory. Other processing variables that may be reliable indicators of persistent reading problems are rapid naming of well-known stimuli such as colours, objects, and, in particular, single digits and letters (Denckla and Rudel, 1976; Bowers and Wolf, 1993; Van Daal and Van der Leij, 1999). Moreover, there is evidence in favour of poor visual perception at low spatial frequencies (Lovegrove, Martin and Slaghuis, 1986) and low contrast (Livingstone, Rosen, Drislane and Galaburda, 1991). However, as was noted by Benton (1962) and Vellutino (1979a, 1979b), the main reason for the earlier rejection of the involvement of visual deficits in developmental dyslexia has been the consistent failure by many researchers to find differences between dyslexics and controls on a wide range of visual tasks. During the last 15 years, however, there have been several developments that challenge this position. A number of studies have demonstrated that dyslexic children may suffer from subtle visual perception problems which fail to lead to measurable consequences on ordinary psychological tests (for reviews, see Lovegrove, 1994; Stein, 1994). Differences between normal and poor readers do emerge once they are compared on visual tasks that are contingent on rapidly changing events in time (Lovegrove, Martin, and Slaghuis, 1986; Williams, Molinet, and LeCluyse, 1989). The findings suggest that dyslexics may differ from controls in the functioning of what is known as the transient visual system. This has led to the hypothesis that developmental dyslexia and many other language-related disorders are due to a pan-sensory timing deficit that affects the speed of processing (Tallal, Miller, and Fitch, 1993). A possible cause of these problems is an impairment based on the distribution of certain types of neurons in the brain called magnocells. Stein and Walsh (1997) have documented the possibility that this magnocellular impairment explains a number of observed multi-sensory characteristics and also co-morbid features found among individuals with dyslexia. The most extensively covered areas are auditory (phonetic), visual and motor problems associated with temporal processing. The cellular impairment means an atypical paucity or reduction in the size of magnocells, for example in the sensory (including thalamic), parietal and cerebellar areas of brain.

The fact that dyslexia is related to impairments on a wide range of abilities involving motor control and time estimation (including motor and timing aspects of speech processing) has led to the suggestion that a cerebellar abnormality may be involved in all these impairments (Nicolson and Fawcett, 1995; Fawcett, Nicolson, and Dean, 1996). According to these authors, reading in dyslexia is only one – albeit a very important – indication of a deficit in the automatization of a wide range of skills (Nicolson and Fawcett, 1990). As a consequence of the co-occurrence of dyslexia with so many other features of development and learning, a wide range of tasks and paradigms measuring linguistic features, working memory, auditory processing, visual perception, temporal processing, motor control, and skill automatization, should be part of the assessment programme. However, with respect to at least some of the associated characteristics, the co-occurrence of dyslexia with other developmental problems (co-morbidity) should also be taken into account because there seems to be considerable overlap with disorders such as dyscalculia and ADHD. Badian (1983), for instance, found that 2.7% of elementary school and junior high school children displayed both mathematical and reading disorders, whereas 2.2 % had only dyslexia and 3.6% only dyscalculia. In the study of White, Moffit, and Silva (1992) these proportions were 10.1%, 4.3% and 2.7%, respectively. In a sample of 80 dyslexic Finnish children (IQ > 80), 28 % were diagnosed as having problems in mathematics, 47% as having attention problems, and 11% as having both (Lyytinen, Ahonen, and Räsänen, 1994). In a current Dutch study using subjects from a complete school district, 15 of 46 12-year old students with learning disabilities and normal verbal intelligence could be called 'pure' dyslexics, whereas 15 combined dyslexia with mathematical disabilities and 16 had mathematical disabilities only (Van der Leij and Van Daal, 2001). Recent twin studies also show that there is a clear genetic overlap between reading and attention disorders (Gilger, Pennington, and DeFries, 1992; Gillis, Gilger, Pennington, and DeFries, 1992). From the findings of August and Garfinkel (1990), Duncan et al. (1994), and Stevenson, Pennington, Gilger, DeFries, and Gillis (1993) it may, in fact, be inferred that 25–50% of the dyslexic population also suffers from attention deficit hyperactivity disorder (ADHD). It is possible that some of the reported non-phonological features are more related to co-occurring disorders and do not belong to the core features of dyslexia, as is tentatively suggested by Wimmer, Mayringer and Landerl (1998).

To make the picture even more complex, the focus should not be restricted to individual features. Although the heritability of developmental dyslexia has received convincing support, according to bio-ecological models (for example, Bronfenbrenner and Ceci, 1994), the influence of the environment should always be taken into account. Hypothetically, at a younger age, the quality of the home environment may be more or less effective for the development of subtle cognitive and linguistic impairments and should be taken into account. Stanovich (1986) argues convincingly that reading-disabled children may undergo developmental changes in aptitude as a consequence of the negative interaction between their deficits and the environment. When the environment is not sufficiently stimulating, impairments that may be quite specific early on may later extend to other domains of cognitive functioning and undermine internal motivation. In fact, it remains doubtful as to whether instruction at a late stage, after some years of failure in regular schools, will effectively remediate the deficits and lags in aptitude. In short, if reading difficulties are not treated early, the prognosis generally appears to be poor.

As a possible pay-off for practice, the study of early precursors may demarcate the guidelines for early treatment. Although nothing is yet known with respect to treatment of genetically at-risk children in the years before they enter school, the importance of early stimulation is further supported by evidence of cortical plasticity in childhood and adolescence, which indicates that early treatment may be more effective. In addition, when treatment is started in kindergarten in the pre-reading phase (age four to six), the cognitive and linguistic prerequisites to reading and spelling skills, which may not develop spontaneously in at-risk children, may still be learned. Several studies have found that intervention at this stage produces significant effects (Bradley and Bryant, 1985; Cunningham, 1990; Ball and Blachman, 1991; Lundberg, Frost, and Petersen, 1988; Borstrøm, and Elbro, 1997). In many cases, considerable gains in later reading achievement are reported. Moreover, the effect on reading achievement appears to be long lasting. It is worthwhile to detect the characteristics of the tools that can be used for preventive purposes at an earlier age.

The Finnish study

The Jyväskylä longitudinal study of dyslexia (JLD) follows children from 106 families with a parental diagnosis of dyslexia and reports of similar problems among immediate relative(s). The follow-up also includes 97 control children from unaffected families. These 203 children have (at November 2000) been followed for 4-7 years since birth. The oldest 49 children entered school during autumn 2000 and the youngest (3) are approaching their 4.5-year assessment. All have participated in a very intensive assessment programme that commenced in the hospital during their first days of life. The comprehensive follow-up has included sensory, motor and cognitive/language assessments at least once per year and during the first two years, and in 2-5 sessions during the first school year. The emphasis has been on language development but a number of cognitive and behavioural assessments have complemented this. In addition, physiological (brain event related potentials, ERP; heart rate, HR) and other experimental (observational interaction) studies have been performed. Furthermore, parents have actively supported the data collection in their completion of developmental diaries and questionnaires. Earlier papers (Lyytinen H, Ahonen, and Räsänen, 1994; Lyytinen H, Leinonen, Nikula, Aro and Leiwo, 1995) furnish more details of the design features. The screening of the affected parents and sub-typing of the associated adult dyslexia has been summarized by Lyytinen H et al. (1995) and documented in detail by Leinonen, Müller, Leppänen, Aro, Ahonen and Lyytinen H (in press). Below, we review the main goals, general design, and outline the methods from which the main findings illustrated in recent publications of the JLD are summarized.

The goals and measures of the Finnish study

A prospective longitudinal study such as the JLD can have numerous ambitious goals. We have sought to ascertain (1) the early *predictors* of dyslexia that help in the identification of those at risk children who are in need of help. Predictive early measures should be simple enough to be implemented during the ordinary practice of child caring. A more ambitious goal is to try to find (2) the *precursors* of dyslexia that will subsequently increase our understanding of its nature. Intervention studies are also required in order to show the causal role played by those factor(s) eligible to be identified as precursor(s). One prospective candidate for the role of a precursor to dyslexia is a speech perception deficit. In our attempts to test this possibility, we have used measures such as brain event-related potentials (ERPs) and experimental behavioural techniques including a head turn paradigm to assess auditory cognition, categorical perception and sensory memory during the first year of life – mainly at six months of age. Because it is difficult to empirically validate causal connections in such temporally distant stages of development – for example, from early perceptual studies to reading acquisition at school age, later replications will be necessary for the validation of more proximal causal connections. In the JLD only relatively late interventions are possible for a number of reasons. Firstly, there are no previous data against which to validate the predictive accuracy of our early measures to help us identify for certain, those children who are in need of preventive measures. Thus, the most serious ethical considerations can be attenuated. Secondly, it is better to delay intervention to avoid affecting our final research criterion (the need to have an estimate of the dependent measure – reading status). Thirdly, any controlled manipulation of the independent variable makes early interventions difficult to interpret before the causal connections between relevant developmental steps are better understood. However, intensive individual interventions (single-case experiments) have been initiated from an age (six years on) when the culmination of signs referring to the potential realization of dyslexia have justified the initiation of remediation. These comprise attempts to assess the role of factors compatible with the potential precursors identified at an early age – such as speech perception (see below), whose relation to the development of phonological skills is apparent.

It is also important to try to figure out the (3) *developmental paths* characterizing the differential development of reading related skills and behaviours. For this purpose, the continuity of and relations between especially language, memory and motor skills have been intensively examined. Early language measures have included intensive follow-up of milestones of vocalization and development of speech production and comprehension with the help of the MacArthur Communicative Development Inventories (Fenson et al., 1991) and the Reynell Developmental Language Scales (Reynell and Huntley, 1987), which have been modified into Finnish for this purpose. At the later stages, from 3.5 years, tests of metaphonology, phonology, orthography, memory and naming have been applied repeatedly every year. The assessment of the development of motor skills has included, for example, measures of automatization at the age of 5.5 years. General language and cognitive skills have been assessed repeatedly using measures such as symbolic play (see Lyytinen P, et al, 1999, for the version used in Finnish) and vocabulary (Peabody Picture Vocabulary test-Revised, PPVT, Dunn and Dunn, 1981), Bayley scales (The Bayley Scales of Infant Development II; Bayley, 1993), and the Wechsler Preschool and Primary Scale of Intelligence (WPPS-R). Neuropsychological status has also been followed with several repeated assessment ages using the Korkman's Developmental Neuropsychological Assessment (NEPSY, 1998) test battery.

An important additional goal has been to uncover (4) *environmental correlates* of developmental features associated with the development of skills known to be potentially relevant for reading acquisition and with the exposure of the child to visual language. Knowledge concerning the supportive role of environmental stimulation might help families with at risk children. For this purpose, parent–child interaction studies have also been executed and the literacy-related environment of the child has been observed.

In addition, an important goal is the examination of mechanisms leading to or providing understanding of the potential development of (5) problems co-occurring with dyslexia (as *co-morbid disorders* such as attention deficit hyperactivity disorders). Behavioural ratings have been collected from an early age. Similarly, developmental patterns leading to the (6) acquisition of *compensatory skills or behaviours* are of great interest. Learning to identify these may assist with finding ways to overcome the problems using natural, supportive measures. One potential factor relating to compensation is intellectual capacity, which has been assessed from a very early age using recognition memory based assessment at the age of six months (for example Rose and Feldman, 1987) and IQ-measures such as Bayley scales at the age of two years. Both co-morbidity and compensation are phenomena known to exist but the conditions associated with their manifestation are as yet, not understood. The JLD provides more than 200 individual developmental paths, the analysis of which may provide relevant outcomes towards increasing our understanding with regard to both of these factors.

The last goal is to examine (7) the potential *biological correlates* of dyslexia in relation to the apparent heterogeneity of the phenotypes revealed by our assessment programme. The behavioural reading-related and possibly also neuropsychological subtyping will be attempted during the first school years. The former is based on our findings that the index parents reveal subtypes according to the dominant feature of the reading impairment. For example, slow or inaccurate reading versus both slow and inaccurate reading subtypes (Leinonen et al., in press). Subtyping based on a wider set of variables identified five subtypes from a sample of the first 52 adults diagnosed as dyslexic in the JLD (Lyytinen et al., 1995). Attempts to define the associated genotypes have been initiated by collecting DNA samples from selected large pedigrees. Measures developed to assess the magnocellular impairment will also be collected at school age. Functional magnetic resonance imaging (fMRI) and magnetoencephalographic (MEG) studies initiated with samples of the index and control parents will complement the psychophysiological data of the JLD children from the ERP experiments executed during the first half a year of life and at 6.5 years.

A summary of the results of the Finnish study

The results based on the first analyses of the whole sample up to the age of 3.5 years have been published in more detail in a number of journal articles. It is, as yet, too early for any definitive results with regard to our first goal – prediction – because our final dependent measure – reading acquisition – is still awaiting its time of assessment. The pre-reading skills such as letter knowledge are relatively successfully predicted by our follow-up measures. However, although the contribution of the group membership (familial risk versus non-risk) fails to show any major additional role, its role is still statistically significant when fed into the regression models as the last variable after the other most accurate predictors (Lyytinen et al., in press). Thus the variance of the known predictors that we have been able to isolate fails to explain all (or overlap totally with) the predictive variance resulting from the familial background with regard to some reading-related dependent measures applicable before the age of reading (Lyytinen et al., in press).

The search for the precursors of dyslexia has motivated very early comparisons of the groups concerning auditory cognition, speech perception and categorical perception. The results reveal reliable differences between groups immediately after birth in ERPs to auditory stimuli (Leppänen et al, 1999; Guttorm et al., in press). Categorical perception of speech sounds differing in terms of the duration of a consonant element was shown to be relatively accurate in both groups using both behavioural (head turn) and brain ERPs. A longer silence was, however, required by the six months old at risk infants to perceive the consonant sound as long (instead of short – a very distinctive feature in Finnish) (Richardson, 1998; Richardson et al. submitted) and also to show an ERP deflection (mismatch negativity, MMN) associated with the brain's detection of difference according to such a lengthening of the sound (Leppänen et al. submitted, see Leppänen and Lyytinen, 1997 and Lyytinen and Leppänen, in press, for a review of related psychophysiological data).

The early development of vocalization or vocabulary failed to show any reliable differences between the groups. The same was true concerning the ages at which milestones in motor development were reached. Also, other early measures taken between the ages of six months and two years failed to show reliable difference (for more details, see Lyytinen P et al., submitted). The earliest direct language measure that reliably differentiated the groups was the maximum sentence length at the age of two years. The mean number of morphemes in the utterances produced by the at-risk group was lower. From age 2.5 years onwards, more differences start to emerge in a number of areas, especially in language-related measures. However, none of the indices of more general cognitive skills, symbolic play, or language comprehension showed any reliable difference (Lyytinen P, Laakso, Poikkeus, and Rita, 1999; Laakso, Poikkeus, and Lyytinen P, 1999; Poikkeus et al., submitted). The most pronounced differences are seen in phonological, morphological and naming measures in all of which the means of at risk children are lower. The risk group scored lower in object naming and inflectional morphology at 3.5 years. Due to the richly inflected, agglutinative nature of the Finnish language, it is no great surprise that the groups differed in their morphological skills. Significant morphemic variation is often confined to a single phoneme(s) in the endings. Thus, the finding that inflections were not mastered as well in the at-risk group is just compatible with the reliable differences in more direct phonological measures consistently observed even at the age of 3.5 years (Puolakanaho et al., submitted). Measures of inflection (such as the Berko type tasks, see, for example, Lyytinen P, et al. in press) may be more natural indices of early predictive language variables because the task characteristics of tests required for the assessment of phonological skills tend to exert their influence on the outcome. This effect may be higher than that of the phonological skills as such at the early age (such as 3.5 years) even if the testing is carried out within the computer animation context that we used (Puolakanaho et al. submitted).

The developmental continuities differ between groups. Children who were early vocalizers displayed better later word comprehension and production than did late vocalizers in both groups (Lyytinen P, Poikkeus, Leiwo, Ahonen and Lyytinen H, 1996). However, children at familial risk for dyslexia showed more perseverance of language delays whereas most children in the control group had overcome their earlier delays. Thus, children with a family history of reading impairment who had low levels of expressive speech at two years, were reliably more likely to exhibit delays on a number of language measures at 3.5 years than did children without this familial status, even if these latter children had shown a similar delay at two years (Lyytinen P et al., submitted). Also, the predictive correlations between specific areas of development such as motor and language skills are often surprisingly more likely to be higher and significant in the data of the at risk group than in that of the control group (Lyytinen H et al., in press). This means that indications of the accumulation of delays, not only in language skills, but possibly also in motor skills, should be taken more seriously if the child has a familial risk of language problems and especially if there exist concomitant delays in more than one area.

The environmental stimulation and behavioural differences observed in the interaction between the children and their parents in reading and task-related situations did not show any consistent differences between groups in the studies covering ages 14 months, three, or five years (Lyytinen P, Laakso and Poikkeus, 1998; Laakso, Poikkeus and Lyytinen P, 1999). Thus, for instance, early exposure to books and parents' reading to children does not differ between the groups. Also, no differences emerged between the groups in terms of the frequencies of maternal interactive behaviours or in children's participation in shared reading at 14 months. Maternal skills to orient the children's attention were, however, found to be positively related to later language development in the control group, while no reliable relation was found in the at-risk group (Laakso, Poikkeus and Lyytinen, P, 1999). Similarly, from a number of gene-environment correlations identified (for more detailed references to the JLD see Lyytinen, H, Ahonen, Aro, Aro, Närhi and Räsänen, 1998), none has yet shown a clear indication of the role of the environment in differentiating the groups in our data. There is some slight tendency for the mother's behaviour to be less beneficial in supporting development in certain areas of cognition in the at-risk group although no differences were found in the behaviour of mothers as such (Laakso, Poikkeus and Lyytinen P, 1999). This is the case although a number of reliable correlations between environmental stimulation and language skills were seen in the analyses based on data of the combined groups.

Co-morbid problems associated with attention can be expected to occur more often among at risk children and some indications concerning this have already been observed in JLD. On the other hand, a substantial number of the children in the at risk group have had absolutely no problems or else have compensated for them very efficiently. A number of children from both groups were already reading by school entry at the level that Finnish children are accustomed to reading at this stage (for more details about the instruction-related paths and learning process typical for reading acquisition in highly orthographically regular Finnish and their reliable predictors see, Holopainen, Ahonen and Lyytinen, submitted a; Holopainen, Ahonen, Lyytinen, submitted b). However, the mean level of pre-reading skills and the number of those showing reading-related skills was substantially lower among the at risk children.

The Dutch study

The prospective study that started in the Netherlands in 1998 will involve a genetic-risk group of 225 children who have a dyslexic parent and a close dyslexic relative, to be followed from birth until the age of nine, when reading problems can be reliably diagnosed. The control group will consist of 120 children, selected in such a way that parental education and gender distribution are comparable. At three locations (Universities of Groningen, Amsterdam and Nijmegen), 75 high-risk children and 40 controls will initially be assigned, all to be assessed according to a single protocol. On the basis of the Finnish experience, attrition is expected to be limited to 20% of the sample, which means that we aim at a final genetic-risk group of 180 subjects and a final control group of 96 subjects. On the basis of the findings of Scarborough (1991) and Lubs et al. (1993), and the estimated posterior probability of developmental dyslexia in the three large family data sets currently available, it is to be expected that the 180 children belonging to the risk group can be divided into two sub-groups: those who manifest with reading problems (40%, which is equivalent to a total of 72 children), and those who, despite their genetic risk, do not show any signs of reading impairment (60%, which is equivalent to 108 children).

The identification of families with a genetic risk for dyslexia started in the middle of 1999 and is still in progress. In contrast to the Finnish study, parents cannot be asked to participate when in hospital for childbirth because most Dutch babies are born at home. Therefore, it is necessary to ask for the help of patient and interest groups, general physicians, midwifes, and health, maternity and post-natal care centres. The first screening consists of a brief questionnaire which parents are requested to complete. They must indicate whether they themselves, their school-age children, or near relatives, have had difficulties in learning to read or write. Next, a thorough assessment of the reading skills of the parents and near relatives is conducted, including a spelling test of pseudo-words, two tests of reading aloud (words and pseudowords), a test for rapid naming (colours, objects, digits, letters), a test for phonological working memory (non-word repetition), and a test for verbal reasoning. Selection is mainly based on the reading tests, the other tests are included to investigate the possibility of different subtypes in the family sample. Selection of the infant requires that at least one parent and one close relative has a score in the lowest decile on one of the two reading tests or in the lowest 25 % on both. In addition, the infants of subjects who show a discrepancy of more than six deciles between verbal reasoning and (pseudo)word reading are included. The latter criterion was added because we noted that some of the parents and relatives with an obvious history of dyslexia perform above the level of the other criteria but very significantly below the level of their estimated verbal intelligence. These cases have a long history of education at the tertiary level (college, university) and, therefore, intense reading and spelling experience that enables them to escape very low levels of performance on these tasks.

The goals and measures of the Dutch study

Although the general goals of the Dutch study overlap with the goals of the Finnish study, the theoretical orientations and specific goals differ slightly. With regard to (1) early *predictors* and *precursors,* the study aims to determine whether early visual, auditory or linguistic markers can be found that are sufficiently reliable in predicting later reading problems and have therapeutic relevance to pre-school children. In particular, we want to (2) evaluate whether developmental dyslexia is associated with a *selective deficit in the magnocellular layers* of the brain that affects speed of processing, either visually or auditory, and may produce attention deficit disorders as well. (3) The study aims to initiate a neurobiologically based *typology* of developmental dyslexia that will enhance or modify existing behavioural typologies, and (4) to explain the possible overlap between developmental dyslexia and attention deficit hyperactivity disorder (ADHD) *(co-morbidity)*.

The assessment paradigms of the Dutch study focus on the development of speech perception, vision, and receptive and productive language skills, in particular those aspects that may give rise to reading problems later on. Since the architecture of the visual system is known to be complete by the age of four months and speech perception develops into a fully operational skill within the first 12 months, we need relatively short assessment intervals during the first year of life. For this reason individual tests have been planned at 2, 5, and 11 months. Afterwards, the number of assessments drops to twice a year until the age of five, giving us a total of 11 sessions per child. Before the age of eight, after the first two years of institutional reading instruction, tests will be administered to assess the development of early reading skills. More specifically, the findings that dyslexia is characterized by a deficit in development of automaticity in reading will be used to differentiate the dyslexic and normal students, using appropriate instruments (Yap and Van der Leij, 1993; Van der Leij and Van Daal, 1999). The study will end with reading tests at age nine that enable us to determine with certainty which of the participating children has been affected by developmental dyslexia. In addition, tests of other relevant skills (spelling, reading comprehension, calculation and arithmetic) will indicate the co-occurrence of dyslexia with other learning disorders.

A major component of the Dutch study is the use of electrophysiological data to assess the development of both the auditory and the visual system, starting at the age of two months and later at the age of five and 11 months and onwards. Our choice of experimental paradigms is based on what is so far known about the cognitive processes involved in normal and impaired reading. The available evidence, based on autopsies and behavioural studies, indicates that developmental dyslexia is characterized by disturbances in the magnocellular parts of the auditory and/or visual systems, both at the cortical and at the thalamic level. These areas will therefore be the principal targets of the assessment programme. The integrity of the (magno)dorsal route to the secondary auditory cortex, which is known to be the central pathway for speech processing, can be assessed by oddball paradigms involving repeated consonant vowel pairs, for example /ba/-/da/, with deviants inducing mismatch negativity. A global test for thalamic integrity is provided by brain stem potentials evoked by clicks. Our hypothesis is that disturbed auditory processing results in a deficient phonological lexicon that ultimately, at reading age, can cause problems in grapheme-phoneme conversion. Because of interaction with the mechanisms for visual word detection, important parts of the magno-cellular visual route will also be examined for integrity, using preferential looking, eye tracking, and evoked potentials as measurements. Among the relevant tests are smooth pursuit, shifting dots, movement detection, and what is known as the cue stimulus paradigm (Johnson, 1990). The latter enables us to assess the integrity of the pathway between V5 and the parietal cortex and is particularly suited to study the functional develop-ment of orienting responses and inhibition of return.

From age 17 months on, the assessment of developmental language skills will play an increasingly important role in the Dutch study. Word recognition will be measured by auditory evoked potentials and a modified version of the LARSP profile chart (Language Assessment Remediation and Screening Procedure; Crystal, Fletcher, and Garman, 1976) will enable us to examine linguistic production. The Dutch revision, known as GRAMAT (Bol and Kuiken, 1989, 1990) is based on an elaborate corpus of spontaneous child language and provides an inventory of morphological markers and syntactic constructions.

The paradigms and tests at later ages are still to be selected but will include assessments of linguistic and phonological development, recep-tive language, non-verbal intelligence, and, after entrance to grade 1, development of basic skills in reading, spelling, arithmetic and reading comprehension. In addition, data from other relevant aspects of develop-ment and the quality of the environment will be gathered by observation and questionnaires.

At this moment (November 2000), 82 babies have been tested, some of them three times already (at 2, 5, and 11 months). Although it took (and still takes) some time to gather the subjects – especially the babies from control families – we feel confident that the target numbers will be reached, albeit with some delay in time. The auditory and visual paradigms function satisfactorily as indicated by preliminary analyses. The study will continue to 2010, which gives us ample time to find additional financial resources.

General conclusions

The study of infant cognitive processes in dyslexia, aiming to identify relevant predictors, precursors, developmental paths, and associated topics, is a challenging enterprise. The Finnish study has already produced an impressive amount of data, published in many articles and book chapters, which the reader may find in the list of references, while the Dutch study is still in its early stages. For a great part designed after taking the Finnish experience into account, the Dutch study will enable us to replicate some of the findings as well as to add additional evidence. As the picture now emerges, both studies of developmental dyslexia are excellent examples of the multidisciplinary research that is needed to understand this multifaceted disorder.

Acknowledgements

The Jyväskylä Longitudinal Study of Dyslexia (JLD) belongs to the Finnish Centre of Excellence Programme (2000-2005), and has been supported by the Academy of Finland, Niilo Mäki Foundation and the University of Jyväskylä. Professor Heikki Lyytinen, who is the main coordinator responsible for JLD, thanks Jane Erskine for polishing the present text concerning the Finnish study. The other senior researchers closely associated with JLD are professors Timo Ahonen, (Niilo Mäki Institute, and national network (Psykonet) providing advanced professional postgraduate training for Finnish psychologists), Matti Leiwo (Department of Finnish Language, University of Jyväskylä), Paula Lyytinen and Anna-Maija Poikkeus (Department of Psychology, University of Jyväskylä). Paavo Leppänen (University of Rutgers), Marja-Leena Laakso (University of Jyväskylä) and Ulla Richardson (University College London) have thus far completed their doctoral studies in the context of JLD.

The Dutch study is part of the national programme *Identifying the core features of developmental dyslexia: A multidisciplinary approach*, initiated and supported by the Netherlands Organization for Scientific Research, and also includes genetic and intervention studies. The co-operating universities provide additional funding. The senior researchers responsible for the longitudinal study are: Pieter Been (University of Groningen), Cecile Kuijpers and Marieken ter Keurs (University of Nijmegen), and Theo van Leeuwen (University of Amsterdam). Professors Frans Zwarts (University of Groningen) and Aryan van der Leij (University of Amsterdam) are chairman and vice-chairman of the national steering committee of the programme.

References

August GJ, Garfinkel BD (1990) Comorbidity of ADHD and reading disability among clinic-referred children. Journal of Abnormal Child Psychology, 18: 29–45.
Badian NA (1983) Dyscalculia and nonverbal disorders of learning. In HR Myklebust (ed.) Progress in Learning Disabilities. New York: Grune Stratton, pp. 235–64.

Ball EW, Blachman BA (1991) Does phoneme awareness training in kindergarten make a difference in early word recognition and developmental spelling? Reading Research Quarterly 26: 49–66.

Bayley N (1993) The Bayley Scales of Infant Development (2 edn) San Antonio TX: Psychological Corporation.

Benton AL (1975) Developmental dyslexia: neurological aspects. In WJ Friedlander (ed.), Advances in Neurology. Volume 7. New York: Raven Press.

Bol G, and Kuiken F (1989) Handleiding GRAMAT: Methode voor het diagnostiseren en kwalificeren van taalontwikkelingsstoornissen [Manual GRAMAT: Method to diagnose and qualify disorders in language development]. Nijmegen: Berkhout.

Bol G, Kuiken F (1990) Grammatical analysis of developmental language disorders: A study of the morphosyntax of children with specific language disorders, with hearing impairment and with Down's syndrome. Clinical Linguistics and Phonetics 4: 77–86.

Borstrøm I, Elbro C (1997) Prevention of dyslexia in kindergarten: effects of phoneme awareness training with children of dyslexic parents. In C Hulme, M Snowling (eds) Dyslexia: Biology, Cognition and Intervention. London: Whurr, pp. 235–53.

Bowers PG, Wolf M (1993) Theoretical links among naming speed, precise timing mechanisms and orthographic skills in dyslexia. Reading and Writing: An Interdisciplinary Journal 5: 69–85.

Bradley L, Bryant PE (1983) Categorizing sounds and learning to read – a causal connection. Nature 301: 419–21.

Bradley L, Bryant PE (1985) Rhyme and Reason in Reading and Spelling. Ann Arbor: University of Michigan Press.

Bronfenbrenner U, Ceci SHJ (1994) Nature-nurture reconceptualised in developmental perspective: a bioecological model. Psychological Review 101 (4): 568–86.

Byrne B (1981) Deficient syntactic control in poor readers: is a weak phonetic memory code responsible? Applied Psycholinguistics 2: 201–12.

Crain S, Shankweiler D (1987) Reading acquisition and language acquisition. In A Davison, G Green, G Herman (eds) Critical Approaches to Readability: Theoretical bases of linguistic complexity. Hillsdale NJ: Erlbaum.

Crystal D, Fletcher P, Garman M (1976). The grammatical analysis of language disability: A procedure for assessment and remediation. London: Arnold. Revised, 1981. 2 edn with additional material 1989, London: Cole and Whurr.

Cunningham AE (1990) Explicit versus implicit instruction in phonemic awareness. Journal of Experimental Child Psychology 50: 429–44.

DeFries JC, Fulker DW, LaBuda MC (1987) Evidence for a genetic etiology in reading disability of twins. Nature 329: 537–9.

De Jong PF (1998) Working memory deficits of reading disabled children. Journal of Experimental Child Psychology 70: 75-96.

Denckla MB, Rudel RG (1976) Rapid 'automatised' naming (RAN): Dyslexia differentiated from other learning disabilities. Neuropsychologia 14: 471–9.

De Weirdt W (1988) Speech perception and frequency discrimination in good and poor readers. Applied Psycholinguistics 16: 163–83.

Duncan CC, Rumsey JM, Wilkniss SM, Denckla MB, Hamburger SD, Odou-Potkin M (1994) Developmental dyslexia and attention dysfunction in adults: Brain potential indices of information processing. Psychophysiology 31: 386–401.

Dunn LM, Dunn LM (1981) Peabody picture vocabulary test -revised. Circle Pines, MN: American Guidance Service.

Fawcett AJ, Nicolson RI, Dean P (1996) Impaired performance of children with dyslexia on a range of cerebellar tasks. Annals of Dyslexia 46: 259–83.

Fenson L, Dale PS, Reznick JS, Thal D, Bates E, Hartung JP, Pethick S, Reilly JS (1991) Technical Manual for the MacArthur Communicative Development Inventories. San Diego: San Diego State University.

Gilger JW, Pennington BF, DeFries JC (1991) Risk for reading disability as a function of parental history in three family studies. Reading and Writing: An Interdisciplinary Journal 3: 205–17.

Gilger JW, Pennington BF, DeFries JC (1992) A twin study of the etiology of comorbidity: attention deficit hyperactivity disorder and dyslexia. Journal of the American Academy of Child and Adolescent Psychiatry 31: 343–9.

Gillis J, Gilger JW, Pennington BF, DeFries JC (1992) Attention deficit hyperactivity disorder in reading disabled twins: Evidence for a genetic etiology. Journal of Abnormal Child Psychology 20: 303–16.

Godfrey JJ, Syrdal-Lasky AK, Millay KK, Knox CM (1981) Performance of dyslexic children on speech perception tests. Journal of Experimental Child Psychology 32: 401–24.

Groenhuis M, Goorhuis-Brouwer SM (1991) De bruikbaarheid van spontane taalanalyse in de klinische praktijk [The use of the analyis of spontaneous language in clinical practice]. Logopedie en Foniatrie 63: 68–71.

Guttorm TK, Leppänen PHT, Richardson U, Lyytinen H (in press) Event-related potentials and consonant differentiation in newborns with a familial risk for dyslexia. Journal of Learning Disabilities.

Holopainen L, Ahonen T, Lyytinen H (submitted a) Prediction of reading accuracy and reading speed in a highly transparent language: different verbal and non-verbal preschool measures as predictors of the instruction time needed for accurate decoding.

Holopainen L, Ahonen T, Lyytinen H (submitted b) The role of reading by analogy in Finnish first-grade readers.

Johnson MH (1990) Cortical maturation and the development of visual attention in early infancy. Journal of Cognitive Neuroscience 2: 81–95.

Korkman M, Kirk U, Kemp S (1998) A developmental neuropsychological assessment. Manual. San Antonio: The Psychological Corporation.

Laakso M-L, Poikkeus A-M, Lyytinen P (1999) Shared reading interaction in families with and without genetic risk for dyslexia: implications for toddlers' language development. Infant and Child Development 8: 179–95.

Leinonen S, Müller K, Leppänen P, Aro M, Ahonen T, Lyytinen H (in press) Heterogeneity in adult dyslexic readers: relating processing skills to the speed and accuracy of oral text reading. Reading and Writing: An Interdisciplinary Journal.

Leppänen PHT, Lyytinen H (1997) Auditory event-related potentials in the study of developmental language-related disorders. Audiology and Neuro-Otology 2: 308–40.

Leppänen PHT, Eklund KM, Lyytinen H (1997). Event-related brain potentials to change in rapidly presented acoustic stimuli in newborns. Developmental Neuropsychology 13: 175–204.

Leppänen PHT, Pihko E, Eklund KM, Lyytinen H (1999). Cortical responses of infants with and without a genetic risk for dyslexia: II. Group effects. NeuroReport 10 (5): 901–5.

Leppänen PHT, Richardson U, Pihko E, Eklund KM, Guttorm TK, Aro M, Lyytinen H (2001). Brain responses reveal speech processing differences in infants at risk for dyslexia. Developmental Neuropsychology.

Livingstone MS, Rosen GD, Drislane FW, Galaburda AM (1991) Physiological and anatomical evidence for a magnocellular defect in developmental dyslexia. Proceedings of the National Academy of Sciences, USA 88: 7943–7.

Lovegrove W (1994) Visual deficits in dyslexia: evidence and implications. In Fawcett A, Nicolson R (eds) Dyslexia in children: multidisciplinary perspectives. New York: Harvester Wheatsheaf, pp. 113–35.

Lovegrove W, Martin F, Slaghuis W (1986) A theoretical and experimental case for a visual deficit in specific reading disability. Cognitive Neuropsychology 3: 225–67.

Lubs HA, Rabin M, Feldman E, Jallad BJ, Kushch A, Gross-Glenn K (1993) Familial dyslexia: genetic and medical findings in eleven three-generation families. Annals of Dyslexia 43: 44–60.

Lundberg I, Frost J, Petersen PP (1988) Effects of an extensive program for stimulating phonological awareness in preschool children. Reading Research Quarterly 23: 263–84.

Lyytinen H (1997) In search of the precursors of dyslexia: a prospective study of children at risk for reading problems. In C Hulme, M Snowling (eds) Dyslexia: Biology, Cognition and Intervention. London: Whurr Publishers, pp. 97–107.

Lyytinen H, Ahonen T, Aro M, Aro T, Närhi V, Räsänen P (1998). Learning Disabilities: A view of developmental neuropsychology. In R Licht, A Bouma, W Slot, W Koops (eds) Child Neuropsychology. Reading disability and more . . . Delft: Eburon, pp. 29–54.

Lyytinen H, Ahonen T, Leiwo M., Gilger J (1994). In search for the precursors of dyslexia. NMI-Bulletin 2 (4): 1–29.

Lyytinen H, Ahonen T, Leiwo M, Lyytinen P, Laakso M-L, Leinonen S, Poikkeus A-M (1992) Early language development and genetic risk for dyslexia. NMI-Bulletin 2 (4): 12–19.

Lyytinen H, Ahonen T, Räsänen P (1994) Dyslexia and dyscalculia in children – risks, early precursors, bottlenecks and cognitive mechanisms. Acta Paedopsychiatrica, Special Issue 56 (1): 179–92.

Lyytinen H, Leinonen S, Nikula M, Aro M, Leiwo M (1995) In search of the core features of dyslexia: observations concerning dyslexia in the highly orthographically regular Finnish language. In VW Berninger (ed.) The varieties of orthographic knowledge 2: relationships to phonology, reading, and writing. Dordrecht: Kluwer Academic Publishers, pp. 177–204.

Lyytinen H, Leppänen PHT (in press) Psychophysiology of developmental dyslexia: a review of findings and results from studies of children at risk for dyslexia. Educational Psychology Review.

Lyytinen H, Guttorm T, Leppänen PTH, Lyytinen P, Poikkeus A-M, Puolakanaho A, Richardson U (in press) Neuropsychology of developmental dyslexia - developmental paths of children with and without family risk for dyslexia during first years of life. Developmental Neuropsychology, Special Issue of Neuropsychology of Dyslexia.

Lyytinen P, Laakso M-L, Poikkeus A-M, Rita N (1999) The developmental and predictive relations of play and language across the second year. Scandinavian Journal of Psychology 40: 177–86.

Lyytinen P, Laakso M-L, Poikkeus A-M (1998) Parental contributions to child's early language and interest in books. European Journal of Psychology of Education 13(3): 297–308.

Lyytinen P, Poikkeus A-M, Laakso M-L, Eklund K, Lyytinen H (2001 in press) Language and symbolic play development in children with and without familial risk for dyslexia. Journal of Speech, Language and Hearing Research.

Lyytinen P, Poikkeus AM, Leiwo M, Ahonen T, Lyytinen H (1996) Parents as informants of their child's vocal and early language development. Early Child Development and Care 126: 15–25.

Mann VA, Liberman IY, Shankweiler D (1980) Children's memory for sentences and word strings in relation to reading ability. Memory and Cognition 8: 329–35.

Mody M, Studdert-Kennedy M, Brady S (1997) Speech perception deficits in poor readers: auditory processing or phonological coding? Journal of Experimental Child Psychology 64: 199–231.

Molfese DL, Molfese VJ (1997) Discrimination of language skills at five years of age using event-related potentials recorded at birth. Developmental Neuropsychology 13: 135–56.

Nicolson RI, Fawcett AJ (1990) Automaticity: a new framework for dyslexia research? Cognition 30: 1–33.

Nicolson RI, Fawcett AJ (1995) Dyslexia is more than a phonological disability. Dyslexia: An International Journal of Research and Practice 1: 19–37.

Olson RK (1994) Language deficits in 'specific' reading disability. In MA Gernsbacher (ed.) Handbook of Psycholinguistics. San Diego: Academic Press, pp. 895–916.

Pennington BF (1995) Genetics of learning disabilities. Journal of Child Neurology 10: 69–77.

Poikkeus A-M, Lyytinen P, Ahonen T, Heiskanen-Nikula K (submitted) Prediction of early language and cognition from 6-month infant visual recognition memory in a follow-up of children with and without familial risk for dyslexia.

Puolakanaho A, Poikkeus A-M, Ahonen T, Tolvanen A, Lyytinen H (submitted). Assessment of 3.5-year old's emerging phonological awareness in a computer-animation context.

Rack JP, Snowling MJ, Olson RK (1992) The nonword reading deficit in developmental dyslexia: a review. Reading Research Quarterly 27: 28–53.

Reynell JK, Huntley M (1987) Reynell Developmental Language Scales Manual II. Windsor UK: NFER- Nelson.

Reed MA (1989) Speech perception and the discrimination of brief auditory cues in reading disabled children. Journal of Experimental Child Psychology 48: 270–92.

Richardson U, Leppänen PHT, Leiwo M, Lyytinen H (in press) Speech perception differences in infants at risk for dyslexia as early as six months of age. Developmental Neuropsychology.

Richardson, U (1998) Familial dyslexia and sound duration in the quantity distinctions of Finnish infants and adults. Jyväskylä: Studio Philologica Jyväskyläensia (Doctoral dissertation).

Rose SA, Feldman JF (1987) Infant visual attention: stability of individual differences from 6 to 8 months. Developmental Psychology 23: 490–8.

Scarborough HS (1989) Prediction of reading disability from familial and individual differences. Journal of Educational Psychology 27: 723–37.

Scarborough HS (1990) Very early language deficits in dyslexic children. Child Development 61: 1728–43.

Scarborough HS (1991) Early syntactic development of dyslexic children. Annals of Dyslexia 41: 207–20.

Shankweiler D, Crain S (1986) Language mechanisms and reading disorder: a modular approach. Cognition 24: 139–68.

Smith SD, Kimberling WJ, Pennington BF, Lubs HA (1983) Specific reading disability: identification of an inherited form through linkage analysis. Science 219: 1345–7.

Stanovich KE (1986) Matthew effects in reading: some consequences of individual differences in the acquisition of literacy. Reading Research Quarterly 21: 360–406.

Stanovich KE (1988) Explaining the differences between the dyslexic and the garden-variety poor reader: the phonological-core variable-difference model. Journal of Learning Disabilities 21(10): 590–604.

Steffens ML, Eilers R, Gross-Glenn K, Jallad B (1992) Speech perception deficits in adult subjects with familial dyslexia. Journal of Speech and Hearing Research 35: 192–200.

Stein CL, Cairns HS, Zurif EB (1984) Sentence comprehension limitations related to syntactic deficits in reading-disabled children. Applied Psycholinguistics 5: 305–22.

Stein JF (1994) A visual defect in dyslexics? In AJ Fawcett, RI Nicolson (eds) Dyslexia in Children: Multidisciplinary perspectives. New York: Harvester Wheatsheaf, pp. 137–56.

Stein JF, Walsh V (1997) To see but not to read: the magnocellular theory of dyslexia. Trends in Neuroscience 20 (4): 508–14.

Stevenson J, Pennington BF, Gilger JW, DeFries JC, Gillis JJ (1993) Hyperactivity and spelling disability: Testing for shared genetic aetiology. Journal of Child Psychology and Psychiatry 34: 1137–52.

Studdert-Kennedy M, Mody M (1995) Auditory temporal perception deficits in the reading-impaired: a critical review of the evidence. Psychonomic Bulletin and Review 2: 508–14.

Tallal P, Miller S, Fitch RH (1993) Neurobiological basis of speech: a case for the pre-eminence of temporal processing. In P Tallal, AM Galaburda, RR Llinás, C von Euler (eds) Temporal information processing in the nervous system: special reference to dyslexia and dysphasia. New York: New York Academy of Sciences. (Annals of the New York Academy of Sciences, 682), pp. 27–47.

Van Daal VHP, Van der Leij A (1999) Developmental dyslexia: related to specific or general deficits? Annals of Dyslexia 49: 71–104.

Van der Leij A, Van Daal VHP (1999) Automatisation aspects of dyslexia: Speed limitation in word identification, sensitivity to increasing task demands, and orthographic compensation. Journal of Learning Disabilities 32(5): 417–28.

Van der Leij A, Van Daal VHP (2001) Cognitive deficits of (sub) categories of 12-year old students with learning disabilities. Paper to be presented at the BDA-Conference, York.

Vellutino FR (1979a) Dyslexia: Theory and Research. Cambridge MA: MIT Press.

Vellutino FR (1979b) The validity of perceptual deficit explanations of reading disability: a reply to Fletcher and Satz. Journal of Learning Disabilities 12: 160–7.

Wagner RK (1986) Phonological processing abilities and reading: Implications for disabled readers. Journal of Learning Disabilities 19: 623–30.

Wagner RK, Torgesen JK (1987) The nature of phonological processing and its causal role in the acquisition of reading skills. Psychological Bulletin 101: 192–212.

White JL, Moffit TE, Silva PA (1992) Neuropsychological and socio-emotional correlates of specific-arithmetic disability. Archives of Clinical Neuropsychology 7: 1–16.

Williams MC, Molinet K, LeCluyse K (1989) Visual masking as a measure of temporal processing in normal and disabled readers. Clinical Vision Sciences 4: 137–44.

Wimmer H, Mayringer H, Landerl K (1998) Poor reading: A deficit in skill automatisation or a phonological deficit? Scientific Studies of Reading 2: 321–40.

Yap RL, Van der Leij A (1993) Word processing in dyslexics: an automatic decoding deficit? Reading and Writing: An Interdisciplinary Journal 5: 261–79.

PART THREE
INTERVENTION

The theory and practice of intervention: comparing outcomes from prevention and remediation studies

JOSEPH K TORGESEN

Practitioners and researchers have been working for many years to develop and implement instructional methods that are effective in helping older children with reading disabilities acquire adequate reading skills (Clark and Uhry, 1995). However, there is consistent evidence from a variety of sources that typical school interventions for children with reading disabilities can most accurately be described as *stabilizing* their degree of reading failure rather than *remediating* or normalizing their reading skills (Kavale, 1988; Schumaker, Deshler, and Ellis, 1986). That is, children usually do not fall farther behind in their reading skills once they are placed in special education, but neither do they 'close the gap' in reading ability with average children of their same age level.

Recently, Hanushek, Kain, and Rivkin (1998) used a very large sample of children from the Texas Schools Microdata Panel to show that typical special education placements during the fourth and fifth grade years of elementary school accelerated reading growth by only 0.04 standard deviations over the rate the children had been achieving in their regular classroom placements. While this represents a positive accomplishment for special education, it is hardly sufficient to normalize the reading skills of children with severe reading disabilities in any reasonable period of time.

The results from the analysis by Hanushek et al., (1998) applied specifically to resource room, or pullout methods of instruction, but nearly identical results have been reported for 'inclusion' interventions with older children. In fact, when summarizing the results from several studies of effectiveness for instructional models requiring that children with reading disabilities be instructed in the regular classroom environment, Zigmond (1996: 187) concluded thus: 'As a field, we have yet to demonstrate what instruction is needed to help students with learning disabilities who are far behind their peers make substantial progress in reading achievement, let alone whether this instruction can be incorporated into the organization and management framework of a general education setting.'

Observational studies of instruction in many special education classrooms (Vaughn, Moody, and Shuman, 1998) have identified several reasons why most placements are not more effective in bringing the reading skills of older children into the average range within a reasonable period of time. First, the interventions are offered with insufficient intensity. The teachers they observed were simply responsible for too many students; they were not able to offer them the individualized instruction required by older children who have struggled for several years in learning to read. Further, there was little direct instruction or guided practice in such critical components as phonemic decoding and phonemic awareness. Most instruction on word-level skills involved 'phonics' worksheets that the children completed independently. A final important element that was missing in the classrooms observed by Vaughn and her colleagues was direct instruction in comprehension strategies, which has been shown to be a very effective form of intervention for older children with reading disabilities (Mastropieri and Scruggs, 1997).

Given that current methods of instruction and implementation are generally less effective than is desirable, what do we know that can lead to improvement in this situation? We actually know quite a lot. First, recent studies of intensive interventions using older children with reading disabilities have demonstrated that it is possible to accelerate their reading growth to a much greater extent than is typically achieved in special education classrooms. Results from this research demand that politicians, educational administrators, and teachers find ways to bring this more effective instruction into the lives of many more children than is currently the case. Second, comparisons of outcomes between remedial and preventive studies are helping us learn more about what we lose by waiting too long to intervene with children who have reading disabilities. These comparisons suggest that, while we must seek to implement more effective instruction for older children, at the same time we must begin to focus more and more of our instructional resources to prevent the emergence of reading disabilities in children who are just beginning to learn to read.

Outcomes from effective and intensive interventions

We have recently addressed the question of whether it is possible to 'normalize' the reading skills of children with severe reading disabilities in a relatively brief period of time in a study that examined the effects of two instructional approaches with the worst readers from several special education classrooms (Torgesen, Alexander, Wagner, Rashotte, Voeller, Conway, and Rose, in press a). The children in the study were between eight and 10 years of age when they received the interventions, and they had been receiving special education services for reading for an average of 16 months prior to entering our study. They were nominated by their teachers as having serious disabilities in acquiring word-level reading skills, and their average score on two measures of word reading skill was more than 1.5 standard deviations below average for their age.

The 60 children identified for the study fit the classic pattern of children with severe dyslexia: their verbal intelligence was in the average range (average verbal IQ = 93) while their scores for phonemic decoding and word reading ability were very impaired (average standard scores for word attack and word identification were 67 and 69, respectively). Passage comprehension scores were relatively higher than word level scores (average standard score for passage comprehension was 83). As a note for the reader, throughout this chapter, I will be describing reading perform-ance in terms of standard scores. The advantage of a standard score is that it indicates where a child falls into the overall distribution of reading ability among children of the same age. A standard score lower than 70 is vary rare; only 2% of children obtain scores that low. If children achieve a standard score of 100, they are exactly at average for their age.

The children in our study were randomly assigned to two instructional groups, and each group was provided with 67.5 hours of 1:1 instruction given daily in two 50 minute sessions, five days a week for eight weeks. Following this intervention, our instructors visited in the child's special education classroom for one 50-minute session a week for eight weeks to help them learn to apply their new reading skills to classroom assignments, and to help the child's teacher adjust the level of assignments to the child's new reading skills. One of the groups received the Lindamood Phoneme Sequencing Program for Reading, Spelling, and Speech (LIPS) (Lindamood and Lindamood, 1998), while the instructional program for the other group was developed locally and was referred to as Embedded Phonics (EP).

These programs both involved explicit instruction in phonemic decoding skills, stimulation of phonemic awareness, building a sight word vocabulary of high frequency words, and applications of these skills to reading and understanding text, but their instructional emphasis was very different. The LIPS program worked intensively to build strong phonemic awareness by helping children discover the articulatory gestures associ-ated with each phoneme. In order to provide a shared language for discus-sion of phonemes and correction of reading errors, each phoneme received a label that reflected a critical aspect of the articulation required to produce it in speech. For example, the phonemes /b/ and /p/ were labelled 'lip poppers' because the lips come together and then 'pop open' when they are pronounced. One of the phonemes (/b/) was referred to as a 'noisy lip popper' because it was voiced, while the other one (/p/) was called the 'quiet lip popper' because the vocal chords are not used when it is pronounced. A large share of the instructional time in the LIPS program focused on teaching children to accurately identify the number, order, and identity of sounds in words.

The Embedded Phonics program was given that name because a relatively smaller amount of focused and explicit instruction in phonics knowledge and skill was provided in a context that involved larger amounts of carefully monitored reading of text. In this program, phonemic awareness was stimulated by asking children to write words they were learning, and to listen for sounds in words as an aid to spelling. Most of the instructional time in this condition was spent reading connected text, with the teacher providing careful error correction and discussion in order to help children generalize effective word decoding strategies to their text reading. There was also considerable discussion of the meaning of passages that were read in this condition.

To provide a clearer picture of the differences in instructional emphasis between conditions, we did a time by activity analysis that produced the following comparisons:

- time spent on training phonemic awareness and phonemic decoding using single word practice was 85% for the LIPS and 20% for the EP program;
- time spent on direct sight word practice was 10% for LIPS and 30% for EP; and
- time spent reading or writing connected text was 5% for LIPS and 50% for EP.

In the context of these important differences in instructional emphasis, it should be noted that both conditions incorporated principles of instruction that have generally been found to be successful for children with reading disabilities (Swanson, 1999). That is, both methods provided:

- ample opportunities for guided practice of new skills;
- very intensive instruction;
- systematic cueing of appropriate strategies in reading words or text; and
- explicit instruction in phonemic decoding strategies.

Standard scores on several important reading measures are illustrated in Figure 8.1. In each graph in Figure 8.1, the children's reading standard scores are presented at the time intervention began (pre-test) and immediately at the close of intervention (post-test), which was an interval of about two months. The graphs also report scores at one and two-year follow-up intervals during which the children received no further intervention from us. About 40% of the children were removed from special education in the year immediately following our intervention.

The top panel illustrates growth in phonemic decoding skills, the middle panel shows growth in text reading accuracy, while the bottom panel shows growth in passage comprehension. The dotted line on each graph is drawn at standard score 90, which is generally considered to be the bottom limit of the 'average' range of reading ability. As can be seen in Figure 8.1, children in both conditions achieved scores either at the bottom of the average range (word reading ability), or solidly in the middle of the average range (comprehension) by the end of the two-year follow-up period.

Figure 8.2 contrasts the growth in reading skill obtained during the intervention with the growth the children were making in special education prior to the intervention. The measure used to assess reading growth was the Broad Reading Cluster from the Woodcock-Johnson Psycho-Educational Battery – Revised (Woodcock and Johnson, 1989) that was obtained before, during, and following the intervention period. The Broad Reading Cluster is composed of scores on the Word Identification and Passage Comprehension subtests of the WJP-R. We obtained scores prior to the treatment from school records, with the average period elapsing between the school tests and our pre-test being 16.6 months. During this 16-month time period, the children received remedial reading instruction within resource room settings. The teacher to student ratio in these resource rooms ranged between 1:8 and 1:18. When the rate of reading growth during the pre-intervention period (when the children were receiving regular resource room interventions) is compared to growth during the intervention period in our study, the effect size for the LIPS group was 4.4, and that for the EP group was 3.9. Not only did the intervention produce powerful acceleration of reading growth during the intervention period, but the children continued to 'close the gap' in reading skill over the follow-up period in which they received no further intensive intervention. At the conclusion of the follow-up period, their standard score on the measure of broad reading skill was 92.5, which places the children at the lower end of the normal range of ability in word reading accuracy and comprehension.

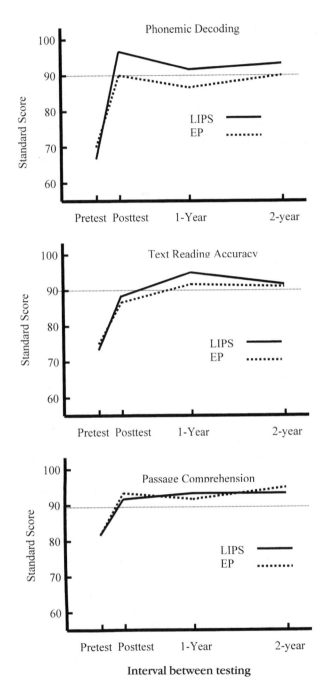

Figure 8.1: Growth in phonemic decoding, text reading accuracy, and passage comprehension resulting from intensive intervention using two instructional methods.

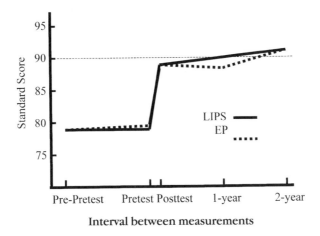

Figure 8.2: Standard scores on the Broad Reading Cluster before, during, and following the intensive intervention. From Torgesen, JK, Alexander AW, Wagner RK, Rashotte CA, Voeller K, Conway T, Rose E (in press) Intensive remedial instruction for children with severe reading disabilities: Immediate and long-term outcomes from two instructional approaches. *Journal of Learning Disabilities.*

Figure 8.2 also suggests that there was little difference in outcome between the two instructional conditions, and that is consistent with more extensive analysis of the outcome data (Torgesen et al., in press a). In fact, the only differences that emerged between the two groups were at the immediate post-test, with the LIPS group performing more strongly on a measure of phonemic decoding accuracy and one of two measures of phonemic awareness. These differences were no longer reliable at the two-year follow-up point.

This study illustrates the power of intensive and appropriate instruction for older children with severe reading disabilities, and it is not alone in showing that we can reasonably expect more progress from children receiving remedial help than is typically obtained in special education settings. One general way to describe the power, or efficiency, of an intervention is to calculate how much the child's reading skills change in standard score points per hour of instruction. Remember, a child's standard score for a given measure of reading skill describes performance in comparison to a large, randomly selected standardization sample. If a child shows improvement in his or her standard scores, it means that the child's reading skills are 'closing the gap' with average-level skills.

Table 8.1 presents gains in the number of standard score points per hour of instruction for measures of phonemic decoding (word attack), context-free word reading (word identification), and reading comprehension (passage comprehension) across several studies. These studies all used measures in which one standard deviation consists of 15 standard score points. The studies by Wise, Ring, and Olson (1999), Lovett, Lacerenza, Borden, Frijters, Seteinbach, and DePalma (2000), Alexander, Anderson, Heilman, Voeller, and Torgesen, (1991), and Truch (1994) all taught children similar to those selected for the present study, while Rashotte, MacPhee, and Torgesen (in press) worked with children of similar ages who were less severely impaired. It is apparent from Table 8.1 that the rates of growth obtained in the study described in this chapter are very similar to other studies of children with severe reading disabilities in the areas of phonemic decoding skills, word reading ability, and reading comprehension.

The consistency in rate of gain across the first five studies in Table 8.1 seems remarkable, and it suggests that the high rates of growth obtained in our study should be generalizable to other settings, with other teachers implementing the interventions. The similarities in growth rate between the LIPS and EP conditions in the Torgesen, et al., (in press a) study suggest that, given the right level of intensity and teacher skill it may be possible to obtain these rates of growth using a variety of approaches to direct instruction in reading. One might even suggest that these rates could serve as a benchmark for 'reasonable progress' in reading for students receiving remedial instruction in both public and private settings.

Table 8.1: Gains in standard score points per hour of instruction for three measures of reading skill

		Phonemic Decoding	Word Identification	Passage Comprehension
Torgesen, et al. (in press a)	LIPS	0.41	0.20	0.12
67.5 hrs of 1:1	EP	0.30	0.21	0.15
Wise, et al., (1999) 40 hrs, sm grp + 1:1 computer practice		0.31	0.22	0.14
Lovett, et al., (2000) 70 hrs., 1:3		0.34	0.18	–
Alexander, et al., (1991) 65 hrs., 1:1		0.34	0.23	–
Truch (1994) 80 hrs. 1:1		–	0.21	–
Rashotte et al. (in press) 30 hours small group (4)		0.50	0.19	0.32

Remaining problems with instructional outcomes from remediation studies

Although the data from the study by Torgesen, et al. (in press a) and the data summarized in Table 8.1 suggest that it is possible to achieve remedial outcomes for children with reading disabilities that are much stronger than is typically obtained in special education, even these results were not all that we might wish them to be. First, the results reported by Torgesen, et al., did not apply to all children in the study. Depending upon the specific reading skill, anywhere from 15 to 60% of the children in the intervention sample obtained standard scores below 90 at the conclusion of the two year follow-up period. Second, outcomes for reading rate, or fluency, were very different from those for reading accuracy. This difference is illustrated graphically in Figure 8.3, which plots growth in text reading accuracy and fluency from the Gray Oral Reading Test-Revised (Wiederholt and Bryant, 1992). At the conclusion of the two-year follow-up period, the average standard score for text reading accuracy across conditions was 90.9. In contrast, the final standard score for rate averaged across conditions was 71.7, a difference of about one-and-a-third standard deviations.

This disparity in outcome for reading accuracy versus reading rate was replicated in another recently completed intervention study with older children (Rashotte, MacPhee, and Torgesen, in press). In this study, struggling readers in grades 3–5 were provided with 35 hours of direct instruction in reading using a method that was roughly similar to the embedded phonics condition from our earlier study. However, in this later study, the instruction was provided in groups of four children, and the children began the study with higher reading skills than those in the earlier study. In the later study, the children's standard score for text reading accuracy at the conclusion of the intervention was 98.3, while their final score for text reading fluency was 85.3. Thus, even in a study involving children with less severe reading disabilities, there was a difference of almost one standard deviation in their scores for accuracy versus rate.

A different outcome for accuracy versus rate from prevention studies

Although we have now obtained substantial discrepancies in outcomes for reading accuracy versus reading rate in two remediation studies with older children, we have found a very different pattern of results from two recently completed studies of preventive instruction in children at-risk for the development of reading disabilities. Prevention Study I (Torgesen, Wagner, Rashotte, Rose, Lindamood, Conway, and Garvin (1999) provided

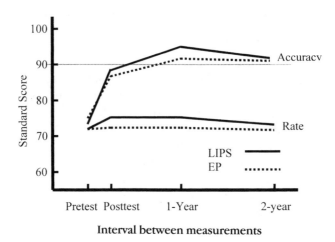

Figure 8.3: Growth rates for text reading accuracy versus text reading fluency in study of two intensive interventions.

88 hours of teacher- and aide-led instruction to children identified as the 12% most at risk for reading failure in kindergarten. The instruction was provided individually in four, 20-minute sessions per week, beginning in the second semester of kindergarten and extending through second grade. The children were randomly assigned to one of three instructional conditions, or to a no-treatment control group. Following the conclusion of instruction at the end of second grade, the reading development of these children was followed over the next two school years.

Prevention Study II (Torgesen, Wagner, Rashotte, and Herron, 2000) provided 92 hours of small-group and computer-based instruction to children identified as the 20% most at risk for reading failure at the beginning of first grade. The children who were randomly assigned to one of the two instructional conditions in this study were seen in four 50-minute sessions (25 minutes of small group teacher-led instruction and 25 minutes of individual computer based practice) per week from October through May of their first grade year. The reading development of these children was followed through the end of second grade.

Outcomes for text reading accuracy and rates from the most effective instructional condition in Prevention Study I are presented in Figure 8.4. This figure shows standard scores for accuracy and rate at the conclusion of the intervention and over the two years of the follow-up period to the end of fourth grade. It is obvious from Figure 8.4 that the children at risk for reading disabilities who received sustained preventive instruction in

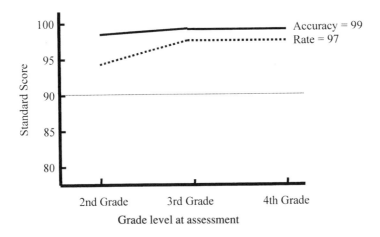

Figure 8.4: Growth in text reading accuracy versus text reading fluency for children who received two-and-one-half years of preventive instruction beginning in kinder-garten and extending through second grade.

this study did not experience the significant disparity in outcomes for rate versus accuracy that were obtained in the remediation studies with older children. The most effective instructional method in this study was based on the Lindamood Phoneme Sequencing Program for Reading, Spelling, and Speech (LIPS) (Lindamood and Lindamood, 1998).

To summarize the differences that we have found in outcomes for text reading accuracy versus text reading rate across two remediation and two prevention studies conducted thus far, final standard scores for accuracy and rate for each study are presented in Figure 8.5. These scores were obtained from the two year follow-up testing for Remediation Study 1, immediate post-test for Remediation Study II, two year follow-up testing for Prevention Study I, and one year follow-up testing for Prevention Study II. For both remediation studies, the differences in scores for accuracy versus rate were statistically reliable and quite large, while the differences in the prevention studies were not statistically significant and very small.

The major finding illustrated in Figure 8.5 is that preventive studies do not show the large differences in outcomes for accuracy and fluency that are manifest in the remediation studies. One possibility might be that noticeable impairments in fluency do not begin to emerge in children with reading disabilities until late elementary school. However, the data from Prevention Study I show that a group of highly at-risk children actually obtained higher scores for fluency in fourth grade than they did in second

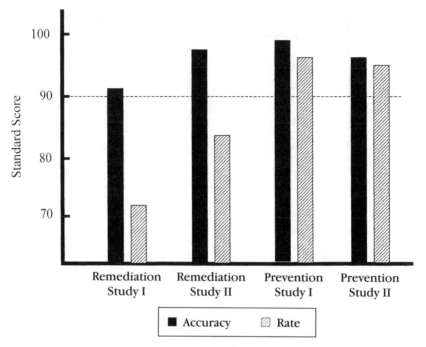

Figure 8.5: Differences in outcomes for rate versus accuracy in prevention versus remediation studies.

grade. It is also possible that the children in the prevention studies may not have been as severely impaired readers as those in the remediation studies because they were identified by risk status rather than actual reading failure. This may be true for Remediation Study I which intervened with children in the bottom 2% of reading skill, but it is less likely for the comparison with Remediation Study II, which served children in roughly the bottom 16% of reading skill. Further, a control group in Prevention Study I that received a variety of school-based interventions, but no research-based interventions, obtained a standard score of 81.7 on the fluency measure. Furthermore, a group of children from a large longitudinal study (Wagner, Torgesen, Rashotte, Hecht, Barker, Burgess, Donahue, and Garon, (1997) who were selected by the same criteria in kindergarten as those in Prevention Study I, but who received no research-based interventions, obtained a standard score of 76 on the rate measure at the end of the fifth grade. Thus, the differences in outcomes for accuracy versus rate measures in remediation and prevention studies cannot be simply ascribed to differences in the severity of reading disabilities of the children being served in the two types of studies.

Deficits in reading practice as a factor in continuing problems in reading fluency

Although a number of factors may be responsible for the continuing problems in reading fluency experienced by children in the remediation studies (Torgesen, Rashotte, and Alexander, in press b), the most important factor appears to involve difficulties in making up for the huge deficits in reading practice that the older children have experienced by the time they reach late elementary school. These differences in reading practice emerge during the earliest stages of reading instruction (Allington, 1984; Beimiller, 1977–8) and they become more pronounced as the children advance across the grades in elementary school. For example, Cunningham and Stanovich (1998) reported evidence suggesting enormous differences in the amount of reading done by fifth-grade good and poor readers outside of school. A child at the 90th percentile of reading ability may read as many words in two days as a child at the 10th percentile reads in an entire year outside the school setting. Differences in reading practice vary directly with the severity of a child's reading disability, so that children with severe reading disabilities receive only a very small fraction of the total reading practice obtained by children with normal reading skills.

One of the major results of the lack of reading practice experienced by children with reading disabilities is a severe limitation in the number of words they can recognize automatically, or at a single glance (Ehri, 1998; Share and Stanovich, 1995). Words that children can recognize easily because they have previously practised reading them in text are sometimes referred to by teachers as the child's 'sight word vocabulary'. A principal characteristic of most children with reading disabilities after the initial phase in learning to read is a severe limitation in the number of words they can recognize 'by sight' or at a single glance (Rashotte, et al., in press, Torgesen, et al., in press a; Wise, Ring, and Olson, 1999).

We have shown elsewhere (Torgesen, et al., in press b) that inefficiency in identifying single words is the single most important factor in accounting for individual differences in text reading fluency in samples of children with reading disabilities. In other words, reading fluency for text is most directly dependent on the proportion of the words in the text that can be identified at a single glance. When these findings are combined with the fact that the number of less-frequent words (words children are less likely to have encountered before in text) increases rapidly after about third grade level (Adams, 1990), it is easy to see why it is so difficult for children who have failed in reading for the first three or four years of school to close the gap in reading fluency with their normally achieving peers. If successively higher grade level passages include increasing numbers of less frequent words, and normal readers are continually expanding their sight vocabularies through their own reading behaviour, it should be very difficult for children, once significantly behind in the growth of their sight word vocabulary, to close the gap in reading fluency. Such 'catching up' would seem to require an extensive period of time in which the reading practice of the previously disabled children was actually *greater* than that of their peers. Even if word reading accuracy is dramatically increased through the more efficient use of analytic word reading processes, reliance on analytic processes will not produce the kind of fluent reading that results when most of the words in a passage can be recognized 'by sight.'

The effect on reading rate of the proportion of words in a passage that can be recognized automatically can be illustrated by data from the intensive remediation study described earlier (Torgesen, et al., in press a). We calculated a words-per-minute score on the two most difficult passages the children read at the pre test, and compared this to their rate for passages of the same level of difficulty at the two-year follow-up test. For the most difficult passage at pretest, rate changed from 38 to 101 words per minute, with a corresponding drop in errors from 10 to two. On the next most difficult passage, rate changed from 42 to 104 words per minute, with a drop in errors from six to one. Thus, for passages that had a constant level of difficulty, the children's reading rate more than doubled from pretest to the end of the follow-up period, presumably because at follow-up, the children could recognize more of the words in the passage easily and automatically. Another way to illustrate this effect is to compare the children's text reading rate for passages that were at their 'instructional level' and which contained many words they had to analyse phonemically in order to read correctly, with passages at their 'independent' level at which most of the words in the passage could be recognized by sight. Their words per minute rate for passages at their instructional level was 78.3, while rate for passages at their independent level was 122 words per minute.

Conclusions

The results from the intervention research described in this chapter have several important implications for both educational practice and for future research. The first implication for practice and educational policy is that schools must work to provide more *preventive* interventions to eliminate the enormous reading practice deficits that result from prolonged reading failure. One of the most important goals of preventive instruction should be to maintain the fundamental word reading skills of at-risk children within the normal range so that they can read independently and accurately. If they can read independently and accurately, and they are also taught to enjoy reading, it is likely that they will experience roughly normal rates of growth in their 'sight word vocabularies' and thus be able to maintain more nearly average levels of reading fluency as they progress through the elementary school years.

The second policy implication from these results is that schools must find a way to provide interventions for older children with reading disabilities that are *appropriately focused and sufficiently intensive*. We have seen a number of examples of the way this type of intervention can produce dramatic improvements in older children's text reading accuracy and reading comprehension in a relatively short period of time.

With this evidence in hand, schools, school boards, and parents need to work toward finding ways to bring more intensive instruction to more children, and we need to adjust our expectations about what constitutes 'reasonable progress in reading' for older children with reading disabilities.

With regard to research, the two most obvious questions arising from the findings considered in this chapter are:

- what is the most appropriate range of intensity and amount of remedial instruction that should be available to older children with reading disabilities; and
- how can reading practice be focused more effectively with older children to help them 'close the gap' in reading fluency with their normally achieving peers?

The first question arises from the fact that, even in the most effective remedial studies, significant numbers of children remain with poor reading skills at the conclusion of the intervention. There is substantial agreement about the elements of effective instruction for children with the most common form of reading disabilities (Lovett et al., 2000; Torgesen, et al., in press a), but there is much less information available about the amount and intensiveness of such instruction that may be required to help all children acquire adequate reading skills.

For children with reading disabilities who have limited sight word vocabularies and limited proficiency in decoding novel words, it seems that the first target of intervention should be to increase the accuracy of their individual word reading skills. More accurate reading at the word level through effective application of a repertoire of word analysis skills is necessary before children can consistently add to the depth and breadth of their sight word vocabulary through independent reading (Share and Stanovich, 1995).

The most successful fluency intervention described to date, repeated reading, (National Reading Panel, 2000) is effective because it provides the kind of repeated exposure to words that leads either to acquisition of new 'sight words' or increases efficiency of access to words that are already in the child's sight vocabulary. Simply providing more reading opportunities for these children may not be sufficient to increase their sight vocabulary at an acceptable rate, because, at higher grade levels, the less frequent words they are trying to learn occur at such infrequent intervals in text (Adams, 1990). Thus, an important question for future research is how to increase the efficiency of reading practice for children whose reading accuracy problems have been remediated through successful interventions. In other words, how should practice be engineered and focused so that it produces accelerated growth in the fluent word-reading processes that are the most critical factor in oral reading fluency?

Acknowledgement

The research reported in this chapter was supported by grant HD30988 from the National Institute of Child Health and Human Development, and by grants from the National Center for Learning Disabilities, and the Donald D Hammill Foundation.

References

Adams MJ (1990) Beginning to read. Cambridge MA: MIT Press.
Alexander A, Anderson H, Heilman PC, Voeller KS, Torgesen JK (1991) Phonological awareness training and remediation of analytic decoding deficits in a group of severe dyslexics. Annals of Dyslexia 41: 193–206.
Allington RL (1984) Content coverage and contextual reading in reading groups. Journal of Reading Behavior 16: 85–96.
Beimiller A (1977–8) Relationships between oral reading rates for letters, words, and simple text in the development of reading achievement. Reading Research Quarterly 13: 223–53.
Clark DB, Uhry JK (1995) Dyslexia: Theory and Practice of Remedial Instruction, 2 edn. Baltimore MD: York Press.
Cunningham AE, Stanovich KE (1998) What reading does for the mind. American Educator 22(Spring/Summer): 8–15.
Ehri LC (1998) Grapheme-phoneme knowledge is essential for learning to read words in English. In J Metsala, L Ehri (eds) Word recognition in Beginning Reading. Hillsdale, NJ: Erlbaum, pp. 3–40.
Hanushek EA, Kain JF, Rivkin SG (1998) Does Special Education raise Academic Achievement for Students with Disabilities? National Bureau of Economic Research, Working Paper No. 6690, Cambridge MA.

Kavale KA, (1988) The long-term consequences of learning disabilities. In MC Wang, HJ Walburg, MC Reynolds (eds), The Handbook of Special Education: Research and Practice. New York: Pergamon, pp. 303–44.

Lindamood P, Lindamood P (1998) The Lindamood Phoneme Sequencing Program for Reading, Spelling, and Speech. Austin TX: PRO-ED, Inc.

Lovett MW, Lacerenza L, Borden SL, Frijters JC, Seteinbach KA, DePalma M (2000) Components of effective remediation for developmental reading disabilities: combining phonological and strategy-based instruction to improve outcomes. Journal of Educational Psychology 92: 263–83.

Mastropieri MA, Scruggs TE (1997) Best practices in promoting reading comprehension in students with learning disabilities: 1976–1996. Remedial and Special Education 18: 197–213.

National Reading Panel (2000) Teaching Children to Read: An evidence-based assessment of the scientific research literature on reading and its implications for reading instruction. Washington DC: National Institute of Child Health and Human Development.

Rashotte CA, MacPhee K, Torgesen JK (in press) The effectiveness of a group reading instruction program with poor readers in multiple grades. Learning Disabilities Quarterly.

Schumaker JB, Deshler DD, Ellis ES (1986) Intervention issues related to the education of learning disabled adolescents. In JK Torgesen, BYL Wong (eds), Psychological and Educational Perspectives on Learning Disabilities. New York: Academic Press, pp. 329–65.

Share DL, Stanovich KE (1995) Cognitive processes in early reading development: a model of acquisition and individual differences. Issues in Education: Contributions from Educational Psychology 1: 1–57.

Swanson HL (1999) Reading research for students with LD: a meta-analysis of intervention outcomes. Journal of Learning Disabilities 32: 504–32.

Torgesen JK, Alexander AW, Wagner RK, Rashotte CA, Voeller K, Conway T, Rose E (in press a) Intensive remedial instruction for children with severe reading disabilities: Immediate and long-term outcomes from two instructional approaches. Journal of Learning Disabilities.

Torgesen JK, Rashotte CA, Alexander A (in press b) Principles of fluency instruction in reading: relationships with established empirical outcomes. In M Wolf (ed.) Time, Fluency, and Developmental Dyslexia. Parkton MD: York Press.

Torgesen JK, Wagner RK, Rashotte CA, Herron J (2000) A Comparison of Two Computer Assisted Approaches to the Prevention of Reading Disabilities in Young Children. Manuscript in preparation.

Torgesen JK, Wagner RK, Rashotte CA, Rose E, Lindamood P, Conway T, Garvin C (1999) Preventing reading failure in young children with phonological processing disabilities: group and individual responses to instruction. Journal of Educational Psychology 91: 579–93.

Truch S (1994) Stimulating basic reading processes using auditory discrimination in depth. Annals of Dyslexia 44: 60–80.

Vaughn SR, Moody SW, Shuman JS (1998) Broken promises: reading instruction the resource room. Exceptional Children 64: 211–25.

Wagner RK, Torgesen JK, Rashotte CA, Hecht SA, Barker TA, Burgess SR, Donahue J,

Garon T (1997) Changing causal relations between phonological processing abilities and word-level reading as children develop from beginning to fluent readers: a five-year longitudinal study. Developmental Psychology 33: 468–79.

Wiederholt JLY, Bryant BR (1992) Gray Oral Reading Tests – III. Austin TX: PRO-ED.

Wise BW, Ring J, Olson RK (1999) Training phonological awareness with and without explicit attention to articulation. Journal of Experimental Child Psychology 72: 271–304.

Woodcock RW, Johnson MB (1989) Woodcock-Johnson Psycho-Educational Battery-Revised. Allen TX: DLM/Teaching Resources

Zigmond N (1996) Organization and management of general education classrooms. In DL Speece, BK Keogh (eds) Research on Classroom Ecologies. Mahwah NJ: Erlbaum, pp. 163–90.

CHAPTER 9

Treating the whole person: emotion, denial, disguises, language, and connectedness

PRISCILLA L VAIL

My dictionary defines *daunt* as a verb: to frighten, discourage, subdue. This is how I felt when asked to write about treating the whole person in a mere 5,000 words.

Any discussion of the people who live with, inside, and around dyslexia must explore emotion, its clout and contagion. Negative emotion frequently branches off into denial and disguise. Denial operates across the generations as well as settling its obfuscating dampness on the hobbled reader. Disguises help people keep their secrets . . . sometimes. While we all wear masks from time to time, sometimes people, particularly dyslexics, put on masks they can't take off. Trapped inside masks of their own making they are often misunderstood or tragically walled off from the available help that could open their lives in new directions. Certainly any discussion of dyslexics would have to consider language, the glorious, uniquely human capacity that is so often underdeveloped in the group we are discussing. And the reason to care about all of the above is the connectedness which can link people with one another as we make that common journey called life. All this in 5,000 words?

I thought my assignment would be impossible until I remembered that small stories can tell big tales. The following vignettes, though set in the United States, transcend geographical boundaries because they explore shared aspects of human nature.

Emotion has the power to open or close pathways, doorways and windows to learning, reasoning and memory. We know from neuroscience that frightened students do poorly. So do adults. Yet how often does fear creep in to the educational process? How many adults (educators and parents) have forgotten what fear feels like and what it can do to cognitive function?

I travel *all* the time and am proud of the smooth routines I've developed. For instance, to prevent impulse packing I make a list of exactly what I'm going to wear and when, choosing items which fit easily in my suitcase, the smallest size Roll-Aboard.

I line up my workshop folders in chronological order, with my speaking notes in the right hand pocket, my airline tickets, and in this instance my passport, on the left side.

The night before a trip, I transfer the tickets to my purse, and put my suitcase and briefcase downstairs by the front door. One more thing. I try to pay all my bills before I fly. You know, wear good underwear in case you get taken to the hospital, and don't leave outstanding debts for the next of kin. Then I usually ask the airport limo driver, who knows me well by now, to stop at the post office in the village. I drop the letters in the slot and prepare to enjoy the newspaper he usually brings for me to read on our hour-plus journey to the airport. So where's the pandemonium the title promises?

In the week of this particular episode, I was excited about going to Victoria BC as I went through the established manoeuvres. My morning flight was due to leave Kennedy at 8:15, meaning airport check-in for an international flight at 6:15 or 6:30, thus my driver and I had to leave my house at 5:00, so I had to get up at 4:15 to wash my hit and run hair, get dressed, and scoff down a quick bite.

My routine unfolded smoothly. In the village, I ran across the 'darkest-before-dawn street to the Post Office, pulled the envelopes out of my purse, dropped them in the curbside mailbox, got back in the car, and we headed for the highway . . . to VICTORIA!

About 20 minutes later, some obsessive / compulsive habit made me put my hand in my purse to touch my ticket folder. No ticket folder. I opened my briefcase, got out the workshop folder to extract my tickets. NO TICKETS. With artificial calm, I said to the driver 'Could you go slowly for a minute? I can't find my tickets. I hope we won't have to go back for them.'

'Better not have to, Mrs. Vail,' he said. 'Traffic's starting to build.'

I fished. I fumbled. I flipped through papers. No tickets.

'Sorry. We have to. Without my tickets, I don't even know the flight number.'

Back at the house, panic mounted. No tickets. Transcribing from my desk calendar, I tried to write the flight information, but my hand was shaking so that the writing was barely legible. The clock showed 5:40. Now we were late.

I got back in the car, close to tears. 'I guess I'll just have to wing it." I said. "Let's see what I can do at the airport.'

'Here' said the driver. 'Use the car phone.'

He gave me the American Airlines phone number. I looked at the car phone as if it were an intergalactic puzzle. 'How does it work?' I asked, my voice breaking.

'You've used this one before, Mrs. Vail. Push Power, punch in the numbers, and push Send.'

'Where?' I couldn't find the buttons.

'The green buttons, Mrs. Vail. You know. Just the way you teach the kids. Green for Go. Remember?'

I pushed the green ones, punched in the numbers, and got a voice mail menu. Trembling still, I pushed # for Additional Assistance, and mercifully heard a human voice.

When I explained my plight, the agent said, 'Lost your ticket? You'll have to buy a new one at the airport. It takes extra time. Get there early. Otherwise you can't go.'

'Can't go?' That phrase unleashed my internal demons and goblins.

'Maybe I should stop travelling. Maybe I can't manage this any more. Maybe I should move to a Senior Citizen's home. Maybe I need custodial care. Maybe I'll have to move in with the children and they won't want me.'

Then, with a thud of terror, I remembered that I had just charged my next six months of business travel tickets. Would my credit card be maxed out? This lost ticket was first class. Would I be able to squeeze its replacement onto this credit card? Why had I brought only one card with me?

'And, please God, don't make me have to do anything complicated such as fill out a form. I can't think. My fingers can't write. I feel guilty, embarrassed, and scared.'

Well, as many of you know, I'm still travelling. American Airlines was kind to me, I bought a new ticket, and they promised me a refund on the old one. I boarded the plane. Tears, this time tears of relief, welled up, and I stopped hyperventilating. I was OK. I haven't had to move in with the children, or submit to custodial care. As an adult, I can quit travelling when I want to, or if I'm incompetent. But what about kids in school?

Students with unrecognized, or unsupported dyslexias face ticketless travel, the potential humiliation of not being allowed to board the academic flight, the shame of not reaching planned destinations, and the loneliness of trying to arrive where everyone else seems to be going, but without any assurance of success or assistance.

Pandemonium comes from the Greek *pan,* meaning *all,* and *daimon* or *demon.* Together, they make the word that means *the abode of all demons,* and, from *Paradise Lost, the palace built by Satan as the capital of Hell.* The word refers to 'any place or scene of wild disorder, noise, or confusion'.

We know from neuropsychological discoveries, as well as from our own parental and clinical experiences, that emotion is the on/ off switch for learning. Scared kids read poorly, if at all. Students without the tickets of skills and seat assignments of trustworthy instruction are left grounded, vicarious observers of others' flights of fancy and of learning. Pandemonium is a paralysing place.

As educators and parents it is our job to create climates in our homes and classrooms that are free of turbulence, fear, motion sickness, wind shear, and overbooking, and which offer the metaphoric pre-boarding of review and systematic overlearning and teaching as dictated by students' needs.

Multi-sensory methods and materials exist, are proven successful, and help students (dyslexic or unburdened) journey through the kingdoms of print. We need to teach teachers how to use them to give students the gift of travel as they earn the frequent flyer miles of successive successes.

As an afterthought, I called home from Victoria to retrieve my telephone messages, and heard, 'Mrs. Vail, this is the Bedford Post Office. We found an envelope of airline tickets in the curbside collection box. We'll save them for you. Hope you got where you were going.'

Denial of dyslexia is closely related to fear: the label itself, disclosure, financial pressure, mistaken association with lowered intelligence, apprehension of blighted opportunity for success, or the guilt with which many of us infuse our obstacles and failures. Under the guise of protection, *denial* of the condition can *deny* the student's right to appropriate teaching and learning.

Three years ago I had a call from a good friend and worried grandmother. I've known Laura and her whole family for forty years. Her oldest daughter Kitty lives in Texas with her husband and children. Eleven-year-old Jeremy was the subject of this call.

'Priscilla, you've got to help us out. Kitty has called and Jeremy is in trouble at school. He failed his history test, he's in the lowest reading group, but the school won't give him any help because they say "he's holding his own and just needs some motivation". His father says he was just the same way at his age, but Kitty is worried. Jeremy hates to read. His handwriting is illegible and his spelling is bizarre. He's started having stomach aches before school but the doctor says there's been a virus going around and also that lots of boys Jeremy's age don't like school because they'd rather be out throwing a ball around or playing computer games. Kitty is usually pretty laid back, but this is really getting to her. Is she right to be worried? Can you talk to her? I hate to bother you, but . . . I mean have you ever heard of anything like this before?'

I asked the obvious questions, inquiring whether there was family history of reading 'reluctance' (I didn't want to scare her away with the term 'disorder' or 'dyslexia'). I asked whether he had enjoyed listening to stories as a little child, whether he had, perchance, been a late talker, what his experience in first grade had been, whether he was a man of action or a man of words, and, most importantly, I asked her to tell me about his passions and his interests.

Like lowering a film into a photographer's developing pan, a picture emerged of an intelligent boy who has always been good with his hands. 'He can make anything, and he's the best fixer in the family . . . all generations!'

As a small child he had preferred trucks and blocks to story hour, and, by age two, was still virtually non-verbal. However, the paediatrician had said, 'Einstein didn't talk till he was four. Jeremy will talk when he's ready. He's right on target for all physical milestones. Don't you go putting pressure on him to talk, Kitty. That'll backfire. Tincture of time. That's what we paediatricians prescribe. Tincture of time.'

Jeremy's first-grade teacher, sweet but green, said that he got on well with other children, and that the main focus of first grade was learning to socialize appropriately. Kitty noticed that he still couldn't read by the end of the year, but the teacher said not to worry.

I asked about second grade to which his grandmother replied, laughing, 'That was the year the Gods intervened in his favour. He fell out of a tree and broke his arm... by the way did I tell you he's left-handed? He was in a cast for six weeks so he didn't have to do any writing. Lucky or what? I guess he did a little reading, but he couldn't write in his journal or whatever they call those things. We were all so happy for him. It was like getting a whole extra vacation.'

When I asked about his passions and interests, the answer was immediate: numbers, sports, art, and friends. 'He's a natural leader. Any group he's in, he's captain. And he's so funny. I gave him a box of crayons when he came to visit. The cover said "assorted colours". He said, "That means they're sorted by colours." Isn't that funny? I told you he's smart!'

'And now?' I asked.

'Now, he's failing. He doesn't understand why. His father has offered him a camping trip if he pulls his grades up. Maybe he's just lazy?' his grandmother said.

In plain English, avoiding any educational jargon, I told her that the profile she had described to me would be consistent with what some people call dyslexia, or, more properly, the dyslexias.

'Oh, no, Priscilla. I'm sure it's not that. You see, he's very intelligent!'

I gave my three-minute talk on the coincidence of dyslexia and intelligence, and suggested some books and article for her to read.

'Yes, good.' she said. 'I'd love to read up on this, but actually I have a lot going on right now. Say, do you think Kitty could just call you? You know, you could explain and everything.'

'I'm always glad to talk with Kitty, but we'll make better use of our time on the phone if she does a little reading first.'

'OK. I'll tell her.'

Several days later Kitty called. No, she hadn't had time to read, but could she just tell me about Jeremy, and see what I thought? An hour and a half later, after a predictable litany, I asked her to send me a few samples of Jeremy's written work, and copies of his report cards.

On one paper, Jeremy had written 'The fyoocher is wats comeing, but mose storys are in the pass tents.'

On another paper, written at the end of his summer at camp, he wrote, 'I was gud at evrthing.'

I told Kitty that, since good diagnosis is the foundation for later prescription, she and her husband needed to arrange a full-scale psych-educational evaluation for Jeremy as soon as possible. Miraculously, I was able to find an excellent person right in her neighbourhood.

Several weeks later, Jeremy's grandmother called me again. 'Well, they got that evaluation and Jeremy's dyslexic. Boy it sure cost a lot of money. And now the person is saying he needs tutoring. Kitty doesn't want to do it. She says it was bad enough taking him to be tested but she certainly doesn't want him branded as different.'

'But if he's dyslexic he already *is* different,' I said.

'Labelling is bad for kids. It hurts their self-esteem . . . by the way did I tell you that Jeremy wrote that as "self of steam". Isn't that cute? I mean it's hysterical, isn't it?'

'Sometimes symptoms look funny' I replied. 'But it's not funny if they're misunderstood.'

'Well, back to that evaluation. It cost an arm and a leg. Oops. Can I call you back? The travel agent's on call waiting. Did I tell you that we've signed on for a round the world trip sponsored by the museum, and we're even springing for the extension. No point going that far just to rush home. We'll be gone nearly eight weeks, and thrifty Jim has even agreed to go first class.'

Several weeks later, Laura called again. 'Listen, I want to run some decisions by you for your blessing. Kitty says she can't bear to wreck Jeremy's life with tutoring. She thinks maybe a summer of swimming and baseball will help him, just, you know, like, . . . grow out of what ever it is he has. Then if he needs tutoring when school gets going, they'll think about it. But definitely not three times a week. You see, if they do that for Jeremy they won't be able to afford that new car . . . SUV . . . they've set their hearts on. They're thinking they could get tutoring half an hour once a week instead of a full hour three times. Doesn't that make sense?'

'Laura, what you're outlining is just a Band-Aid, and a mini Band-Aid at that. If finances are the issue why don't you help her out? What better investment could you make?'

'Oh, goodness, I don't think we could do that. Jim would say they should make it on their own the way we did. Besides, we don't believe in spoiling grandchildren with expensive presents. And, if we do this for Jeremy, what will the other grandchildren say they need?'

Nothing I said changed the situation.

The following February, Laura called again. 'There was vandalism in the library at Jeremy's school. He was accused but Kitty says he would never do anything like that.'

In April, a group of Jeremy's new friends was accused of bullying/terrorizing two younger boys in the locker room. Kitty said that Jeremy had left before the incident turned ugly.

The following October, Jeremy was found in possession of drugs, and also with an amount of money in his back pack that exactly matched the amount stolen from his hall of lockers.

Laura and Jim would not pay for counselling. Kitty said 'Maybe he didn't do it.'

In spite of all the family surrounding him, Jeremy is as neglected as a latchkey child. Afraid, failing, and desperate to be accepted, he would rather be wicked than be invisible. Unable to do with effort what his classmates can do with ease, he is drifting further and further to the fringes with no visible means of return.

Prevention is always easier than remediation. *An ounce of prevention is worth a pound of cure.* Jeremy's ounces were in drug packets he bought.

For want of a nail the shoe was lost. Jeremy's nail would have been the tutoring no one wanted to pay for.

Penny wise, pound-foolish. Jeremy's penny wasn't the good luck kind, and his pound turned out to be the pound of his flesh.

A stitch in time saves nine. Jeremy's stitch was the ache in his side from not being able to read. Nine? Cats have nine lives. Jeremy has only one.

Disguises are an extension of denial, usually used by people who don't know (yet) that there are methods and materials to help learners of all ages.

It's a question of figure/ground: some people see the shape of the vase; others see the silhouettes of two profiles. I'm proud when I can switch back and forth – a visual equivalent of Double Dutch in jump rope. Some people can solve the puzzles in the books with page after page of multi-coloured dots. With prolonged scrutiny, the dots melt into the background and the figure of a wheelbarrow or a parade or an owl emerges. I can't pull off the miracle; for me, the page of dots remains a page of dots.

Similarly, people have varying abilities to see dyslexia in children *and* adults. Some see the students in a class as a 'vase' of ninth graders or as 'profiles' of first graders. A trained eye can see both the vase of intactness and profiles of dyslexia.

Many people, be they employers, family members, or physicians see other people as the variegated dots on the page of workplace, home or community. People whose awareness is heightened by training, exposure or personal experience initially see the coloured dots, and then are able to give the concentrated look through which the figure of the dyslexic emerges against the background of the general population.

Dyslexic students usually show up quickly, their errors jump off the page, claiming attention. Adults, no longer under academic scrutiny, are harder to recognize. Some choose lives or jobs that exercise their talents and leave their disguises intact.

New York Judge Jeffrey Gallett, who navigated law school because his roommate read assignments aloud to him, disguised his dyslexia when he went out to eat by pretending to read the menu and then asking the waiter for 'lasagne, please, or whatever you have that's closest to it.' He wonders that he didn't die of lasagne overdose.

Fred Epstein, Chairman of the Neurosurgery Department at New York's Beth Israel Medical Centre and Director of the Institute for Neurology and Neurosurgery, survived the agonies of school until he could use his spatial skills, nimble fingers, and high intelligence to save lives and return hope to young patients and their families.

One of New York's most acclaimed fashion designers draws, drapes fabric but needs an administrative assistant to manage her letters, contracts – and money!

George Dawson, first-time published author at age 102, who didn't read until he was 98, worked with heavy machinery in a dairy throughout most of his working life. Whether he is dyslexic or whether he was simply untaught is less important than his ultimate victory in understanding and using print.

A soccer Mum who still keeps her dyslexia secret volunteers to be chair or president of the various groups she belongs to. She is a good thinker, crafty strategist, careful planner with an excellent memory. She has learned to delegate, Delegate, DELEGATE. Her children are old enough that she responds to notes from school: 'Read that to me will you, Honey, I can't read while I'm driving', or 'My hands are full.'

Less fortunate are those who live on the lam, shifting employment, running from emotional entanglement, evading the closeness that might lead to exposure. Others tangle with the criminal justice system but maintain their denial or disguise even during incarceration. It's as though an inner coach is whispering 'it's hard to catch a moving target. Keep your chin down, your hands up, and your feet moving forward.'

Then there's Charlie. At the conclusion of a session I had given for a group of mental health professionals in community medicine, a participant told me a story.

'When you were talking I thought about Charlie. I think I've done something very cruel.

'I live in a fairly modest apartment building. Even though it's not grand, we have a doorman . . . for security. Charlie's young, energetic, funny and very personable. I've often wondered why he isn't a lawyer or a brain surgeon, but it's our luck to have him.

'Last Tuesday I was expecting an important piece of mail, and kept checking the hall outside my front door. No mail. I called downstairs and told Charlie. He told me that the guy who sorts the mail hadn't come in yet. He didn't know why. I explained my plight and asked him if he would just thumb through the mail and fish out my letters. He said that wasn't his job. I said I knew that, but I needed a favour, would he please help me out. He replied that he gets paid to wear his uniform and stand by the door. I didn't actually remind him of the big tip I had given him for Christmas but I said that I had been good to him and now was his turn. He said he wasn't going to do it. He didn't even say he was sorry. So I lost it. I yelled at him over the phone "Damn it Charlie. What's the matter with you?" When I came downstairs later, he wouldn't make eye contact.

'Now I think I know what's the matter. Maybe it's just a question of strict union rules, but maybe the reason such a bright young man is in such a menial job is that he can't read. Here I am a doctor, and I've just hurt someone very badly.'

Adults who can't read are prey to shame, embarrassment, guilt, anger, and depression, prompting evasion, avoidance, aggression, denial, or criminal behaviour.

How many people are we talking about? Roughly 20% of the population fits somewhere on the reading disability continuum. What should we do?

- Raise the general 'index of suspicion'.
- Publicize the statistics.
- Recognize the symptoms.
- Replace shame with specific help, thus hope.
- Improve teacher awareness and training so dyslexic children don't slip by to become misunderstood dropouts or self-loathing adult evaders.
- Endorse screening for dyslexia in juvenile justice procedures and support literacy programs in rehabilitation and correctional facilities.

• Inform people about BDA in the UK, IDA and Literacy Volunteers in the US, and reading instruction programmes on television for young and adult viewers.

Several years ago a seventeen-year-old boy invited me to see his Grateful Dead recordings. After I had 'admired' (?) the art on the record jackets, he pulled out a record and pointed to the small gold lettering around the bottom arc of the label. 'I've never understood this', he said. 'What does it mean? "All rights reversed."'

What a profound question. Did he mean all rights reversed, as in all letters which should face right are reversed for dyslexics and face left instead? Or, on a deeper level, did he mean that all rights, meaning privileges, are reversed as in the judicial sense of denied. Non-readers are barred from access to the knowledge and beauty contained in the kingdom of print. Are their rights reversed?

Those of us fortunate enough to be well taught or self-taught readers need to acknowledge our great privilege, and through teacher training and personal alertness, see to it that adults who have slipped through the cracks have a second chance to have 'all rights reserved'.

A wise person once said 'for many dyslexics, language itself is a second language.' Most people use language automatically. But the word *dyslexia* comes from the Latin *dys* meaning *difficulty* and *lex* meaning *words* or *language*. Thus, this tool that underlies communication, supports conceptual development, bestows the ability to query, disagree, persuade, or tell of love, facilitates the mechanism for filing recollections and associations, and permits one to retrieve words and information for use in thinking and reasoning is blunt, bent, or virtually absent.

Those with language confusion misperceive, misunderstand, misuse, misplace and misrepresent. These aren't misprints and I'm not a misanthrope.

These five verbs describe the way in which increasing numbers of students (and adults) use language today. I don't decry the glorious sprawl and tangle of legitimate language growth. I'm neither a Luddite nor a verbal ostrich. I even admire and chuckle over some of the cybervocabulary we get from geek speak. These new words are anchored in meaning and make sense. What worries me is imprecision; slippery words that slosh around sounding like other words. Human beings absorb vocabulary and the rhythms of language through their receptive language capacities: listening and reading. They exercise what they think they have learned through their expressive capacities: speaking and writing. Speaking and writing are windows to internal confusions.

Misperceive

People who misperceive make 'slips of the ear' as in transforming the funereal (or nymphomaniacal!) folk song phrase 'she laid him on the green' into the royalty wannabe 'Lady Mondagreen'. The title of Malachy McCourt's book *A Monk Swimming* comes from mishearing the Hail Mary phrase 'Blessed art thou amongst women' as 'Blessed art thou, *a monk swimming.*' Do these affirm the promise in the 23rd Psalm: 'and surely *good Mrs. Murphy* shall follow me all the days of my life'?

Some who misperceive make unintentional puns, intelligent errors:

- A fifth grader wrote, 'I read the books over vacation. Here is my *summery.*'
- A nanny wrote home 'The Mom's OK. She just wants to cuddle the baby so she doesn't get *post part 'em depression.*'
- A tenth grader e-mailed his grandmother 'I'm getting ready for the Hallowe'en *mask-a-raid.*'
- A teenager reviewed a movie: 'This *sinema* is rated R.'

Misunderstand

Other errors are bulletins from 'bedlam' which, as we know from *The Professor and the Madman,* Simon Winchester's book about the writing of the *Oxford English Dictionary,* is a foreshortening of Bethlehem, the name of a hospital for the insane.

Infrequent readers lack the visual burglar alarm system that would warn them when incorrect spelling steals meaning from phrases. Because they misunderstand words themselves, their written expression makes no sense or, as one person wrote, 'no cents'. Does that mean their jottings aren't worth a 'plugged' nickel? They don't know where words come from, or even that words, like families, have origins, roots and branches. Consequently, they write, and we try to read, such gobbledegook as:

- 'Jimmy is so smart. He's started the ABCs and nearly knows the whole *awful bit.*'
- 'The problem with this Greek hero is that he suffered from an *edible complex.*'
- 'Everywhere you looked there was another cigarette *bud.*'

In response to a spoken assignment to write a paragraph about the Greek goddess Aphrodite, an eleventh grader wrote '*Afro deity* was very beautiful.'

Asked to define 'hugger-mugger' a middle school girl said with certainty 'someone who hugs you and then steals your money'.

The teacher said 'My lesson misfired. I was trying to help Rebecca understand herself better so I told her she was dyslexic and what that meant. Later that morning she was in a small reading group with Anna and Salonica. They started reading. Anna said 'Rebecca, you can't read.' Rebecca replied 'That's because I'm *selective*.' 'But you're so slow,' said Anna. Rebecca trumped: 'That's because I'm more *selective* than you.'

A sixth grader wrote: 'I don't want to do this. It will be bad for my *self of steam*.'

Misuse

People with word retrieval problems, which frequently accompany dyslexia, often use phrases or expressions that are 'a half bubble off plumb'. In so doing, they make trouble for themselves, retard their own progress, or appear ridiculous. As they say in rainy Scotland where boots are called 'Wellies', short for Wellingtons, they are 'peeing in their Wellies'.

For example, a father, mother, and two sons live in a mid-Western town with a sizeable German population. The father is particularly active in the German/American Club and wants his wife and children to accompany him to club events. Tom, the younger son, doesn't enjoy these outings, feels self-conscious about being there, and doesn't see why he should have to us his free time on something he finds distasteful and embarrassing. A 'dress German' party was in the offing, each male family member has a pair of grey lederhosen with green trim, and the mother has a dirndl. Exhorted to come along to round out the family group, Tom resisted as long as possible, but finally capitulated, blurting out 'OK I'll go. But I'm NOT wearing those wiener schnitzel!'

There are expressions that initially sound incorrect or senseless, but which, on consideration, are very clear. An eleven-year-old dyslexic in a class of rapid, powerful readers, said 'I feel like a worm in a bowl of spaghetti. We're the same in lots of ways, but also I'm really different.' At the end of the next academic year, after receiving good help, the same kid said, glowing, 'I'm in a bowl of worms.'

Misplace

What has become of 'there are' as in 'there are' six web sites, 'there are' four pieces of sushi in the fridge, or 'there are' 12 unanswered e-mails and 'there are' two videos that have to be back at Blockbuster before 10:00. We've lost 'there are'. It's misplaced, replaced by 'therza' and 'therza lotta':

therza lotta Web sites out there, *therz* four raw fish under that lemon juice, *therza lotta* e-mail to do and *therz* two videos for Blockbuster unless we want to pay the fine.

Misrepresent

So, like, why should we, like, care? Robust language is a mighty human tool. We must not blunt it. Our words, heard, read, spoken and written must not misrepresent our intentions. Because language is highly contagious, we need to soak ourselves, our students, and our progeny in the vocabulary, structures and cadences of strong, reliable, sweet, melodious, evocative correct language. Otherwise, believing we are connecting with others, we are simply delivering monologues into our own mirrors.

Connectedness rescues us from our own mirrors, broadening our vistas to include, scenery, perspective, and, of course one another. This is what happened to me.

I thought I could predict every moment of that tightly planned day. My note cards were in order. The outlines were at the auditorium, ready for distribution. I looked forward to presenting a six-hour session on reading comprehension, helping readers connect with writers, with ideas, and with themselves, and how to join printed words with the knowledge, emotions, and questions we carry inside. While some kinds of comprehension develop spontaneously, most students need instruction from teachers who understand the processes themselves.

I was wearing my Worry Doll necklace. Classically, these individual, colourful, tiny Guatemalan figures are kept in a jar or on a plate. When their owner puts a few under the bed pillow at night, their job is to worry on the sleeper's behalf, thus providing tranquil slumber. But, lore says, when Worry Dolls are joined in pairs on little bits of wood (as in my necklace) they become Amigos, friends to the world and to each other.

With 30 minutes to spare before being picked up, I planned to sit in the lobby and polish the new introduction to my talk. As I relished this bubble of private time, a man came down the hall, saying to the woman behind the registration desk, or perhaps to the world at large, 'I can't work my phone. How do I get long distance?'

She replied, rather curtly 'It works just like any other phone. Just get into AT&T or whoever your carrier is. You'll have to use your PIN.'

His face told me her words didn't make sense to him. 'I have a family emergency. I need to make a call.' The woman shrugged and turned away. 'Just use it like any other public phone.'

He was pale, and seemed perplexed and overwhelmed. I got up and crossed over to him, explaining that I couldn't help overhearing, that I had often been confused by telephone terminology myself. I held out my cell phone and offered to place the call for him. He stepped back, hesitant but clearly wanting to say yes. I said that my prepaid phone plan let me call anywhere, any time, with no long-distance charges.

'It's free.' I said. 'Please just tell me the number so I can call it for you.'

When the number started to ring, I handed him the phone and turned away to give him the illusion of privacy. I heard him tell the person on the other end that his daughter had spent 12 hours in surgery, the doctors were doing their best but she was very weak and in grave danger of infection so the children must not come to visit for the next several days. He said he didn't know when he would be able to call again, or how he would get the news to the rest of the family. Then his voice cracked. He said he had to go, and handed the phone back to me because he didn't know how to hang up.

He started to tell me about his daughter who had caught her right sleeve in the machinery of a leaf blower; the machine had devoured not only the cloth of her jacket but had torn off her right forearm. With that, his whole body trembled and he choked in sobs. I put my arms around him, and, with one hand, cradled his head against my shoulder. I didn't know what to say. How stupid it would be to tell him that everything would be all right. All I could think of was to say that I could tell he loved his daughter very much. That reached him. 'Yes I do. I love her very much.'

He raised his head from my shoulder and stopped short. 'I shouldn't be doing this. I shouldn't be crying like this. I should be strong. I'm a cop.'

'Yes you should be crying like this. You love her, she's hurt, you're worried and you're probably exhausted. How did you get here? Are you alone?'

He explained that his daughter had been brought to the hospital by a Medi-vac helicopter, that he and his wife had come by car. She had seen the helicopter pass over their house but had no idea who the passenger/patient was. He told me that his wife was waiting in their room to hear whether he had been able to make a call. I asked him to bring her, and their list of family telephone numbers, to the lobby. I would place the calls for them, as many as they wanted, for the next thirty minutes. I emphasized it would be free. He looked at me, dazed, reluctant, embarrassed, ambivalent, frightened and aching for someone to make the decision for him. 'Let's do this for your wife. We can help her.'

Several minutes later he reappeared, holding her hand. Her hair was rumpled, her eyes red from sleeplessness and tears. They looked like Hansel and Gretel, lost in the woods. I didn't press her with the manners of introductions, I just asked her to tell me the number of someone she thought they should call. When the connection was made, I gave her the phone. Her husband slipped his hand into mine rather the way you fit a plug into an outlet to get power. I held his hand while his wife talked. For the next call, he talked. She held my hand. And thus it went, alternating on the phone, telling the news.

When bad things happen we need to tell the story out loud. It's how we come to realize that it's true. Finally, they had called all the people on the list, and it was time for me to go. I kissed each one, and wished their family the best of luck.

At the podium, I put aside my carefully crafted introduction.

First, touching my necklace, I told the conference goers how the dolls had once represented worry but, coming together in pairs instead of alone, they were now Amigos, symbols of friendship.

Next, I told the story of the two frightened, grief stricken people, and how, through them, I had just been given a great gift: a piece of black plastic, a cell phone, had been my passport into the inner reaches of two other human souls. I had been privileged to stand in the presence of so much love, from parents to child, and back and forth between husband and wife. These people gave me the gift of allowing me to help when they were in trouble. Proud, habitually competent people often don't know how to do this. These two almost didn't dare but, in desperation, they took a chance.

Finally, I relayed the physician's credo that is carved on the base of a statue of Dr Livingstone Trudeau in Saranac, New York: 'To cure *sometimes,* to relieve *often,* to comfort *always.'*

This same credo can belong to us all. With educators, parents and students, we can *sometimes* cure ignorance by offering knowledge. In classrooms, we can *often* relieve anxiety by demonstrating successful strategies. And in our dealings with other human beings, we can comfort *always* by being intellectually and emotionally available.

There is no more solemn trust.

There is no greater privilege.

This is what it is to treat the whole person.

CHAPTER 10

International perspectives on dyslexia

SUSAN A VOGEL, STEPHEN REDER

The overall goal of the project reported in this chapter was to advance our knowledge and understanding of the magnitude and complexity of the problem of dyslexia from an international perspective. A team of distinguished researchers in the field of dyslexia/learning disabilities representing nine countries is currently investigating the impact of a wide range of factors on the International Adult Literacy Survey (IALS) findings. Unlike previous comparative studies, which were based on a variety of different assessment measures, this project is unique in using an identical measure, the IALS, administered under the same conditions in each of the participating countries. Data will be extracted from nine nations, including disability status questions in the IALS. These nations are Belgium, Canada, Germany, Great Britain, Ireland, New Zealand, the Netherlands, Sweden, and the US. In this chapter, we present the overall plan for the project and some preliminary data regarding the five English-speaking countries. Factors to be examined will be differences in phonological, morphological, and orthographic aspects of different languages, and differences in public policy, special education, pedagogical theory, and the practice and teaching of reading and reading intervention among the countries surveyed. Findings will be reported for each nation and then compared cross nationally in order to understand the impact of the identified differences on the prevalence of dyslexia, age and gender distribution, literacy proficiency, and educational attainment of those with dyslexia in each country. Finally, prevalence of self-reported learning disabilities for the nine nations will be reported as well as preliminary findings on this population in comparison to the general population in the five English-speaking countries.

International perspectives on dyslexia

In this chapter, we report progress towards an innovative venture that allows researchers worldwide the opportunity for the first time to undertake a multinational comparison of adults with self-reported learning disabilities as compared to the general population in each country on a variety of parameters such as prevalence of learning disabilities, literacy proficiency, educational attainment, employment, and income, using the extraordinarily rich data gathered via the International Adult Literacy Survey (IALS).

With the technological advances and sophistication of instantaneous and real-time electronic communication, researchers worldwide have expanding opportunities to collaborate. The International Adult Literacy Survey project was designed to capitalize on these technological advances in order to enhance our understanding of the complexity and magnitude of the problem of dyslexia by bringing together a group of internationally known researchers in the field of dyslexia/learning disabilities and literacy (see for example, Vogel and Reder, 1998 for reviews of adult literacy). This group of collaborators will start by identifying cross-national differences by sharing relevant information about the phonology, morphology, syntax, and orthography of their languages, and about public policy, legislation, awareness and understanding of dyslexia and learning disabilities, availability of special education services, pedagogic theory, and the methods used in teaching reading and reading intervention. The participants in this project will work together to interpret new findings from the International Adult Literacy Survey (IALS), a measure of prose, document, and quantitative literacy, which to date has been administered to a representative sample of individuals aged 16 and older under the same conditions in 21 countries. In our first year of collaboration we will focus on the first wave of data collection in the nine countries that addressed the disability questions, namely, Belgium (Flanders), Canada, Germany, Great Britain, Ireland, New Zealand, the Netherlands, Sweden, and the United States.

International perspectives regarding dyslexia/learning disabilities have been described by a number of experts from Canada, Italy, and New Zealand (Chapman, 1992; Fabbro and Masutto, 1994; Wiener and Siegel, 1992). Even from this limited number of studies, it is apparent that one source of the complexity in conducting cross-national research is differences in the definition of key terminology (See Opp, 1992 for a case in point in which the term 'learning disability' in Germany referred to mild mental retardation.) However, in Germany the term 'dyslexia' is defined in much the same way it is defined in the US (Lyon, 1995) and is an area of considerable research interest (Klicpera and Schabmann, 1993, Wimmer, 1999). There is also a growing body of comparative researchers, for example, Goswami and Wimmer (1994) and more recently Landerl, Wimmer and Frith (1997), who are investigating the impact of differences in orthographic, phonological, syntactic, and morphological aspects of language in English and German. In an earlier study, Lindgen, De Renzi, and Richman (1985) compared developmental dyslexia in Italy and the US. However, good as these attempts were, there have been very few such studies and, for the most part, they have been focused on a specific aspect of linguistics.

To date, the only systematic multinational co-ordinated research effort in the field of dyslexia has been a collaboration among 15 countries co-ordinated by the European Cooperation in the Field of Scientific and Technical Research (COST A8) over a three-year period. The main object-ive of this project was to investigate early reading failure with a focus on language and other cultural differences (Olufsson and Stromquist, 1998). Because of the specific focus of the COST mission, the project did not address cross-national differences in public policy, legislation, special education services, and pedagogic theory and practice in teaching reading.

There is some urgency in initiating this project to accomplish the tasks described above. Were the IALS findings to be released in a future technical report it is unlikely that they would be accompanied by the inter-pretative information that is being proposed here. The release of such data could very well result in a 'literacy Olympics' mentality or, worse, could result in the premature abandonment of good practice rather than the adoption of research-based intervention strategies (Stahl, Higginson and King, 1993).

The purpose of this project is as follows:

- To interpret the IALS findings for each nation in terms of prevalence, gender ratio, literacy proficiency, and educational attainment of individuals with dyslexia as compared to those without dyslexia in light of the background information described for each nation.
- To compare these findings cross-linguistically and cross-nationally in light of the shared and unique features of the nine nations.
- To develop a series of international, broad-based, and specific recom-mendations for future comparative research collaborations, reading instruction and intervention, provision of special education, and teacher preparation.

The IALS data

In addition to the national background data that each participant was able to bring to this project, the data source common to the participants which provided new insight was the public-use IALS data set based on the first two administrations of the IALS (OECD, 1997). The first-wave database contains responses to the background questionnaire items including disability status and assessed prose, document and quantitative literacy proficiencies of the 38,358 adults age 16 and above sampled from the Organization for Economic Co-operation and Development (OECD) countries participating. Further technical description of the IALS design, instrumentation, assessment and sampling techniques are available elsewhere (Murray, Kirsch and Jenkins, 1998; OECD, 1997, 1995).

For the current project, secondary analyses will be conducted on data from the nine countries that included the relevant disability questions in their survey questionnaires: Belgium, Canada, Germany, Ireland, The Netherlands, New Zealand, Sweden, the UK and the US. The background question of particular interest here asked whether respondents ever had a learning disability. The sampling, weighting and other aspects of the survey design permitted nationally representative, comparable data to be produced and analysed.

The IALS database also contains rich information about individuals' educational background, language background, reading and writing activities at work, adult education and training experiences, general reading and writing activities, family literacy activities, household information, and parental labour force participation. This research database contains no individual or local geographic identifiers, and thus satisfies ethical requirements in terms of confidentiality.

The initial tasks of the participants include the following:

- To provide an overview of the linguistic and orthographic features of their language and the relationship of these features to dyslexia/reading disabilities in their nation.
- To identify and analyse the terminology used in the IALS questionnaires in each participating nation in relation to prevailing technical and popular understandings of this terminology, and to place the use of this terminology within a time frame in each respective country.
- To provide an overview of the legislation and public policies regarding individuals with dyslexia/learning disabilities.
- To describe the procedures for identification of individuals with dyslexia/learning disabilities, the eligibility criteria, and the special

education services available (from kindergarten through twelfth grade) within an historical perspective.

• To provide an overview of the prevalence and gender ratio of dyslexia across the life span as well as the method of identification used to generate these data in each country.

• To describe the methodology and practice of teaching reading and dyslexia intervention within an historical perspective to the present.

It is expected that one of the major outcomes of this project will be to prevent the misinterpretation and/or misuse of the IALS results by pitting one nation against another based on a superficial understanding of the results. Such misuse could result in premature adoption of an intervention method or reading methodology that is not research-based such as occurred with the adoption of the whole language approach (Noah, 1984; Stahl, Higginson and King, 1993).

The IALS survey and tasks

The IALS surveyed random samples of individuals age 16 and older (the upper limit in most countries was 65) in 21 countries in a unique combination of questionnaire and educational methodologies. Home interviews and assessments of functional literacy proficiencies were conducted on prose, document and quantitative literacy scales (scores 0–500). Key design features common to all countries included the administration of a rich background questionnaire (taking around 30 minutes to complete) and an initial screening, based on the criteria of passing 2/6 components in order to progress to the assessment proper. This screening ensured that all respondents were sufficiently skilled in the spoken language of the interviewer to attempt the full assessment. The background questions addressed an extensive range of information on ethnographic factors, current employment, self-assessment of literacy skills, and reading habits. The approach adopted in administering the questionnaire and literacy items was to allow respondents unlimited time to complete each booklet which contained about 45 questions per booklet. This reading comprehension measure was based on the ability to extract information from text of all types. Skills assessed included using printed and written information to function in society, to achieve one's goals, and develop oneself as an individual. Proficiencies were estimated on a 0–500 point scale based on difficulty level of the items respondents answered correctly or incorrectly. These scores are often reported in five levels ranging from 1 to 5 with poor (level 1) and excellent (level 5). Scoring utilized a weighting system based on item response theory (Murray, Kirsch and Jenkins, 1998, which produced efficiency estimates and took into account non-responses.

Method

The population age 16 and older in these nine countries totalled approximately 293 million, from which a sample of 31,375 was drawn. The IALS sampling design and sampling weights were used to construct comparable nationally representative population estimates for self-reported learning disabilities in these nine countries. Although self-report is certainly not an infallible indicator of clinically identifiable learning disabilities it appears to have served as a useful and reasonably valid method of sample ascertainment in several large scale surveys in the US, including the data set regarding the percent of students with disabilities enrolled in US colleges and universities (for in-depth discussion, see Vogel, 1998a, 1998b; Vogel and Reder, 1998).

Results

In the nine nations, there were an estimated 9.85 million adults who reported having learning disabilities, representing 3.4% of the population age 16 and older. Figure 10.1 shows the corresponding rates for the nine countries in the IALS. The prevalence rates of self-reported learning disabilities based on our preliminary analyses varied widely among these countries, ranging from the highest rate of over 7% in New Zealand to the lowest rate of less than 1% in Sweden. The prevalence rate for the US in these IALS data was 3.3%, very close to the 3.4% rate for the entire set of nine countries.

Although it was the country with the lowest prevalence rate, Sweden was also the country with the highest level of literacy proficiency in the IALS (OECD, 1997, 1995). The international correspondence between population levels of literacy proficiency and the incidence of SRLD is far from perfect in the IALS data. New Zealand, for example, had the highest prevalence rate for SRLD but also very high levels of literacy proficiency in its adult population. Apparently the factors associated with the incidence of LD are distinct from those associated with the acquisition of literacy proficiency, although it is also clear that LD is often a major barrier to the acquisition of these same literacy skills and knowledge (Reder, 1995; Vogel and Reder, 1998).

We were also interested to know how those who had a self-reported learning disability compared to the general population on years of schooling, completion of secondary school, document literacy proficiency, and the percentage performing at the lowest level on document literacy. In order to increase the power in making these comparisons, we collapsed the SRLD groups in the five English-speaking countries into one group, namely, Canada, Ireland, New Zealand, the UK and the US (Reder, 2000).

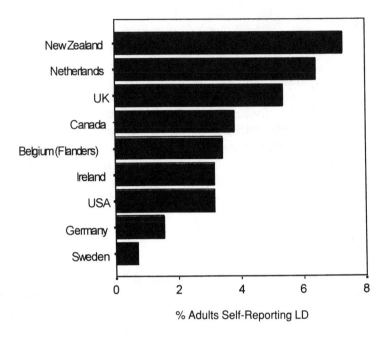

Figure 10.1: Prevalence of self-reported LD in adults. Source: Reder S (1998).

Using the collapsed data across the five English-speaking countries, it may be seen (see Table 10.1) that there are striking and significant differences between those with self- reported learning disabilities (SRLD) and the general population.

The respondents with self-reported learning disabilities had almost two years less schooling than those in the general population. About half as many had completed secondary school – failure to do this being, in most countries, a significant impediment to finding and maintaining a job. There was also a highly significant difference in document literacy proficiency with more than half among the SRLD respondents scoring at the lowest level on the document literacy as compared to about one-fifth in the general population. Deficits of this magnitude are very likely to impact on all aspects of life.

Implications

These initial findings point to some important international differences in the prevalence of learning disabilities in adult life and in the SRLD group compared to the general population. Previous research has found strong

Table 10.1: Analysis of SRLD respondents compared to the general population in the five English-speaking countries

	Years of schooling	% completed secondary school	Document literacy proficiency score	% at lowest level of document literacy
SRLD	10.7	29	209	55
General population	12.2	58	277	19

relationships among LD, educational attainment, literacy skills, and the social and economic dimensions of adult life in the US (Reder, 1995; Reder and Vogel, 1997; Vogel and Reder, 1998). There is good reason to expect that similar analyses of these relationships within the comparative international framework of the IALS would shed important new light on LD. Particularly valuable would be modelling studies that link statistical analysis comparing the SRLD groups by country with the IALS database within a comparative historical framework regarding public policies, legislation, special education services, reading pedagogy, teacher preparation, and so forth. The IALS project holds the promise of enhancing our understanding of how to effectively educate those with dyslexia/learning disabilities and rather than competing with one another, learning from one another so that those with dyslexia are better able to compete in the global economy and lead more satisfying lives.

Postscript

At the time when this chapter was written (November, 2000) we had just begun to work together on the analysis and interpretation of the IALS data. Following a successful symposium at the International Dyslexia Association International Conference in Washington DC, we planned the time line for the first year of this project. It seems to us that initiatives of this type have untapped potential for influencing outcomes, particularly for adult dyslexics and those with learning disabilities, a hitherto much-neglected area. By April 2001, the time of the BDA conference for which this chapter has been prepared, we are hopeful that further strides will have been made in our understanding of dyslexia and adult literacy worldwide. We look forward to sharing these insights with you in the IALS symposium at the British Dyslexia Association Conference at York University in April, 2001.

Acknowledgements

The authors gratefully acknowledge the assistance of the International Dyslexia Association, which provided a grant that allowed us to initiate this project.

References

Chapman JW (1992) Learning disabilities in New Zealand: Where Kiwis and Kids with LD can't fly. Journal of Learning disabilities, 25, 362–70.

Fabbro F, Masutto C (1994). An Italian perspective on learning disabilities. Journal of Learning Disabilities 27(3): 138–41.

Goswami U, Wimmer H (1994) The influence of orthographic consistency on reading development. Word recognition in English and German. Cognition 51: 91–103.

Klicpera C, Schabmann A (1993) Do German children have a chance to overcome reading and spelling difficulties? A longitudinal survey from second until eighth grade. European Journal of Psychology of Education 8: 307–23.

Landerl K, Wimmer H, Frith U (1997) The impact of orthographic consistency of dyslexia: a German-English comparison. Cognition 63(3): 315–34.

Lindgen SD, De Renzi E, Richman LC (1985) Cross-national comparisons of developmental dyslexia in Italy and the United States. Child Development 56: 1404–17.

Lyon GR (1995) Toward a definition of dyslexia. Annals of Dyslexia XLV: 3–27.

Murray TS, Kirsch IS, Jenkins LB (1998) Adult literacy in OECD countries: technical report on the first International Adult Literacy Survey. (Technical Report NCES 98-053) Washington DC: US Department of Education, National Center for Education Statistics.

Noah HJ (1984) The use and abuse of comparative education. Comparative Education Review 28(4): 550–62.

Olufsson A, Stromquist S (eds) (1998) COST A8 – Cross-linguistic studies of dyslexia and early language development. Luxembourg: Office for Official Publications of the European Communities.

Opp G (1992) A German perspective on learning disabilities. Journal of Learning Disabilities 25(6): 351–60.

Organization for Economic Cooperation and Development, and Human Resources Development Canada (1995) Literacy, economy, and society: Results of the First International Adult Literacy Survey. Paris: OECD.

Organization for Economic Cooperation and Development, & Human Resources Development Canada (1997) Literacy skills for the knowledge society: Further results from the International Adult Literacy Survey. Paris: OECD.

Organization for Economic Cooperation and Development (1998) Technical report on the first International Adult Literacy Survey (Technical Report NCES 98-053). Washington DC: US Department of Education, National Center for Educational Statistics.

Reder S (1995) Literacy, education, and learning disabilities. Portland OR: Northwest Regional Educational Laboratory.

Reder S (1998) International comparisons of the prevalence of self-reported and school-identified learning disabilities. Portland OR: Portland State University.

Reder S (2000) An overview of some IALS findings in English-speaking nations. Paper presented at the conference of the International Dyslexia Association, Washington DC, 11 November 2000.

Reder S, Vogel SA (1997) Lifespan employment and economic outcomes for adults with self-reported learning disabilities. In P Gerber, D Brown (eds) Learning Disabilities and Employment, Austin TX: Pro-Ed, Inc, pp. 371–94.

Stahl NA, Higginson BC, King JR (1993) Appropriate use of comparative literacy research in the 1990s. Journal of Reading 37(1): 2–12.

Vogel SA (1998a) Adults with learning disabilities: what learning disabilities specialists, adult literacy educators, and other service providers want and need to know. In S A Vogel, S Reder (eds) Learning Disabilities, Literacy, and Adult Education. Baltimore MD: Paul H Brookes Publishing Co, pp. 5–28.

Vogel SA (1998b) How many adults really have learning disabilities? Paper presented at the conference of the International Dyslexia Association, San Francisco CA, 11 November 1998.

Vogel SA, Reder S (1998) (eds) Learning Disabilities, Literacy and Adult Education. Baltimore MD: Paul. H Brookes Publishing Co.

Wiener J, Siegel L (1992) A Canadian perspective on learning disabilities. Journal of Learning Disabilities 25: 340–50.

Wimmer H (1999) Developmental dyslexia in regular orthographies. Paper presented at the conference of the International Academy for Research in Learning Disabilities. University of Padova, Italy, 5 September 1998.

PART FOUR
GOOD PRACTICE

CHAPTER 11

Pre-school children and dyslexia: policy, identification and intervention

MIKE JOHNSON, LINDSAY PEER, RAY LEE

The ability to use language and to communicate effectively is the basis of successful social interaction and learning. The relationship between phonological awareness at the onset-rhyme level and the development of literacy is now well established. For example:

> Phonological awareness is rooted in the early experiences of childhood prior to embarking on formal learning of literacy skills and is thought to arise partly as a result of hearing and chanting nursery rhymes. Normally progressing pre-schoolers begin to recognise that words or streams of speech sounds can be divided into smaller segments. They notice similarities between some of these segments and are particularly aware of those that rhyme. Later as apprentice reader/spellers they go on to recognise the relationships between sound patterns and spelling patterns.
>
> (Layton, Deeny, Upton and Tall, 1996: 3)

This view owes much of its empirical foundation to the work of Bradley and Bryant (1983), Goswami (1986) and Bryant and Goswami (1987) establishing that the acquisition of literacy is dependent on the integration of a number of strategies that develop out of a child's experiences, notably those that heighten an awareness of rhyme and alliteration. The National Literacy Strategy in the UK has recognized this by introducing the teaching of phonological awareness to all children in their first year of schooling. The aim is to close any gaps in the child's processing system before failure sets in. It is recognized that there are a number of children who find the acquisition of language skills a barrier to learning. Of these, there is a subgroup that 'unexpectedly' experiences difficulty and suffers, often dramatically, in the education system. Bradley and Bryant (1983), Stackhouse (1986), Kamhi and Catts (1986) have suggested that these children may have a history of phonological deficits perhaps accompanied by ongoing difficulties with rhyme and alliteration judgements (Bradley 1988).

As detailed later in this chapter, research indicates that it is possible to identify children with these specific learning needs at a very young age. If appropriate remediation follows, difficulties can often be overcome or ameliorated. Lundberg and colleagues (1988) have shown that training phonological awareness in pre-school children promotes literacy development and may even prevent the emergence of literacy difficulties in some children. Other writers, such as McArthur and colleagues (2000) suggest that language impairment is the fundamental difficulty. Together with, or reflected in, weaknesses in speed of processing and short-term memory, organizational, sequencing and fine motor skills it can lead to limitations in the development of specific aspects of reading, spelling, writing and sometimes numeracy. None of this is necessarily related to low intellectual ability and/or poor teaching. For some pupils there may be added problems of attention and concentration. Others may have developed unacceptable behaviours as a result of frustration.

One of us (Peer) is currently investigating the relationship of otitis media (or 'glue ear') with the weaknesses described above. Results to date indicate that many young children with the above 'symptoms' have suffered significant bouts of upper respiratory tract infections leading to this condition. Over 70% of those studied were significantly affected in later stages of schooling (Peer, 2001 in preparation).

There is a further issue that is only just beginning to be discussed. That is of children for whom English is an additional language (EAL). Of these there is a sub-group who are also dyslexic. Cline and Shamsi (2000) claim that most children with EAL do not encounter particular problems in deciphering print at the word level, even in their second language. They go on to state (in relation to dyslexia) that 'it is probable that many such children go unnoticed and are treated as though their problems are solely to do with limited knowledge of the language in which they are trying to read' (p. 3).

Peer (1997) demonstrated that there are large numbers of such young children who need to be identified, and then offered appropriate language input and dyslexia teaching. There is virtually nothing done in the UK to work effectively with this group. A full discussion of the issues involved can be found in Peer and Reid (2000).

By 2004, the UK government intends that there be universal provision for all three year olds whose parents want it. They are currently developing a programme of measures to ensure provision of quality. They will then put in place a package of training for 35,000 providers of early year's provision. The UK has a system for testing all pupils on entry to school called 'Baseline Assessment'. This is being examined to determine which elements may be suited to inclusion in a pre-school 'baseline'.

The Curriculum Guidance for the Foundation Stage (DfEE, 2000) details current thinking and policy:

> The foundation stage of education will make a positive contribution to children's early development and learning. During this time we cannot afford to get things wrong. The early years are critical in children's development. Children develop rapidly during this time - physically, intellectually, emotionally and socially. The foundation stage is about developing key learning skills such as listening, speaking, concentration, persistence and learning to work together and co-operate with other children. It is also about developing early communication, literacy and numeracy skills that will prepare young children for key stage 1 of the national curriculum.
>
> (Hodge, 2000: 4)

Hodge goes on to say:

> All children should be given the opportunity to experience the very best possible start to their education. We need to ensure that our children enter school having established solid foundations on which they can build. This will help to ensure that they continue to flourish throughout their school years and beyond.

The Qualifications and Curriculum Authority (QCA) are drawing up practical guidance to support the document in recognition of the need for greater understanding among a range of providers to support pre-school and early years children.

In the UK, access to additional support for pupils with Special Educational Needs comes though the procedures detailed in the Code of Practice (DfEE, 1994). This is also currently under review. It is hoped that the review will result in a firmer grip being taken by authorities on the early identification of dyslexic children. It is important that local authorities remain obliged to determine and meet the special educational needs of each child, not just 'all children' as in Para. 1.4 of the proposed revised Code (DfEE, 2000). We are concerned that 'practical realities' in terms of reduced funding, changes in local authority responsibilities across the country and the lack of experience and knowledge of early years educators in special educational needs issues generally, and dyslexia specifically may lead to degradation of what is already barely adequate provision.

For example, DfEE (1994) stated in 5.10 that:

If the educational and/or developmental progress of the child under five gives rise to concern, the child's teacher, if the child is at school, should prepare a written report setting out the child's strengths and weaknesses and noting evidence for the concern. The use of parent assessment material and developmental checklists should be considered.

The proposed revised Code is less clear. The nearest it comes to this statement is Para. 4.7, 'Early Years Action', which states, inter alia:

The triggers for intervention through Early Years Action could be the practitioner's concern about a child who despite receiving appropriate early education experiences:

- makes little or no progress even when teaching approaches are particularly targeted to improve the child's identified area of weakness
- continues working at levels significantly below those expected for children of a similar age in certain areas
- presents persistent emotional and/or behavioural difficulties, which are not ameliorated by the behaviour management techniques usually employed in the setting
- has sensory or physical problems and continues to make little or no progress despite the provision of personal aids and equipment
- has communication and/or interaction difficulties and requires specific individual interventions in order to access learning.

(p. 20)

There are references to various sources of information scattered through the Draft Code. However, this diffusion and the emphasis above on the responses of the child to current teaching and management practices increase the likelihood that failure rather than prediction through careful identification will actually be the 'trigger'. The result will be delay in appropriate teaching and the need to overcome damage to the child's self-concept as a learner. A review of the content of initial teacher training for primary school teachers, where there is evidence of a significant lack of time to deal with SEN issues, may also be indicated.

Recently the British Dyslexia Association together with AFASIC, the association representing children with speech and language impairments, have produced a training pack entitled Language and Literacy: Joining Together (Wood, Wright and Stackhouse, 2000). This package is designed to enable early years practitioners from all agencies to work effectively with each other and with parents in order to identify and support children with speech, language and literacy difficulties. The two organizations recognize that health visitors are key people in identifying weaknesses. They have the advantage of being able to monitor children's progress over the early years, long before anyone in the education system sees the child. Training of this group of providers is of clear importance.

So how may we identify, at young age, those pupils who will need particular forms of teaching if they are to attain the literacy levels necessary for success in mainstream schools? In other words, those pupils who have dyslexia in some form or severity. 'Dyslexia is evident when accurate and fluent word reading and/or spelling is learnt very incompletely or with great difficulty' (Pumfrey and Reason, 1999: 18).

Unfortunately this, the latest definition from the BPS is unhelpful in relation to young children. It presumes that, until failure has occurred, assessment cannot be attempted. If a child is too young to have begun formal reading instruction clearly this definition does not apply. Further, it is not in agreement with work to be cited later, indicating that dyslexia is much more than a reading difficulty.

A more useful description is Peer (2000a: 4):

> Dyslexia is best described as a combination of abilities and difficulties which affect the learning process in one or more of reading, spelling, writing and sometimes numeracy/language. Accompanying weaknesses may be identified in areas of speed of processing, short-term memory, sequencing, auditory and/or visual perception, spoken language and motor skills. Some children have outstanding creative skills, others have strong oral skills whilst others have no outstanding talents, they all have strengths. Dyslexia occurs despite normal intellectual ability and conventional teaching. It is independent of socio-economic or language background.

Even with this more comprehensive statement identification of dyslexia in young children still poses many problems.

Firstly, there is the fact that the younger children are the more unreliable are any statements made about them. Any identification method should therefore relate to a basic part of the child's functioning. Another is that, because of the increased likelihood of 'false positives', identification should result in interventions that would be of value to any pupil. It is better to give support if there is any question rather than wait for failure to be sure. The only codicil is that support must be given in such a way as not to suggest potential failure.

Two important aspects of any assessment methodology are its 'sensitivity' and 'concordance'. The former relates to the proportion of correctly identified individuals, the latter to predicted and observed group membership. Thus 'sensitivity' is a stricter criterion as it refers to specific individuals. There must also be an acceptable balance of 'false' and 'true' positives and negatives. For example, by including a large number of predictors, Badian (1988) was able accurately to predict 14 out of 15 subsequent poor readers. However, this was at the expense of a relatively high number of 'false alarms' in that 10 out of the 24 pupils predicted to have later difficulties developed as normal readers.

Elbro, Borstrom and Petersen (1998) further comment:

> High prediction rates must not be achieved by including a large number of predictions. Not only is it unlikely that each will relate to some outcome measure, but because of the effects of randomness within each element replication of the measure will produce different results.

Thus we are seeking methods of identification that relate to a clear theoretical model, are robust in their predictive value whilst conservative in the number of measures and associated with interventions which enhance the attainments of all pupils. Frith (1995: 8) produced a useful 'basic causal model'.

Methods of identification can be mapped on to this model. Starting at the biological level, Frith states: 'In my view dyslexia is a condition with a genetic origin' – quoting Pennington's (1990) review as a powerful source of evidence. Later work by, for example, Cardon et al. (1994) has identified the relevant chromosomes (see Chapter 1 in this book for further information).

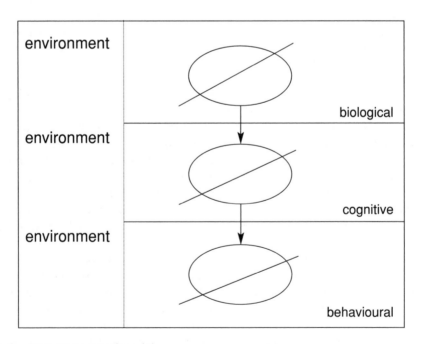

Figure 11.1: Basic causal model.

Thus, an initial 'pointer' to possible future dyslexia is a family history of reading, speech or language problems (see the chapter by van der Leij, Lyytinen and Zwarts). A sensitive taking of a family history may in itself be beneficial. As Peer (2000b: 6) points out: 'Through their children's diagnosis the parents understand their own difficulties and feel a surge of relief as they realize why they experienced difficulties at school.' She goes on to say that the first essential is to assure them that early intervention will help their children in ways which were unknown in the past. Both Auger (1998) and BDA (1999) give clear guidance on activities that parents can use to support their children in developing literacy.

These activities can and should be made a part of normal parent/child interactions. They aim to draw the child's attention to symbol–sound relationships, commonalities between sounds and ultimately to the fact that complex sounds are made up of combinations of simpler ones. They also introduce the concept of multisensory work so that the child comes to recognize the integration of the information from various sources and that inputs can support each other. Frith (1995) suggests that, at this biological level, there are abnormalities in the brain. The aims of the methods quoted above are to create an 'environment' that will ameliorate the effects of these abnormalities.

There is now a wealth of literature in the area of neuropsychology and dyslexia. Robertson (2000) presents an up-to-date overview of the area. Of particular interest in relation to pre-school children is the work of Dirk Bakker (for example, Bakker, Licht and Kappers, 1995) and Angela Fawcett and Rod Nicolson (for example, Fawcett, Nicolson and Dean, 1996). Bakker, working in Amsterdam, Netherlands, considered that in the early stages reading is primarily a right hemispheric activity, only later transferring also to the left. In an effective, mature reader a balance between the hemispheres has developed. Robertson (2000: 44) provides a useful table (Table 11.1 below) indicating the characteristics of children who have failed to develop this correct balance:

Table 11.1: Reading behaviour of P-types and L-types (Robertson, 2000)

	P-type	L-type
Preferred Modality	Auditory	Visual
Reading Route (Morton, 1969)	Indirect	Direct
Reading Behaviour	Slow/Accurate	Fast/Inaccurate
Balance of Hemisphere Activity	Right	Left

> The L-type dyslexic pupil attempts to read with little regard to the perceptual features of the text. Reading is fast and may demonstrate many inaccurate responses to surface features of the text . . .
>
> These pupils find it difficult to assimilate the fine perceptual differences between the alphabetic symbols and attempt to access the text by global access to meaning.
>
> The other sub-type, the perceptual P-type pupil, is equally disadvantaged but in a different way . . . Reading is characterised by slow and fragmented reading. The quality of the message between the writer and the reader may be lost in the midst of individual sound/symbol conversion.
>
> (Robertson, 2000: 42–3)

This refers to reading per se, but there is no reason to believe that a pupil will not take a similar approach to pre-school activities making similar types of demands. Clearly there could also be emotional and 'personality' connotations. However, if, in the pre-reading activities cited above, children are found to be markedly quick but inaccurate or very slow and over-concerned with detail in their responses it may be worth considering possible 'balance' effects.

Bakker proposed direct stimulation of the 'inactive' hemisphere to restore the balance and Robertson (2000: 44) lists a range of critical studies relating to such interventions. At the pre-school age it is probably sufficient to select games requiring an approach in the 'weak' area. For instance, for a child who is fast and inaccurate (L-type) matching and difference games requiring attention to detail would be useful. For the slow fragmentary P-type, guessing games for objectives in a feely bag (using the left hand only), 'creativity' games, thinking how many different things an ambiguous shape might be could be useful. Again, we stress that this is just an emphasis in a normal set of play activities and not 'therapy'.

Nicolson and Fawcett at Sheffield University in the UK (Fawcett, Nicolson and Dean, 1996; Nicolson and Fawcett, 1999) suggest that there may (also) be difficulties with cerebellar functioning. They have taken the term 'language dexterity' coined by Leiner, Leiner and Dow (1989) as analogous to motor skill acquisition and execution, and applied it to impairments in dyslexia. Their initial work involved tests of balance and time estimation. This was later developed into a clinical battery tapping wider functions (Fawcett, Nicolson, and Dean, 1996). Children with dyslexia showed highly significant impairment on all the cerebellar function-related tests and, importantly, significant differences compared with reading age-matched controls.

Leiner and colleagues postulate that because, in humans, the cerebellar cortex connects not only to the motor cortex but also to Brocca's area of the brain it therefore 'is critically involved in the automatization of any skill whether motor or cognitive' (Fawcett, Nicolson and Dean, 1996: 262). Fawcett and colleagues propose that cerebellar abnormality in dyslexia is the start of the 'causal chain' leading to difficulties in reading, writing and spelling (see the chapter by Fawcett and Nicolson for the ontogenetic causal chain).

The first battery to come from this work was the Dyslexia Early Screening Test (DEST) (Nicolson and Fawcett, 1996):

> The DEST comprises 11 simple sub-tests – speed, phonological skill, motor skill, cerebellar function and knowledge – which together provide an 'at-risk' judgement, together with an ability profile that indicates the particular area of difficulty.
>
> (Nicolson and Fawcett, 1996: 248)

It is suitable for pupils of 4.6–6.6 years old and takes half an hour at most to administer.

However, this has now been followed by a more appropriate battery for the children we are considering here – the Pre-school Early Screening Test, or PEST.[1] At the stage of writing, this was in a prototype version, but the normed test is due for publication in September 2001. It has more tests than DEST, but they are shorter, which is very appropriate for young children. The average four year old can complete the tests in one 20-minute session, although if concentration is poor the testing can be split into two or even three sessions.

The earliest work of Fawcett (1990) involved the gross motor skill of balance and the use of a 'dual-task' methodology. Balance is 'one of the most practised of all skills and the one most likely to be automatized' (Fawcett, 1990: 160). The tasks were performed under two conditions: one where only balance, the primary task, was involved and a dual task where the child had to balance whilst performing a secondary task – for example, counting (another very early and practised skill). Because of the cerebellar abnormality the child cannot rely on balance being maintained automatically so greater involvement of the cerebral cortex must take place. This is quite unconscious but revealed when a greater 'load' is put on the cortex by the addition of the counting task. This is analogous to a computer slowing down when the memory becomes overloaded. Fawcett and Nicolson call this ability to maintain normal performance by working harder 'conscious compensation'.

Whilst a modified test of the ability to maintain balance when gently pushed in the back forms part of both DEST and PEST other subtests have been added to enhance overall 'concordance' and 'sensitivity'. However, preliminary results from Kelly (1993) with pupils with little or no English

suggest that the version of the original balance test alone may be an effective and robust indicator of some of those pupils who may have dyslexic-
type difficulties in the attainment of fluent English. In this case 'false
positives' would receive additional support rather than being 'selected
out' from normal curricular activities. We return to the issue of bilingual
children below.

Referring to intervention (in contradistinction to Bakker) Fawcett,
Nicolson and Dean (1996: 278) state:

> The fact that cerebellar difficulties are a useful symptom does not mean, neces-
> sarily, that they are a valuable method of remediation. The appropriate remedi-
> ation depends upon the behaviour to be remedied. If the problem is reading,
> then the appropriate remediation is reading support targeted on the particular
> difficulties shown . . . We would certainly confirm the importance of phono-
> logical support as the central component of a structured programme of reading
> remediation.

Finally at this level there is an interesting study by Livingstone et al.
(1993). They looked at the relationship between season of birth and
predisposition to dyslexia. Examining a clinic population of 558 boys they
found a smooth curve of frequency of diagnosis of dyslexia peaking in May,
June and July suggesting true 'seasonality'. 'For different 5 year cohorts,
early summer birth accounts for 24% – 71% of cases of dyslexia.' They
suggest that

> 'Viral infection, especially influenza, during the second trimester of pregnancy
> (February, March, April) is the most attractive hypothesis to account for these
> findings. Immunisation of women of child bearing age could reduce the
> incidence of dyslexia' (Livingstone et al., 1993: 612).

They go on to say, and we would agree, that it would be useful to
observe carefully against a checklist any child with an early summer
birthday, particularly if his or her mother reports having 'flu earlier in the
year.[2] This brings us to the second level of Frith's model – the cognitive.
She concentrates on the importance of phonological deficit, associating it
at the biological level with abnormality in the perisylvian region of the
cortex (Frith, 1997).

Nicolson and Fawcett (1996) see this as the major line in their more
comprehensive structure. Phonological processing is broadly defined as the
ability to process sounds in spoken language. Frith (1995) suggests that:

Individuals who are diagnosably dyslexic . . . generally have the following signs:

- delayed speech acquisition and problems in early speech production
  (Scarborough, 1990)

- object naming and word retrieval difficulties (Wolf, 1991)
- poor verbal short-term memory (Shankweiller and Cain, 1986)
- difficulty in segmenting phonemes (Kamhi and Catts, 1986)
- poor at non-word repetition (Snowling, 1987)

Catts (1991: 11) also generalized his earlier findings:

> A reading disability is much more than a problem of recognising and making sense of written language. It appears to be a more extensive disorder that is present well before children are confronted with formal reading instruction. In fact, in many cases the disorder is better described as a development language disability that interferes with the acquisition of spoken and written language.

Most recently, McArthur and colleagues (2000: 873) with a sample of Australian children aged between 76 and 167 months have shown that:

> The reading and language scores of 110 children with specific reading disability (SRD) and 102 children with specific language impairment (SLI) tested over seven experiments revealed that 53% of children with an SRD and children with an SLI could be equally classified as having an SRD or SLI, 55% of children with an SRD had impaired oral language and 51% of children with an SLD had a reading disability.

These studies and other work suggest that problems with oral language may well precede and foretell reading disabilities.[3] Elbro, Bornstrom and Petersen (1998: 40) introduced the concept of the quality of phonological representations or phonological 'distinctness':

> Distinctness means degree of separation – that is the relative distance between a phonological representation and its neighbours. It may be relatively hard to segment and perform phonological operations on words that are represented in a less distinct form. The Automatic extraction of grapheme – phoneme correspondences may be directly dependent on the quality of the phonological representations.

Thus the clearer the speech and language surrounding children, the better that speech and language can be associated with its detailed representations, the easier it will become for the children to 'find' the letter or word they need when speaking or reading. This may well be one of the mechanisms underlying the effectiveness of multi-sensory methods. It certainly implies, again, that if there is a suggestion of possible dyslexic-type difficulties we should be careful in how speech and language are handled even in otherwise very unusual and informal situations.

Elbro et al. (1998) tested their hypothesis with the use of a multiplicity of measures with a group of kindergarten children against a criterion of future identification of dyslexia in 'grade 2' three years later. Sophisticated multiple regression techniques were used to separate out the most powerful predictors. Phonological representations were tested. 'In addition, early speech and language skills predicted individual differences in literacy outcome and genetic risk accounted for unique variance over and above those factors.'

Thus reflections of the cognitive level in terms of phonology (through whatever neural mechanism), motor skill and automatization can be seen reflected at the behavioural level in a variety of ways. Many of these behavioural reflections can be the subjects of careful observation if guidelines are given to 'aware' and knowledgeable staff. Others may require deliberate screening via, for example PEST, DEST or COPS, Cognitive Profiling System.

'In the final regression model, three measures were found to contribute independently and statistically significantly to the prediction of dyslexia. They were letter naming, phoneme awareness and distinctiveness of phonological representations. (This latter) was also predictive of phoneme awareness in early Grade 2 even after controlling for early phoneme awareness, articulation and production vocabulary.'

This result would reinforce the view outlined above that 'risk' factors for dyslexia include a genetic predisposition to dyslexia, a summer birthday and/or early indications of difficulty in speaking or learning language. In such cases, care should be taken to use and develop speech as distinctly as possible consistent with the child's stage of development. As Elbro et al. (1998) state:

> An indistinct representation may serve the purposes of everyday communication perfectly well, but may be very hard to segment into phonemes and use as the basis of further phonological manipulations.
>
> Phonological representations were tested by a simple naming test using pictures selected from a children's picture lotto (Picture naming and speed) and a test of phonological distinctiveness to elicit the child's most distinct pronunciation of single words. The child was shown a hand-held puppet and told that the puppet had speech difficulties. It did not pronounce words too well and the child was to teach it to speak more distinctly. A picture was then shown to puppet and child and the experimenter pronounced it for the puppet, e.g. a picture of a crocodile would be accompanied by 'co-dile'. The child was to tell the puppet the correct pronunciation.

Finally, Gallagher, Frith and Snowling (2000) showed that: 'Letter knowledge at 45 months was the strongest predictor of literacy at 6 years.'

As a postscript, tentative mention might be made of a rather surprising finding from the latest work of one of us (Johnson) (Johnson and Kelly,

2000). Earlier work, extending Kelly (1993), suggested that a bilingual child might reliably be identified as being dyslexic, using a screening device for an automaticity deficit in balance, at around eight years of age. However, the test appeared to produce an unacceptable number of false positives at age seven or below.[4] We therefore wished to find an alternative method of identifying younger children, based on the same theoretical principles.

It is well known that dyslexic students frequently use avoidance tactics when put under pressure with reading and writing tasks. Based on the assumption that this instinct develops at an early age we set out to test the hypothesis that young children who 'avoid' certain activities in free play situations will later develop literacy difficulties and exhibit automaticity deficits, as measured by the screening device.

A class of reception age (4.5 to 5 years) was observed on a daily basis over two terms in free-play situations for periods of 15 minutes and the length of time spent on each activity available was recorded. Observations made were later compared with test results on National Curriculum Standard Assessment Tests (SATs) at age seven. On entry to the junior school the school staff administered standardized reading and spelling tests. The following year profiles were built up on each child that included National Curriculum Levels at age seven (SATs results) and English Language Stages from the annual Needs Analysis Survey. They were also tested for dyslexic automaticity deficits.

On examining the observation schedules, three years later, clear differences in play patterns between boys and girls were noted. The boys tended to spend most of the time in construction, choosing jigsaws, sand play, and fine motor activities to a lesser extent, with least time spent on reading/writing activities. The girls spent most time on reading and writing activities, with less time on jigsaws and fine motor activities, rarely had the opportunity for sand play (as they tended to get 'pushed out' by the boys) and spent least time in construction. It seemed, initially, that finding a pattern to fit the 'dyslexic' profile would be difficult. Closer examination of the data, separating them into two distinct groups, seemed more promising.

Only one girl at age four, avoided reading activities consistently (she had a 0% reading score). Instead she spent all her time in large construction or Lego, following the pattern established for boys. At age seven, she was the only girl with an uneven profile on National Curriculum levels (with English lower than mathematics and science). She was one of two girls found to have an automaticity deficit on the screening test in year three.

Time spent on reading activities was generally much lower in boys at age four, but there were only five boys who avoided reading tasks consistently. At age seven all of them were more than a year behind their chronological age in reading, but only two of them had uneven National Curriculum profiles. These two were amongst the four pupils found to have automaticity deficits in year three.

On the surface, although it looked as though the study of early play patterns might predict later literacy difficulties, it seemed more likely to pick up problems of a 'specific' nature in girls than in boys. The boys were more likely to be influenced by friendship groups and this sometimes affected choices. The relationship between the time spent reading at age four and reading scores at age seven did not seem as strong in boys. One particular child, who spent only 3% of his time on reading activities at age four, had one of the highest reading scores at seven. He was then 1.6 years above his chronological age in reading.

The strength of the relationship between percentage scores for reading in pupils aged four years and the reading scores on standardized tests at seven years of age was analysed statistically. Three analyses were made: girls' scores, boys' scores, and boys' and girls' scores combined. The association for girls was 0.76, significant at the 0.01 level. The relationship for boys was 0.78, significant at 0.005 level. For the boys and girls group combined it was 0.57, significant at 0.01 level.

This analysis established a relationship between the percentage of time spent on reading activities at age four and reading scores at age seven. The next stage was to examine the link between percentage reading scores at age four and automaticity deficits at age seven.

Firstly, two separate analyses were carried out on the data:

- The reading patterns of dyslexics and non-dyslexics were compared at age four. The differences between them were significant at the 0.01 level.
- The automaticity deficits of dyslexics and non-dyslexics were compared at age seven. The differences were also significant at the 0.01 level.

Analysis of reading patterns and automaticity deficits showed significant differences in the scores of dyslexics and non-dyslexics and an association between the length of time spent voluntarily on reading activities at age four and automaticity deficits at age seven of -0.43, significant at the 0.05 level.[5]

Clearly, caution must be exercised as this study relates to one class of pupils in one school, nevertheless these are fully longitudinal data. A statistically significant relationship was found between the length of time spent on reading activities at age four and reading scores at age seven. The difference in the length of time spent on reading activities by dyslexics and non-dyslexics was also statistically significant. Relying on reading habits alone to identify dyslexia at an early age, however, may result in some over-identification. Of the six children who appeared to avoid reading at four years of age (they had 0% reading scores) only three turned out to be dyslexic. Thus in this part of the study there were three false positives but no false negatives.

Observing young children at play, then, appears to be an effective method of monitoring children who might be 'at risk'. All six children who avoided reading in their early years turned out to have some form of literacy difficulty at age seven. Giving additional support to these children during their first few years at school would be critical for future success. There is therefore no ethical dilemma in producing false positives.

The data suggested that specific learning difficulties (dyslexia) might be easier to identify in girls than in boys at the age of four, as only two out of the five boys who avoided reading activities at the age of four were later identified as being dyslexic. Correlation analysis showed a statistically significant relationship between the length of time spent on reading activities at age four and dyslexic automaticity deficit scores at age seven. Avoidance of reading activities in young children can also be considered to be a good predictor of later reading difficulties including dyslexia.

Clearly, at the pre-school stage, as proposed in the UK Draft Code of Practice, policy should result in a seamless web of identification, intervention, monitoring and modification. One of us (Lee) outlines a case study of a school demonstrating a successful model of such practice.

Middleton in Teesdale Primary and Nursery School is situated in the Pennine Hills in north-east England. It is at the centre of the largest rural catchment area in County Durham. Although there is a rich blend of backgrounds, the area has generally been identified as having a large group of children presenting with poor oral, reading and written language skills.

Strag (1972: 52) stated:

> When diagnosis of dyslexia is made in the first two years at school then 82% can be brought to chronological age standard. If diagnosis occurs later, towards the end of primary education the success rate falls to 10/15 %.

This statement led staff at the school to conclude that strategies must be developed in the nursery that would maximize the language development of the children. These strategies were to involve assessment, screening and intervention.

The three stages of assessment policy in the nursery are:

- initial profiling at three years on entry;
- continuous assessment between three and four years;
- skill screening/screening for dyslexia on the child's fourth birthday.

It was decided that assessments should occur in line with the causal model framework (Frith, 1995) detailed above.

Initial profiling at entry to nursery aged three years

Records containing a sensitive, pertinent, developmental profile are created to enable patterns of difficulties to be identified and so that targeted help can be given. These initial data are collected using a simple, confidential interview based on Portwood (1996) completed when the parents have their introductory meeting at the nursery. The questions they are asked reflect the levels in the Frith (1995) model.

Biological factors include:

- Family history of dyslexia – Cardon et al., (1994) have identified regions on three chromosomes that may cause a predisposition towards dyslexia (see Chapter 1).
- Problems in pregnancy – Galaburda and Kemper (1979) has reported cases of two dyslexic girls who, on post mortem, revealed scars suggestive of injury in late pregnancy. Thomson (1989: 148) states 'That by investigating birth history the teacher is looking for possible neurological damage. If there is an "at risk" birth and this is associated with events such as difficulties in early sucking, continued crying and also paediatric involvement during the first year or two of life, one should look carefully at the child's test profile for signs of minimal neurological dysfunction.' Such dysfunction may be responsible for later learning difficulties.
- Relevant health problems – Pumfrey and Reason (1991) suggest that infections of the middle ear in early life (such as glue ear) and other auditory problems might adversely affect learning (see the comments by Peer above).

Cognitive factors include articulation patterns – Scarborough (1998) states: 'Children who have a better mastery of phonology, as exhibited by their ability to articulate speech sounds clearly and to hear spoken words accurately, can readily gain metalinguistic appreciation of the phonological structure of words.'

Behavioural factors:

- Irritability – irritability in a child can be a symptom of stress. Gentile and McMillan (1987) have demonstrated that stress is implicated in learning difficulties.
- Avoidance behaviour – this can be another symptom of stress. Some children who encounter difficulty with language avoid literacy tasks so that they will not experience the mortification of failure. Stanovich (1986) claims that 'the resultant lack of opportunity to develop underlying competencies can then contribute to specific learning difficulties.'
- Motor problems – Nicolson and Fawcett (1999) argue that dyslexic children will often present with motor problems because of cerebellar impairments. Often children's later problem with fine motor skills can be predicted through their earlier competence at crawling, walking and feeding habits.
- Concentration – the cerebellar impairment hypothesis (Nicolson and Fawcett, 1999) is a generalized learning theory that predicts that there will be a wide range of behavioural symptoms concerned with any skill associated with dyslexia. Among these symptoms is the ability to concentrate, because processing is more effortful and thus more difficult to maintain.

Continuous assessment between the ages of three and four years

As the child progresses in nursery a continuous assessment of progress is made using Aspects of Achievement (Norfolk County Council, 1996). It details:

(1) social emotional development;
(2) physical development;
(3) aesthetic and creative development;
(4) communication;
(5) reading;
(6) science and technology;
(7) maths.
(8) written language.

Each section is split into a series of descriptive progression points that can be used to monitor progress and can be broken down into finer categories if needed for an individual child. For example if 'effective control of writing implements' is not developing then the following questions are asked:

- Can the child make accurate and controlled shoulder, elbow and wrist movements?
- Can the child make accurate and controlled finger movements?
- Has the child got a sensible pencil grip?
- Can the child relax whilst holding a pencil?
- Has the child been through the repertoire of writing exercises (Graphisme) (De Forge, 1976) to maximize pencil control?

Teachers keep special note of pupil progress in those areas identified and, through experience, staff have come to recognize patterns that might indicate a child might be 'at risk' of specific problems such as dyslexia. They will also ensure that the child's day is structured so as to ensure that he or she is involved in appropriate activities. If a need is deemed to be severe a teacher with special responsibility for that skill area or an outside specialist will be involved. Use is made of the Letterland (Wendon, 1997) scheme to assist letter/sound correspondences. An assessment sheet has also been devised to track each child's progress with phonological awareness.

Dyslexia screening on the child's fourth birthday

Staff also use a school-based screening procedure – Middleton Screening Test (MiST) (Lee, 1996). Scarborough (1998) analysed screening procedures and showed that a sensitive battery of tests was more accurate than any single measurement. MiST attempts to follow her recommendations. The subtests are listed below and reflect theories significant in dyslexia research:

- Memory. Rack (1994) states, 'One of the most reliable and often quoted associated characteristics of developmental dyslexia is an inefficiency in short-term memory.' Nicolson and Fawcett (1996) in their Dyslexia Early Screening Test assert that: Memory difficulties are one of the most pervasive problems for dyslexic children.' The MiST memory tests include:
  - following instructions;
  - repeating two sentences;
  - digit span;
  - Kim's game;
  - sequencing.

- Motor skills. As early as 1985 Auger reported gross motor co-ordination problems in dyslexic children. Levinson (1988) noted a link between mild cerebellar damage, motor skill deficits and dyslexia. This link has been refined in an elegant causal theory outlined in Nicolson and Fawcett's (1999) cerebellar impairment hypothesis. The motor skills tests included the following.
  - fine motor skills;
  - gross motor skills;
  - graphisme;
  - free drawing;
  - colouring;
  - writing;
  - picture copying.

- Rapid naming. Denckla and Rudel (1972) carried out the background research that justifies the inclusion of this test in the MiST battery. They demonstrated that 'rapid automatized naming' is an indicator of dyslexia.
- Rhyme. The rhyming test is based on research by Bradley and Bryant (1985) who found that the ability of nursery children to process rhyme and alliteration is predictive of the level of literacy ability four years later.

Parts of MiST have now been incorporated into a shorter normed test, the Baseline Early Screening Test (BEST) (Fawcett, Nicolson and Lee, 2000). One advantage of this new test is that it offers a visual-processing subtest. Until this test is published a specialist optometrist is consulted if visual processing problems are suspected.

Rationale for intervention

General nursery policy is:

- that detailed initial and ongoing assessment should inform all teaching and learning activities;
- that teaching and learning activities should be available for all children; the special needs child being given enhanced opportunities to practice.

Intervention strategies

Handwriting. Thomson (1984) recommends the introduction of cursive writing to all children with specific learning difficulties. Pumfrey and

Reason (1991), describing Thomson's contribution, state: 'Cursive writing is simpler in terms of starting and finishing strokes, in its lack of straight lines and confusable forms. Its connectedness helps in the assimilation of word patterns as gestalts.'

The main scheme used to develop cursive writing patterns is the French scheme, Graphisme (Yves de Forge, 1976). The system is designed to assist nursery children to develop an efficient pencil grip. Flexibility of shoulder, elbow, wrist and fingers are encouraged with a series of exercises. Children use scissors to cut straight lines, spirals and circles. Whenever they are drawing they are encouraged to shade using patterns rather than scribbles. The scheme presents many designs, which must be shaded using particular repetitive pencil strokes. The patterns naturally progress to cursive letter shapes and blends higher up the school.

The school has adapted the phonic programme Letterland (1997) so that letter-sound correspondence is taught using cursive letters. The children associate the shape of the letter with its sound by saying it as they write the letter in the air, write the letter large on a velvet wall, join dotted letters, trace the letter on sandpaper or felt, trace the letter in sand and copy the letter on paper.

In line with policy, all Letterland and Graphisme skills are available for all children. A child with special needs, however, is given enhanced opportunity to participate and improve.

Kinesthesiology. Paul Dennison (1997) described kinesthesiology as the physical aspect of brain organization. He reports that 60% of his clients with learning disabilities were mixed dominant, for example left eyed and right handed and eared. He suggests that this factor can contribute to a child's failure to read and write.

Specific language difficulties are known to correlate with all varieties of mixed dominance profiles.

> The beginning reader when encoding and decoding words, needs the linear, left to right, beginning to end auditory component in order to see the relationship of the phoneme (sound pattern) with the grapheme (written symbol). Without this, reversals, transpositions and disorganised visual performance often persist. Lost and unable to mentally master his environment, the child with this profile often seeks kinaesthetic and tactile experience to help him organise his sensory world. (Dennison (1997: 6)

Young children are naturally multi-sensory and use organized movement to attempt to reinforce a skill. Scarborough (1998) reports that co-ordinated hand and arm movements generally accompany babbling activity in babies. Dennison described a series of exercises that are designed to balance brain activity and enhance progress. If children have problems with fine motor control then they are given a daily session of kinesthetics prior to Graphisme exercises. This session will involve gross motor and balance activities interspersed with games to reinforce and practice the same skills in a more 'open' context. Crossover movements, for example left hand to right shoulder, elbow and ear and so on, are emphasized as are the reverse of earlier movements. Such activities have a long history in 'remedial education'.

Full details of this highly structured and integrated programme can be found in (Lee, 1996).

As well as these more specialized activities, all the normal nursery activities such as interaction with books, messy play, imaginative play, and so forth, take place each day as normal.

Management issues

For a programme such as this to work well the leadership in the school must be 'special' and staff training is vital. As far as possible each member of staff has knowledge of all areas of the curriculum. All staff have a fluent knowledge of phonics and phonological awareness. One member of staff specializes in educational kinesthesiology, another in graphic representational techniques. All staff encourage parents to develop attitudes and techniques, which will enhance their ability to help their own children. Parents are shown how to play multi-sensory games and issues such as screening and teaching techniques are explained and discussed at regular parents' meetings.

Conclusions

In this chapter we have endeavoured to demonstrate that if the needs of children with dyslexia are to be met in an inclusive setting, identification at an early age of both those children and their needs is vital. It is clear that their difficulties will manifest themselves in the language area. Their roots lie at the biological level in the malfunctioning of the brain. This may be caused genetically, or through maternal infection or birth trauma. Its main effects are seen in the phonological system but associated effects may be noted in speed of processing and degradation of automated functioning.

Interventions should be language based and, in the main, consist of activities that will benefit all pupils. Screening procedures related to known correlates of dyslexia may therefore be used with confidence as any children identified, even if ultimately as a 'false positive', will be offered more intensive teaching and enhanced curricular access. There can be no excuse for 'waiting for failure' or even delaying identification procedures until the start of formal reading instruction. This can only result in adding damage to the self-concept to the existing difficulties faced by a child.

Notes

1. The prototype PEST has been renamed the BEST, the Baseline Early Skills Test in response to input from the publishers, the Psychological Corporation.
2. Children born in May-July start school later and therefore have only one term in reception (see the chapter by Lindsay in this book).
3. Recent research has established considerable commonalities between the developmental disorders of dyslexia, specific language impairment, ADHD and dyspraxia. A key requirement is to establish whether or not there are subtypes of each disorder, with both 'pure' and co-morbid exemplars.
4. The editors have found that this relates to the normal development of balance skills in children, which are naturally variable in children of seven and under, whether or not they will later go on to show automaticity deficits.
5. It is important to note that lack of practice will be a contributory factor in this finding. A predisposition to have problems with literacy coupled with avoidance techniques is likely to generate a reciprocal interaction.

References

Auger J (1985) Guidelines for teachers, parents and learners. In Snowling M (ed.) Children's Written Language Difficulties. Windsor UK: NFER Nelson, pp. 147–71.

Auger J (1998) BDA Factsheet. Reading: British Dyslexia Association

Badian N (1988) Predicting Dyslexia in a Pre-school Population. In: Masland, M. (ed.) Pre-school Prediction of Reading Failure. New York: York Press, Parkton MD.

Bakker DJ, Licht R, Kappers EJ (eds) (1995) Hemispheric Stimulation Techniques in Children with Dyslexia. Advances in Child Neuropsychology. New York: Springer Verlag.

Bradley LL, Bryant PE (1983) Categorising sounds and learning to read – a causal connection. Nature 301: 419–521.

Bradley LL, Bryant PE (1985) Rhyme and Reason in Reading and Spelling. Ann Arbor: University of Michigan Press.

Bradley LL (1988) Making connections in learning to read and to spell. Applied Cognitive Psychology 3: 2–18.

British Dyslexia Association (1999) Briefing paper on BPS report. Reading: BDA.

Bryant PE, Goswami U (1987) Phonological Awareness and Learning to Read. In Beech J, Colley A. Cognitive Approaches to Reading. Chichester: Wiley.

Cardon LR, Smith SD, Fulker DW, Kimberling WJ, Pennington BF, DeFries JC (1994) Quanititative trait locus for reading disability on chromosome 6. Science 266: 276–9.

Catts HW (1991) Early identification of reading disabilities. Topics in Language Disorders 12: 1–16.

Cline T, Shamsi T (2000) Language Needs or Special Needs? The assessment of learning difficulties in literacy among children learning English as an additional language: a literature review. London: DfEE Publications.

De Forge Y (1976) Le Graphisme Technique. University of Lille France. Atelier Reproduction des Theses.

Denckla MB, Rudel RG (1972) Rapid automatised naming (RAN): Dyslexia differentiated from other learning disabilities. Neuropsychologia 14, 471–79.

Dennison PE (1997) The physical aspect of brain organization. Educational Kinesiology Foundation UK Newsletter (June): 5

Department for Education (1994) Code of Practice on the Identification and Assessment of SEN. London: HMSO.

Department for Education and Employment (2000) Curriculum Guidance for the Foundation Stage. London: Qualifications and Curriculum Authority.

Elbro C, Borstrom I, Petersen DK (1998) Predicting dyslexia from kindergarten: the importance of distinctiveness of phonological representations of lexical items. Reading Research Quarterly 33: 41.

Fawcett AJ (1990) A Cognitive Architecture of Dyslexia. Unpublished PhD thesis Department of Psychology. Sheffield, University of Sheffield.

Fawcett AJ, Nicolson RI, (1996) Dyslexia Screening Test (DST). London: The Psychological Corporation.

Fawcett AJ, Nicolson RI, Dean P (1996) Impaired performance of children with dyslexia on a range of cerebellar tasks. Annals of Dyslexia 46: 259–83.

Fawcett AJ, Nicolson RI, Lee R (2000) Baseline Early Skills Test (BEST). London: The Psychological Corporation.

Frith U (1995) Dyslexia: can we have a shared theoretical framework? Educational and Child Psychology 12: 8.

Frith U (1997) Brain, Mind and Behaviour in Dyslexia. Dyslexia: Biology, cognition and intervention. C Hulme, M Snowling (eds). London: Whurr.

Galaburda AM, Kemper TL (1979) Cytoarchitectonic abnormalities in developmental dyslexia: a case study. Ann Neurology 6: 94–100.

Gallagher A, Frith U, Snowling M (2000) Precursors of literacy delay among children at genetic risk of dyslexia. Journal of Child Psychology and Psychiatry 41: 203–13.

Gentile LM, McMillan MM (1987) Stress and Reading Difficulties: Research, assessment and intervention. Newark NE: International Reading Association.

Goswami U (1986) Children's use of analogy in learning to read: A developmental study. Journal of Experimental Child Psychology 42: 73–83.

Hodge M (2000) Curriculum Guidelines for the Foundation Stage. DfEE London.

Johnson M, Kelly K (2000) Early Identification of Dyslexia through Observation. Submitted for publication.

Kamhi AG, Catts HW (1986) Towards and Understanding of Developmental Language and Reading Disorders. Journal of Speech and Hearing Disorders 51: 337–47.

Kelly, K. (1993). Assessing Bilingual Pupils with Specific Learning Difficulties. School of Education, Manchester Metropolitan University. Manchester, unpublished thesis.

Layton L, Deeny K, Upton G, Tall G (1996) Phonological Awareness and the Pre-school Child. Birmingham: University of Birmingham.

Lee R (1996) Middleton Screening Tests (MiST) Unpublished PhD Thesis 1996/2000

Lenvier HC, Lenvier AL, Dow RS (1989) Reappraising the cerebellum: what does the hindbrain contribute to the forebrain? Behavioural Neuroscience 103, 998–1008.

Levinson HN (1988) The cerebellar-vestibular basis of learning disabilities in children, adolescents and adults: hypothesis and study. Perceptual and Motor Skills 67: 983–1006.

Livingstone R, Balkozar SA, Bracha HS (1993) Season of birth and neurodevelopmental disorders: summer birth is associated with dyslexia. Journal of American Academy of Child and Adolescent Psychiatry 32: 612–16.

Lundberg I, Frost J, Peterson OP (1988) Effects of an extensive programme for stimulating phonological awareness in pre-school children. Reading Research Quarterly 23: 263–83.

McArthur GM, Hogben JH, Edwards VI, Heath SM, Mengler ED (2000) On the 'specifics' of specific reading disability and specific language impairment. Journal of Child Psychology and Psychiatry 4: 869–74.

Morton J, (1969) Interaction of information in word recognition. Psychological Review 76, 165–78.

Morton J, Frith U (1995) Causal modelling: a structural approach to developmental psychopathology In D Cicchetti, DJ Cohen (eds) Manual of Developmental Psychology. New York: Wiley, pp. 357–90.

Nicolson RI, Fawcett AJ (1999) Developmental dyslexia: the role of the cerebellum. Dyslexia 155–177.

Nicolson RI, Fawcett AJ (1996) Dyslexia Early Screening Test (DEST). London: The Psychological Corporation.

Norfolk County Council (1996) Aspects of Achievement. Assessing and Recording of Achievement in the Early Years. Internal Report.

Peer L (1997) Dyslexia and Bi- Multi-lingual: In a class of their own. Unpublished Masters dissertation, Institute of Education, Manchester Metropolitan University.

Peer L (2000a) Assessment into Action. Reading: British Dyslexia Association.

Peer L (2000b) What is dyslexia? In Smyth I (ed.) The Dyslexia Handbook 2000. Reading: British Dyslexia Association.

Peer L, Reid G (2000) Multilingualism and Dyslexia: A challenge for educators. London: David Fulton.

Pennington BF (1990) The genetics of dyslexia. Journal of Child Psychology and Psychiatry 31: 193–210.

Portwood M (1996) Developmental Dyspraxia Identification and Intervention. A manual for parents and professionals. London: David Fulton.

Pumfrey P, Reason R (1991) Specific learning difficulties (dyslexia). Challenges and responses. London and New York: Routledge, p. 93.

Pumfrey P, Reason R (1999) Dyslexia, Literacy and Psychological Assessment. Report of the Working Party of the Division of Educational and Child Psychology of the British Psychological Society. Leicester: BPS.

Rack J (1994) Dyslexia. the phonological deficit hypothesis. In Fawcett AJ and Nicolson RI (eds) Dyslexia in Children Multidisciplinary Perspectives. Harvester Wheatsheaf. Hemel Hempsted.

Reason R (1999) Dyslexia, literacy and psychological assessment. DECP Newsletter 92: 3–12.

Robertson J (2000) Dyslexia and Reading: A Neuropsychological Approach. London, Whurr.

Scarborough HS (1998) Early identification of children at risk for reading disabilities. Phonological awareness and some other promising predictors. In BK Shapiro, PJ Accardo and AJ Capute (eds) Specific Reading Disability: A view of the spectrum. Timonium MD: York Press, pp. 75–119.

Scarborough HS (1990) Very early language deficit in dyslexic children. Child Development 61: 1728–63.

Shankweiler D, Cain S (1986) Language mechanisms and reading disorder: a modular approach. Cognition 24: 139–68.

Snowling M (1987) Dyslexia: A cognitive perspective. Oxford: Blackwell.

Stackhouse J (1986) Segmentation, Speech and Reading Difficulties. In Snowling M. Children's Written Language Difficulties. Windsor: NFER- Nelson.

Stanovich KE (1986) Matthew effects in reading: some consequences of individual differences in the acquisition of literacy. Reading Research Quarterly 21: 360–407.

Strag GA (1972) Comparative behavioural ratings of parents with severe mentally retarded, special learning disability and normal children. Journal of Learning Disabilities 5: 6312–635.

Thomson M (1989) Developmental dyslexia. 3rd edn. Studies in Disorders of Communication. London: Whurr Publishers.

Thomson M (1984) Developmental dyslexia: its nature, assessment and remediation. London: Edward Arnold.

Wendon L (1997) Letterland. London: Collins.

Wolf M (1991) Naming speed and reading. Reading Research Quarterly 26: 123–40.

Wood J, Wright J, Stackhouse J (2000) Language and Literacy: Joining together. Reading: British Dyslexia Association.

CHAPTER 12

Identification and intervention in the primary school

GEOFF LINDSAY

In this chapter I shall consider how children with significant difficulties in the development of literacy may be identified and how this identification links with intervention.

The context

My focus is the primary school, or rather the primary period, although both concepts are problematic. Compulsory education in the UK starts in the term after a child becomes five years of age, but many children will start primary education during the term in which they are five, and often at the start of the year. This difference is important as, by the end of key stage 1 (seven years) children may have experienced between six and nine terms of education, with the youngest children tending to be those who have had less.

Similarly, the period of primary education varies from one county to another, with the United Kingdom being a country with an early start (i.e. 4 to 5 years), while others start at 6, even 7 years. Furthermore, while the start of compulsory education in the UK has not changed, the introduction of the foundation stage is an attempt to influence conceptualization and pedagogic practice between primary and pre-school stages. The introduction of the foundation stage with its own curriculum guidance (Qualifications and Curriculum Authority, 2000) has included the Reception year with pre-school, to cover the period up to the start of key stage 1.

The second contextual issue is the legislation and practice with respect to special educational needs, and in particular the guidance provided by the Code of Practice on the Identification and Assessment of Special

Educational Needs (DfEE, 1994), and the revised Code currently out for consultation (DfEE 2000). The Code of Practice offers guidance on all aspects of special educational needs, including dyslexia and hence it provides an important framework. Furthermore, the concept of 'special educational needs' must be considered with respect to 'dyslexia', with both having been found to be problematic.

The Code of Practice incorporates a stage-model of assessment and decision-making, presently comprising five stages, but these become four stages in the new Code. The aim is to take a broad view of special educational needs, which results in it being expected that quite large numbers of children, one in five has been the level commonly quoted in the past (for example, Croll and Moses, 1985), will have SEN at some stage in their schooling, although for different reasons. However, this level of prevalence, derived from epidemiological studies (see the Warnock Report: DES, 1978) has now been superseded. The numbers of children at any stage of schools' registers of SEN was recently found to be 26.1%, an increase of 38.8% compared with a study of the same schools in the early 1980s (Croll and Moses 2000). The main group of children on SEN registers may be characterized as having learning difficulties (88.7 % in this recent Croll and Moses study), and literacy difficulties made up the bulk of these. Croll and Moses report that, of those children identified as having a learning difficulty, 84.2% were considered to have all-round difficulty with learning, whereas only 15% had difficulties specific to one aspect of learning. Of this latter group, the majority (70%) had reading difficulties. Hence, with respect to literacy difficulties, the majority of children as reported by teachers have all round learning difficulties, and so comprise the most prevalent group.

Finally, it is important to consider bi- and multi-lingualism issues. In some areas, schools may include children with very many family languages, and the degree to which English is the first or additional language will vary. Schools in Wales also will have different numbers of children with Welsh as their first language. The interaction of bi- and multi-lingalism and literacy difficulties raises many theoretical and practical issues, which are now being addressed (for example, Peer and Reid, 2000).

Consideration of a model of identification and assessment

In this section I shall review the different elements of a model for the identification and assessment of children with difficulties in literacy development.

Although presented separately, these elements interact, and the final part of this section will attempt to draw the elements together.

Why assess?

Although this may seem a redundant question, it is worth asking. Unless action is to occur then assessment is redundant, so before assessing it is important to consider the possible action outcomes and their likelihood of occurring.

There are a number of possible reasons for assessment, depending upon the model used. As will become apparent, one traditional approach, diagnostic or assessment for classification is not recommended. Rather the purpose advocated here is to guide teaching and the provision of educational intervention in general. This includes screening, assessment through and for teaching, and investigation of a range of factors related to literacy development.

Which children?

The determination of which children are to be considered is not straightforward and is discussed in other chapters. This is an important issue for different aspects of the field. For example, researchers who wish to compare the differential effects of interventions may need to separate children into coherent and valid groupings. Within the domain of practical application, the difficulties with definitions have been a continuing theme.

For present purposes I shall take the definition prepared by the Working Party of the Division of Educational and Child Psychology of the British Psychological Society (1999: 18): 'Dyslexia is evident when accurate and fluent word reading and/or spelling develops very incompletely or with great difficulty.' This definition focuses on literacy learning at the 'word level', and implies that the difficulty is severe, and that it persists. As with other earlier definitions, it is susceptible to confusion – for example, no operational specification is given to 'very incompletely' or 'great difficulty'. However, this definition appears to have achieved support among educational psychologists.

This definition differs from the main approach of recent years, based upon a discrepancy model. Here, children might be designated as dyslexic on the basis of a difference between their actual level of reading and/or spelling, and that predicted on the basis of a well established assessment of general cognitive ability using, for example, the Wechsler Intelligence Scale for Children (now in its third edition – WISC III) (Wechsler, 1992) or the revised British Ability Scales (BAS II) (Elliott, 1996).

This approach lends itself to 'precision' in the sense that exact discrepancies to define dyslexia v. non-dyslexia can be proposed, and in the US such a formulaic model has been popular. However, it has often been misused or at least poorly used. For example, given that reading tests and tests of general cognitive ability do not correlate perfectly and are not perfectly reliable, then these factors affect the predicted score and the discrepancy needed. When this is done, interesting – and for the unwary rather unexpected – outcomes are found. For example, a child with an IQ on the BAS II of 130 may on the face of it be expected to have a predicted reading quotient at this level also, above the 97th centile. However, when the predicted score is calculated correctly, it is found to be 118. Further, the child's actual score must be significantly different from this, requiring a score of 111 or lower (at the 95% level of probability) before a significant discrepancy between IQ and reading score can be claimed. Hence, on the basis of the statistical properties of the tests, discrepancies need to be substantial before they can be considered significant.

The use of a discrepancy approach has been popular, and it will be found both in the literature and the reports of assessments on individual children. Related to this approach is the use of profiles, and in particular the view that dyslexic children have an ACID (arithmetic, coding, information and digit span) profile. This is derived from the proposition that dyslexic children are characterized by scores on the arithmetic, coding, information and digit-span subtests on the WISC (whichever version used) that are lower than their scores on the other subtests. Again, this approach requires statistical analysis as each subtest is not perfectly reliable, and hence the determination of whether the child's discrepancy is reliably different must take into account normal variations resulting from error. As with the model comparing IQ against reading standard score, practice reveals that quite substantial differences are required in order to show this is indeed an ACID profile.

Such statistical analyses have been aided by better manuals, and computer scoring and analysis systems, but also require a level of sophistication with psychometric theory and practice not within the training of teachers, and hence even less accessible to parents. However, a more problematic aspect is that increasingly researchers and educational psychologists have come to the view that such discrepancy and profile approaches have limited usefulness per se. For example, Frederickson (1999) has made a strong case against the usefulness of the ACID profile, and the DECP[1] Working Party (Division of Educational and Child Psychology Working Party of the British Psychological Society) reports a special issue of the journal *Dyslexia* (vol. 2, no. 3, 1996) where contributions, were 'representative of the current balance of opinion in the research literature strongly weighted against the validity of discrepancy definitions' (DECP, 1999: 58).

Hence, while the definition used here may be criticized on the grounds of a lack of specificity, this may not necessarily be important. Specificity is required if a diagnostic approach is undertaken, whereby the purpose is to assign children precisely to categories, in this case dyslexia or non-dyslexia, where non-dyslexia may be subdivided into normal (no significant difficulty) or another literacy difficulty. Such approaches are most useful, and indeed may be essential, if there are differences in the implications of the diagnosis and such differences are highly reliable. However, in the field of dyslexia and literacy difficulties, such direct and exclusive relationships between diagnosis and intervention have not been shown. The approach advocated here, therefore, is that of assessment related to intervention, a more fluid and dynamic model – see below. For the present, the main point is to stress that this approach changes from one of diagnosis, with implications of certainties, or at least high probabilities of the child being correctly and appropriately classified (for example, as 'dyslexic'), to one where information is gathered and hypotheses are generated which are tested. This is a very different approach to the task.

Which domains?

The traditional model of dyslexia, as of disabilities in general, stresses the problems that are 'within child'. Research and professional practice have clearly shown that there are indeed such difficulties in some children, and that their struggle to develop literacy is not simply due to absence from school, disaffection, poor teaching or other external factors. Earlier chapters in this book as well as other recent publications have indicated the importance of cognitive and of biological factors (for example, Hulme and Snowling, 1998; Gallagher, Frith and Snowling, 2000). However, the evidence also is clear that external factors can and do affect children's literacy development. Consequently it is necessary to consider assessment in a wider sense, not just of the child's development in literacy and general cognitive ability. The model presented here has been promoted before as a general approach to conceptualizing children's development difficulties, and their assessment, but for the present discussion the focus will be on literacy (Wedell, 1978; Lindsay and Wedell, 1982; Lindsay, 1995; Adelman, 1992).

The domains for assessment follow directly from the definition above: assessing and evaluating accuracy and fluency of word reading and spelling, assessing learning opportunities in the classroom and within the National Literacy Strategy, and assessing persistence (DECP Working Party, 1999). However, this three-domain model will be expanded upon in the following discussion.

Assessing and evaluating accuracy and fluency of word reading and spelling

The first domain is that of the target skill – literacy. Here the aim is to assess the child's abilities on the range of literacy tasks, appropriate to his or her age and functional level. There are three types of question pertinent here, and generally each may be addressed by a different method of assessment.

Normative

How discrepant is the child's literacy from that typically found for their chronological age? This question may be addressed by standardized reading tests, which provide reading ages or standardized scores. It must be remembered that with increasing chronological age (CA), the spread of scores also increases amongst the population. At age eight, the reading age equivalent to a child being at the tenth and second centile for Neale Accuracy are 6:02 and < six years respectively, i.e. 1:10 and more than two years respectively below CA. However, by age 10, the reading ages for those centiles are 7:01 and 6:05 years, translating into 2:11 and 3:7 years respectively behind CA.

Normative assessments have gone in and out of fashion as they do not, of themselves, provide direct information on what to teach (although see Whitworth and Sutton, 1973, for an example of teaching ideas based on WISC III profiles). However, it is argued here that an estimate of the reading level and variation from the mean score for the age groups provides useful information in its own right.

Several tests are available to teachers and psychologists but choice will be determined by two factors: the nature of the test (for example, single word reading or continuous prose) and the technical quality of the test (for example, its standardization and reliability measures). Probably the most popular individually administered tests with satisfactory technical qualities are the Neale Analysis of Reading Ability – Revised (Neale, 1997), the New Reading Analysis (Vincent and de la Mare, 1985) and the Word Reading scale from the BAS II (Elliott, 1996).

Criterion referenced

A separate assessment process addresses the specific, absolute skills and knowledge of the child rather than their relative performance against their peers. This includes sound recognition, letter symbol sound (grapheme-phoneme) correspondence, and recognition of specific words. Again, the focus here is on the target skills of reading and spelling. Criterion-referenced approaches to assessment are more directly related to teaching. The assessment may target a specific aspect of knowledge or skill. If the child achieves success, there is no need to teach as a new element. Where a lower level is achieved this may indicate the element is suitable to be taught next or, that preliminary work is necessary before tackling this.

These two methods of assessment are complementary, providing information about normative status and mastering of specific skills.

In the present model, the first domain to be examined is the target skill. However, the traditional role of other assessment, for example of general cognitive ability, is also included.

Hypothesis-testing and prerequisite skills

The present model changes the emphasis for the use of an assessment by a test of general cognitive ability. Such tests, which in the UK will most likely be the Wechsler Intelligence Scale for Children III (WISC III) or the British Ability Scales II (BAS II), have traditionally been used to obtain an IQ, against which to compare the reading and/or spelling standard score. From this difference it is possible to determine whether the actual reading level is statistically below that provided by IQ. However, as argued above, this approach becomes redundant if the discrepancy model is not valid, the position argued here. Nevertheless, tests such as the WISC III and BAS II do provide the psychologist with a series of subtests or scales that allow a more analytic approach. For example, different aspects of verbal cognitive ability may be compared.

Both the WISC III and BAS II, and indeed some other comparable tests, allow analyses at the level of individual subtests or scales, and of groupings of these. For example, the WISC III has four factors: verbal comprehension, perceptual organization, freedom from distractibility, and processing speed.

These factor scores, comprising more items are more reliable than the individual subtest scores. Also as they comprise subtests that cover some similar aspects of cognition, analyses at this level allow investigation of the generality of a strength or weakness across different tasks.

The use of such tests for this more analytic approach can be helpful, but there are also dangers. Firstly, it is important to recognize the statistical limitations. For example, a single subtest score will typically be less reliable than factor scores, with IQ being most reliable. This has implications when interpreting differences between scores. Indeed the issue is compounded as not only must the reliability of each score be taken into account but also the reliability of the difference. This is a technical matter, but it is common to find interpretations of differences between scores that are simply not sustainable, purely at the level of statistical reliability.

Secondly, assuming differences are statistically significant, are they educationally significant? This is, of course, a very different question, and it is here where evidence of educational correlates of test problems, and the experience of the psychologist, come into play. Further guidance on the technical aspect of this approach can be found in Kaufman (1994) for the WISC III.

In addition to tests designed to measure general cognitive ability, there are also methods of assessment that are closer to the target skills of literacy. For example, the Phonological Awareness Battery (PhAB) (Frederickson, Frith and Reason, 1997) comprises tests to assess alliteration, naming speed, rhyme, spoonerisms, rhyme and alliteration fluency, and non-word reading. This battery was developed to assess aspects of phonological processing ability, which is now firmly established as having a significant relationship with the development of literacy skills. Indeed, there is now firm evidence that difficulties in this domain may fairly be interpreted as a proximal cause, not just a correlate, of literacy difficulties. Although fairly recent, and so not subject to extensive research, evidence has been accumulating for the usefulness of the PhAB (for example, Dockrell and Lindsay, 1998). The Phonological Abilities Test (Muter, Hulme and Snowling, 1997) also addresses phonological skills, with subtests for rhyme detection, rhyme production, word completion and phoneme deletion but its target age range is five to seven years, compared with six to 15 for the PhAB (although the main use of the latter is likely to be with younger children).

The third test to be considered here is the Graded Non-Word Reading Test (Snowling, Stothard and McClean, 1996). This is a relatively quick test that assesses a child's ability to read strings of letters that allow acceptable pronunciations but are not real words. This test attempts to assess a child's ability to process strings of sounds against letter symbols, and so is at a higher level than single letter-sound relationships as measured by the PhAB, for example. Furthermore, when the strings produce two syllables, assessment is made of the child's ability to make use of other principles or rules, for example the most likely place(s) to split the string into syllables.

The Children's Test of Nonword Repetition (Gathercole and Baddeley, 1996) also uses non-words but here the task is one of repeating the non-word after it is given aurally, by a tape recorder. This is essentially a test of short-term memory, but unlike tests such as digit span, where number strings must be repeated, the material is closer to the target skills in literacy. However, note that in both tests non-words are used, so reducing information, semantic knowledge, which might help the child with either task.

These four tests have been mentioned specifically as they are all relatively recent, and have been developed in the UK, with clear rationales based upon evidence from studies of literacy development, and hence are theoretically driven. Moreover, they have each been standardized on reasonable samples, and show acceptable psychometric properties. Their usefulness, beyond the evidence produced by the respective authors, will be confirmed over the next few years.

These tests are good examples of how non-target skills may be assessed. The rationale for the abilities focused upon is that these are correlates of, at least, or even prerequisite skills for effective reading and spelling. As such, these tests provide a range of information that does not explain a child's reading difficulties but does provide the basis for sound hypotheses for explanation and action.

This is not simply circumlocution, but represents a fundamental difference of approach. Essentially, this approach recognizes that we are dealing with probabilities and not certainties. For example, it has been known for many years that although many children who lack what are considered to be prerequisite skills for literacy struggle greatly in learning to read, some children do progress to reading with less, or no such difficulty.

For example, work on children with cerebral palsy has shown that, for many, a visual processing difficulty is very predictive of reading difficulties, but some children buck this trend (Wedell, 1973) and visual perceptual deficiencies are not necessarily limited to reading difficulties (Wedell, 1977). Individual case studies also support this. For example, one child I worked with had major visual perceptual and spatial awareness problems, and scored very low on traditional tests of general cognitive ability (below the second centile) and a test of visual perception. However, by focusing on reading and writing, and not trying to remediate these deficient supposed prerequisite skills, we were able to develop his early reading at a rapid rate. Similarly, a girl with very limited spoken language skills, including the use of no more that three word utterances, was helped to read by focusing on reading itself, while a separate programme addressed her language problems.

Accuracy and fluency

Most of the assessments discussed have focused upon accuracy as the prime measure. This is clearly essential but, as Haring and Eaton (1978) have argued, there are other important skills to develop; they propose five in total namely, acquisition, maintenance, fluency, generalization, and adaptation. For present purposes, I shall focus on fluency.

Research has indicated that acquisition, demonstrated by accuracy, is not enough as a teaching goal. While developing a skill there is a substantial amount of information processing capacity focused on that skill and associated factors at the time. Typically, as fluency increases, less information processing capacity needs to be allocated, and eventually the skill becomes 'automatic' (see Samuels, 1999). For example, studies of effective readers indicate that their rate of reading is faster, they can gain information more effectively, and they will not notice some minor errors.

What is very noticeable with children with reading difficulties is that their fluency is less than that of their peers at similar levels of accuracy. As a result they gain less information from the text as they spend more on ensuring accuracy (Samuels, 1999). Consequently, it is important to build fluency as well as accuracy goals into a programme. This will include a higher degree of overlearning (repetition) than typically developing readers/spellers. The use of time targets (e.g. words read correctly per minute) can be easily assessed and recorded.

Precision teaching, despite its name, is an effective method of recording and charting children's progress. This approach, also called daily measurement, lends itself to daily probes, taking only one or two minutes, to assess progress. The probes comprise items specifically from the teaching programme, and so are criterion referenced (for example, a list of the 10 words currently being learned, in random order, on a page of perhaps 50 or 100 words). The child's accuracy and fluency are assessed by number of words read correctly and number read correctly per minute respectively. Practice may take place at other times, but the probe, an assessment device, may also act as a learning device as it is another opportunity for the child to practise the specific skill.

Nicolson and Fawcett (1990) have presented a useful rationale for the importance of automaticity, and the impact of its inadequate development in children's reading ability. See also Kolligian and Sternberg (1987) for a fuller model of learning disabilities, specifying automaticity as a key element.

Summary

The focus of this section has been on 'within child' factors. The primary focus has been on target skills, with assessment of other skills being supportive. The task is not one of diagnosis – coming to a categorical decision (for example, dyslexia/non-dyslexia). Rather, it is essentially a process of hypothesis testing, starting with target skills and using other assessments to provide further clues that support or challenge likely explanations.

All assessments must be of sound technical quality, otherwise results are dubious and may mislead. This is particularly true of standardized tests of the type discussed above, but also of criterion-referenced assessments, a point often under-recognized. While there is no need for standardization samples, criterion-referenced assessment must still meet general technical considerations – for example, whether the assessment process is valid as a means of ensuring that the child's true ability will be revealed. Hence, practitioners must be aware of statistical and other technical factors with respect to specific instruments and procedures. The type of knowledge of psychometrics mentioned here is not typically available to teachers as it is not part of their training. However, the British Psychological Society is developing a scheme specifying competencies in educational assessment that may lead to further training to allow teachers to be assessed and awarded recognition. (Such a system has operated for occupational assessment for several years). In the interim, and probably well into the future, there is a need for joint professional practice in assessment with educational psychologists acting as advisers on the choice and use of instrument and methods, delivered by teachers, advisers and collaborators in the interpretation of results; and direct assessors when instruments require skills and training that they alone have, but where interpretation and plans for action are discussed and developed together with teachers.

Assessing learning opportunities

In addition to children's inherent characteristics, it is necessary to consider the impact of the learning opportunities available. The two main factors are teaching and the curriculum, but others will be considered below.

When the 1988 Education Bill was being debated, the stress was on the curriculum. Teachers, it was argued, would be left to decide how to teach it. Subsequently, this has changed and the centrality of the way a curriculum is taught has been not only increasingly recognized but also regulated. The OFSTED framework of inspection, for example, includes quality of teaching as one area for inspection (Ofsted, 1999).

National Literacy Strategy

Probably the most important factor for literacy has been the implementation of the National Literacy Strategy (NLS), which sets out both curriculum and teaching methodologies. Schools are expected to follow this, although some choose not to – see discussion of the Essex research below. Hence, any assessment of learning opportunities must start with the NLS.

It is reasonable to conclude that the NLS is based upon research on effective literacy development (Beard, 1999). However, as the DECP Working Party (1999) argue, there are two independent questions: to what extent is the curriculum appropriate to children having difficulty acquiring literacy, and to what extent is the teaching (or 'instructional approaches' in their terminology) appropriate for these children as well as typically developing children?

The DECP Working Party provide a useful review of the NLS in terms of its appropriateness on each question, and Piotrowski and Reason (2000) have provided a comparison of materials designed for use at the word level by typically developing children, by those making slower progress, and by those regarded as having difficulties of a dyslexic nature.

Pietrowski and Reason (2000) argue that special education has had a major influence on the NLS. By this they mean that many of the factors traditionally stressed in practice with children with literacy difficulties, and identified from research with such children, have a role in the NLS, a change from the days when there was a substantial gulf between approaches for these compared with typically developing children. However, differences remain.

Their review of materials asks eight questions including whether there is progression and whether they are based on mastery learning. They conclude that there are differences between the materials. For example, the strongest linking between assessment and teaching ('assessing to teach') was formed from the materials for children making slower progress compared with those for all children and dyslexic children.

Mastery learning, however, is evident in materials from both the dyslexic and slower development groups, but only implicit in materials from the general programme. Hence, assessment must include examination of the materials; the review by Piotrowski and Reason (2000) is useful for guidance.

Effective instruction

The NLS incorporates a range of teaching approaches as well as a curriculum content. However, aspects of effective teaching have been identified that subsume and expand upon these.

There are distinct traditions in research and practice in this area. One may be characterized as child centred, or romantic in that it stresses creativity, encouragement, individualization, respect for the child, and facilitation by the teacher. Another is grounded in behavioural psychology and is often referred to as 'instruction'. This approach stresses structure, targets and evidence from studies based on the predictions from learning theory.

The concern for those working with children with literacy difficulties has been that the approach typically used in primary classrooms was insufficiently structured to ensure success. Children with such problems might be offered approaches based on a therapeutic model, for example to reduce anxiety and increase motivation. However, whatever the approach, there is a need to assess these teaching or instructional components – their presence and effectiveness.

Ysseldyke and Christensen (1987) have set out an Instructional Environment Survey. This examines the learning environment of the classroom as characterized by the interaction between teacher and individual child. Twelve aspects of effective instruction are proposed and presented in a modified form below:

- Instructional presentation – for example, is instruction presented clearly? Is the child's understanding checked before moving on?
- Classroom environment – for example, is time used productively? Is classroom control efficient, effective?
- Teacher expectations – for example, realistic but high? Communicated clearly to the child?
- Cognitive emphasis – for example, are thinking skills necessary for the task explained?
- Motivational strategies – for example, are there a variety of effective strategies?
- Relevant practice – for example, opportunity to practise with relevant materials, sufficient time for overlearning?
- Academic engaged time – for example, is the child engaged on the task? Is the task appropriate?
- Informed feedback – for example, is this immediate, informed, corrective?
- Adaptive instruction – for example, is there appropriate differentiation of the curriculum and method of delivery?
- Progress evaluation – for example, is there direct and frequent assessment of progress? Is this recorded and used to plan?
- Instructional planning – for example, is instruction planned appropriately to student's needs? Are needs assessed accurately?
- Student understanding – for example, do children show they understand?

These 12 elements provide a sound basis for assessment of the child's learning environment as characterized by interaction with the teacher and instruction method. Each can be operationalized and assessed, and hence can potentially be modified.

Further possible aspects of the learning environment may be examined:

- Ecological – for example, noise levels; visual aspects such as glare, poor lighting; ventilation; space.
- Support – for example, presence of learning support assistants; volunteers; bilingual support.
- Groups – for example, grouping within NLS; withdrawal or in-class support arrangements.

- Other professionals – for example support from educational psychologists, advisory teachers, medical officers and so forth.
- Parents – for example parental involvement, especially for intervention.
- Training – for example skill and knowledge development opportunities; methods for example courses, shadowing other colleagues.
- Community for example support, tensions, further learning opportunities.

Each of these is important as a contribution to the learning environment of the school, from the child working alone, through classroom to school and community factors. It is based upon a systematic view of the factors that affect children's development (Bronfenbrenner, 1979) and hence of the elements which must be assessed although the 'distance' between each of the elements specified and literacy per se varies.

Persistence

The third element to assess relates to time. Children's difficulties may be assessed with respect to their own characteristics and the learning opportunities available, but each of these elements and, importantly, their interaction vary over time.

This approach challenges the view that children's abilities are necessarily stable. For instance, the variability of IQ over time has been well established (for example Hindley and Owen, 1978). However, although children's abilities may change in absolute terms, and relative to those of their peers, there is also evidence for persistence, for some children, although some may move in and out of categories (see, for example, Share et al. 1987).

Evidence is also building up for a developmental pattern starting from early childhood, and characterized by language difficulties, later presenting as reading difficulties (for example Gallagher, Frith and Snowling, 2000; Dockrell and Lindsay, 1998; Dockrell and Lindsay, in press). Hence there are two issues for assessment: persistence over substantial periods of time for example one or more years, and changes with respect to intervention in the short to medium term. The former is best approached by normative measures to gauge relative standing over time.

As stated above, these assessments require technically sound, well-standardized instruments. However, it is also important to recognize the limitations resulting from change of test. For example, some tests are appropriate only for younger or older children so necessitating comparisons on the basis of different tests, with different standardizations.

Moreover, over a period of 10 years a test may be revised, in which case the norms are likely to be different such that a child may achieve different scores on the old and new version if the general standard of reading, as indicated by the standardization sample, has increased or decreased.

With respect to short- and medium-term assessment, the aim is to monitor the effectiveness of an intervention in order to modify it as necessary, or to remove a child from a special programme. Normative measures are of limited usefulness and criterion-referenced measures are to be preferred.

The model of precision teaching or daily measurement discussed above is helpful here – see Solity and Bull (1987) for an accessible account of its use. It appears to have gone out of fashion (DECP Working Party, 1999) yet it provides a relatively simple method for monitoring progress, and providing direct feedback to children to give a sense of success and improve motivation.

Early identification

The early identification of literacy difficulties is a separate but substantive issue for assessment and intervention.

There can be little doubt that educationists and parents would wish to see effective early identification programmes in operation. The parallel with medical screening, to identify 'cases' at an early stage of an illness, or preferably at a pre-symptomatic stage, is often made.

In practice, educational screening, and indeed medical screening in many cases, has been found to be more problematic than hoped.

To take a medical parallel that is topical, it appears that screening for prostate cancer in men is possible through a simple test, but the rates of false positives and false negatives would be unacceptably high, so causing unnecessary anxiety in some and unwarranted relief in others. With respect to early childhood development the situation is similar in that accuracy is usually not high, but for a different reason. Here, we are dealing with a developing child, where normal development is highly variable across children, who show various trajectories (for example Law et al, 1998, for a review of screening for speech and language delivery).

Attempts to develop early educational screening have proven problematic (see Lindsay 1995 for review). However, there is evidence for predispositions to literacy difficulties and some evidence for the usefulness of screening instruments. The former comes from studies such as that by Gallagher, Frith and Snowling (2000) mentioned above. They compared the literacy skills of 63 children selected as being at genetic risk of dyslexia with 34 children where there was no family history. The study indicates that those children at genetic risk were indeed more likely to have literacy difficulties at age six years.

This applied to 57% – a very high probability – but far from perfect prediction. Indeed, eight of the 63 children scored above the mean on a literacy component standard score, and one child scored above 125 – in about the top 5%. Further analysis, however, indicated that this literacy-delayed group tended to have significantly slower speech and language development at 45 months, albeit that again the match was not perfect.

The point to stress, therefore, is that early identification programmes for literacy delay should be sequential and regarded as probabilistic.

At risk factors from family histories, or from birth can be used in a model, which then includes language development at about three to five years and literacy at about five to seven years. At each stage the process would recognize that a child's likelihood of developing literacy difficulties can only be estimated as a probability, and hence a definite 'diagnosis' is not appropriate (see above).

All schools in England must conduct baseline assessment on children within seven weeks of school entry, and this has potential for an important contribution to a sequential model of early identification. Unfortunately, the current national arrangements do not ensure a quality system (Lindsay, 1998; Lindsay and Desforges 1998; Lindsay, Lewis and Phillips, 2000).

Most importantly, there are no requirements for the 91 accredited schemes to demonstrate their technical quality meets an acceptable standard (for example with respect to reliability, standardization) or even that this has been evaluated, although a minority, reviewed by Lindsay and Desforges (1998) do have such data.

On the other hand, Lindsay, Lewis and Phillips (2000) found that reception teachers are keen to use baseline assessment and find it helpful in planning their work, albeit that only 47% of schools stated they used baseline assessment for identification of special educational needs 'a great deal', a figure that rose to 72.4% when 'quite often' respondents were included. Hence, at present, the national scheme's status as an element in the proposed sequential model cannot be considered well-established across infant and primary schools as a whole. Baseline assessment to meet the Qualifications and Curriculum Authority's criteria, must be broader than literacy assessment, although schemes must assess aspects of language and literacy. Examination of the content of schemes suggests that their assessment of these domains is not consistent, even if covering similar domains (Lindsay, Lewis, and Phillips in preparation). However, there are also a small number of screening instruments specifically for dyslexia, of which two will be considered.

The Dyslexia Screening Test (DST) (Fawcett and Nicolson, 1996) and the Dyslexia Early Screening Test (DEST) (Nicolson and Fawcett, 1996) derive from research by these authors, with the former designed for children 6:5 to 16:5 years, and the DEST for children 4:5 to 6:5 years.

The tests are designed to identify children at risk of dyslexia, and are a combination of subtests assessing current target skills (for example reading), as well as others, phonological skills, for example. Of interest, and unusually, the tests include items involving balance, which derives from the authors' research on automaticity and cerebellar functioning, and their argument that there is a more general skill automatization problem for dyslexic children.

As discussed above, attempts to compare scores of the subtests must be treated cautiously, with regard to statistical and educational significance of differences, and the results from the DEST and DST must be seen as probabilistic indicators, not clear-cut 'diagnostic' indicators. The usefulness of these tests will become more apparent with research on interventions deriving from the profiles obtained.

Indeed the authors claim the DEST and DST are designed to identify learning disabilities of all types, and hence further assessment is required to identify needs. However, Fawcett, Singleton and Peer (1998) report an overall hit rate of 90% (18/20) of children predicted to have reading difficulties by the DEST at mean C.A. 5:4 years against reading attainment on the WORD at mean C.A. 7:9 years. There were 10.7% false positives (designated at risk on the DEST but whose reading was satisfactory at 7:9 years) and 2.0% false negative (designated not at risk, but who had reading difficulties at 7:9 years.

The CoPS Cognitive Profiling System (Singleton, Thomas and Leedale 1996) is a computer-based standardized assessment instrument, with emphasis on phonological awareness, memory and auditory discrimination. It derives from a research study by the author, which investigated the predictive power of the instrument, and indeed led to the selection of specific subtests. 'Hit' rates are reported to be high, when comparison of CoPS given at age five was compared with reading assessed at eight years. For the cut-off scores selected, overall hit rate for poor readers was 96%, with 16.7% false negatives (children who were designated not at risk, but who had reading difficulties at eight), and just 2.3% false positives (children designated as 'at risk', but where reading was satisfactory at eight years). As with the DEST/DST, further independent evidence is necessary, but with the same provisos as above, the CoPS appears to have potential usefulness.

However, in both cases, and indeed in all cases of predictive assessments, altering the cut-off points for 'at risk' or 'reading difficulties' (for each is a question of judgement, there being no sacrosanct cut-offs) has *opposing* impact on false positive and false negatives rates. By reducing the number of false negatives, and so maximising the number of children later identified as having reading difficulties, the proportion is also increased of children incorrectly identified as at risk who later have satisfactory reading (false positives). Practitioners often argue that it is better to maximise the capture of children at risk, so offering the opportunity for alternative intervention (e.g. Fawcett, Singleton and Peer). This is understandable, but a balance is needed as children incorrectly identified as at risk of a problem may be disadvantaged e.g. by unnecessary assessments and inappropriate interventions.

Conclusions

This chapter has addressed the assessment of children at the primary stage, key stages 1 and 2, with reference to intervention. The starting point has been a view of dyslexia that is broader than traditional approaches. This derives from much recent work on the nature of literacy difficulties and the lack of evidence for distinct differences between children designated as dyslexic by previous discrepancy approaches, where IQ is used as a predictor of expected literacy ability (for example Stanovich, 1991; Siegel, 1989).

The approach taken by the Division of Educational and Child Psychology Working Party of the British Psychological Society is commended, and has formed the basis of the approach here. However, this has been expanded upon in several ways. In this final section I shall propose a model of assessment which brings together the strands previously discussed. It has the following elements.

Compensatory interaction

As argued by Wedell (1978), Wedell and Lindsay, (1980), and Lindsay (1995) children's developmental difficulties must be considered as a result of an interaction between their own strengths and weaknesses and those of the environment. Furthermore, the balance of each of these changes over time, as does the interaction between them.

Wedell has termed this model one of 'compensatory interaction', whereas Adelman (1992) has proposed a similar approach albeit without the time dimensions, but referring to a transactional view of the locus of primary instigating factors (see Lindsay, 1995 for discussion of these models) – see Figure 12.1. This approach requires the assessment of:

- within child factors;
- external factors – both learning opportunities within the classroom, and wider environmental elements;
- progress over time, short, medium and long term.

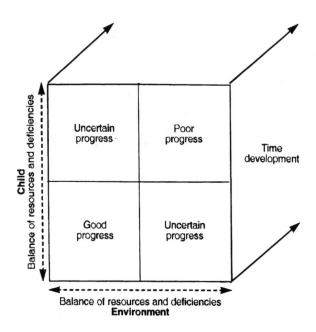

Figure 12.1: A model of compensatory interaction Source: Wedell and Lindsay (1980).

Componential assessment

The majority of approaches to assessment used with children with literacy difficulties incorporate assessments of elements within the overall instrument, for example the Phonological Assessment Battery comprises six subtests. Implied in this approach is that these more specific elements are sufficiently discrete to be worth examining, and that the resulting profile is helpful. Furthermore, the elements may fit together in a coherent fashion such that impairment or underdevelopment in one has implications for another.

Hence some form of hierarchical relationship may be hypothesized. This approach is often implicit in that different researchers have investigated different elements, and perhaps devised assessment for the domain on which they have focussed. Others have attempted to postulate a more coherent system.

For example, Kolligian and Sternberg (1987) have used Sternberg's theory of intelligence to prepare a componential model for learning difficulties.

This incorporates acquisition (for example phonological awareness) at a basic level, with analytic skills (for example phoneme–grapheme correspondence) building upon these, and with higher order skills such as automaticity and meta-cognitive ability at a higher level still. Such a model also fits into a causal model, with biological, cognitive and contextual elements (for example Sternberg and Spear-Swerling, 1999; Hulme and Snowling, 1998).

Here, biological causes may be viewed as more fundamental, but also more distal (further removed from the target skills of reading). The cognitive element is more proximal, but within this some elements will be more proximal to reading than others (for example word recognition compared with memory for non-literary material).

An assessment model should build upon this approach, which is theory-and-research driven, and also comprehensive.

Sequential assessment

The implementation of assessment, and decisions concerning the status and needs of children, should be part of a sequential strategy. Relevant data may be available from family histories as well as at birth, both biological (for example birth weight, birth order), social (for example social disadvantage or social class) and family (for example maternal depression). Rigby, Sanderson, Desforges, Lindsay, and Hall 1999) have demonstrated how medical and educational databases, with perinatal and baseline assessment data respectively, can be combined and indicate risk factors. Further information could be gathered in the pre-school, especially the early foundation stage period, with a particular emphasis on speech and language assessment. An improved national baseline assessment scheme at school entry could be linked to further investigation with assessment to follow. A new end of foundation 'baseline assessment' could provide further evidence, while daily assessment of specific learning could take place over the reception and early key stage 1 periods.

The importance of the link between language and literacy difficulties emphasizes the need for close, coherently organized collaboration between front line educational professionals, especially teachers, learning support assistants and educational psychologists, and colleagues in health, especially speech and language therapists. Similarly close collaboration is necessary for strategic planning of identification and intervention systems between SLT managers and their counterparts in LEAs (see Law, Lindsay, Peacey, Gascoigne, Soloff, Radford, and Band, 2000).

This sequential approach should derive from a componential model – that is, the elements to be assessed should have a coherent relationship with each other and a more encompassing model of assessment, as proposed here. One aspect of sequence is chronological time (for example birth versus school entry data) while the second is derived from the componential model (literacy-related before more general cognitive abilities).

Practical consideration must also apply, for example observing the child before an individual assessment to try to prevent the form being affected.

Probabilistic judgement

All assessment procedures for children's development have less than perfect prediction or categorization power. Moreover, children's natural trajectories vary, and may be altered by interventions. Consequently, all data must lead to probabilistic, not absolute, categorized judgements.

With respect to the current model, probabilistic analyses may be used to identify especially high risk children but attention should not be limited to these. At each stage, the net must be spread more widely than the predicted 'at risk' group.

Intervention

With respect to intervention, the nature of this will depend on age as the model here applies to pre-school, even birth, and genetic counselling. In the pre-school period, the focus should be on speech and language development while at school age the main intervention will be via the National Literacy Strategy. However, there are two issues of relevance here.

First, the NLS, and the materials produced to support it, while apparently having aided the raising of general standards of literacy, does not fully incorporate the good practice elements for children with difficulties in literacy acquisition.

Secondly, the NLS may not be the most effective approach. Research in Essex (The Essex Early Reading Research (ERR) programme) appears to be making more significant gains, especially in reducing substantially the numbers of children with literacy difficulties by the end of year 1, than the NLS (Solity, Deavers, Kerfoot, Crane and Cannon, 2000), although this paper lacks full data on the statistical analyses substantiating this claim.

Concluding comment

In this chapter I have taken a deliberately broad perspective on assessment of intervention with children with literacy difficulties. The approach is non-diagnostic and non-categorical, depending upon a comprehensive model of reading, and hence a comprehensive model of assessment, which must be implemented according to a sequential strategy.

This model, it is proposed, has general applicability across all children with literacy difficulties, with variations deriving from individual differences. However, a further element to consider is the absolute number of children with literacy difficulties, and what the term actually means. The NLS, and the Essex programme therefore provide a further interesting element in the debate over assessment, but particularly the nature of literacy difficulties.

Prevalence rates for literacy difficulties, whether of dyslexia as traditionally defined or poorly developed reading more generally, vary according to the precise definition and study, but tend to be high, especially in areas of social disadvantage. Yet the NLS, and, it is claimed even more successfully the Essex ERR, can apparently reduce prevalence rates substantially.

In the case of the Essex ERR, Solity et al (2000) claim that in one study only 2% of ERR children who would be classified as lower achievers (bottom 25% of their group) would be classified lower achievers in a non-intervention comparison group, whereas 65% of the comparison group children would be classified lower achievers in the ERR schools. Moreover, the mean reading age (British Ability Scales Word Reading) at mean chronological age of about 6:4 for each group, was 6:10 for the ERR against 6:3 for the comparison.

Furthermore, in a second study, the ERR schools children outperformed those in schools following the NLS (RA 7:2 years against 6:8 years) at the end of year 1.

Hence, the NLS appears to be reducing the number of children with literacy difficulties whereas the ERR appears to be reducing the numbers even more dramatically – a trend also reported in the US by Vellutino et al. (1996) in a different intervention study. If these results can be sustained, and generalized to other schools, our conceptions of prevalence rates must change. Our assessment and intervention model must adjust to take account of these different numbers, and the differential need for approaches for all children (for example the NLS and ERR) compared with more specific variants or more fundamentally different approaches.

The assessment and intervention model presented here is an attempt to incorporate recent research on risk, correlates of literacy difficulties, more recent conceptualizations of literacy difficulties and dyslexia, and also a more comprehensive model of assessment going beyond 'within child' factors. The tension between evidence from groups and manifestations in individual children must be acknowledged. Any assessment intervention model must be sequential, probabilistic rather than absolute, flexible and recognizing teaching as an 'art' as well as a 'science'.

Notes

1. Some researchers advocate maintaining the discrepancy definition (see the debate in Nicolson, 1996).

References

Adelman HS (1992) LD: the next 25 years, Journal of Learning Disabilities 25: 17–22.

Beard R (1999) National Literacy Strategy: Review of Research and other Related Evidence. Sudbury: DfEE Publications.

Bronfenbrenner U (1979) The Ecology of Human Development. Cambridge MA: Harvard University Press.

Croll P, Moses D (1985) One in Five. London: Routledge & Kegan Paul.

Croll P, Moses D (2000) Special Needs in the Ordinary School: One in Five? London: Cassell.

Department for Education and Science (1978) Special Educational Needs, London.

Department for Education (1994) Code of Practice on the Identification and Assessment of Pupils with Special Educational Needs. London: DfE.

Department for Education and Employment (2000) SEN Code of Practice on the Identification of Pupils with Special Educational Needs – draft. London: DfEE.

Division of Educational and Child Psychology (1999) Dyslexia, Literacy and Psychological Assessment. Report of a Working Party of the DECP. Leicester: British Psychological Society.

Dockrell J, Lindsay G (1998) The ways in which speech and language difficulties impact on children's access to the curriculum. Child Language, Teaching and Therapy 14: 117–33.

Dockrell, J.E. and Lindsay G. Specific speech and language difficulties and literacy. In P Bryant and T Nurses Handbook of Children's Literacy, London: Kluwer.

Elliot CD (1996) British Ability Scale. 2 edn. Windsor: NFER-Nelson.

Fawcett AJ, Nicolson RI (1996) The Dyslexia Screening Test. The Psychological Corporation: London.

Fawcett AJ, Singleton C, Peer L (1998) Advances in early years screening for dyslexia in the UK. Annals of Dyslexia 48, 29–60.

Fredrickson N (1999) The ACID test – or is it? Educational Psychology in Practice 10(4): 195–206.

Fredrickson N, Frith U, Reason R (1997) Phonological Assessment Battery. Windsor: NFER-Nelson.

Gallagher A, Frith V, Snowling MJ (2000) Precursors of literacy delivery among children at genetic risk of dyslexia. Journal of Child Psychology and Psychiatry 41(2): 203–14.

Gathercole SE, Baddeley AD (1996) Children's Test of Nonword Repetition. London: Psychological Corporation.

Haring NG, Eaton MD (1978) Systematic instructional procedures: an instructional hierarchy. In NG Haring et al. (eds) The Fourth R. Research in the Classroom. Ohio: Charles Merrill, pp. 23–40.

Hindley CB, Owen CF (1978) The extent of individual changes in IQ for ages between 6 months and 17 years in a British longitudual sample. Journal of Child Psychology and Psychiatry 19, 329–50.

Hulme C, Snowling M (1998) Dyslexia: Biology, Cognition and Intervention. London: Whurr.

Kaufman AS (1994) Intelligent Testing with the WISC III. New York: Wiley.

Kolligian J, Sternberg RJ (1987) Intelligence, information processing, and specific learning disabilities: a triarchic, synthesis'. Journal of Learning Disabilities 20(12): 8–17.

Law J, Boyle J, Harris F, Harkness A, Nye C (1998) Screening for speech and language delay: a systematic review of the literature. Health Technology Assessment 2 (9).

Law J, Lindsay G, Gascoigne M, Peacey N, Soloff N, Radford J, Band S (2000) Provision for Children with Speech and Language Needs in England and Wales. London: DfEE.

Lindsay G, Wedell K (1982) The early identification of educationally 'at risk' children: revisited. Journal of Learning Disabilities 15: 212–17.

Lindsay G (1995) Early identification of special-educational needs. In I Lunt, B Norwich, V Varma (eds) Psychology and Education for Special Needs. Aldershot: Arena.

Lindsay G (1998) Baseline assessment: a positive or malign influence? In B Norwich, G Lindsay (eds) Baseline Assessment. Tamworth: NASEN, pp. 8-40.

Lindsay G, Desforges M (1998) Baseline Assessment: Practice, Problems and Possibilities. London: David Fulton.

Lindsay G, Lewis A, Phillips E (2000) Evaluation of Accredited Baseline Assessment Schemes 1999/2000. Coventry: CEDAR, University of Warwick.

Muter V, Hulme C, Snowling M (1997) Phonological Abilities Test. London: Psychological Corporation.

Neale MD (1997) Neale Analysis of Reading – Revised Windsor NfER – Nelson.

Nicolson RI, Fawcett AJ (1990) Automaticity: A new framework for dyslexia research. Cognition 35, 159–82.

Nicolson RI (1996) Developmental Dyslexia: Past, present and future. Dyslexia: An International Journal of Research and Practice 2, 190–208.

Nicolson R, Fawcett A (1996) Dyslexia Screening Test. London: Psychological Corporation.

Office for Standards in Education (1999) Handbook for Inspecting Primary and Nursery Schools. London: The Stationery Office.

Peer L, Reid G (2000) Miltulingualism, Literacy and Dyslexia. London: David Fulton.

Pietrowski J, Reason R (2000) The National Literacy Strategy and dyslexia: a comparison of teaching methods and material. Support for Learning 15 (2): 51–7.

Qualifications and Curriculum Authority and Department for Education and Employment (2000) Curriculum Guidance for the Foundation Stage. London: QCA.

Rigby AS, Sanderson C, Desforges MF, Lindsay G, Hall DMB (1999) The Infant Index: a new outcome measure for pre-school children's services. Journal of Public Health Medicine 21: 172–8.

Samuels SJ (1999) Developing reading fluency in learning-disabled students. In RJ Sternberg and L Spear-Swerling (eds) Perspectives on Learning Disabilities: Biological, Cognitive, Contextual. Boulder, Colarado: Westview Press.

Share DL, McGee R, McKenzie D, Williams A, Silva PA (1987) Further evidence relating to the distinction between specific reading retardation and general reading backwardness. British Journal of Developmental Psychology 5: 33–44.

Siegel LS (1989) IQ is irrelevant to the definition of learning disabilities. Journal of Learning Disabilities 22: 469–78.

Singleton CH, Thomas KV, Leedale RC (1996) Lucid Cognitive Profile Systems (CoPS). Beverley: Lucid Research.

Solity J, Deavers R, Kerfoot S, Crane G, Cannon K (2000) The Early Reading Research, the importance of instructional psychology. Educational Psychology in Practice 16(2): 109–30.

Solity J, Bull S (1987) Special Needs: Bridging the Curriculum Gap. Milton Keynes: Open University Press.

Snowling MJ, Stothard SE, McClean J (1996) Graded Nonword Reading Test. Bury St Edmunds: Thames Valley Test Company.

Stanovich KE (1991) Discrepancy definitions of reading disability: has intelligence led us astray? Reading Research Quarterly 26(1): 7–29.

Sternberg RJ, Spear-Swerling L (eds) (1999) Perspectives on Learning Disabilities: Biological, Cognitive, Contextual. Boulder CO: Westview Press.

Vellutino FR, Scanlon DM, Sipay ER, Small SG, Pratt A, Chen RS, Denckla MB (1996) Cognitive profiles of difficulty-to-remediate and readily remediated poor readers: early intervention as a vehicle for distinguishing between cognitive and experiential deficits as basic causes of specific reading disability. Journal of Educational Psychology 88: 601–38.

Vincent D, de la Mare M (1985) New Reading Analysis. Windsor NfER – Nelson.

Wechsler D (1992) The Wechsler Intelligence Scale for Children. 3 UK edn. London: Psychological Corporation.

Wedell K (1978) Early identification and compensatory education. Paper presented at the NATO International Conference on Learning Disorders, Ottawa.

Wedell K (1973) Learning and Preceptor-motor Disabilities in Children. London: Wiley.

Wedell K (1977) Perceptual deficiency and specific reading retardisation. Journal of Child Psychology and Psychiatry 18(2): 191–4.

Wedell K, Lindsay G (1980) Early identification procedures: what have we learned? Remedial Education 15: 130–5.

Whitworth JR, Sutton DL (1993) WISC III Compilation. Novato CA: Academic Therapy Publications.

Ysseldyke SE, Christensen SL (1987) Evaluating students' instructional environments. Remedial and Special Education 8(3): 17–24.

CHAPTER 13

Good practice in secondary school

MICHAEL THOMSON, STEVE CHINN

Introduction

This chapter has grown out of two conferences. The first was a conference at East Court School for parents of dyslexic children, held in October 2000. This was aimed at giving parents some ideas of what it is like living with dyslexia and how schools adapt to dyslexic difficulties. This forms essentially the introductory and general comments of the first half, which provides an overview of the consequences of dyslexia (MT)

The second conference, upon which the second half of the chapter is based, was held at Mark College in November 2000 and organized by Jean Jamieson for dyslexic pupils from Nailsea Comprehensive school in North Somerset. After a day of lectures and workshops (and food!) the pupils, aged from 11 to 17 years, sat down in groups and discussed what helped them in their mainstream school and what hindered their work (SC).

Schools that specialize in teaching dyslexic pupils (not necessarily exclusively) are subject to changes in research, awareness and definitions as our understanding of learning difficulties evolves. Sometimes new developments and theories create positive influences on education, but not always so. Schools have to try to remain pragmatic and continue to offer an education that is effective for the individual.

Within the past few years the definition of dyslexia (or learning disabilities in the US) has undergone a change in emphasis. Both the British Dyslexia Association and the International Dyslexia Association have focused the definition on difficulties with language, as has the somewhat controversial definition from British psychologists. In the 1980s, America took a broader view and listed difficulties in listening, speaking, reading, writing, reasoning, mathematics and social skills as part of their definition. Experience in the classroom would lead most teachers to this wider realization of the impact of dyslexia on the academic and social development of the pupil.

This issue is further clouded by the recent recognition of other specific learning difficulties such as dyspraxia, ADD, ADHD, Asperger's syndrome, dyscalculia and the frequent comorbidity of these difficulties with dyslexia. Schools are now facing a wider spread of identified difficulties and the more subtle consequences of inclusion are beginning to show. Perhaps we should avoid mentioning one further major influence on special education – the influence of litigation.

Within this changing framework, the authors have tried to describe the range of provision that can be made available to dyslexic pupils from early years to GCSE (the National examinations set in England and Wales for 16 year old pupils) drawing on the pupils' own observations.

Consequences of dyslexia

Although this chapter has been written by two principals of specialist schools for dyslexic children, we hope that some of the general principles we discuss below are relevant to dyslexic children in any school. The British Dyslexia Association has been trying to develop, with the DfEE, the notion of 'dyslexia-friendly' schools. This really is the start of providing good support for dyslexics, whether in a specialist school, a school with a unit, or a school with just some tutorial help for dyslexics. It seems to us that there are two main issues in provision for dyslexics at school. The first is recognition of dyslexia with school systems that then support this recognition and secondly, of course, there is the specific help that should be given for dyslexic learning difficulties.

The first stage of recognition is understanding the child's written language difficulties. For some children that means scant literacy skills at all. Thus for severe dyslexics provision of alternative notes, assignments and evaluations are essential for subjects. In English the focus will be on basic spelling and decoding skills in reading. Even the 'remediated' dyslexic will need recognition however. We will optimistically assume that by secondary school the child will have *some* basic written language skills.

This means that every subject teacher needs to be aware that the children will need a longer time to read assignments, will have difficulties copying from the blackboard, will need their essays and written work marked for content and knowledge of the subject, rather than for punctuation and spelling, and so on. All these are fairly well known, or should be, at a school that purports to help dyslexic children. However, what is less well recognized, is that dyslexia is not just about reading, writing and spelling. It reflects a number of difficulties that a child may have, often linked to organizational problems. Table 13.1 demonstrates a number of these difficulties around the school and it is important to be aware of and provide additional support for children in these areas.

It is important to note the positive features in Table 13.1. It can be very easy to assume that dyslexia is all doom and gloom. In contrast, as may be seen, dyslexics have qualities that can be better than in other children and it is important to encourage and provide support for these. The work effort and determination comments in Table 13.1 refer to children who have been given appropriate study skills and help.

Another important aspect, of course, in developing a dyslexia-friendly school is self-esteem and confidence. This is a key area for any child, but absolutely fundamental to helping the dyslexic. Children's response to their low self-esteem and confidence can range from depression and withdrawal through frustrations, attentional problems, being the class clown, to more serious behavioural difficulties. It is important to recognize these at both ends of the extreme and to provide appropriate classroom management and pastoral care for them.

Table 13.1: Some difficulties around the school.

Organization:	Timetables; 'prep' and assignments; completion of work.
	Finding the way around school.
	Personal organization.
	(Parents' organization!).
Co-ordination:	Ball games - cricket/squash etc. for some (see below).
	Fine motor skills versus gross motor skills.
Note-taking:	From blackboard.
	From dictation.
Project Work	Extraction of information from source.
	Time to complete assignment.
Positive Features	
Often good skills in:	Work effort and determination, if helped in study skills.
	Global "gestalt" thinking; logically applied, sometimes Maths.
	Computer studies.
	CDT inc. technology/design/art skills/engineering.
	Good Games ability viz. 'balance', 3D skills, often Rugby as opposed to Soccer.
	Science, esp. experimental laboratory skills, but difficulties with note taking and sequencing skills!

As far as the second element of good practice is concerned – specific teaching techniques – it is beyond the scope of this chapter to go into any detail, but some general principles are given in Table 13.2.

Before we look at specific areas of the curriculum, we shall look at aspects of the National Curriculum and how this can be modified to help dyslexics.

The National Curriculum

Schools such as Mark College and East Court, which are specialist schools for dyslexics, offer the National Curriculum, but with teaching modified to enable full access. This has the following implications:

- The need for high/low material – presenting information in such a way that it meets the child's own levels of reading and writing and spelling. For bright dyslexics this means providing, for example, source material that is easy to read but has the same informational knowledge content as their non-dyslexic peers.
- Associated with this is our appropriate use of worksheets. For example, science and humanities worksheets can consist of cloze procedures that link to English, or provide a framework. Rather than getting a child to copy down experimental procedures and tables and diagrams, which may be difficult for some dyslexics, this is provided and the results instead are analysed and discussed. In other words, one is looking at content and knowledge, not low-order skills of reading, writing and spelling.
- That reading from text and essay writing need to be appropriate (see discussion below).

Table 13.2: General principles of teaching

1. Established teaching methods:
   - multi-sensory approach, sight, hearing, speech and touch
   - overlearning
   - analytical: meaning/logical

2. Success in areas of strength.

3. Reward – correct responses, mark what is right.

4. Small sequential steps (many routes to same objective).

5. Memory aids.

- Expectation should be high for content and knowledge of the subject matter, but lower for spelling and writing speed.
- Careful consideration should be given to the subjects that dyslexics are encouraged to do. In our experience, IT, laboratory-based sciences, CDT and so on, are rather better than, for example, history, which may require a lot of reading and writing essays. Careful consideration needs to be given to the undertaking of a foreign language. Many schools for dyslexics disapply French. One possibility is for a child to start another foreign language at 13, starting at the same level as other children. This might be Spanish, which is much more widely spoken than French and is more regular.

Some aspects of the National Curriculum are quite problematic for teachers to evaluate in dyslexics. English is a very good example of this. For example, in reading, attainment target three suggests that pupils should be able to read text fluently and accurately and attainment target two suggests that they should be able to use more than one way of reading – for example, phonic, graphic, syntactical and contextual cues. Many dyslexic children, even at 13 or 14, may not be able to do this, but on the other hand are quite able to deal with other aspects of higher attainment targets. For example, attainment target five refers to understanding key themes and characters in reading and attainment target six states that pupils should have a personal response to literacy text, understand layers of meaning and comment on significant facts. Even attainment target seven, awareness of themes and structures and linguistic features, could be within some children's grasp. We could go on, but the main implication is that some lower order skills in reading, writing and spelling are bracketed together with more complex ones. Dyslexic children could often understand these latter if only they could decode the alphabet or if they were allowed to use the work orally. Which does one use to evaluate the child in terms of their attainment targets?

The same thing, of course, happens in writing. For example, in attainment target six, where a pupil could use specific features or expressions to convey effects, to address the reader or, as in attainment target seven, with appropriate choices of style. Yet, on the other hand, more difficult for dyslexics would be attainment target three, which comments that spelling should usually be accurate, including that of common, polysyllabic words!

As far as English is concerned, it is well known that dyslexics as described above need a multi-sensory structured programme of phonics. It would be impossible to go into greater depth here, except just to comment that we also need to focus on many other aspects of written language. Table 13.3 gives an example of essay planning which is linked in general to many other subjects, as well as English.

Table 13.3: Essay planning

Linear plan (following a line).

The idea is to develop a logical and systematic plan. Starting at the beginning and developing, in a sequential manner, towards the conclusion or end.

a) Detailed planning is important.
b) Logical progression in sequence must follow.

Ask these questions and follow these steps:

1. How long have I got?
2. How many pages are needed? (My speed of working).
3. Can I, at the start, see my way to the end?
4. How many paragraphs to a page? How many sentences to a paragraph?
5. Begin working on plan - spend approximately 5–8 minutes in 60 minutes.
6. Draw 'Linear plan' outline, e.g. division of line into pages, paragraphs.
7. Jot down ideas; 'sketch out' aim for key areas', words, major headings.
8. Fill in paragraph headings.
9. Remember –   Intro: 'setting scene'
                          Development: 'expansion'
                          Conclusion
10. Don't panic! Remember that you are attempting to paint an accurate picture using words.

Classroom needs

The following are comments from dyslexic students, about issues affecting them in the mainstream. They act as a consumer's view of the educational needs of dyslexic pupils in a mainstream setting. The headings (in italics) are theirs. The comments are SC's.

What hinders?

Teachers who go too fast and expect too much. Being expected to produce the same amount of work (as non-dyslexic pupils) in a given time.

Speed of working is a problem for dyslexic pupils and must not be confused with the traditional meaning of being 'a bit slow'. Speed of working is not a function of IQ, but of factors such as reading skills, writing speed, spelling and the search for the alternative word that the pupil feels he can spell correctly and slowness in getting started. Slow speed can also mean lower output. It is easy to underestimate the huge effort that went into that 300-word essay, when peers have written 1,000 words. Expectations are powerful. Powerful as motivators and equally powerful as demotivators. The balance is crucial and relies on knowing the pupil well and on the ability to constantly adjust the expectations appropriately.

Teachers who don't stick to the point.

When a pupil has short-term memory problems, especially if they affect the absorption of sequential information, the last thing needed is for the teacher to go off at a tangent. Clear, focused information, presented visually and orally helps. It is better still if the presentation includes a preview and review.

Teachers who know I am dyslexic but don't help me enough. Being patronized.

Some teachers don't help at all. Sometimes they claim they 'don't believe in dyslexia'. Sadly that problem can run through to higher education. Against this need for help is the balance needed in helping without patronizing or overtly helping 'my little dyslexic friend'.

Too much copying off the board and/or dictating notes. Rubbing work off the board too soon.

I could add with some personal embarrassment, 'teachers with poor handwriting'. I once taught a pupil with a short-term memory that allowed him to copy just one letter at a time from the board. Looking up at the board, looking down at the page, writing the letter, and looking back at the board, hopefully at the right place. It was a devastating handicap. Ready-made notes would have been such an enormous help. Even for pupils with slightly longer short-term memories, copying from the board or textbooks is a slower process. (I realized then that I wrote 'slower', returning to the issue of speed. The comparison is, of course, with peers and with expectations that attach to those peers. In the absolute, slower is harder to define. Certainly I have always puzzled at the need for fast work in mathematics and for time limits in examinations. Fast is part of the culture of education and, within reason, that's fine, but 'within reason' may have to be redefined for dyslexic pupils).

Having test results read out loud. People who make fun of me or who are sarcastic.

Often a dyslexic pupil's self-esteem has been eroded by years of negative feedback. For that feedback to be so publicly revealed is an additional insult to the injury of knowing you are poor at tests. Sarcasm and poking fun also attack self-esteem. It rarely improves performance.

Being told off when I'm asking a friend for help.

This is a good example of a reasonable, but inappropriate response from a teacher. Greater awareness and positive use of the 'problem' could change it to a positive situation. Talking in class can disrupt, can suggest that pupils are not relying on their own input and could suggest that a pupil is not listening. But for a dyslexic it may be an essential survival strategy. If the friend was a designated mentor or buddy, then this need has official recognition and could be a very effective and economic form of support.

Not being allowed to use my laptop in lessons.

Why not? This can sometimes be the result of poor liaison or ineffective advocacy. Voice recognition technology could transform a pupil's work output. Information and communication technology can be one of the best ways to help dyslexic pupils access the curriculum. Hardware should come with appropriate software and training. For example, we have found that voice recognition software on its own is not enough but becomes truly valuable when used alongside Keystone. Again, a positive classroom response could improve working conditions for a dyslexic pupil. Teachers could help pupils manage their laptops efficiently and effectively.

Confusing 'dyslexic' with 'stupidity'. Lack of understanding/empathy for dyslexia (from teachers and other students).

Hopefully if the understanding is there the confusion goes away. Awareness and empathy can go a long way to help dyslexics survive school. They are a good start, cost nothing and will improve the learning experience of all pupils.

Being made to read aloud in class.

This has to be the ultimate in unawareness. Again self-esteem is eroded publicly.

What helps?

Help being given discreetly (and quietly) to individuals.

At whatever level the help is given, whether a brief extra explanation from a teacher or more extended help from a learning support assistant, if it is not managed sympathetically, then any academic gains may be outweighed by loss of self-esteem. It may result in the pupil not asking for help when he needs it.

Being given more time.

This also suggests that the dyslexic pupil is prepared to give more time, a characteristic that should be encouraged.

Handouts with summaries of work.

This circumvents the need for note taking and ensures that accurate notes are there for revision. In these times of ever increasing technological advances it should be possible to give notes on disc (floppy or CD), so the pupil can edit, modify or personalize them.

Marking work in dark colours, tidily. Praise!

This reduces the negative impact of any work that has to be marked wrong. Red ink is not a good feedback and a book generously covered in red ink crosses does not build confidence. Conversely, praise, if not patronizing, is a great moral booster and motivator. Success is an even better motivator. Allowing the dyslexic to genuinely succeed is a true mark of positive awareness. This is differentiation at work.

Working in smaller groups.

And having the right composition in these groups. Placing a dyslexic in a special needs class with a wide range of needs, such as ADHD (attention deficit hyperactivity disorder), EBD (emotional and behavioural disorder), or slow learners will not increase the quality of teacher/pupil contact time.

Trained teachers. Awareness of dyslexic difficulties. Teachers who care.

Pupils know when a teacher knows how to help them. Training may be at the awareness level for say a geography or science teacher, but should be at British Dyslexia Association recognized levels for English and possibly for mathematics. It has been said before, but bears repeating, that knowing how to teach dyslexics helps in the teaching of all pupils. There is a wider impact.

Grades that show individual improvement.

At Mark College we separate our effort grades and achievement grades by a term. The two measures do not always marry well. A good effort grade accompanied by a low achievement does not give an encouraging message. If grades are related to the individual then a grade for improvement may be more appropriate.

Marking that is clear and helpful.

Marking, as well as being in subtle pen colour, can also be constructive and diagnostic. Just to be told that something is 'wrong' only gives a negative message. Some guidance on how to put the work right helps the individual. Although this applies to any pupil, it is probably more important for many dyslexic pupils who bring a long experience of negative marking to the classroom.

Catch-up exercises.

This is such a good idea. It should be obvious, of course, but then the obvious can be overlooked. If a school is to become dyslexia friendly, then having resources for catch-up is an essential requirement. This might well include a collection of flash cards that can be bundled for individual needs. It could also include worksheets (possibly on CD or floppies) where writing is minimized.

Work judged for content, not spelling.

It is not just having the spelling marked wrong that is a problem. It is the pupil restricting the vocabulary he uses to the words that he thinks may be spelled correctly rather than using his wider oral vocabulary. Avoiding the words that the dyslexic pupil knows he cannot spell will drastically reduce the maturity, quantity and content of his written work. It is not an unusual occurrence for a pupil from Mark College to achieve an A grade for the listening and speaking component of the GCSE English language examination and be awarded a D grade overall.

The pupils spoke with feeling and conviction about their experiences and needs. Secondary education makes enormous demands on dyslexic pupils, probably more than they will experience at any other time in their lives. The Nailsea pupils' suggestions are rational, reasonable and sensible, and within the reach of any school which has a commitment to educate all its pupils to their full potential.

CHAPTER 14

Identification, and intervention in adults

JANE KIRK, DAVID MCLOUGHLIN, GAVIN REID

Background

This chapter aims to provide some insights into dyslexia in adults, particularly focusing on factors related to employment and education. Crucial issues such as screening, assessment, careers advice and preparation for work and study will be discussed. This chapter will therefore have implications for tutors in further and higher education as well as employers and employment services staff.

Understanding dyslexia

It is important that those engaged in work with adults with dyslexia, whether in employment or at college, are comfortable with their understanding of dyslexia. In our experience we appreciate that this is not always the case and this may represent a major obstacle to achieving equity for dyslexic people in education and the workplace.

It is important to highlight the individuality of dyslexia, which also means that in different work and study contexts the extent to which the dyslexic difficulties affect the person's performances will vary. Dyslexia should therefore be seen as contextual implying that in some situations the difficulties associated with dyslexia will be minimal and in some situations dyslexia may well be advantageous.

It is often however more difficult to diagnose dyslexia in adults than in children. Many adults with dyslexic difficulties develop coping and compensatory strategies and usually can become quite adept at disguising the presence of dyslexia. Due to this many remain unfulfilled, often underestimating their abilities, perhaps working in an occupation that does not use their real abilities or even declining promotion for fear that their dyslexic difficulties are exposed (Reid and Kirk 2001).

Legislation

The Disability Discrimination Act 1994 should ensure that the rights of dyslexic adults are protected. The Act covers all disabilities. Although dyslexia may not be as readily obvious as, for example, a physical disability, it may have no less social, emotional and personal consequences for the individual. It may even be suggested that dyslexia is the best known but least understood of the disabilities referred to in legislation.

Perceptions

There are many different perceptions of what dyslexia is among the general public, the media and employers. This is not entirely surprising, as there is no definable consensus among professionals in the field. For example the British Psychological Society examined how educational psychologists perceive dyslexia and how assessment should be conducted. The working report (BPS 1999) suggested that the key aspect in recognizing dyslexia in children relates to the identification of phonological difficulties, with the role of IQ being fairly irrelevant. Miles (1996) suggests that the concept of a global IQ can be misleading. The cognitive profile, however, which an IQ test can yield, can be extremely informative (McLoughlin, Fitzgibbon and Young, 1994).

Others in the field (Eden et al, 1996; Wilkins, 1995) emphasize visual factors, and some others look at motor co-ordination (Blyth, 1992), perceptual aspects (Davis and Braun, 1997) and auditory sensitivity (Johanson, 1992). Indeed the BPS in their report described 10 different hypotheses associated with dyslexia. Many researchers strongly suggest qualitative factors associated with phonological processing as the core difficulty in dyslexia and that such difficulties cut across the full range of IQ scores (Stanovich, 1996). In adults, however, phonological difficulties may not be the most prevalent as through exposure to print at level of functional literacy has often been achieved. For that reason it is important that assessment should be tailored to an individual's context in the workplace or at college.

With a disparity of views among researchers and professionals it is little wonder that the media reports on 'cures' for dyslexia often in sensational fashion. Recently among the cures reported have been fish oil capsules, massage therapy, vitamins, coloured lenses, neurolinguistic programming, reorientation of the brain and many others. Although it is not the purpose of this chapter to evaluate or to pass qualitative judgement on these views, it is sufficient to suggest that the almost weekly addition of dyslexia 'cures' is not helpful to the working practices of professionals and the perceptions of employers and certainly do not help to quell the anxieties of dyslexic people.

Implications for employment

The majority of dyslexic adults experience a variety of difficulties in employment. Not only do they have difficulties in finding and retaining work – their transition from school to work also causes concern (Faas and D'Alonzo, 1990). Clearly this has implications for careers advisers (Reid, 2001), as well as tutors at college and university (Singleton, 1999). It also has implications for the Employment Service and particularly staff involved with disability. It is important for example that those dyslexic people who are unemployed realize their rights for assessment and support to assist them in securing employment.

The context for assessment

Dyslexia in the adult years needs to be understood within the context of changes that occur throughout the lifespan. During periods of transitions demands and expectations can increase. This may occur when dyslexic people change jobs or seek promotion. Sometimes, in fact, it is when dyslexic people have been successful that they need help in order to meet the new demands of responsibility in employment or promotion. In many instances adult dyslexics are self-referred but it is sometimes tutors or employers who recognize discrepancies in their performance and suggest an assessment.

Assessment and diagnosis

The process of assessment and diagnosis addresses the issue of why dyslexic people find tasks difficult. It involves several stages including:

- information gathering;
- screening – which formally identifies the existence of the behavioural characteristics;
- psychological testing – which tries to explain the existence of the behavioural characteristics.

These stages should be followed by:

- developing self-understanding; and
- taking action.

The first step in the process involves gathering information in a structured way. If this information indicates that the client is likely to be a dyslexic then the next step is formal screening. One of the biggest improvements in identifying dyslexia during the adult years has been the development of relevant screening tests so that we no longer need to rely on those designed for the younger age group. Two of the best examples are Study Scan/Quick Scan and the Dyslexia Adult Screening Test (DAST).

In assessment it is important to identify positive factors as well as investigating the adult's difficulties. This applies equally well to interviewing, using checklists or screening tests.

When using such instruments, it is imperative that they are not administered in isolation. The principle of 'specificity', that is, the notion that dyslexic people have an underlying neurological inefficiency, is central to the screening and assessment process. Consequently, the accurate diagnosis of dyslexia requires the measurement of general ability and working memory. Any procedure that fails to incorporate appropriate cognitive tests is likely to produce both false positives – that is the incorrect identification of a person who has low intelligence as dyslexic – and false negatives, which is the failure to identify a dyslexic person as such because they have developed strategies that compensate for their dyslexia. The reliance on the assessment of literacy skills alone as the sole or main diagnostic procedure is inappropriate and uninformed.

Study Scan and Quick Scan

Quick Scan (Zdzienski, 1997) is a short questionnaire, designed for use on a computer. It is suitable for adults who want to find out about the way they learn. Quick Scan will outline individual learning preferences and study styles, and produce a useful printed report on personalized study guidelines. It will also indicate whether the student shows any significant possibility of being dyslexic and may result in a recommendation to go on to complete the full assessment in Study Scan.

Study Scan is a comprehensive range of tests that covers most aspects of a full educational assessment. It will give an indication of general levels of attainment and highlight specific areas of strengths and weakness. It will automatically analyse the individual performance of students in different tests and produce a printed diagnostic dyslexic report. Study Scan contains the following tests:

* memory (auditory and visual) and coding;
* literacy (including reading and listening comprehension, spelling and punctuation);
* numeracy (including calculations and applications);
* cognitive abilities (including verbal and non-verbal reasoning, as well as vocabulary);

- proficiency tests (speed of reading and speed of copying);
- free writing.

Dyslexia Adult Screening Test (DAST)

The Dyslexia Adult Screening Test is an individual administered scale that consists of eleven individual subtests, including :

- rapid naming;
- one-minute reading;
- postural stability;
- phonemic segmentation;
- two-minute spelling;
- backwards digit span;
- nonsense passage reading;
- non-verbal reasoning;
- one-minute writing;
- verbal fluency;
- semantic fluency.

The DAST provides an 'at risk score'. It is a thorough and useful first step in formal identification.

Formal diagnosis

The purpose of a formal diagnosis is not to identify people as being dyslexic but to explain their difficulties. Formal diagnosis involves psychological testing, careful observation and clinical judgement. Although discrepancy definitions of dyslexia have been rejected, the word 'discrepancy' remains useful in the identification process because our understanding of the etiology of dyslexia is now such that we can identify relevant discrepancies in an individual's cognitive profile.

The process of investigation using tests is intended to identify areas of fundamental weakness. If the individuals being examined are dyslexic they will perform poorly on certain tests, particularly those that tap working memory. Such weaknesses will, assuming the individual is of average or above average intelligence, stand in marked contrast to their functioning in other areas. The tests used in diagnosis must cover a wide range of abilities otherwise the disparity between general functioning and functioning in specific areas cannot be measured and there is a risk of misdiagnosis. In addition to identifying a discrepancy the procedure should allow the examiner to specify what weakness is causing it.

Testing intelligence

The test most widely used in the diagnosis of adult dyslexia is the Wechsler Adult Intelligence Scale (WAIS), originally developed in 1955, revised as the Wechsler Adult Intelligence Scale-Revised (WAIS-R UK) in 1986 and now republished and much improved as the Wechsler Adult Intelligence Scale – Third Edition (WAIS-III, 1997).

The WAIS-III is a normed test – that is to say there is information contained in the manual relating to how specified groups perform on the subtests. It can be used with individuals between the age of 16 and 89 years. It examines different kinds of intellectual functions and allows the examiner to rule out, or diagnose, intellectual disability. When acquainted with the subtests the examiner can, with careful observation, become sensitive to behavioural nuances. This is a particularly important skill in the assessment of dyslexia, where individuals may be completing certain tasks using compensatory strategies that can only be detected by careful observation of how they are responding.

A considerable amount of research has been devoted to identifying 'typical' dyslexic profiles of Wechsler subtest scores. Bannatyne (1974), for example, has proposed four groups of subtest combinations on which dyslexics and non-dyslexics are presumed to differ. They are Spatial (Picture Completion, Block Design and Object Assembly), Verbal Conceptualization (Comprehension, Similarities, Vocabulary), Sequential (Digit Span, Arithmetic, Coding or Digit Symbol) and Acquired Knowledge (Information, Arithmetic, Vocabulary). Dyslexics have been found to be equal to, or better than, non-dyslexics in spatial ability and conceptual ability but they do less well in sequencing ability and acquired knowledge.

A large number of studies have identified what is known as the ACID profile of WISC scores and this has proved very useful in diagnosing dyslexia. That is, arithmetic, coding (digit symbol), information and digit span have been shown to be the subtests on which dyslexics typically do less well than non-dyslexics. Each of these subtests places a demand on phonological skills or working memory and the pattern of weak scores reflects inefficient working memory skills.

The identification of adult dyslexics using the Wechsler Adult Intelligence Scale has not been as well researched as the identification of dyslexic children using the WISC. There are, however, several studies that have provided support for both Bannatyne's clusters and the ACID profile (Cordoni et al., 1981; Salvia et al., 1988; Katz et al., 1993).

Some adult dyslexics will readily exhibit patterns of scores that fall into the ACID profile and it is an obvious indicator. It is important to reiterate, however, that clinicians, should not just examine the subtest scores of the

WAIS-(III) with a view to determining if this profile exists. They should make behavioural observations during the administration procedure.

The overwhelming reason for the continued use of the Wechsler Adult Intelligence Scale is that it is a neuropsychological test that identifies strengths and weaknesses. There is increasing evidence for a neurological difference between dyslexic and non-dyslexic people, one of the sources being neuropsychological testing. Further, the neurological differences that characterize dyslexia persist throughout the lifespan (Bigler, 1992). Studies have, for example, demonstrated that similar profiles are evident when the Wechsler Intelligence Scale is administered to both dyslexic children and adults. (Katz et al., 1993).

Attainments in literacy and numeracy

It is perhaps inevitable that the understanding and assessment of literacy skills is always placed in an educational context. It has been said that whereas children learn to read, teenagers read to learn (Chall, 1983). Adults do read to learn but they also read to work. One might add that they read to play, as being able to read underlies many social activities. Although the assessment of reading skills of adults will resemble that of the assessment of reading skills of children, the aims and process can be quite different. Moreover, the testing of adults will depend on context.

The aims of assessment

There are essentially three aims in assessing an adult's reading skills, especially in the work setting:

- establishing whether the reader has sufficient competence in all aspects of reading as to enable them to deal with a particular occupation, or at least the programme of study leading to that occupation;
- diagnosing reading difficulties and establishing a starting point for remedial instruction;
- measuring progress on reading programmes.

Levels of attainment

Where standardized tests have been used to assess the reading levels of children, scores have been expressed as reading ages, grade norms or percentile equivalents. The first two of these are clearly inappropriate for adults, particularly as many tests limit themselves to student populations. It is not helpful for adults to know they have a reading age of 10 years, for example, and is in fact quite demoralizing. The same can be said of percentiles. Knowing that one has scored less well than 80% of the population could do on a particular reading task is not encouraging, to say the least. Further, it might not be relevant to the particular individual. We only need the reading skills that enable us to deal with the demands placed upon us by our educational, work and social programme. The most enduring and important situation in which adults need reading skills is their work environment. Criteria for establishing levels of attainment amongst adults are, therefore, best derived from work tasks.

Adult literacy and numeracy skills can be rated as being at one of four levels. These are professional, technical, vocational, and functional.

The components of reading assessment

The assessment of adult reading skills should therefore include measures of decoding, reading and listening comprehension, as well as reading rate. Each subskill should be evaluated separately, particularly when the aim of an assessment is to diagnose reading difficulties and plan remedial instruction. This is not as easy as it should be as there is a dearth of good tests designed for adults.

Metacognition

An additional area that should be considered, particularly when working with readers operating at an advanced level is metacognitive skills – peoples' own thinking about the way they learn and work. Brown (1980) first applied the concept of metacognition to reading and underscored its crucial role in effective reading. Metacognitive skills related to reading can be described as reading for meaning (comprehension monitoring) and reading for remembering (studying or learning). A good reader possesses metacognitive skills in reading, is aware of the purpose of reading and differentiates between task demands. When reading text for a study assignment, for example, or reading a magazine for pleasure, the reader actively seeks to clarify the task demands through self-questioning prior to reading material. This awareness leads to the use of suitable reading strategies. A good reader varies their reading rate and comprehension level as a function of materials being read. The altering of reading rate according to the purpose of reading and the difficulty of the text is flexibility. This can be tested, by calculating and comparing rates of reading for simple and difficult materials (Manzo and Manzo, 1993).

Awareness can also lead readers to monitor their reading comprehension. When good readers encounter a comprehension difficulty they use 'debugging' strategies. These attempts at problem solving reflect self-regulation. Good readers evaluate their own comprehension of material and this has important consequences. If readers do not realize that they have not understood a particular part of given material, they will not employ suitable 'debugging' strategies such as back tracking or scanning ahead for possible cues to solve the difficulties. The fluent or mature reader is rarely conscious of his overall comprehension monitoring. When a comprehension failure arises the fluent reader immediately slows down in reading and either reviews the difficult sections or reads on seeking clues in subsequent text. Metacognition therefore does have two components: one is on-line monitoring of comprehension; the other is taking corrective action when encountering difficulty (Wray, 1994). The assessment of metacognition in reading involves investigating two subskills: first, whether someone has a reasonably correct estimate of his or her own abilities, and second, whether or not he or she is comprehending what is read or heard.

Readers should be encouraged to ask questions such as:

- When I read a book how often do I go back to a passage or sentence and re-read it so as to clarify things?
- How often do I ask a fellow student or tutor for clarification of ideas?
- Am I able to get the main idea of a passage after reading it ?
- How often after an examination do I feel I have done well but find the results are disappointing?

If the answer is rarely to the first three and often to the last, it might be that the reader is not good at comprehension monitoring (Wong, 1986).

Writing and spelling

A sample of the client's writing should also be examined. A simple topic can be suggested or they can choose one of their own. Many dyslexics find this difficult and it is important to suggest something that they do not have to think too much about. Something such as their journey to the assessment centre or a description of hobbies minimizes thinking time. The Basic Skills Tests include specific tasks – that is, writing a postcard and writing a letter.

Arithmetic

The testing of arithmetic skills can be helpful, particularly when difficulties with these have been raised by a client or an employer. Dyslexic people do not usually have a conceptual problem with mathematics and the specific difficulty with mathematics known as dyscalculia is rare. This does not, however, mean that dyslexic people find mathematics easy, but that their difficulties are 'manifestations of the same limitations which also affect their reading and spelling' (Miles and Miles, 1992).

Some of the potential areas of difficulty described by Chinn and Ashcroft (1993) include:

- directional confusion;
- sequencing problems;
- problems arising from weak working memory skills;
- the language of mathematics;
- problems arising from reading difficulties.

Those clients identified as dyslexic should be offered support and guidance. Step three involves raising awareness and understanding of what dyslexia is. Most dyslexics will benefit from knowing how their dyslexia has affected them in their early life, how they have coped with it to date, how it continues to influence their life and how they can acquire new behaviours that will enable them to overcome the difficulties they face. The last step involves agreeing on what action is necessary and how to implement it.

Feedback to client

Acceptance and understanding have been identified as essential factors in determining whether a dyslexic is able to take control and overcome their difficulties. Providing feedback is therefore the most important part of an assessment. The goal is to enable individuals to understand their condition and how it affects them in order that they can take appropriate action. This is a part of the assessment that requires special attention, as dyslexics are people who have problems with the organization and processing of information. It is through a proper explanation that the client will be able to start developing their awareness and understanding. If, following an assessment, clients leave without a greater understanding of the nature of their difficulties and what they can do to overcome them, then it has been a waste of their time.

Feedback should take two forms. Immediately after testing this should involve a careful explanation of the test results and their implications. A simple operational model, preferably one that can be illustrated graphically, can be a useful aid to understanding. The client's strengths and weaknesses should be described and strategies for dealing with the latter outlined. It is important to be positive. Many adult dyslexics will have already developed their own strategies and the way these can be applied constructively to deal with other areas of difficulty can be explained. Practical information about sources of further help including agencies and appropriate literature, tapes and videos should be provided. It can be particularly helpful to the client if the clinician records the feedback session on tape so that they can listen to it again at their leisure.

Verbal feedback should be followed by a written report. Essentially this should reiterate what the client was told at the end of the assessment session. In writing the report attention should be given to the educational level and literacy skills of the client. The inclusion of an abstract and interim summaries can aid comprehension as can other factors that improve readability, such as large print. Production of the complete report on tape as well as in the written form could be valuable.

Too many assessment reports written about adults are based on the format used by educational psychologists when describing their assessments of children. It should be remembered that they are being written for quite a different audience. Dyslexic adults should be able to derive benefit from the report themselves and should feel comfortable about showing it to people such as their personnel managers, who will not necessarily be trained in test interpretation. It has become regular practice to begin assessment reports with a page giving test results. Because of the different audience and the increased likelihood of misinterpretation this should not be done. It can be helpful for specialist teachers who might work with the client being assessed to have the test results, but these should be on a separate sheet so that clients can make them available at their own discretion.

Assessment follow up

As well as developing people's understanding it is important that they know where they can get further assistance and support. It is essential to help them establish real and achievable goals. They also need to be informed of their rights under legislation such as the Disability Discrimination Act as well as the support that might be forthcoming in educational work settings. In our experience individual programmes directed towards each person's very specific needs are more beneficial than courses addressed to a group. Dyslexic people have much in common but they are also individuals.

Preparation for employment – job choice

It is common for dyslexic people to find themselves in employment or on a course of study that highlights their weaknesses, which can, of course, undermine their confidence. This highlights the importance of informed careers advice that clearly indicates the demands of the workplace or a particular career/course at the outset. The implications of this are:

- the need to make careers advisers aware of dyslexia;
- the need to ensure that college open days and course introductions are user friendly in terms of the demands of the courses and that this can be fully appreciated by the student;
- the need to ensure that those with dyslexia are fully aware of the extent of their dyslexic difficulties; and
- the need to ensure that employers have an informed awareness of dyslexia so that they can appreciate both the strengths and the difficulties of the dyslexic person and the implications of this for the workplace.

There are also implications for employers in relation to training and sometimes retraining the dyslexic person in their employment. In some cases the full nature of a job is not made clear to the applicant at the interview stage.

Careers staff

Careers staff also have a key role to play and they need to consider the following:

- how to obtain at least an awareness training in the area of dyslexia;
- not all dyslexic people will display the same strengths and difficulties;
- the need to obtain information on the assessment that will clearly indicate the person's strengths and weaknesses;
- the need to consider the dyslexic person as an individual and his or her needs and ambitions and preferences should be acknowledged.

Liaison between education and work

In the study conducted by Kirk and Reid (1999) this aspect was raised as being of crucial importance. The relevance of the mainstream school curriculum to employment skills is a key factor to the success of adult life. Research findings have provided striking conclusions concerning the transitional period of dyslexic adults to successful employment. Hoffmann and colleagues (1987) identified a mismatch between curricular and employment needs and according to Nosek (1997) two of the top determinants for work success are work experience and vocational education during secondary school. Vocational education and work experience also provide opportunities to inform the employer and the dyslexic student about dyslexia and the nature of the accommodations that can be made in the workplace.

A technical report prepared by the National Joint Committee on Learning Disabilities in the United States (Orton Dyslexia Society, 1994) suggests that careful planning is essential in the transition from secondary to post-secondary education and such planning involves contributions from four groups – the student, the parent(s), and secondary and post-secondary professionals. The report outlines specific roles for each of these groups – for example, the student should have an understanding of his or her specific disability and have realistic work goals; secondary school personnel should form a transition team and develop an appropriate package of materials to record the student's progress and to facilitate service delivery to the post-secondary school; and the post-secondary staff should be responsible for negotiating reasonable adjustments within the faculty. This report is clearly far reaching and the many recommendations and suggestions highlight the importance of this transition period for the young person with dyslexia. Similarly the Adult Dyslexia for Practice and Training Report (ADEPT, Kirk and Reid, 1999: 113) that was commissioned by the Employment Service recommended that workplace assessment is an important aspect in the development of both a diagnostic and support programme for the dyslexic adult and that this should 'include career aspirations, job-related tasks and a matching process between the job and the profile of the dyslexic person. This has implications for the career service and for heightening the awareness of dyslexia among employers.'

The integration of the diagnosis and treatment aspects within training programmes can be demonstrated in the training of job-seeking skills, job interest, working habits and practical work skills such as filling in job applications and following directions (Hoffmann et al., 1987). It will only be when such vocational aspects of training have been integrated into the school programmes that dyslexic people will be able to enter the world of work equipped to deal with the varying demands of the workplace.

Dyslexia in post-school education

Due to the greater understanding of dyslexia and the need to ensure wider access to further and higher education both in the US and in the UK, the number of students with dyslexia entering post-school education is increasing. In the UK an increasing number of disability support centres in higher education have been established (Singleton, 1999). This has been accompanied by an increase in the number of students with dyslexia entering university courses. Additionally, in the UK funding has been made available from the Higher Education Funding Council and other bodies for projects to help students with disabilities.

In the US 8.4% of graduate students reported a disability (Brinckeroff, 1997). In 1994 the National Board of Medical Examiners received four hundred requests for alternative assessment and threefold increases have been noted in Law Faculties for special admission considerations.

It is important therefore that university and college personnel make themselves available to school staff and to potential recruits before the student decides on a particular course.

Supports

Although it is important to ensure that adults with dyslexia benefit from available supports it is also important to attempt to facilitate a degree of autonomy in learning and compensating for their dyslexia. Employers and course tutors therefore have a responsibility to attempt to do this as sensitively as possible. It is important that dyslexic people if they are to attain a degree of self-sufficiency become familiar with the nature of dyslexia and how and why it affects them. They need to understand how they actually process information; to devise strategies to cope with what for them is a different way of thinking; and to deploy tactics to deal with day-to-day living.

For example in relation to training or indeed re-training some of the key areas will include:

* organization, both in terms of materials and resources, and the 'cognitive organisational' aspects of learning;
* reading strategies: it may be too time consuming for the dyslexic person to read fully reports or documents, so they may need to employ strategies, involving skimming and scanning, which can help them understand and retain the meaning of the texts;
* note taking: it is important that they are familiar with strategies such as mind mapping and the use of key words and concepts which can help to structure note taking;
* presentations: quite often dyslexic people may have to make presentations to colleagues in the workplace and this can be quite challenging as many of the skills in making presentations such as organization and structure and identifying key points can be difficult for dyslexic people;
* study techniques: there are many strategies and techniques that can be used by dyslexic people but it is important that the technique should be one selected by the dyslexic person her/himself as each may have their own preferences for learning.

Knowledge of the importance of learning styles can be useful for employers, course tutors and for dyslexic people. Many adults with dyslexia are not aware of how they learn and perpetuate the same inappropriate learning pattern throughout their life. Learning styles are comparatively easy to identify through questionnaires (Dunn and Dunn, 1996; Lashley, 1995; Hobson, Anderson and Kibble, 1998). Additionally The QuickScan Screening Test (Zdzienski, 1997), discussed earlier in this chapter, provides a learning styles profile, although this is has been criticized (Sandison, 2000). Learning styles can also be identified through observation and reflection. After a task is completed it is important for the adult with dyslexia to reflect on the manner in which it was accomplished. It is extremely important to consider the process of learning as well as the outcome. It is only by doing this that an individual can identify which components of the task were easy, which were difficult and why. Asking and answering these questions can inform the learner about subsequent learning.

It is therefore important for the employer and the course tutor to be aware of how learning styles can affect job performance or course success. Therefore, work procedures and course teaching can influence the quality of the experience for the learner. For example, a visual learner may have difficulty in following auditory instructions or a person with a kinaesthetic preference needs to have a 'hands on' learning experience rather than being shown what to do.

Conclusion

There may be some debate regarding the degree of dyslexia experienced by the adult. For example employers may ask the question whether someone is mildly, moderately or severely dyslexic as this can have a major influence on the resources made available to the dyslexic person. Determining 'levels' of dyslexia is however very difficult. Do we focus on the extent of the processing difficulty or the behavioural characteristics? In determining degree the focus should probably be on the skills people have and those they need, addressing questions such as 'what does this person require to meet the demands upon him or her?' Even then we must take into account the complex interaction between cognitive processes, achievements and affective factors such as confidence, anxiety and self esteem.

It is important for adults with dyslexia to gain a full appreciation of their strengths and indeed their rights and therefore a self-advocacy role should be encouraged. Reiff (1998: 324) suggests that self-advocacy is 'embedded in the model of employment success' and that self-disclosure accompanies self-advocacy. It is important therefore to encourage adults with dyslexia throughout the assessment and intervention process to discuss the extent of their dyslexia and to be able to articulate that to an employer if necessary. To establish this type of autonomy is one of the functions of professional involvement throughout the whole process of assessment and support.

References

Bannatyne A (1974) Diagnosis: a note on recategorization of the WISC scaled scores. Journal of Learning Disabilities 7: 272–4.

Bigler ED (1992) The neurobiology and neuropsychology of adult learning disorders. Journal of Learning Disabilities 25: 448–506.

Brinckeroff L (1997) Students with learning disabilities in graduate or professional programs: emerging issues on campus and challenges to employment. In Paul J Gerber, Dale S Brown (eds) Learning Disabilities and Employment. Pro-ed Publications. Austin Texas.

British Psychological Society (1999) Dyslexia, Literacy and Psychological Assessment, Report by working party of the division of Educational and Child Psychology of the British Psychological Society. Leicester: BPS.

Blyth P (1992) A Physical Approach to Resolving Specific Learning Difficulties. Chester: Institute of Neuro-Physiological Psychology.

Brown AL (1980) Metacognitive development and reading. In RJ Spiro, B Bruce, WF Brewer (eds) Theoretical Issues in Reading Comprehension. Hillsdale NJ: Lawrence Erlbaum.

Chall JS (1983) Stages of Reading Development. New York: McGraw-Hill.

Chinn SJ, Ashcroft JR (1993) Mathematics for Dyslexics: A teaching handbook. London: Whurr.

Cordoni BK, O'Donnell JP (1981) Wechsler Adult Intelligence Score Patterns for Learning Disabled Young Adults. J Learning Disabilities 14(7): 404–7.

Davis RD, Braun EM (1997). The Gift of Dyslexia. London: Souvenir Press

Dunn R, Dunn K, Price GE (1996) Learning Style Inventory. Lawrence KA: Price Systems.

Eden GF, VanMeter JW, Rumsey JM, Maisog JM, Woods RP, Zeffiro TA (1996). Abnormal Processing of Visual Motion in Dyslexia revealed by Functional Brain Imaging. Nature 382: 66–9.

Faas LA, D'Alonzo BJ (1990) WAIS-R scores as predictors of employment success and failure among adults with learning disabilities. Journal of Learning Disabilities 23(5): 311–16.

Fawcett AJ, Nicolson RI (1998) The Dyslexia Adult Screening Test. London: The Psychological Corporation.

Hoffmann FJ, Sheldon KL, Minskoff EH, Sautter SW, Steidle EF, Baker DP, Bailey MB, Echols LD (1987) Needs of learning disabled adults. Journal of Learning Disabilities 20(1): 43–52.

Hopson B, Anderson J, Kibble D (1998) Learn to Learn. Leeds: Lifeskills Publishing Group

Johanson KV (1992) Sensory Deprivation – A Possible Cause of Dyslexia. Oslo: Scandinavian University Press.

Katz L, Goldstein G, Rushdin S, Bailey D (1993) A neuropsychological approach to the Bannatyne recategorization of the Wechsler Intelligence Scales in adults with learning disabilities. J Learning Disabilities 26: 65–72.

Kirk J, Reid G (1999) Adult Dyslexia for Employment, Practice and Training (ADEPT) A report commissioned by the Employment Service UK. Edinburgh: University of Edinburgh.

Lashley C (1995) Improving Study Skills. London: Cassell.

Manzo AN, Manzo UC (1993) Literacy Disorders. Orlando FL: Holt, Rinehart & Winston.

McLoughlin D, Fitzgibbon G, Young V (1994) Adult Dyslexia: Assessment, Counselling and Training. London: Whurr.

Miles TR (1996) Do dyslexic children have IQs? Dyslexia 2(3): 175–8.

Miles TR, Miles E (1992) Dyslexia and Mathematics. London: Routledge.

Nosek K (1997) Dyslexia in Adults: Taking charge of your life. Dallas TX: Taylor.

Reid M (2001) Dyslexia and the careers service. In L Peer, G Reid (2001) Successful Inclusion in the Secondary School. London: David Fulton.

Reid G, Kirk J (2001) Dyslexia in Adults: Education and Employment. Wiley: Chichester.

Reiff HB (1998) Off the Beaten Path: A model for employment success for adults with learning disabilties. In SA Vogel, S Reder (eds) Learning Disabilities, Literacy and Adult Education. Baltimore MA: Paul Brookes.

Salvia J, Gajar A, Gajria M (1988) A comparison of WAIS-R profiles of nondisabled college-freshmen and college-students with learning-disabilities. Journal of Learning Disabilities 21(10): 632–6.

Sanderson A (2000) Reflections on study scan. Dyslexia 6(4): 285–90.

Singleton CH (1999). Dyslexia in Higher Education: Policy, provision and practice. Report of the National Working Party on Dyslexia in Higher Education. Hull: University of Hull.

Stanovich KE (1996) Towards a more inclusive definition of dyslexia. Dyslexia 2(3): 154–66.

Wechsler D (1955) The Wechsler Adult Intelligence Scale. New York: The Psychological Corporation.

Wechsler D (1986) The Wechsler Adult Intelligence Scale – Revised (UK. edition). Sidcup, Kent: The Psychological Corporation.

Wechsler D (1997) The Wechsler Adult Intelligence Scale – III. San Antonio: The Psychological Corporation.

Wilkins AJ (1995) Visual Stress. Oxford: Oxford University Press.

Wong BYL (1986) Metacognition and special education: a review of a view. Journal of Special Education 20: 19–29.

Wray D (1994) Comprehension monitoring, metacognition and other mysterious processes. Support for Learning 9: 3107–13.

Zdzienski D (1997). Study Scan. Limerick: ISL.

Index

precision teaching, 265
reading aloud, 288
Reading recovery, 20
Repeated reading, 200, 265
spelling disability and chromosome
    15, 55, *see* genetics
time targets, 265
reasoning ability, 101
recessive, 42
redefinition of dyslexia, 89, 281
regression, 15
reliability, 13, 115
remedial and preventative, 186
research based intervention, 220,
    185–202, 115–6
research design, 148
resources, 19
rime and rhyming, 7, 112, 114, 117, 263
RITA (Readers Interactive Teaching
    Assistant), 19
Rodin Remediation, 23

school failure, 17
screening 8, 24, 118, 292, 294
secondary 116, 281–291
    self esteem and confidence, attention,
        283,
    behavioural difficulties, 283
    depression, frustration, 283
segmentation, 95, 109, 113, 121, 161,
    241, 263
self advocacy, 306
sensitivity and concordance, 235
sensorimotor/ magnocellular 23, 101,
    65–88
    amplitude modulation and speech
        sounds, 76, 81
    and nonword reading, 76, 263
    auditory confusion of letter sounds,
        83
    auditory magnocells and phonology,
        95, 65, 75, 76, 81
    auditory magnocells and post
        mortem, 78
    auditory temporal processing and
        phonology, 76
    balance, 79
    basic physiological processes, 77

binocular vergence control, 74
causal chain, 71
cerebellar tumours, reading
    difficulties, and language, 80
cerebellum as magnocellular, 79
cerebellum, 65, 69, 79, 81, 83
changes in sound frequency
    (frequency modulation), 75
clumsiness, 65
coherent motion detection, 70, 71
contrast, 69
controlling eye movements during
    reading, 69, 73
development of visual magnocells, 69
discriminating pure tones at low
    frequencies, 77
eye movements, 68
fatty acids, 66
fixations, 67
flicker sensitivity, 70
focusing visual and auditory attention,
    66
functional imaging, 71
genetic control of magnocells, 65
immunological attack, 66
immunological system and fatty acids,
    65, 82, 83
individual differences in brain, 77
inner speech, 75, 79
intervention for unstable visual per-
    ception, 73
IQ and reading ability, 65
low level sensory processes, 77
magnocells, 65, 83, 95
metabolism, and magnetic resonance
    spectroscopy, 80
motion sensitivity and reading ability,
    71
occlusion, 74
    randomized control studies 75
    rate of reading, 74
orthographic and phonological
    abilities, 66
parvo and magno pathways, 69
phonological choice, 118
poor sequencing, 66
poor visual memory for orthography,
    65, 81